THE ULTIMATE SALES BIBLE

THE ULTIMATE SALES BIBLE

Sales Secrets Born from Pool Halls, Poker, and Gambling: The Framework that Scales People and Companies to 9-Figure Success

TODD SPECIALE

Clovercroft Publishing

The Ultimate Sales Bible: Sales Secrets Born from Pool Halls, Poker,and Gambling:
The Framework that Scales People and Companies to 9-Figure Success

©2023 Todd Speciale

All rights reserved. No part of this book may be reproduced or transmitted
in any form or by any means, electronic or mechanical, including photocopying,
recording, or by any information storage and retrieval system,
without permission in writing from the
copyright owner.

Published by Clovercroft Publishing, Franklin, Tennessee

Edited by OnFire Books

Edited by Ann Tatlock

Cover Design by Suzanne Lawing

Interior Design by Suzanne Lawing

Printed in the United States of America

ISBN: 978-1-956370-14-0

ENDORSEMENTS

Add to cart folks, ADD TO CART, buy the book and get one for all your friends! And once you've done that, add one more. Todd Speciale has knocked this one out of the park and the true secrets to sell (the right way) are all INSIDE THIS BOOK!

Every high achiever, every big hitter, every human who lives their dreams, understands that the secret to winning everything is mastery of one skill… sales.

Although many try, the truth is many fail, because no matter how many books, courses and conferences someone will partake in, the real tactics are rarely ever taught. And if I'm being honest, after decades in the industry the truth is that many who teach simply haven't won big enough to know how to help others duplicate their success… UNTIL NOW!

Todd and "The Ultimate Sales Bible" are the true exception! No marketing gimmicks, no fluff, this book shares the actual tactics needed to close on your best life. This is not mere motivation and promises, this is artistry, mastery of a craft and mentorship to all willing to go the distance, all delivered from the heart of a superhuman who cannot stand to see people lose when they could win.

Not only has Todd won in all areas of his life, business, sales, family, health, faith and finances, from the exact skills he teaches here, he has also duplicated it with the masses and can guarantee the path to success. Those he teaches, win big. Actually, they win HUGE! The teams he trains break records. The teams he trains cultivate an unmatched culture. There is a noticeable difference in the minds, skill sets and results of all those who have experienced the Speciale Effect.

If you want to learn and master the art of sales, if you want to win big or maybe even just believe in and sell yourself, start here and stop reading anything else! This is your new best friend, your secret code and the way to never lose again. All you want can and will be yours if you'll learn and apply the tools in this book!

The world is in a mid-epic-shift and we know only the skilled will make it. It's time to skill up here. Read it daily, live the habits, practice what it preaches, and this life is yours for the taking.

Thank you Todd for living addicted to your impact. Thank you for taking your success and using it to give back. It's winning season and I cannot wait to see this movement in full effect. You truly did, Make Sales Great Again.

Danelle Delgado, *The Millionaire Maker*

* * * * *

I am writing this endorsement to Todd Speciale's book *The Ultimate Sales Bible* first and foremost because of the man he is.

We are in tumultuous times these days. Who to believe? Who to learn from? Who to TRUST? We have shifted from the Information economy to the TRUST economy.

Consuming BS every 15 seconds for the last decade has made every one of you a world-class BS detector. I think that is a good thing.

So why buy yet another sales book? The answer. You shouldn't. You should INVEST in THE sales book. *The Ultimate Sales Bible*!

Skepticism is a wizard-level intelligence indicator. You should be skeptical! I am. Big Time!

Here's my rules that may help you.

- Do I need to get better at the skill of sales to feed my family and create more distance from broke?
- Is the information coming from someone who has been in my shoes?
- Has this person or these strategies performed in a real company, created real results, and been SYSTEMATICALLY trained to a wide array of people who were able to get consistent results?
- Lastly. And this is the most important question. Can I TRUST this person and their strategies?

The answer to all of these questions and more with Todd and his information from his company, Make Sales Great Again, is a wholehearted, enthusiastic YES!

I have known, traveled with, hired, watched and partnered with Todd on many projects. Every single time, the result is the same. Wild sales success. Not just for Todd or for the company, but also for the most important people to him, the sales reps, sales leaders and business owners!! Thousands of families fed, thousands of great sales and business minds empowered to gain a real craft that they can use for life and in any setting or economy.

I would TRUST Todd with my family, my money, and my companies, and have! So can you!

INVEST in yourself right now, get this book… absorb the information and take immediate and direct action with it! Knowledge without action is worthless.

This book was written with the same passion Todd applies to his family, his friends, his business and to helping every sales pro and business owner he meets! You'll be glad you did!

With Love and Trust,
JASON SISNEROS
Chairman - Anton Jae Global

FOREWORD

This book should come with a warning label, "Do not read unless you are prepared to hear the truth about selling." If you've chosen to ignore the warning, I want to congratulate you. You are about to read the definitive guide on mastering sales in today's intensely competitive landscape.

The market landscape is evolving, and consumers are savvier than ever. The arsenal of tools needed to excel as a top-tier salesperson keeps growing. The rise of Generative AI tools, enhanced Sales Enablement Platforms, and the advanced sophistication of Intelligent Revenue Platforms are just some indicators of the arsenal a modern salesperson needs to stay ahead of.

However, a crucial reminder for all salespeople is this: while having the latest tools and tech stacks can be an advantage, if we fail in basic one-on-one or group sales, no amount of tech will salvage those deals.

The Ultimate Sales Bible encapsulates the finest sales techniques available today, aiming to guide you in advancing or sealing the deal. If you know Todd Speciale, you're aware that he isn't just any typical sales expert. He's blunt, decisive, astute, perceptive, and relentless—the epitome of a top sales performer. If you don't know Todd, you're about to find out why he's one of the industry's leading sales expert in the world today! Don't let those tattoos fool you!

In this book, Todd lays out the best sales strategies to both resonate with today's modern buyers and close more sales consistently. He's acutely aware that in today's market, setting yourself, or your product apart from your competition isn't getting any easier. Why? Well, most product offerings in the market today have reached a point of similarity, making them seem interchangeable. With small businesses and enterprises desperately trying and failing to find ways to differentiate their products, where should they turn? The answer is clear: focus on the only differentiator left — the salesperson.

In this hypercompetitive environment with shrinking budgets and increasing uncertainty, a salesperson's ability to frame value in a client's mind can spell the difference between landing or losing a deal. *The Ultimate Sales Bible* is about gaining the right mindset, using the right toolset, and acquiring the right skillset to kick your competitor's ass! Let's Make Sales Great Again…one deal at a time!

VICTOR ANTONIO, *Sales Velocity Academy*

DEDICATION

Before you can become more, you have to believe that you can. That takes people in your corner. It takes the love and support we all need to evolve into the best versions of ourselves. You have to literally remove any form of negativity, non-believers, and the ones who say it can't be done in order to reach the goals you know you're capable of.

For me, that was the hardest move to make. I've had the luxury of being on stage with and knowing some very powerful people in the business and speaking world, and they all have many things in common that define their successes. The most powerful one, to me, was how without hesitation they've eliminated even family if need be… with intention, to become the one-percenters that thrive at that highest level.

I learned that skill and implemented it IMMEDIATELY! As difficult as that was. As crazy and stupid some told me I was for doing it, it set me on a course of growth that I could've never imagined possible.

I have many friends in my life to thank that have never left my side through thick and thin. No matter what I faced, you were there. For that, I thank you. Without "REAL" friends and not just the fake ones who say what you want to hear and talk behind your back right after… I mean the authentic ones who checked on me when I needed it most and inspired me to do more when they knew I wasn't fulfilling my life's passion in helping others be the best versions of themselves, while teaching them to scale their businesses through leadership and how to sell the right way, with integrity and honesty.

Then there were the "influencers," if you will. The people who dedicated their time to help me grow, knowing deep down that I could add massive value to the lives of others the right way. They knew I wanted to write a sales book that would undoubtedly "Make Sales Great Again."

To Jason Sisneros and Joe Calo, two men I call brothers. Your expertise in business has allowed me to understand why it's important to share your secrets with others to make this world a better place. The inspiration, generosity, and true compassion you've both had by taking me in as one of your own, I don't know how to ever repay. Thank you for giving me tools and confidence, and for supporting me through my journey. I personally believe that without your guidance, I wouldn't fully understand the importance of giving back or the impact that sharing our knowledge and gifts with others has on this world. For all of this and so much more, I'm grateful for you both.

To Danelle Delgado, who has been and always will be one of the most influential people in so many lives. Not only is she one of the best speakers in the world, but she's also one of the most servant-minded sales- and businesswomen in the world today. She gave me an opportunity to run side by side with her and coached me to uncover talents and release fears. With her sound advice, she put me in the most powerful mindset! Danelle's one of the best mothers in the world and has extended that same compassion to others, giving us all hope that we can make all our dreams come true. She's a massive gift that the world needs, and I want to thank her for everything she's done for me. I'm forever grateful.

To Victor Antonio, who to me is one of the most powerful sales trainers and just genuine humans anyone should be lucky enough to meet. My first time seeing him on stage was at Grant Cardone's first 10x Growth Conference in Miami, Florida, in 2017. He was electric on stage and added more sales value in 30 minutes than I had learned at that entire event. Victor proved to me that day that I needed a lot of work, but that becoming a master closer and sales trainer is possible.

He drove me to fight even harder to perfect my craft, not just in sales, but in speaking as well and he probably didn't even know how he impacted me. Fast forward years later. I've been on stages with some of today's most powerful people, keynoted major events, coached, trained, and consulted multiple companies including CEOs and sales teams worldwide. I want to personally thank him for his wealth of knowledge and getting to know him. I owe a lot of my success to Victor, so thank you.

To Brandon Biskie, my partner and one of the most dedicated life grinders, one of the baddest closers, exceptional trainers, and extraordinary business minds I have the luxury of running with EVER! The world should know that I owe a lot of my success and growth in this industry to you for fighting through the trenches together. You've been a brother, a friend, and a person I learn from daily. Thank you for all that you do, all that you are, and it's comforting knowing you're in my life. Love you brother, and we are and always will be better together.

To Art & Karen, my in-laws who have always believed in their entire family, supporting us, and helping every single one of us accomplish our goals. I thank you for being true role models that I look up to more than you probably know. You have my heart and loyalty always.

To Nick & Carolina and now my perfect nephew Carlo! There are people out there that say they want others to win, but you two mean it. You've always been your family and friends' biggest fans, as we are yours. Watching you two love one another and seeing your success and accomplishments come to fruition has motivated me to do even more. I know I may not say it enough, but you both inspire me. Thank you for being in my life and I love you very much. I can't wait to be Carlo's sponsor on the PGA tour. ☺

To my mother, Maryjane. You define strength in every way. You're the strongest woman I know, who's beat cancer more than once, lost the love of your life, and still always finds a way to smile through the hard. Your presence is proof that love for everyone exists. I love you, Mom.

To my brother and his family, Rob & Kim. You've given me hope when I didn't think there was anything left in me. Your love and gift of friendship I cherish every day more and more as we get older and I need everyone to know how much you've helped me thrive over the years, just loving me and giving me your unconditional support when I was at my lowest. To say I'm lucky to have you in my life would be a drastic understatement. To Tristan, Krista, & baby Kinsley, Uncle Todd loves you!

To Abriella, I don't even know where to begin. You are a light in all of our eyes and just an enormous blessing to us all. When you're old enough to read this, I need you to know that because of you, you've pushed Daddy to not only become a better man, but to guarantee that you, your mother, and sisters live a privileged and fruitful life of abundance long after I'm gone. Your smile is contagious. Your laughter is something I can't wait to hear every day. I'm so lucky God gave you to us. Daddy loves you; you are perfection in every way.

To Addyson, you are me. Hardheaded, stubborn, but VERY strong! I respect you and love you probably more than you'll ever know. You're one of the smartest people I know, and in spite of anything we may go through, my love for you will and forever be eternal. I'm proud of you. I love you and I hope you know that Daddy will always be here for you, right by your side until the day that I die. Follow your passions, live your life, and don't settle. I'm so grateful God gave you to me and I'll always be your biggest fan rooting for you. Through thick and thin, good times and hard, I'll be your rock when you need me. Love you.

To Averigh, the emotion that runs through me even typing your name is so powerful and has been the ultimate catalyst for success in my life since the day you were born, and even shines brighter today than it ever has before. YOU have NEVER left me. You've been by me, with me, and for me since day one. I've laughed with you. I've cried with you. You've seen me at my worst and my best, giving me your entire heart always. I just want you to read this decades from now and know that without your continuous support and selfless dedication to empowering me to be more… I wouldn't be where I am today. So I just want to thank you for being my daughter, a friend, and someone I can undoubtedly count on without hesitation. Daddy loves you. You need to know my success is a lot because of you.

To my wife, Michelle. We've been through it all. The happy. The hard. The tears. The joy. The mistakes. The wins. The heartache. And finally the massive amount of LOVE that has allowed us to fight through it all side by side. Not many couples can say they've been through it all and came out on top. We did JUST THAT! You are my best friend. My soulmate. My heart beats for you, and without you, I wouldn't be the man I am today. We've suffered and prevailed.

You came into my life when I didn't have much. You instantly became a mother to two daughters at a young age and filled that role better than anyone in the world could've. You have supported me and poured your commitment and trust into me when many wouldn't have. You've given me hope and belief that I can be more and because of that, that's exactly what we have become: more. I just want you to know that you are equally the BEST MOTHER IN THE WORLD and THE BEST STEPMOM ON THE PLANET, and without you giving each and every one of us all that you have… we wouldn't be able to live the life we are living.

You are our rock. You are the glue that holds us together. You are a true example of fighting through everything, sticking by our side regardless of what comes our way. I could go on and on and on about you, but I just need you to know not only who you are, but what you have done for us all is recognized, noticed, and we ALL are forever grateful for you. I love you SO MUCH!

I'm sure anyone who knows me knows this was coming, to my father Bob Speciale. He's always been and always will be my hero and I know he's looking down smiling from the heavens above. My life has been worth living because of the love and strength you continue to inject into my soul. Every move I make, I look up to the sky and say, "Dad, this is for you" and it drives me to do things others say can't be done. Until we meet again, I thank you daily and I love you.

Lastly, to the supporters, the real friends who have always applauded my wins and believed I could do more. Fortunately, I can say there's been quite a few of you. Not the fake ones who say they support me but whose tune changes the minute they talk to someone else. I mean the authentic ones! I wish I could name you all, but you know who are. There's not a day that goes by where I'm not extremely grateful for you. From me to every one of you, I'm forever in your debt. Without all of you, I wouldn't have had the guts to do any of this.

INTRODUCTION

You're probably asking yourself where the title *The Ultimate Sales Bible* came from and why, so let me explain. I started a leadership and sales consulting company called "Make Sales Great Again" because I've written millions of dollars in the sales world, helped train thousands of people, and have had the luxury of speaking on some large stages, with some of the biggest names, in the most lucrative sector in the world called "sales" for decades now. Unfortunately, saying you're a salesperson is becoming a horrible title to hold, due to the many who call themselves "master closers" who are actually "master liars."

My style of selling combines what I've learned growing up on the streets with books I've read and training from legends I've paid thousands of dollars for. Now I'm using what I've learned to give you the ultimate selling formula. I truly believe the best salespeople are a combination of both street smarts and book smarts.

I could go into all of my accomplishments and accolades, but this book is FOR YOU; it's not about me. I want to concentrate on giving you all the lessons I've learned over the years, so you don't make the same mistakes others do. You'll learn tools and tips that are authentic ways to sell from decades of education I've received from people like Brian Tracy, Jordan Belfort, Danelle Delgado, Victor Antonio, Zig Ziglar, Grant Cardone, Tom Hopkins, Brad Lea, and so many more.

I'm extremely passionate about this and, to be honest, I wasn't even going to write a sales book this soon, but I'm tired of good people being lied to and taken advantage of. I'm going to help people realize that sales is the best industry in the world and is most profitable when done right!

I want to teach people that honesty is the ONLY form of sales! You should be able to learn from those who have massive amounts of integrity and become a master salesperson the right way. It's not only possible, it's easier than you think.

The hardest part for those in the sales world is understanding the difference between "selling to serve" and "selling to survive," which we'll get into later in this book. The hard truth is, most are being told to sell to earn a paycheck. They have bills to pay or just want to get rich, or the owners of the companies just have to reach their goals and don't care about the well-being of those they should be grateful to have the opportunity to sell to, in order to hit those goals. It ends up defining the sales role as the "I just want your money" role, rather than what it should be, the "I just want to add value to your life" role. I hope that makes sense.

Within these chapters, you're going to hear a lot of passion-based ways to empower the world to Make Sales Great Again! I am going to take the sales title and prove that it doesn't belong to the con-artist, to those who only want my money, those whom I can't trust, those who will tell me anything to get the sale. Instead, the title of salesperson is a very integrity-based luxurious role that, when handled correctly, is one you should and will be proud to have!

It's time to take back what's ours. It's time to fight the liars, not closers, of the world and prove what real skills and good people are made of. I want to thank you and applaud you for wanting to learn how to sell the right way!

I personally believe this book is needed and will help others see the value in Making Sales Great Again! I hope you enjoy this book, share it with others, and if you get one takeaway from it, it's a win for me!

CONTENTS

Chapter 1	A Master Closer and A Master Liar: There's a Big Difference	21
Chapter 2	Sales: The Ultimate Profession	28
Chapter 3	Rising Above the Rest: Characteristics of the Elite Performers	34
Chapter 4	The Grit Factor: Mental Toughness	48
Chapter 5	Vision, Goals, and Sales: A Symbiosis	59
Chapter 6	Dominating Sales: From Credibility to Authority	75
Chapter 7	Serving vs Selling: The MSGA Way	90
Chapter 8	The Death of the Alphabet	96
Chapter 9	Be Direct	100
Chapter 10	There's Only One First Impression	108
Chapter 11	Strategic Tonality: Using Your Voice as a Tool	121
Chapter 12	Mastering the Art of Mirroring	134
Chapter 13	Play the Person, Not the Cards	143
Chapter 14	Shut Up and Sell	153
Chapter 15	Solution-Driven Sales	165
Chapter 16	Elevating Equity: The Pathway to Building Value	176
Chapter 17	How Kaffee Got Jessup: How to Ask the Best Questions!	187

Chapter 18	Securing the Win: Tie Downs & Trial Closes	214
Chapter 19	The Takeaway: People Want What They Can't Have	234
Chapter 20	Objections: Block First, Handle Later	250
Chapter 21	Logic and Emotion: The Balancing Act	315
Chapter 22	The Choice Close	335
Chapter 23	Don't Talk $h!t	342
Chapter 24	Your Negotiation Arsenal	350
Chapter 25	The "T.O." Process That Changed My Life	377
Chapter 26	Urgency: The Sales' Unicorn	390
Chapter 27	Suggestive Numbers	401
Chapter 28	Mastering the Close	407
Chapter 29	The Greatest Lead in All of Sales	438
Chapter 30	Follow-Up: How to Actually Do It	450
Chapter 31	Sales Scripting	457
Chapter 32	Reviews and Testimonials: Using the Psychology of Social Proof	477
Chapter 33	Don't Let the Sponge Dry	488
Chapter 34	Be Coachable: The Most Underrated Skillset	505
Chapter 35	Know Your Numbers	512
Chapter 36	Culture Is King	517
Chapter 37	Don't Give Up Ever!	532
Chapter 38	Get Rich. Stay Rich	543

CHAPTER 1

A MASTER CLOSER AND A MASTER LIAR: THERE'S A BIG DIFFERENCE

If you're a veteran in sales or just starting out, it's imperative that you understand why sales is truly an ROR (Return On Relationships). We have salespeople, leaders, and business owners so worried about hitting the numbers they need to hit that they're allowing their sales teams to do "whatever it takes" to close a deal. It's 2023, and unfortunately so many of the talented individuals who have been in the sales game for years, including the newcomers, have relied on "tactics" to sell rather than integrity and honesty. They tried to "catch up," if you will, due to the lack of income suffered in 2020 because of the pandemic (COVID). But to be fair to the newcomers in sales, this is not something new. Liars lie, closers close. They are not the same.

I'm VERY passionate about this because I've been in it. I've seen it and good people are getting robbed. The only difference between a bank robbery and someone lying about what their product or service can do for someone just to get paid, is the mask and gun. The liars in the game have no mask on that you can see (believe me, it's there) and they use their mouths rather than guns to hold you up.

The fear of a personal financial crisis made people second-guess customer-relationship building, the R.O.R., and many started utilizing sleezy methods of embellishment and lies so they could earn a commission. The money was all that mattered to them, not the prospect. The customer-care portion of the presentation seems almost eliminated in some sales industries, and this has truly brought down how people are thought of if they chose sales as their profession.

The hard part about teaching people to lie rather than sell is that when they get a taste of the high commission/pay, it's like being addicted to a drug. They see how easy it is to lie and earn, so they get even more creative, figuring out new ways to manipulate rather than just educate themselves on how to do it the right way. Then it becomes a domino effect. One liar teaches a new hire to lie, then that new hire tells their friends how to lie to earn, and in a matter of no time you have a team of liars rather than a team of closers.

Then you have the enablers, as I mentioned earlier. They are the leaders or business owners scared to get rid of those individuals stealing from good people to earn a living, because they are afraid to rebuild the right way. They are condoning the weak that are providing the volume of business they need because it's giving them a paycheck or allowing them to maintain growth for investors to see. This is COMPLETELY wrong and should be considered criminal, in my eyes.

IT IS NOT OK when you're aware of malicious tactics being used, just so you can fill your pockets, while blatantly taking advantage of a client or prospect. Let me repeat that. IT IS NOT OK WHEN YOU'RE AWARE OF MALICIOUS TACTICS BEING USED, JUST SO YOU CAN FILL YOUR POCKETS WHILE BLATANTLY TAKING ADVANTAGE OF A CLIENT OR PROSPECT!

If you're a leader allowing this to happen—using lies to sell, embellishing what a product or service offers simply to close a deal, completely disregarding a prospect's well-being, knowing you're selling them something they either don't need or that doesn't do what you say it will—then SHAME ON YOU! It makes you the weakest type of leader. The weakest type of salesperson—or should I say, a strong liar. Most importantly, it makes you a company that clearly doesn't understand how getting rid of these thieves will help you scale at a much higher level.

If you see something like this happening in your environment, you can do a couple of things. You can run, and I mean get the hell out of there, if a leader is allowing this. I'm sure you've heard the phrase "guilt by association," right? Well, that'll be you if you're not careful. Your name, your reputation, your bond, and care for others should always trump a paycheck. Or you can stand strong—if the opportunity and product or service you're offering is sound and adds value to others—by presenting/selling it the right way, proving how it can be done while teaching others to do the same.

My experience over decades in sales has shown me that those allowing this have a really hard time stopping it, because it will instantly affect their financial status when rebuilding. You have to vet every company and their processes if you're working with (I say *with*, not *for*) someone.

If you're a leader or owner of a company or organization, you need to step up your integrity game. The key to success is truly living by the core values your company says they live by. Not just telling someone what they are, but by implementing them daily and staying real to what they mean to you. I promise you this, if you get rid of the top "liars" in your company, you'll take a brief hit in production, BUT long term you'll see that creating a strong foundation doing things the right way will guarantee growth in ways you could've never imagined.

Understand this, it takes one person to poison a team. One person doing things the wrong way can impact an entire company. It takes one deal paying high commission through lying to make people think "I'll just try it once," and then good people are being stolen from and your company isn't a sales organization anymore, it's a crime syndicate stealing from the masses. DO NOT let this happen and if you're reading this and you know deep down this is you, CHANGE! It's never too late.

I've worked with CEOs of major Fortune 500 companies who had to answer to some high-level investors. They were very apprehensive about getting rid of the people who were providing the numbers they needed to show high efficiency. I don't blame them! It's scary when you're writing $10 million a month in business and I'm telling you to cut out the "top liars" who are usually 60% plus of that nut. Those CEOs looked at me like I was insane, but they got rid of the "top liars." And yes they took a hit initially, but within 6 months, they completely blew that $10 million number out of the water and doubled their sales growth DOING IT THE RIGHT WAY!

I have multiple examples of this, working with some of the most talented and well-respected salespeople in the world. This isn't my method. I didn't create the "sales honesty" bible, but what I did do was realize the profitability in selling with integrity. There's no better way. You may get the quick cash by lying, but the long-term high-level production and consistent growth comes from honesty.

Have you ever thought about the repercussions from clients who are lied to? Do you know the impact it can have financially in obtaining referrals and future business? Have you thought about maintaining that client base you've already built and how having liars in your organization will force long-term existing clients to cancel, leave, or decide you're not the right fit anymore?

It takes one bad move to destroy all you've worked for. Your reputation as a salesperson, leader, or company precedes you, and once you're deemed as dishonest, you have to find new people to lie to. Instead you should be building a brand on trust, integrity, and hardcore honesty behind every opportunity and prospect.

Here's another golden nugget for you. If you don't know, it's OK to say, "I don't know." The problem is, our egos get in the way when we don't know something, so we make something up to sound like we do. It's the worst move ever! First, you're lying. Secondly, they know. People can read you, like you can read them. You want the solution? Are you ready for it? It's way easier than you think. Try saying this next time you don't know something:

> *"I actually don't know the answer to that, but I know it's important to you which means it's important to me. So give me one second and I'm going to get the right answer for you from someone who does know."*

THAT'S IT! That simple! The amount of respect, trust, and care you're giving your prospect will help you earn their business. "I don't know" is the key to the close when you don't know the answer to a question. People want the truth, not a bullshit answer.

Here's a fun fact for you. New business is 80% more likely to add-on, upgrade, or be sold additional services or products through you when you nurture them and prove that they matter as a client. A new client or prospect that hasn't heard of you is a much harder close, and a prospect that's heard of you but has also heard negative reviews will take much more time to sell as you'll need to explain all the bad reviews and unhappy previous prospects.

Moral of the story: SELL TO SERVE rather than SELL TO SURVIVE! Don't lie. Don't steal. Don't embellish. You don't have to resort to these tactics, and if you are, it's actually costing you more than you think. If you've been taking advantage of good people, there's still time to fix this and earn your integrity back.

If you're wondering why timeshare people say, "I'm in real estate," or why car sales individuals vaguely say, "I'm in the automotive industry," or why insurance agents say, "I'm in the financial industry," or why salespeople at times aren't completely honest about their title when asked what they do for a living, in my personal opinion, it's because of one of these two things:

1. They're embarrassed to use the real title or industry they're in because of the malicious tactics used in that specific field even if they sell the right way; or

2. They're lying to sell and they don't want people to find out what they really do because they might know someone they've done business with in the past.

Why wouldn't you just say…. "I'm in timeshare," "I'm a used car salesperson," or "I sell insurance." Let's be honest, if you're scared to say what you do for a living, then you know deep down something's not right or the reputation of that field isn't good for a reason.

Now this doesn't mean those industries aren't great! It just means, be STRONG and set the tone of who you are and how you're going to sell in that field to help MAKE SALES GREAT AGAIN!

I'll end this chapter with this. Over the years I've personally been in business and seen several different organizations blatantly lying and stealing from people to earn a living. If that's you, the questions I have for you are… How do you lay your head down at night knowing you're a thief? Would you like what you're doing to clients to happen to you or the people you love most? And finally, how do you look at yourself in the mirror every day, getting up knowing you could be crippling a family financially if you're selling a high-ticket item you promised would add value when you knew it wouldn't? I know people who lie and say, "I don't care at all. I'll rob them all." Then when I asked them what they'd do if it happened to them, the answer was not surprising: "I'd be infuriated if someone did that to me." Yet, you still do it to others? Weird.

The worst part about all of this is that people suffer. The prospects, the clients, the ones who trusted you and believed that what you're offering can add value to their lives. It's not OK!

I will teach you how to SELL RIGHT.

I will teach you how to LEAD RIGHT.

I will teach you how to LIVE YOUR CORE VALUES and stand by them.

I will teach you that HONESTY, INTEGRITY, and AUTHENTICITY is the key and the most profitable way to sell and build your business and brand.

Put your seat belt on if you're driving, sit up if you're reading this, because you're about to get sales lessons that you'll commit to, take massive action on, and embrace the change that will ultimately give you all the riches in the world the RIGHT WAY! And what I mean by riches isn't JUST MONEY, it's the heart, soul, and mind, so you can wake up proud of who you are and what you do!

Remember, there's NO FAST TRACK TO SUCCESS! You have to put in the work to build long-term sustainable profitable relationships where you are the obvious choice to do business with because of HOW you do business, not just what you're selling.

CHAPTER 2

SALES: THE ULTIMATE PROFESSION

The undeniable difference that a sales career has to offer over any other profession in the world is more apparent today than ever!

I want you to understand how proud I am of you for taking the time to read this book and how important it is to truly educate yourself to master the art of sales, because when you do, you'll begin to earn more money than most doctors, attorneys, or any other profession we are conditioned to pursue as children. I've made millions in sales. It's changed my life in ways I never thought possible.

I started in sales selling vacuum sweepers door to door at the age of 15 years old. Imagine knocking on doors, lugging a huge vacuum around for 10-12 hours a day. At first I was wondering what the hell I was thinking, trying to sell a $2000 vacuum sweeper in 1991! UNTILLLLL, I sold the first deal and made 35% commission. I'm sure you can imagine my excitement while walking the 3 miles back to where my mom was going to pick me up. I was smiling cheek to cheek, and even at that young age I was thinking…. "This is it for me, I'm never doing anything else ever again!" A fifteen-year-old kid in one day made $700 in 1991. This was the beginning of understanding how unlimited income, no-cap pay, could affect the rest of my life.

I've sold a ton of different things throughout the years, which eventually led to me training, consulting, and sharing with the world why sales is a truly unmatched opportunity. I just want you to fully grasp and be fully engaged reading this book to prepare yourself for the opportunity of a lifetime, if used right!

Victor Antonio said, ***"If a company caps you, LEAVE and LEAVE FAST!"*** Sales is only the *most lucrative* position in the world when the compensation plan allows it. DO NOT, I repeat, DO NOT work with a company that caps your pay. In other words, limits the amount of money you can earn.

The reason why I love sales is because I can create my own paycheck. The harder I work the more I make. The more I put in, the more I get out. The more I learn, the more I can educate and build a team, giving them the same opportunity. As a sales professional, you have the right to literally say, "I'm gonna make $20,000 today." And it's actually possible. You dictate the outcome of your success. NO ONE but you! If you win, it's because you hustled and stayed dedicated to the process. If you don't, it's your fault and yours alone.

I hate excuses. Some things you should never ever do. One of the most important ones I live by is to never point fingers or blame anything or anyone but yourself. It's a cop out. It's the holy grail of excuses to place blame. Unsuccessful salespeople like to find excuses rather than solutions. Here are some of my favorite excuses when people don't succeed or are struggling in sales:

1. **"The product/service sucks."**
What they should say: "I should've done more research on the product/service before I took this job."
or

"I need to know everything about this product/service before I do another presentation to make sure what I'm offering adds value to my prospect."

– *Your fault*

2. "The leads suck!"

What they should say: "I'm not dedicated or motivated enough to learn how to get my own leads and because of that it's way easier to blame the leaders and the company for not handing me deals on a silver platter."

or

"I suck at getting referral business and too proud to ask for help from people who are good at getting referrals."

– *Your fault*

3. "Are they stupid? Everything I said makes complete sense!"

What they should say: "I need help presenting or explaining what we offer, so next time I have a prospect I can add value to by offering my product/service, they'll understand me better."

– *Your fault*

4. "There's too many competitors."

What they should say: "I need to learn about my competitors and find out why we are different and what makes us a better choice to do business with. And even if what we're offering is identical, I need to make the prospect understand why working with me is worth choosing us!"

– *Your fault*

5. "They didn't have time for me."

What they should say: "I don't know how to create enough urgency to get them to spend their valuable time with me. I know people will make time for things they want to make time for. I just need help showing them why time spent with me is worthwhile."

– *Your fault*

6. "No one's showing up! I keep getting ghosted."
What they should say: "My show rate for appointments sucks. I need to humble myself and finally get the help I need to create more urgency, so people will want to meet with me."
– *Your fault*

7. "Not enough people know who we are."
What they should say: "Marketing and selling are two different things. I chose sales. I haven't maximized the opportunities I've had the luxury of receiving."
– *Your fault*

8. "There's only so much time in the day and I'm too busy."
What they should say: "I need to be more organized and prioritize every minute of the day to maximize my success. I don't know what to pay or how to hire help to create more time to grow myself and the company."
– *Your fault*

9. "It's impossible to reach the levels they've set for me."
What they should say: "I know I have what it takes to achieve anything, but because I won't ask for help to be more efficient, I'll just blame my bosses. It's definitely not my fault. What they're asking for is just unrealistic."
– *Your fault*

10. "No one is returning my texts, emails, or calls. It's not my fault."
What they should say: "I tried contacting them once or twice and now every attempt sounds desperate because I don't know the right things to say to get them to return my message. Their loss, not mine."
– *Your fault*

11. "I handled their objection, but they just wouldn't let it go."

What they should say: "I thought I handled their objection. Obviously I didn't or they wouldn't have used it as a way out on the back end. My ego is way too big to ask someone to teach me how to approach objections."

– *Your fault*

12. "Marketing sucks"

What they should say: "I'm not skilled enough, nor do I have the business mind or competence to take the time to be able to present and sell my product or service the right way, so I'll have to blame the marketing for not doing my job. It's easier to blame them."

– *Your fault*

13. "Our price is too high."

What they should say: "I don't know how to create enough need through value so price won't be the easy way out."

– *Your fault*

Obviously these aren't all the excuses salespeople make, but it's a damn good reference so you don't fall into the web of finger pointing.

Understanding this NOW will remind you what not to do in the best industry in the world, when the going gets tough.

I want to be completely honest with you, though—it's not easy. The most lucrative sales positions are commission ONLY! I've had $100,000 days. I know others who've had million-dollar days and then there are some that have had zero-dollar days. People will have opinions on commission-only roles and will try to sway you away from them, but it is undoubtedly the highest paying position to hold over anything else you can do! You can make as much or as little as you want. You can work as hard or as little as you want, but when truly dedicated… the riches you can obtain by mastering sales is unmatched!

Every day is different when working in sales; you will meet so many different people and personalities. You'll have the chance to travel all over the world if you'd like, and have multiple workspaces. BUT, you have to sell to be successful. There are unlimited job opportunities when you master this skill. When you do that, you can work for any company, anywhere.

When you're in sales, it offers unlimited options for growth, both in leadership and compensation. There are no limits – you can sell as much as you want and be promoted and compensated accordingly.

If you're wondering if you should be in sales, just know that you already sell every day of your life. Being able to master the art of sales is a skill that you will be able to use in everything you do! Selling requires patience, learning how to listen, knowing how to ask good questions, having exceptional people skills, and being willing to work hard. These are all the skills necessary to be successful.

Warren Buffet was doing a closing speech to a graduating class at Harvard and at the end of his speech he had a Q & A. One of the students who graduated top of her class asked him a question and his answer shocked the world. Now let me put this in perspective. Here's Warren Buffet, one of the world's wealthiest men, speaking to a brilliant class at Harvard, all of whom have graduated with very high-level degrees. The question asked was, "What do you think the most important skill for us to learn will be entering the real world after graduation?" His reply… "Learn how to sell. If you don't learn how to sell, nothing you've learned here will allow you to maximize the success you're truly capable of."

DAMN IT! That should get you as excited as it did me! So, let's teach you how to sell and how to sell the RIGHT WAY!

CHAPTER 3

RISING ABOVE THE REST: CHARACTERISTICS OF THE ELITE PERFORMERS

Sales individuals have changed so much over the years. What a good salesperson was 20 years ago is quite different than what they are today. Some characteristics have dramatically changed, and some haven't. The handshake that used to mean the deal was done is now a 100-page contract that requires notary and more. Why? Because the characteristics of a salesperson have changed and it's your responsibility as a salesperson to bring the good ones back to the surface!

Let's dive into what I KNOW to be the top characteristics you must have to be a high-performing sales professional.

SALES TRAIT #1: HONESTY

I know I went hard into this in Chapter 1. The dishonest sales individuals in the world over the past two decades have destroyed the sales profession and I'm not going to go on a rant again about it, but if you're a dishonest person and need to lie to close deals, stop reading this book right now. The traits of an exceptional sales professional begin and end with honesty.

A "real" sales professional will tell you if the product or service they're offering is for you or not. They'll be honest. They won't take your money just to earn a commission. When your job is to persuade people for a living, it tempts some to not be honest. You do this to earn a living. I've seen it happen a million times where a salesperson's bills get higher and higher and they're sitting with that one family and they think, "I'll just embellish a bit," because they need the money so badly. Dishonesty manipulates people, instead of serving someone.

Look, yes, there are many horrible people lying their asses off robbing people for a living, and although it gives them wealth, it'll terrorize your soul. It's just not worth it. Be a good person. Be an honest person. Because when you do, honesty will win every time and you'll be able to look at yourself in the mirror every day! You can lie your way to the top or bag a big client by over-promising, saying stuff that just isn't true, but ultimately people catch on and your success ends. Your name gets trashed and more than anything, you hurt people. Don't do that. There are far too many good families getting robbed that don't deserve it. In some cases, your being dishonest can affect their family for generations to come.

SALES TRAIT #2: BE AMBITIOUS

You have to have heart, drive, determination, and pure grit to be successful in anything, but having a sales career can really put you to the test. If your goals aren't high, you'll always be mediocre. Let's not sugarcoat anything here. Ambition is dead center in the heart of sales.

Being ambitious means you'll not only fight harder for you, but for the client as well. You'll do more than expected. The old saying is "under promise and over deliver." Nah, ambitious sales individuals don't under promise anything anymore. They promise and then do more!

SALES TRAIT #3: HAVE INTEGRITY

Can I be honest? I strongly dislike anyone who doesn't have integrity, ESPECIALLY when it's in a sales transaction costing money. If you're one of those people, once again, stop reading and go give this book to someone who has integrity immediately please.

How you make money is MORE important than the money you make. Many of you experienced sales representatives have big goals; just don't do anything shady to get there. Because the only thing you've accomplished when you do that is proving you don't care about anyone but yourself or the fact that you may be hurting others.

Honesty and integrity are the two most important reasons I wrote this book and titled it *The Ultimate Sales Bible*. Too many of you will take the path of least resistance, the weak route. Don't do that. Just do the right thing and it'll create success and riches that will last a lifetime.

SALES TRAIT #4: PERSISTENCE

Data shows that 80% of sales close after at least 5 follow-ups, yet 66% of sales reps give up after only one or two!

Kind of says it all, really. Closing deals takes time and requires persistence.

Salespeople who willingly and systematically stay in touch and on top of their clients have way more success than those just in it for the quick cash or looking for the low-hanging fruit.

SALES TRAIT #5: HAVE HUMILITY

When you see a sales professional hit great numbers and start to walk around like they own the place, arrogant as hell and never sharing the juice (good sales techniques), get away from them fast. They don't last.

This kind of individual who never claps when others win.

The type of person who needs to be in the limelight, who has to be the center of attention always.

When you're humble in sales, it means you recognize areas you need to grow in. It means you're OK saying to a prospect, "I don't know, but I'll find out the right answer," instead of bullshitting your way through a prospect question or concern.

With ultimate humility you never take your strengths for granted, but you are grateful for the lessons and open to learning from anyone, at any tenure or age, at any time.

All of this is absolutely essential to growing individually and to building a dominant humble sales team.

SALES TRAIT #6: BE ORGANIZED

Here's the hard truth about salespeople. Most hate administrative or organizational tasks.

We have so many different clients, at different stages in the sales cycle, who need to be continuously contacted to make sure they know they matter. BEFORE and AFTER THE SALE!

The most successful salespeople in the world move and they move fast. It's imperative that you slow down and set up daily tasks. Use a calendar religiously so you don't waste someone's time by missing an appointment. It's the worst thing you can do. You MUST be early every single time. Answer when they call or message you and prove that they are that important to you.

If you can't stay organized, leads will undoubtedly fall through the cracks. There are a ton of good CRM (Customer Relationship Management) systems out there that can send you automated texts and emails for upcoming appointments or events throughout your day. I highly recommend them or simply get a virtual assistant. You'd be surprised how cheap they are and they manage everything for you.

If you're disorganized in sales, your time management will suffer when it comes to addressing customer demands, meeting deadlines, and forming deep, lasting relationships that are directly related to your success and future referral business. Organization is also a key element of sales success because it translates to focus and planning.

Simply put, word gets around. If you're the sales individual who can't follow up or be on time, and who never gets back to people… you, your brand, and your company will suffer much more than you think.

SALES TRAIT #7: EMPATHY

Empathy puts you in the buyer's shoes. Great sales professionals feel what a customer feels, knows what's important to them, and respects and understands their thoughts.

They know what motivates their prospects. They know and are OK with customer changes, knowing that in a fast-paced world pivoting is necessary, and they don't complain about helping their clients.

Yes, you need to ask the right questions. You need to listen carefully. Just know that having empathy builds the best long-term relationships by building trust, making the bond between you and the client stronger than ever.

Whatever their pain points are, they need to be yours. Your job through empathy is to build credible solutions for each client and this alone will result in tremendous sales success from a servant standpoint, rather than just trying to "close" someone.

Harvard Law did a study about the world's top sales professionals, the elite, and what their top 7 traits were. Now if you asked them, they'd give you quite a bit different answer than the consumer would. But the consumer says these are the top traits that make a high-level achieving salesperson:

1. Modesty

Harvard found that 91% of the best sales professionals had medium to high scores of modesty and humility. Is that shocking to you?

I mean, yes, the majority of salespeople in the world aren't classified in the top tier, which is the reason why the stereotype of a salesperson is usually that they're pushy and egotistical. The study also shows that ostentatious salespeople who are too confident and show it, alienate themselves from the mass clientele that are reached by those salespeople who are modest.

2. Conscientiousness

This study showed that 85% of top salespeople were reliable, responsible, and always stayed in contact with their clients, which ultimately proved their desire to be serious about their role. These people take control of the sales cycle and the process all the way through until the customer is pleased and very satisfied that they've done business with you. Being conscientious is a very in-demand trait for an up-and-coming sales leader.

3. Achievement Orientation

84% of this study proved that the best salespeople in the world have a passion, desire, fixation, if you will, on achieving their goals and most of the time, these are goals that most people think aren't attainable. They love and welcome the challenge, but constantly stay in a state-of-growth mode looking for more. They constantly measure performance against the goals they're trying to reach.

4. Curiosity

Having curiosity as a sales professional, to me, is essential to become one of the elite. You listen to give value and tailor each of your next moves to make sure you're doing the right thing for the customer, rather than looking for that one moment to go in for the kill.

It also makes you more personable, easier to talk to, and releases the tension as curiosity proves you care. Curious salespeople also know their product or service better than anyone and there is nothing better than that when dealing with a prospect.

Usually these individuals have a massive hunger for learning new things. They need more knowledge constantly. As a matter of fact, in this Harvard study 82% of the entire study scored really high on their curiosity levels.

It's just a fact that top sales professionals are way more eager to learn than less successful sales individuals. The hard truth is that most of the salespeople in the world really limit their ability to grow, win, and become the best version of themselves by allowing ego to slow their learning ability down. Like thinking that just because on paper they might outperform someone, that they can't learn from them. This is ego at its finest and if you let that happen, expect a mediocre sales life.

5. Lack of Gregariousness

Gregariousness: fond of company; sociable. Here's a cool statistic from Harvard's study. The top 30% of sales professionals in the world were less sociable or fond of company, than the remaining 70%. Wait… are you telling me the that the top salespeople in the world don't like being around people much?

I used to have a theory and then I did my own study. I wanted to prove that a prospect would rather cut out the bullshit and just have someone be honest with them—they don't want to feel like someone is putting on a show for them. Eighty-seven out of 100 reps who made it clear that they were there to do business closed more deals than the ones who tried to build life-long bonds quickly.

Now don't get me wrong, you need to build relationships. But there's a time when the conversation is forced to pivot into asking for the business of the prospective client. You need to make that clear. Being friends, having life-long relationships, building rapport… ALL very important. BUT one of the biggest traits I would ask you to remember is that of knowing when and how to make that transition from the buddy-buddy chat to "it's time to do business" conversation. It seems as though Harvard agreed.

6. Lack of Discouragement

Harvard University did a study that proved 91% of the top 10% of the best sales professionals in the world stay encouraged. An astounding 94% listened to something motivational for over 30 minutes a day. The study also showed that less than 10% experienced sadness or lower levels of feeling discouraged.

Talented salespeople handle emotional disappointments better than most, bounce back from hard days, weeks or months, and are just mentally prepared for the next opportunity, never letting a previous situation dictate the outcome of the next sale!

You have to be encouraged. The mental aspect alone in sales is hard, which we get into later in this book, but knowing deep down you will keep going through any peak and valley this career brings you is essential to your success.

7. And Lack of Self-consciousness

Listen to this number. FIVE PERCENT, yes, I said 5% or less of the top sales professionals showed extremely low levels of being self-conscious in front of anyone at any time. The best salespeople in the world don't have this problem.

If you want to be one of the elite, don't be embarrassed, ever. Be you. Be corky. Be fun. No, you're not going to be for everyone, but neither is the person trying to act all professional and looking like they have a stick up their ass 100% of the time.

The best of the best have no problem fighting for their cause and what they believe in. These types of people have no problem cold calling anyone at any time, walking up to random strangers and pitching themselves, or even speaking to a high-level prospect that others likely don't have the guts to approach.

Be not afraid, my people! This way is the only way to grow your brand. Don't be too aggressive, but definitely be OK going after it all professionally and with no fear.

Oh, and P.S., when you do this, they'll tell others. Their telling others means more business! It's not that one person is lucky and you're not. It's that the more successful sales professionals of the world just have more of the traits above.

Look, I'm highly aware that there are all sorts of different personalities in sales. What one person does, the other may do it differently. Doesn't matter your background, styles of serving, or what your personality is. Treat people right. Show you care. Be honest and make damn sure they know that what matters to them is to you the most important thing. Period.

Let's talk some more truth, shall we?

MOST, and I say MOST for a reason, because MOST sales professionals have this desire to conquer! A lot of your top producers in the world have a thing called EGO DRIVE. But let's distinguish the difference between good and bad ego and what ego really is in general.

EGO: a sense of self-esteem or self-importance.

Good ego isn't about needing to be seen as the coolest all the time, having some enormous personality, or being pushy; good ego is literally just being conscious of a person's self-esteem. You're way nicer when you feel like you're adding value to someone's life or offering a product or service you passionately believe in. The best salespeople define good ego as their ability to listen and understand a customer's needs better than others. They feel confident that their product or service will add value to a prospect's life, but recognize there may be times when it doesn't or won't. Then the honest salesperson will politely tell the prospect (good ego) and guide them to someone who can add value to them (self-confidence).

Bad ego, or having a lower self-esteem, forces less talented or less trained salespeople to behave poorly. They start spewing things to look confident and strong, but don't really know their product or service well enough to earn the prospect's trust. Think about it. Who do you want to work with—someone who doesn't know that much about what they're offering or the person who knows it like the back of their hand?

Have you ever met a salesperson you liked because they were friendly and could confidently say that no one knows what they're offering better than they do and then prove that throughout the presentation? I don't know about you, but... Wait, yes, I do know what you'd say here... we ALL would want to work with that person over a less knowledgeable one.

There are many common traits of the bad ego or low ego salesperson. They constantly interrupt your questions and never take constructive criticism well. This forces them to get defensive fast and become combative with prospects who have concerns or objections. The truth is it's not really their fault most of the time. It's how they were trained.

Let me give you an example:

Prospect: "OK, I understand what you're offering. So how much is it?"

Low-Ego Salesperson: "Look, you've probably heard we're not the cheapest or maybe you looked online and saw some higher prices, but don't be misled. What I'm offering you is very affordable."

Prospect: "So how much is it?"

The prospect is probably pissed or frustrated now because this bad or lower ego-based salesperson wasn't confident enough to answer authentically and with strength. So, let's see how a stronger sale professional with a good ego would've handled this scenario.

Prospect: "OK, I understand what you're offering. So how much is it?"

Good-Ego Salesperson: "That's a great question. Is price a large factor in deciding to move forward with us today?"

Prospect: "No, I was trying to get an idea."

Good-Ego Salesperson: "No problem at all and completely understandable. The range is between x and x amount and I'll explain that in detail when we find the right solution for you."

See the difference? Night and day. Not even close. So good and bad ego are directly related to client retention, presentation, and confidence (not arrogance). The worst part about having less of an ego is that you waste a ton of time on what has nothing to do with the client, you, or the product or service you're offering. All because you didn't take the time to prepare yourself to be one of the elite presenting for you or your company.

The more tools you have, like:

- the more you listen
- the more you train
- the more you learn
- the more you're lifted up by others
- the culture you're in
- having positive people around you constantly
- getting a good night's rest
- learning not to be fearful of rejection; understanding it's a part of the business you're in
- having a sales process and following it
- learning to empathize with a prospect
- being coachable

… the more you will feel confident and build that GOOD EGO up daily. It'll also help you gain a prospect's trust much faster and it will definitely help you transition to the close on the back end.

There's no room for big egos in sales. There's no room for arrogance. There's no room for being too cocky. All you're really showing the world is you have an exaggerated sense of self-importance that others may or may not see, so you feel the need to flaunt or exaggerate who and what you really are. No wants to do business with people like this ever.

The hard part in sales is that you can have a great person, highly motivated, who has all the right traits, and they pop a few big sales and their ego goes through the roof. What they don't know is they get knocked down hard and it's way harder to come back up if people know you as that arrogant ego-based asshole who thought they knew everything and better than everyone.

Don't do or say things like this and you'll keep it under control:

- Don't be arrogant ("I know more than you" smirk with eye-roll face. You all know what I'm talking about… LOL). This is the worst.
- Don't talk down about others (usually masking your own insecurity to boost your ego).
- Don't treat people disrespectfully.
- Don't act like you know more than you do.
- Don't fake or lie about your stats.
- Don't make fun of others (you don't know them or what they're truly going through).
- Don't gloat when you have a good day, week, month or whatever (be proud, not arrogant).
- Don't let money or success change your level of humbleness.

Let's put it into very simple terms for you. Good Ego = BIG INCOME. Bad/Low Ego = little to no income.

Good Ego, combined with empathy, will pave a clear path to victory in the sales world. I've seen way too many talented people end their sales careers because the word got out about how arrogant they were. But if you stick to authenticity, empathy, honesty, and all of the willingness to grow that I've mentioned in this chapter, your GOOD EGO will guarantee you a long and successful future in the sales world!

This will help get you referrals, which is more business. It'll help you on all levels of efficiency. It will also help with retention and keep your deals and relationships on the books, when most BAD EGO deals are made for claps, not cash, and end up canceling or relationships don't allow for future business.

MORAL OF THIS CHAPTER: Just be a genuine, always humble person, who never thinks you're better than anyone else. Just have confidence, know your product or service better than anyone and present it in a way that's heartfelt, always putting someone's needs on a pedestal. Whether it be team members or clients.

The days of the ALPHA PERSON is the old way to lead and sell, not the new way. The assumption that someone has to have a BIG EGO (thinking they're better than others) to be great in sales is SO FAR FROM THE TRUTH. If you're a recruiter, don't look for the "aggressive sales performers." Look for the "motivated people ready to serve."

You want to always maintain a good ego, be open minded, a team player, curious about opportunities on all platforms without judgment, collaborate with like-minded people—all of this will keep you right on track.

I'll end with this: One of the best GOOD EGO moves that we will talk about more in the leadership portion of this book has to do with stepping in as T.O. (take over) to close a deal when a prospect had no intention of buying. Even if you're a leader in your organization and you step in, keep in mind that someone else started the deal. Give credit to the representative you helped for getting the customer to that point. Coach them on what you would've added to help them grow in their presentation, but DON'T YOU EVER SAY THESE WORDS when someone asks you about the deal: "I got the deal for them." Damn, I hate that. Literally the biggest bad ego move ever. Let that team member hear you say that and watch how fast you'll lose them.

Give credit. Applaud wins. Help with compassion. This is the way to attaining massive success with your good ego. People with good egos don't need the credit; they know the value they've added.

Go back and read or listen to that sentence again. Then move on to the next chapter.

CHAPTER 4

THE GRIT FACTOR: MENTAL TOUGHNESS

How tough are you? Do you think you have what it takes to be one of the elite sales professionals in the world? Do you have the grit to keep going when things aren't going the way you'd like them to? The real question is, can you learn to be mentally tough to thrive in the highest caliber sales environment? Let me help you answer this. The answer is YES!

It doesn't matter if you've never sold before. It doesn't matter if you've had any type of training at all. What matters is your ability and openness to listen, not just hear, but utilize the tools and honest integrity-based techniques that will literally guide you to becoming a thriving salesperson.

What is mental toughness? Many have different opinions on what this means, so let me give you mine. Mental toughness is a pattern of thoughts that become constant, habitual moves that allow you to overcome the emotions when you don't close deals and equally as much when you do.

Challenges always arise in the sales world. New prospect problems that need to be solved or guided through in a way to where your client sees the value of what you're selling.

Mental toughness is also "doing the right thing" always. What do I mean by that? Unfortunately—let me say that again, unfortunately—in today's world, there are many so-called sales professionals who hold the title, but don't move accordingly when it comes to serving the prospect.

They will try to convince someone to buy something, even when deep down inside they know that the product or service they're offering isn't the right fit and won't add value to that person's life. Mental toughness is crucial at this moment.

A lot of salespeople work on commission, no salary, no guarantee, and sometimes on a salary plus commission basis, where even in this sense the majority of their income comes from the commission side. So let's say you have bills to pay. You had a rough month the month before, some extra expenses may have come up, or you're looking to buy something and you need an influx of cash. For some, this means they force people into something they don't need because of the money they will earn from closing that deal.

This is not OK. It's arguably the hardest mental toughness for some to learn, because of the income a large deal can provide. I am begging and hoping that if you're reading this book, you understand that what comes around goes around. Treat people right. Do the right thing! Be strong enough to let a deal go when you know it's not right for the client. Even if the client is buying what you're saying and maybe trying to figure out a way to put your product to good use, selling them something they don't need is not the right way to serve people.

If it's not right for them, tell them it's not, even if you know you can push them into the deal. The referrals, appreciation, and trust you earn from treating your client or prospect like humans will give you the opportunity to serve them in the future. You'll be the first person they call, because you put them before the money.

"Put the people before the paycheck" is something I've lived by for decades in this industry and I personally believe it's given me the majority of my success.

People who serve others all have some common traits, such as:

- Honesty
- Integrity
- Servant mindset
- Emotionally detached for the yes and no. Handling the peaks and valleys in sales.
- Maintaining a positive attitude
- Daily habits that keep them focused on what's important
- Practice daily gratitudes
- Speak to themselves with zero limiting beliefs

If you know me or are just getting to know me by listening to or reading this book, you know that honesty, integrity, and serving people in anything in life is what's most important to me. I'll be touching on all three of those throughout this book. So let's get into detaching yourself emotionally.

THE NO

In many sales industries, you hear the word "no" way more than you hear the word "yes." You have to be able to navigate and understand how a "no" is moving you toward the "yes," but in some cases the "no" just may be a "no."

Most companies I've trained, and I mean large Fortune 500 companies with massive nationwide sales teams, don't train on this enough or even at all. They are sacrificing so much when they don't, because even the untenured salesperson can have huge amounts of success by using the "no" to gain the information they need to serve the prospect properly.

Unfortunately, most of the untrained sales individuals today get defensive when someone says "no." They go through their entire presentation not getting the answers they want. The prospect isn't engaging the way they'd like them to, and the end result is that dreadful word we all hate to hear, "NO."

For the trained, they use the "no" to gather information. To dive deeper into the discovery which we will talk about later in this book. But hearing "NO" sets a lot of people off track. Some even get defensive. They worked so long trying to present something to you and it's just a no.

Some give up here. Some get mad here. Some get combative with the prospect here which, by the way is the worst of all moves; that never gets you the deal. Then there are the ones who understand the value of the "no." They've been mentally prepared to hear it and know that if used properly, they are that much closer to serving someone—in other words, getting the deal!

The "no" also detours many salespeople from their next opportunity. They do a presentation, they don't get the deal, and then the attitude for the "no" moves to the new opportunity or prospect. I call this the trickle-down effect. This relates to anything in life, really. When you're arguing with someone or having a heated conversation, when you're just upset because you've recently had bad news, all of this can affect the next person(s) that you come in contact with.

For instance, you work extremely hard with one of your prospects or clients, get a "no" and then you immediately have another opportunity, which goes south because of the negative mindset you're still in from your previous conversation or presentation.

Being mentally tough, brushing off the "no," starting fresh, smiling, being ready to serve someone is CRUCIAL to your sales career. This is an "art," in my opinion. You have to be mentally strong to just move on. Learn from the "no," get rid of any limiting beliefs, doubt, or negativity, and be ready to serve at your highest.

Now I know what you're thinking: "This is easier said than done, Todd," and you're right. BUT here's my promise. If you can get used to understanding the value behind the "no" and starting fresh, brand new as the powerful person you are, starting off every opportunity ready to serve with energy, confidence, and happiness, your career will scale to exponential levels.

THE YES

What if I told you that lack of success can come from not understanding how to emotionally handle the "yes" in your sales career too? Would you agree? Well, let me explain.

Cornell did a study on how getting the "yes" too often in a salesperson's career can have a tremendous impact on whether they're successful or not, if understood incorrectly.

They tracked the results from thousands of salespeople over a 6-year period, in many different types of sales environments. They used different products and services to measure how successful a salesperson is, if they don't allow the yes to limit their performance. They found that ego, in many cases, crippled the success of a salesperson's career, when they went from numerous "yes's" to just a few "no's" in a row.

The Cornell study found that:

After hearing "yes" more than 3 times in a row, an individual's ego started allowing them to believe that it was "too easy" to sell. So inevitably, they started short cutting their process. They started not to do the things they got them to the "yes" in the first place. Ego driven presentations, thinking they were just too great of a salesperson, diminished their performance once they received only 2 NO's after getting 3 Yes's.

Think about that. Think about how important it is to being mentally strong enough, never to allow your ego to get in the way of your career. This is another instance where it's easier said than done.

Things are going so great. The yes's are flowing. Everyone's happily buying what you're offering and then just a couple NO's come and you start questioning yourself:

- "What am I doing wrong?"
- "That prospect just didn't get it."
- "That lead sucked."

Being mentally tough in sales comes with the "yes's" too. You have to be able to always stay humble and, most importantly, when you're winning, keep your process sharp.

Just like the "no," when you're done serving someone, move into the new opportunity with energy, confidence, and happiness, where just the simpleness of habit puts you in the best position to win.

Hearing "yes" too often can create ego and cause you to get too cocky. Now don't get me wrong, there's a HUGE difference between being "cocky/arrogant" and having "confidence." If you're a top salesperson, you definitely need to have confidence, but don't let the "yes's" get to your head. I've seen way too many extremely talented people get knocked off their high horse and never get back on because they weren't mentally prepared to handle the peaks and valleys that come in this very lucrative sales world.

Maintaining a positive attitude is a must. In some sales industries, if you're closing at 30% you're considered a superstar. These individuals understand that even though they are considered the top of the top salespeople in their industry, THEY are still going to hear "no" 7 out of 10 times. It's simple math. 70% of the people they speak to aren't going to do business with them.

It's hard to get up over and over again like that. It's pure rejection and for many, it's difficult to take, which ends a lot of sales careers much too early.

So how do you combat a defeated mindset? Good daily habits. Practice daily gratitudes, listen to something motivational or inspirational, constantly educate yourself by reading or listening to books, and most importantly, speak positively to yourself daily.

My daily habits keep me going. Without them, I don't think I'd be where I am today mentally, which inherently adds to the success in my life financially too.

This is my personal routine. You don't have to do the same; just have a routine that adds value and positivity to your life. Oh and yes, I do all of this before even looking at my phone. I know, I know. For real, Todd? Yes, for real. When I get up, it's a focused habitual routine that leads me to success and it doesn't include looking at my phone first. We all need that disconnect, trust me.

So here's mine:

1. The moment I wake up, I pray. Thanking God, regardless of how good or bad my day was prior, for another opportunity to be alive with the ones I love most and the ability to serve others.

Prayer doesn't have to be your thing. We may not believe in the same things and that's OK. But this is my first thing, because without God, I'm nothing. I choose, just my choice, to put him above all else and make sure he knows that I know that without him, I don't have anything.

2. I then write down 10 things I'm very grateful for. Every. Single. Day!

Funny story. I was working with the amazing Danelle Delgado, to me one of the most prominent and extraordinary humans on the planet, who mentors, teaches, serves all sorts of people from beginners to CEOs of billion-dollar companies, guiding them and their sales teams to success. She also teaches anyone willing to move with intention on how to create a successful business.

So, one day I had a very unsuccessful, rough day. The next day I called Danelle, complaining about all the "hard" in my life. Her response: "Did you write your gratitudes today?" I had not and I told her that. So she told me to stop talking, stop complaining, go grab my gratitude book and write not 10 gratitudes, but 100 of them. Yep, you read it right. One HUNDRED gratitudes. It took me 3 hours to think of 100 things that I was grateful for, but I did it.

I realized that when I think about life's hard, compared to the good in my life, it's easy to forget all that I have. When you focus on the hard, it's what you think about. If you focus on gratitude, it's easier to move past the hard.

It was a great lesson for me to learn. To not complain, but to live every day full of gratitude and love for all that I've been blessed with.

This practice has been second to prayer for me, as far as the biggest catalyst in my career and life.

3. Write down 3 attainable/semi-challenging goals for the day

I write down 3 goals to achieve daily. It can be work based, life based, fitness, finance, anything you'd like. I don't make unrealistic goals. I make realistic goals.

For instance, I wouldn't make a goal to lose 10 lbs today (although I'd like to … LOL).

My goals are similar to this:

Goal #1 - Workout for 1.5 hours. 45 minutes of cardio. 45 minutes of weights.

Goal #2 - Write for 2 hours

Goal #3 - Create new leadership training outline.

Very attainable, but accountable goals. Accountability is key to your daily routine, but the sense of accomplishment and productivity you get from setting this goal practice is essential for your mindset to be focused and sharp. This practice also reduces the opportunity for decreased daily production if you stick to it.

4. Working out daily

Some think otherwise, but there's a statistical direct connection between success and fitness. When you feel good physically, you perform better in business.

There was a study done on over 200 self-made millionaires and 200 individuals who weren't nearly as successful. The results were astonishing as 76% of the most successful business individuals in the world exercise for a minimum of 30 minutes each day.

British entrepreneur Richard Branson, actor Chris Hemsworth, and others swear that the success of their businesses and careers have a direct correlation to fitness and the habit of fitness.

Richard Branson actually said in an interview, "I definitely can achieve twice as much by keeping fit."

Chris Hemsworth (Thor) said in an interview, "Fitness has awarded me many opportunities in my life. It's not just the physical attributes that bring abundance, but how I feel every day, makes me work harder mentally as well. Mentally, I'm stronger than ever, because of the efforts I put in my life physically."

This just means that extraordinary people in business have great fitness routines. Additional studies have shown that our mental capability is directly linked to exercise, regardless of someone's age. When you work out, you have a stronger lifeline due to increased immune systems, more energy, and a greater sense of well-being. Not to get technical, but exercise increases serotonin levels that go to our brain. The evidence is there, so make this a part of your daily routine. You'll feel less lethargic and ready for the day.

5. Listen to something educational or motivational daily.

Finally, what you listen to matters! Not one day goes by that I don't listen to or read something motivational or educational. A lot of people say they don't have the time, but you do. It's just not important enough for you to care or you'd make time.

Your car is a mobile university. You drive, which means you have time. You can get up earlier to make the time. The moment I made this a daily routine, I learned more, felt more confident in training and leading people, and it took my company to a whole new level.

Now some of you read that "motivational" word and may have thrown up in your mouth a little and I promise you I get it. I wasn't always the guy who believed in it and I suffered because of it. Some people on social media, big time coaches and entrepreneurs, will tell you that motivation isn't real, that consistency is.

There is some truth to that, but you have to be motivated by something to create consistency, in my humble opinion. Maybe it's to learn something more about perfecting your craft. Maybe it's you wanting to become a better person. Maybe it's just listening to something positive to pull you out of a rut. Whatever it is, something either pushes you to want to have powerful words of inspiration or education in your life, or you just don't, and you listen to music all the time.

Studies have shown that the best salespeople and leaders in the world are consistent on what they listen to or read. Motivation, consistency, dedication are all attached to success on every level.

Find something. Your why. Family, friends, loved ones, maybe it's to succeed to prove others wrong and prove yourself right. Whatever it is, I know this. You can't change your life by not listening to or reading something that can enhance your life.... so why not try? This practice has helped me work with some of the highest-level companies and people that I would never have been able to work with had my mind not been right or had I not educated myself on my craft to become the obvious choice to work with.

Tony Robbins and other world-renowned coaches will tell you to look in the mirror and say something positive about yourself rather than always critiquing how you look or where you're at in life. I don't know the exact science behind it like those guys do, but it's definitely made an impact in my life. I speak to myself with intention and am clear on my expectations daily.

Finally ...

6. Send 3 Gratitude Text Messages Daily

Send three texts to someone not expecting it. Yes, it can be family and friends, but what about the random person who isn't really a part of your world? Maybe you've seen them on social media and you just want to be that person to lift someone up.

You never know what people are going through in life, and I've personally seen my life change just because I cared enough to care about other people. I don't do it for that, but I know personally I've gone through some serious things in my life, and having someone there impacted me tremendously. Serving them, serves you.

Whatever your thoughts are on how you want to live is on you. I didn't write this to convince you to change. I didn't tell you my routine to tell you how I live. This was an example of how every day starts for me and the studies behind how it helps not just sales professionals but people on all levels become the best versions of themselves.

Have a routine and stick to it. Period.

CHAPTER 5

VISION, GOALS, AND SALES: A SYMBIOSIS

If you don't know how you're getting there, why even start? If you don't have goals to attain, what are you trying to achieve? These are two questions I asked myself a long time ago. I put myself in some very rough situations throughout my life. I've had my back against the wall so often that I actually took a personal assessment test that proved I worked best under pressure. Not because I enjoyed it, but because I had to.

I took a test with a buddy of mine named Paul Blanchard, who owns a company called Habit Finder. Paul is without a doubt one of the most intelligent people I have the luxury of knowing. He breaks down everything scientifically through what he's called the "The Un-Personality Test." It takes about 10 minutes and, no, I'm not here to plug Paul, but you and your team should truly go take this free test. It revealed so much about my life, I was shocked! Paul worked with me personally and told me about my entire life in a nutshell. It was so accurate and he basically said that throughout my life, I've been mentally trained and forced to be successful.

As good a trait as I thought that was, he said something that rocked my world. He said, "You've created massive success with your back against the wall your entire life, but what if you just learned how to create a little space between the wall and your back." Now once again, Paul uses words I don't understand that he thinks is normal ... LOL ... but he broke it down to this.

If I just created a vision, set some goals, and then created a path that led me there, it would release the pressure to succeed. If the way I move is intentional, I will get there even if I were methodical in my movement and stayed the course.

Is it really that easy? It is. The assessment went much deeper, but the moment I put my vision on paper and created short-range, mid-range, and semi-long-term goals, I started to achieve WAY MORE than when I was forced to succeed. The pressure was released. I felt more at ease. When I achieved my goals, I set new ones. When my vision was created, I added to that vision. I like working on myself to where I'm satisfied, but not so much that I can't fight for bigger things. Some call it the "never satisfied" mindset. I like winning and the feeling of achievement, as I believe we all do, but I'm definitely always pushing myself to do more.

If you want a sales and leadership career, you have to lead yourself first. You need a vision. It doesn't matter how old you are, where you are in your career, how long you've been crushing it or not. There are new levels to success when you have a vision and create goals to obtain.

So how do you create a vision?

A sales vision is a statement that dictates where you want yourself or your sales team to be within a certain period of time. If you don't have this vision, several unproductive things happen.

For instance:

- **It's hard to prioritize things**

You work on too many things at the same time, which means minimal production in each. Don't get me wrong, I believe you have to be capable of multi-tasking so you can form multiple streams of income, but master one thing, then move on to the others until you create a process where your presence in one area isn't needed as much, so you can start to concentrate on the next task at hand.

- **Lack of focus**

When you're intentionally focusing on a vision board or something set, planted, created to achieve, it's proven to be achieved more often. When you know why and what you're going after, you end up getting there.

- **No man's land**

Without a clear vision, most salespeople drift. They float in the unknown space on whether what they're doing is enough or not. Even if they become the best in their field, without having a vision of your personal goals to achieve, you'll always be wondering if there's more you can do and how you can get there.

I've had multiple visions set up for many individuals, CEOs, salespeople, sales teams and small to major Fortune 500 companies where we go in to elevate their efficiencies when they're trying to scale. When that vision is clear, I have direction. Which means I can teach, lead, energize anyone personally or an entire team to scale with an action plan that will net the highest results for growth.

What is a vision statement and what's the best way to build yours?

My definition might be different from others, but truthfully, when building vision statements I define it around goals to achieve, the outcomes I'm expecting from those goals, and having an organizational purpose (a road map) to guide me to reach those bars I set for myself or a company.

All of this gives you direction. It helps you realize and visually see the road map to your success through all the necessary components. Now when you combine that with the right mindset and eliminate limiting beliefs, you've set yourself up to scale on an exponential level.

When you're clear on movement, you can see the goal and how to get there. Your vision becomes motivating rather than being in a constant state of chaos, not knowing what needs to be done and when, and not prioritizing moves to be most efficient.

A vision statement is not the same as a mission statement. Don't get the two confused. The easiest way to understand them is that a Vision Statement looks to the future of what you're going to achieve. A Mission Statement speaks more of the present, such as daily goal setting and speaking positively to yourself. Also a Vision Statement is something you're aspiring towards, something you're looking forward to accomplishing and inspire teams and those around you to do equally. A Mission Statement is more of a day-to-day operational status that keeps you active and moving intentionally.

When creating your Vision Statement, set bars that are challenging and that can, and will, net you your biggest achievements yet. I don't believe in setting goals that are small enough to constantly achieve. Some say that, if they don't hit their goals, that the bar was set too high and they feel unaccomplished. For me, the path to success should always be challenging, the times you do hit those higher-level goals, the feeling you get is worth all the times you didn't hit those goals. It paid off. The hard work was worth the effort and that feeling of accomplishment pushes you to reach even higher!

Most of the sales teams we assist in creating Vision Statements for companies set a time frame of 6-12 months max. It's enough time to achieve said goals and brings urgency in accountability to map out proper steps to get there in a specific time frame.

Your Vision Statements don't have to be some long, drawn-out scenario-based paragraphs or essays either. They should be short and extremely intentional based on what you're trying to achieve.

Here are a couple examples of Vision Statements:

- To increase sales revenue by 20% over the next 6 months
    - Simple, but intentional. This type of vision statement also MUST BE tracked weekly and monthly, recalculating metrics based on lack of production or increased production. This is crucial to the success of hitting your goals.

- Decrease rescission standards by 15% over the next year. (Keeping more business.)
    - To use this Vision Statement, you have to calculate how much business you're losing, and how much money it will net the bottom line by keeping this business.

Just two very simple but intentional Visions Statements. Then the mission statement should be present in day-to-day operations in achieving the Vision Statement success.

Ideally you should break down both statements into small smarter goals, with the right leaders (not by title, but by individually who the person is) to achieve their portion of the goal. When you put people in place, owning their portion of what you're trying to achieve overall, it's statistically proven that achieving that goal will increase by almost 78% more efficiency. Yep, it's true. Breaking down plans of actions for each person to focus on guarantees your overall success.

If you're an individual with a Vision Statement, the same applies. Break down the goal into segments and use people that move with you, such as your spouse, friend, or co-workers where their sole responsibility may be to hold you accountable to achieve your success.

Once you've identified the right people to run with, you have to create ACTIONABLE STEPS to reach your goal. Setting these steps to success is extremely important daily, weekly, and monthly to obtain any goal. It's the easiest way to guarantee success. The one-percenters who do are the ones we all try to be like, but their effort and goal setting with a definable road map is why they succeed. They also adjust accordingly to move differently week to week with personal or team reviews of where they stand in production to hit the goals they set. This accountability is why the ones who win at high levels do so consistently.

Finally, evaluating performance weekly, monthly, and quarterly with accountability plans set in place such as personal performance reviews and team performance reviews, keeps the goal always on your mind and pushes you to catch up when struggling to hit the bars you've set for yourself and/or your team. Once those reviews are complete, you can readjust, assist, and serve yourself and the team better to get them to be more efficient. This is not to come down on anyone, but to SERVE, to ASSIST, to HELP. Never ever ever does coming down on someone help you achieve your goal. SERVING is the best remedy for everything. When you come from a servant leadership level, including SERVING yourself, do it empathetically and with an accountability level of compassion.

You have to find the balance of not being too hard on yourself or your team and pushing yourself with an actionable plan to give yourself the big wins. Otherwise, you'll get bummed out and burnt out. That doesn't help anyone ever.

Be conscious of how you move in setting your goals and vision statement, and then adhere to your mission statement to be the best version of a sales individual, better yet the LEADER YOU WILL BECOME!

Once you have all the important steps of creating your vision ironed out, you need to set goals and set them accordingly. So what's the best way to set a goal? Let's dive in!

First of all, reaching goals doesn't happen overnight. As much as the new world mindset believes that to be, it's not realistic. It takes hard work, determination, grit, and a full sense of understanding that there is no short road to success. So setting your goals needs to be somewhat realistic, while pushing yourself further every time you achieve the goal set. You have to stay committed, through the good and the bad times. Consistency will mean more than skillset.

You could be fighting for a promotion, more sales, serving people in your community, or even trying to win some sort of award. You might want to be better at speaking, giving morning meetings, networking, or you might want to just become a better communicator.

When setting a goal you have to be specific. You need to see the timeline and fully understand what it's going to take to get there. What do you want to achieve? Is the goal you're setting worth your time? Is sacrificing the time and effort going to give you the feeling of accomplishment you're looking for? Can you measure your goals? Are you able to recalculate your goals based on inefficiency, such as a slow week or obstacles that may occur? Being prepared about the unknowns is very important when setting your goal. Think about all that could happen that might get in the way or stall your production.

I always recommend setting short-term and "semi" long-term goals. I don't personally like 5-year plans. I like setting weekly, monthly, quarterly, and annual goals. Life changes, things happen, and it's next to impossible to predict the future. I like being realistic about the shifts and pivots that happen in life. I have fallen into the trap of believing life's all sunshine and rainbows, only to get knocked down and finding myself having to reevaluate every time I set super long-term goals. Annual goals are the longest I set, but if you feel the need to set longer goals, just follow through using the same mindset as you would for an annual assessment, just extended with increased goals to reach.

Having short-term and annual goals is important because you'll always be evaluating both and where you stand. So if you hit a short-term goal, your long-term goal is still something you're striving to hit, while resetting short-term goals to hit along the way.

THE OUTLINE

- **Know what your goal is!**
    - I can't tell you how many times I've asked someone in multiple industries, "What's your goal? What's your vision statement?" And they don't have a clue. If someone asks you what your goal or vision statement is, it should be so ingrained in your head that you INSTANTLY recite it to them. No stuttering, no thinking about it, no fumbling over your words. COMPLETE and utter intentional understanding of what you're setting out to accomplish now, in the near future, and IN LIFE!

- **Is your goal in writing?**
    - Put everything in writing. When you can see it, that means it's real. Too often, people just talk about goals, mentioning them in general conversations. Nothing is written anywhere, so when they're asked about their goals, they seem to change constantly. There's no real written commitment on what to achieve. Writing your goals down is essential to achieving them.

- **What's it going to take to hit your goal?**
    - What moves do you need to make to have the best possible outcome? Have you set parameters on intentional dedicated pivots from what you're currently doing, to what needs to change? Understanding what it's going to take and actually writing it down gives you visual clarification. Again, put it someplace where you can see it, constantly reminding yourself of how you're going to feel when you achieve said goal.

- **What sacrifices need to be made?**
    - How much time (scheduled in) will it take for you to hit your goals? Daily, weekly, monthly, and quarterly? Who

will you have to sacrifice time with? Is it worth the sacrifice to achieve your goal? How much money will it take? What relationships will you have to sacrifice—family, friends, or co-workers—whether it be time or cutting people off?

- **How long will it take you to hit your goal?**
  - Have a start date and end date. Make sure you have the time it will take broken down into segments daily, weekly, monthly, and quarterly, and be sure to constantly evaluate your performance to recalculate the time it will take to complete your goals.
    - When you're trying to achieve your goals, mapping out performance on when, where, and how you're going to accomplish your goal is essential to your success.

- **What steps do you have in place to give yourself the best outcome?**
  - A detailed step-by-step, day-to-day process should be in place to stay focused. The first step is the most important one. Most people have ideas that they think are goals, but never even take that first step that forces you to cross that invisible line in the sand. One side is the hard work that leads you to an unmatched life payoff of accomplishments. On the other side are all the people who talk a big game, but forget to move. Creating a process and having steps to accomplish your goals forces you out of your comfort zone. You've spent all this time preparing; now just take that first step! The road map to a new life is easier navigated when you create the steps. It's like your own personal navigation system. Create one and then have more than one person review it that you trust, because someone will see things that you might not. Once they've reviewed it, then you can start to MOVE!

- **Is your goal setting trackable?**
  - There are so many benefits to tracking your goals, such as:
    - Gives you the chance to recalculate your weekly, monthly, quarterly, bi-annual, and annual goals based on your daily production.
    - Keeps you accountable. If you have a bad day, use the above and force yourself to catch up. If you have a good day, stay the course. Keep your foot on the gas pedal. You're ahead of the game! This type of accountability gives you a chance to surpass the goal you've set!
    - When you constantly see it, log it, and review your performance, you're more conscious of and reminded of what needs to be done in order to hit your goals.
    - Tracking your progress keeps you motivated, but most importantly, I like to attach my goals to certain "why's" for each one. Such as: "I need to reach 10 sales this week, so it will allow me to get my daughter that car she's always wanted." When you do this, it's for something bigger than money and pushes you to accomplish more.
    - When you review your performance daily, consistently logging your progress, it keeps you much more engaged than a person who doesn't respect the goal-setting process as much. Your plan is your life.
    - Finally, for decades I've been tracking every move I make because it gives me direction and focus, and gives life to the words and plan I have in place. It's without a doubt the main reason I've accomplished so much.

- **Are the steps to achieve your goal prioritized properly?**
  - Prioritizing your goals is SO IMPORTANT to scaling your life on all levels! It reduces stress, it's the best time saver, it increases production, and more. If you don't prioritize the moves you make, the steps to achieve your goal(s), it's likely you'll forget certain essential factors to increase the chances of accomplishing everything you set out to do. This part of the goal-setting process takes time. Do NOT rush through this. It's equally as important to get another set of eyes or two when prioritizing the steps to success in your goal-setting process.
  - Remember, if you're an entrepreneur, most of the time you're working 8-10 hours a day at a job, then if you're motivated and dedicated to doing bigger things, you're coming home and working another 5-8 hours on your personal goals to get out of your 9-5. With all of this going on, you MUST figure out a way to use your time the most efficiently and that means prioritizing! Without this, your mind gets scrambled and you start giving each step 30% of you rather than focusing on one step at 100% of you. You have to know what you want to achieve and then set up your steps accordingly by importance.
  - There are three known processes when doing this:
    1. *Urgent Steps:* To many, this might mean steps that must be done right away, set with a deadline, weighed based on an outcome need promptly. The truth is, it doesn't always mean that. You need to ask yourself, "If I didn't do this right away, how would it affect my progress?" If the answer is a lot, then it's categorized in the urgent steps. If the answer is NOT a lot, then move it to one of the other categories below.

2. *Significant Steps*: Most of the time people will go back and forth with certain steps wondering if they should be in the "Urgent Steps" section or this one. Significant steps usually have a strong presence in your long-term goals. Urgent steps are mostly day-to-day moves that keep you moving towards your significant steps that hold more foundational presence in your goals.

3. *Advantage Steps*: You have to give yourself the best outcome in goal-setting steps, which means evaluating two tasks that seem equally as important, but which one will get you closer to the end game? For instance, you might have an opportunity to close a sale as a leader in your organization, but the prospect can only meet with you during a sales training you are doing for your sales team. So the question is, is it more important to get one deal? Or to train others to be better at their craft which in the long term will net you more overall sales? Depending on the timing, such as end of the month trying to hit your monthly performance or the beginning of the month starting fresh may sway the weight of your decision on which one nets you the biggest advantage in accomplishing your goal.

- The truth is most people don't prioritize their goals. They just take what comes and live by this "I'll get there one day" mindset that limits possibility for so many. They procrastinate more. They usually work on the urgent tasks, forgetting about the significant and advantage steps. They always seem to have the highest anxiety and are doing a thousand things at once, while accomplishing very little. On the other hand, when you follow the process and respect why it's so important to prioritize your goals properly, you'll reduce obstacles and roadblocks that others who don't prioritize their goals will face throughout their lives. Makes for a healthier life financially, mentally, and physically. As they say at Nike, JUST DO IT!

- **What possible obstacles might you face while going after your goal?**
  - Make a list of all possible obstacles that might occur or arise. Personally and professionally. There's no judgment here. Just be real about the problems you could face and list ALL OF THEM. When you do this, you're way ahead of the pack. It's like blocking objections. Surface the issues before they arise. Own them. Have a game plan for each if they occur. Carve out the max possible time and what resources it'll take to handle each obstacle. I know it seems tedious, but when you're aware of what could come at you, your preparation will pay off big time. Again, when you make this list, have a couple sets of eyes review possible problems that may occur and get their opinions. I've never set a goal, broken it down in detail, without having someone I trust give me their honest opinion. So many times I've missed something that they've managed to catch. Understanding possible outcomes keeps you prepared and ready for almost anything that comes your way. Eliminating risk tremendously!

- **Who are you working with to hit your goals?**
  - THIS is the most productive or most goal-crushing section of goal setting. Yes, we've all heard this saying, "You are the sum of those you surround yourself with" or "If you hang out with five idiots, you'll be the sixth." These statements are accurate, by the way, but some people don't take them seriously. Who's around you? Who's helping you? Who are you taking advice from?

- I personally have made a list of people I hang out with or who are in my circle and determined what value they had in my life. Was it good? Bad? Stagnant? Were they negative? Positive? Complaining all the time? Happy? Motivated? I have a detailed list and don't sway from what's important to me. Like, what are your core values and do the people around you stand for similar? Or are they so far off track that you wonder why you're still allowing them in your life? Some people never critique their surroundings, and it keeps them stuck in mediocrity. Take the time to really dive into the people in your life, make sure their alignment is within the structure of the life you're trying to create. If not, talk to them and try to explain the support you're looking for, because it's OK if others' lives don't align with yours; it just means you have to keep some at arm's length or even remove them when you're trying to accomplish bigger things.

- **How would your life change when you hit your goal?**
  - This is so much fun. Start writing out the perfect life you'd create if you just crushed all your goals. Like, you actually visualize the car you'd drive, the dream house you want, the vacations you could take, serving the people you love most. How happy would you be? Would it help eliminate stress and give you the chance to do more? Would your health get better, due to less stress? Whatever's important to you, whatever dream life you've ever wanted, write it out in detail, create a vision board and put it someplace where you can see it every day. That motivation specifically took my life to new levels because it was in my face EVERY SINGLE DAY. It was a constant reminder of what I knew my life could be if I just kept going. Then I'd read once a week what my perfect life would be when, not "if," I hit my goal. Doing this consistent-

ly motivated me and helped me to be disciplined in a way few people are.

Finally and most importantly…
- **Who does it affect if you don't hit your goals?**
  - Ouch. If I'm being honest, this is personal. We all have people in our lives we love— relatives, kids, spouses, friends, family. If you gave up, how would it affect your loved ones? If it is just you and you alone, how would it affect you if you didn't make it? Whose life would it impact and how? Be specific. Mine was so detailed, I hated reading it because it made me cry and angry thinking about the life I'd create for them if I gave up. Would I really be OK looking into the eyes of someone I loved and saying, "It was too hard; I had to give up"? Was I really OK with people I loved looking at me as someone who folds during the hard life offers up? How would I feel if my children wanted something that I couldn't afford? Would I want to live a life where I couldn't spend time, the most valuable, non-replaceable thing, with the ones I love most? I want you to really take time and write out how failing, not succeeding, would affect YOU and THOSE you love. This plays a huge role in your journey towards a powerful and fulfilling life. It's why I never gave up. I've been at the bottom and I know how it feels, so there's ZERO CHANCE I'M GOING BACK or SETTING MY KIDS AND FAMILY UP TO LIVE LIFE feeling the way I did when I had nothing. No way. No chance. You want to be motivated? You want to be disciplined? Write this one out and read it once a week. Call it "Who suffers if I give up?" Be detailed and I promise you, you'll be the most determined person on the planet if you take the time to be real with this step. It changed my life.

There are so many reasons why goal setting is important. I personally like the emotional guide to goal setting, because my family is my world and I'll never let them down. But that doesn't need to be everyone's motivator. Goal setting gives you more focus, keeps you disciplined by following the processes above, gives you properly outlined direction, more clarity, more time, more freedom, and more productivity. Goal setting keeps you accountable. You can control the outcome of your life better since you have more control over your movement. You can make better decisions. You're inspired to serve more and that means serving yourself too. Motivation comes easily when you combine a proper goal-setting and vision-statement model, creating a foundation of success so you can be stable and excited to do things others only talk about.

I'm proud of you for getting this far, for taking the time to read or listen to this book when others miss out on so much education that can take them from zero to 100 real quick and the right way! I wanted you to feel the importance of this chapter and to start implementing what you've learned not only in business and in sales, but in your lives as well. It doesn't matter how far you are in life, you always have room to push yourself to achieve more. And guess what? It's possible. Read this chapter 10 times in a row if you have to. Take notes, highlight the stuff that resonates with you and remember, there's no process I've created here, it's what the elite do. It's what they've done for decades. I just added what moved me personally, which moved my career to leave a ripple effect of succession to the lives I have the luxury of touching. Goal setting is THAT important!

CHAPTER 6

DOMINATING SALES: FROM CREDIBILITY TO AUTHORITY

Have you really thought through how important your credibility is? Did you know that being credible helps with authority? Not just in sales, but your reputation, the time it takes to build one, and how fast you can ruin it if you're not careful. Credible people are serious listeners. They shut up when being criticized. They don't get defensive ever and they think before they speak. They want to be served and they love to serve. In other words, they don't mind asking for help, receiving it, and giving it. Your credibility rises when people know you listen in order to learn and are never above growing.

A credible sales professional will read body language and assess how to address their prospect even before a prospect says a word. To a client, that proves you know what they're feeling and it builds credibility when you're right.

Being an expert in your field might mean knowing more about your product than anyone, or credibility can also be created when you admit you "don't know" the answer to a question your prospect asks. Too many salespeople try to embellish or fluff their way through a question they may not know the answer to, when a credible one will just say, "That's a good question and I have no clue what the right answer is. BUT I'm going to ask someone who knows right now, instead of telling you something that may not be accurate." SEE, now that right there builds trust and credibility in your character, which plays a huge role in the decision-making process.

How do you think prospects define credibility? How hard is it to prove that you're credible, honest, real, and that you're there to serve them whether your product or service is for them or not? The answer, in today's sales world is: HARD! There are far too many liars and scam artists tarnishing the character of and opportunities for the authentically good people who are trying to elevate their lives in this unmatched earning industry that is sales!

Bad assumptions destroy credibility! In order to build credibility, you MUST do what you say you're going to do. If you promise something, deliver! If you're ready, I'm about to share with you the move of all moves. The holy grail of defining how credible others think you are. I had to figure out a way to unleash the truth without having people tell me what I wanted to hear.

I was training a large Fortune 500 sales team one day and I had a thought. *I wonder what these people really think of me?* So I asked myself that question and created a process to get the truth that I needed to hear.

So the question was, how do people see me? Like, really be honest. What do they think of me as a person? Are you the obvious choice to do business with? Should they trust you based on previous business moves or sales you've made? Sounds tough, right? Well, I don't want you to answer this. If you're really serious about your personal and professional growth, I want you to ask people you trust to anonymously type out how they think others view you as a person. Yes, type it, so you won't be able to try to guess who wrote it by the handwriting. I know, I know. Scary, right? Well, if you need honesty in how credible you are and you're OK with being critiqued, this is the best way to find the real in how others see you.

Your ego is about to take a hit, believe that. A lot of you won't even do this exercise because you're not willing to hear where you need to grow to achieve a high level of credibility. But it's the best way. It's the right way. It's what taught me most of my areas I need to concentrate on to grow.

Anonymous critiques are the best. Here are some about me I'm happy to share. Some of it we know about ourselves and don't want to admit it. Other stuff, we don't know about ourselves and we need to admit it.

These were some of my anonymous critiques:

1. "Todd, you need to change this…"
2. "Todd, people think of you like this…"
3. "Todd, you talk too much."
4. "Todd, you talk too fast."
5. "Todd, you cuss too much."
6. "Todd, you sound like you're trying to swindle everyone when you sell."
7. "Todd, because of the mistakes you've made, people don't trust you."
8. "Todd, your past makes people choose someone else."
9. "Todd, you cater to certain people."
10. "Todd, you just care about the money."

I want to be clear here. You're putting yourself in a very vulnerable scenario, but it was necessary for me to reclaim my personal credibility. I wanted to be better in all aspects of life and I was ready for anything anyone said, but I will tell you this, not everything everyone says is always true. Some people like to judge or bring people down, BUT perception, my friends, is reality. If they're saying it, it could be malicious, but something prompted them to say it. Is there validity to it all? Could be and maybe not, but just KNOWING that people put me in any of the above categories gives me a clear path to what I need to do to make sure they see me differently moving forward.

My personal and business credibility was worth the ego punch. If you want to change, like truly check yourself, this process is so big. On the other side of this is freedom and the ability to connect with people so your credibility is never questioned again.

Your name is everything. Your movement is everything. How you serve others is everything. So if you think you can become a powerful sales professional without credibility, you're dead wrong. But it takes deep reflection most aren't willing to do.

So let's dive into how you can create better credibility. Here are some simple tips that aren't hard, but are VERY affective in gaining life-long credibility.

1. BE ON TIME.

I'll tell you a little story about being punctual. My girlfriend at the time, Michelle, who's now my wife, set up a golf tee time for me to go golfing with her dad. The tee time was set for 8:42 a.m. I was notorious for being late and, like all other times in my life, I was running late again. Can you imagine what an idiot I was to show up late to the first tee time of meeting her dad to play golf? I think back in disgust now, because I remember pulling in the golf parking lot and there was Art (her dad) sitting in the golf cart waiting as I was parking. I had to get out, then put my shoes on and then get my clubs out to bring them to his golf cart. As I'm walking up, I say, "Hey, sir, I'm so sorry I'm late but it was unavoidable. There was so much traffic and there was an accident. [There wasn't. I was just scared to say I was late.] Sorry for the wait, sir." There was nothing but silence. He didn't respond to anything I was saying until I loaded up the cart and sat next to him. Then he said, "Son, I'm gonna only say this to you one time in our lives so I want you to listen carefully. Being late is disrespectful. You said it was unavoidable, but you're wrong. Get up earlier. Leave earlier because you respect me enough to get here on time regardless of whether there was an accident or not. No professional person in the world should be late. So if you ever show up late for anything with me or my family again, I'll take that as a sign that you don't care or respect us enough to be on time. And that, son, will be the last time we do anything together."

Sheesh. Harsh much? Or was he.... Here's what I learned that day. Regardless of whether it was my fault or not, I don't want anyone ever to think of me like that again. I also want people to respect my time equally as I should respect theirs.

If you can't even be on time, how credible are you as the person I want to do business with? The answer is, not very. I was never late again. Fourteen years later, I'm always on time. When someone sets something up with me, they know I'll be there. Credible.

2. HAVE A SERVANT MINDSET.

People need to know you care. They need to know that if they need something, you're ready and willing to help always. I pride myself on being available, personally and in business. How does serving have anything to do with credibility? Simple. If people wonder if someone else is ready to help them or they KNOW you are, who do you think they're calling? Go above and beyond your title or scope of work. "Under promise, over deliver" is a real accurate business, life, and sales accelerator.

3. DO WHAT YOU SAY YOU'RE GOING TO DO.

Here's the thing. There's nothing that bothers me more in today's world than this: When I ask someone to do something for me and they respond, "I got you," and then they take their time getting it done or, worse, they never do it. Here's what people know about me. You ask me to do something, I get it done and I always get it done in a timely manner. Usually immediately. You have the time. I constantly say, "Don't tell me you don't have the time; just tell me it's not important enough for you to care about." At least you'd be honest and not tell me you're too busy. You want quick credibility. Do what you promise to do always!

4. BE REAL.

Authenticity is lacking so bad in this world right now, especially in the sales industry, that being honest doesn't seem to be a real thing anymore. Hence my company's name *Make Sales Great Again*. It's crazy to me that if you're being honest, you're considered "different."

Here are a few pro tips for your life and business:

- If you don't know the answer, tell them you don't know the answer.
- If your product or service isn't for them, tell them it's not for them.
- Never ever lie about anything. Lying about your offer will add crazy rescission issues, end any chance at referral business, and destroy your character and credibility.
- Listen to serve, don't sell to survive.
- Care about the outcome of what you sold to prospects. Don't serve them and leave them.

If people know you as a liar, you won't scale in life. BUT if they know you as the person who's always going to do the right thing, putting others before themselves when serving, you'll be the one whom others search for to do business with.

5. BE CONSCIOUS OF HOW YOU SPEAK.

Harvard Law did a study on how salespeople speak and what were the defining factors that turned them off from working with someone. They found that it wasn't just the cussing or the language they used, but having bad grammar in general. The statistics proved that 53% of prospects were bothered by bad grammar and chose not to do business with the salesperson. Now is this something I agree with? I'll say that grammar is important and you should always work on elevating your vocabulary, but using big fancy words, as impressive as some are, isn't the reason why people don't do business with you. Being conscious of how you speak, leaving a good impression, being professional, courteous, and kind with your words is why they will or won't make you the obvious choice to work with.

6. HOW YOU MOVE MATTERS.

Body language is something we get into later in this book, but in this credibility portion, you need to understand that people will judge you before one word comes out of your mouth. How's your posture? Are you sitting up straight like a stiff person, slouched like someone who doesn't value your prospects' time, or are you just being you, sitting intentionally, intent on listening and proving to your prospects that you are there to serve them? How's your eye contact? Are you looking away when they're speaking? Are you staring down at the material you're using to pitch them 70% of the time? Or are you intentionally looking them in the eye, respectfully letting them know that they have your undivided attention? Are you crossing your arms, leaned back like you don't care whether they're there or not? Or are you sitting forward, arms normal, intently there to assist them if you can?

All these moves matter. You don't want to be judged before you speak and you may even hate hearing that it happens, but it does. You need to be prepared and conscious of this, so when they do judge you, you'll be judged in a good way, creating the type of credibility that makes you stand out from others without even saying a word.

7. ALWAYS CARE ABOUT WHAT MATTERS TO YOUR PROSPECT AND UNDERSTAND HOW THEY FEEL.

You might wonder why this has anything to do with credibility, but too many untrained sales individuals spew information. This doesn't help you. You need to ask good questions and stop wasting time on stuff they "might" be interested in. Value them enough to talk about what "definitely" matters to them. It's about them, not you. If they have questions, stop and don't you dare move forward until you've taken the time to prove that how they feel matters most. Not the sale. Not the commission. Not the close. Just them, how they feel. When you do this, credibility skyrockets, since most sales individuals just sell for the cash, rather than to serve.

8. KNOW YOUR PRODUCT OR SERVICE.

You should always educate yourself to be the go-to expert in your field. You should dig deep into what you're offering someone, so you can help your prospect better than most. That being said, credibility is equally built by not knowing. If you're asked a question that you don't know, don't bullshit your way through. People these days can see that coming a mile away. Remember, people expect you to lie, so don't. Be the different. Be the real. Be truthful. Say you don't know, but you're going to get the right answer. Knowing and not knowing are crucial components to building credibility.

9. YOUR REPUTATION MATTERS.

This is one that I had to learn the hard way. I've made a lot of horrid mistakes in my life and take full accountability for each and every one. I'm perfectly OK admitting to my times of struggle and bad moves. I'm finally free from hiding behind who I was. Notice how I said, "who I was"! Yep, that's right. You can change.

Living in the past won't get you the future you deserve. NO ONE besides the man upstairs is perfect. Not me. Not you reading or listening to this book. The truth is, I lost many opportunities due to stupid errors in my life, and I want to teach you not to make the same mistakes I did.

That being said, don't you EVER let someone tell you that change isn't possible. I went from broke to having a life of abundance. I went from a salesperson to one of the leading experts in sales and leadership in the world. I went from the drunk guy, running illegal poker games for a living for a decade, to becoming a 3-time bestselling author and one of the most sought-after keynote speakers, earning the nickname The Culture Creator when no one believed I'd ever leave the streets.

Here's some proof of how time and proper movement heals. I didn't mention all of that above to boast. I did it because over 15 years ago, I was running card games out of penthouses, apartments, and houses. We had security, waitresses, catered food, and I made my money on the card tables. It's how I lived. I was doing steroids, drinking all the time, divorced. I was living the night life that I thought was "the life." Man, was I wrong.

One day I was sick of it and I posted a motivational post on Facebook. I got like 10 dm's instantly saying things like:

- "Bro, take that down. That's not you."

- "Todd, is this a joke? You're no motivational speaker."

- "Todd, did your account get hacked?"

See, the thing is, 15 years ago had I told people I would have all the accolades I listed above and how I've helped numerous companies write billions of dollars in business, helping them scale through motivation, life principles, and training… Do you think anyone would've ever believed that I'm the man I am today? The answer is NO! Every time I talked about getting out of the game and going legit, they told me that people like me don't change. My reputation was the poker guy who fights downtown and rages drunk. To be honest, I don't blame them for thinking that. That was my fault and on me.

BUT, it also motivated a guy like me to prove them wrong and most importantly prove to myself I was worth more.

Fast forward to today:

- **Chief Executive Officer** – Make Sales Great Again, Inc. Created billions in revenue for multiple companies.

- **Chief Sales Officer** – Apex Roofing & Restoration; $150 million dollar company

- **Author** who wrote three books. You're reading the third one now.

- **Co-Host** – Gutcheck Uncut Podcast

- **International Keynote Speaker** – Been on stages with some great names in the world.

The question is, as cool as all that sounds above, would ONE PERSON who knew me 15 years ago, the man I was, for even a second believe me if I said I was going to accomplish anything I just listed above? The answer is NO!

Let's switch it up, though. If TODAY, I told anyone who knows me with all the accomplishments I just listed above, that I:

- Had a drinking rage problem

- Ran illegal card games for a living for over a decade

- Was a cheater

- Treated people like trash

- Wasn't the best father

- Was robbed at gunpoint 3 times

- Had multiple cars repossessed

Do you think for even a second that they'd believe I was all those things I just listed, if they know me as the man I am today and never knew of my past? The answer is NO!

So can people change? THAT ANSWER IS YES! Change is very possible. Credibility can be rebuilt. Your reputation can change from the person no one should trust to the only person they should trust. Recommended by many.

Your reputation can either gain you success or cost you success. That choice is yours and you have no excuses anymore. If I can do it and did it, you can too.

My reputation for years was embarrassing, but I take pride in constantly growing and now being known as the person who has persevered and helps others to do the same. In sales, when your reputation is that you are a good, honest, and real person to do business with, your customer base will grow by leaps and bounds, far beyond the people faking or lying their way to the cash. Be honest about who you were, who you are now, and who you're trying to become. Your story matters to your prospects. Share it with them so they get to know who you really are. That type of credibility is irreplaceable.

I want you to stop and ask yourself this question right now. Would I rather do business with someone who is the expert in their field with a reputation as the expert or someone who isn't the expert in their field or known as one? Really think about what I just asked you. Most people don't prepare for their careers properly and that's one of the biggest mistakes you can make as a sales individual or entrepreneur.

The most successful and dominant people in business master the field they're in before they even think about moving on to something else. They know that if they aren't the industry name, if they aren't known for constantly learning the new trends in their field, if they can't confidently answer a question a prospect or a buyer has, then they will NEVER reach their full potential. It's just not possible to skate through a profession when you're trying to dominate.

Most people, not just salespeople, take the path of least resistance. In other words, they just learn as they go. The law of averages, which most untrained managers will preach to you, says, "Just see enough people and it's inevitable that you'll close some." They say it's just a numbers game. When the truth is, the elite concentrate on increasing the efficiency of those numbers. They aren't content with the average; they live to create the new standard. These are the people at the highest level.

You MUST KNOW that having exceptional product knowledge is essential to your growth. Be fully in front of industry changes. Constantly learn the ins and outs of what's coming, as this will show how ahead of the curve you are compared to other options a prospect might have.

So, if we know this is the key to guaranteeing your success, why don't most people put in the time to do the work it takes to be an elite? Simple answer. They're lazy. Let's call it what it is. Let's not sugarcoat anything here. EFFORT is the difference between winning and losing. Most people just don't put in the time, and don't have the guts or courage to learn what they need to learn to be the obvious choice people want to work with.

Let's be honest. You're saying a couple things right now. The first thing you're saying is, "When do people have the time to put in all this extra effort, when I'm working all day?" Let me reply to that in a direct fashion. PEOPLE MAKE THE TIME FOR THINGS THAT THEY WANT TO MAKE THE TIME FOR. Period. Don't tell me you don't have the time! Just be honest and say it's not important enough for you to care to make the time. For instance, if you're closing a deal that will change your life, it's the deal you've been waiting for your whole life, but you get a call that a loved one is hurt bad and being transported to the hospital, would you still finish closing that life-changing deal? We all know you wouldn't. You wouldn't even hesitate to get to that family member's side, because you chose at that moment what was more important. It's time vs. value. If you see that value doing something else is more important than what you're doing now, you'll MAKE THE TIME for it!

Yes, there's instant value in being by a loved one's side, which is why you'd choose that. If you're being completely transparent right now, fully vulnerable, you'll call yourself out right now! See, most don't make the time for things that don't have an **immediate value.** They don't want to put in the effort if the reward isn't instant. It's the biggest obstacle the untrained effort of a potential industry giant faces during their ascent.

The other excuse people make is, "I don't have the time." That's a complete lie. You're lying to yourself, you're lying to your team, your family, and anyone else that's in your presence if you use the biggest excuse in the world of "I don't have the time."

We all see specific high-level names on social media, in the news, the cover of magazines, and say, "It must be nice being them," but what you never see is the effort it took to get there. Those elite individuals would work their 9-5 job all day and then come home and work another 8 hours on their passion. They'd be zoned and dedicated to work on what'll allow them to write their own paychecks. It's crazy to me how much people will work "FOR" someone else, but won't take the time to work on their own businesses or work on themselves to be the master in their industry. It just makes no sense. Most would rather go home and watch Netflix than build a business, a brand, a new life where they have full freedom and happiness.

When you take the time to know more about your field than any other person that your co-workers, prospects/clients, friends, and family have ever heard, the word gets out. They'll not only be impressed, but even the ones who question what you do will have no other option than to go, "Damn, Todd really knows his shit." This, without a doubt, will earn you business. Even if not with the immediate crowd, people will refer others to you. Now what if they asked you about your field and you weren't confident in answering questions? What if you didn't have the answers to what they were asking? What if you didn't know about the NEW in your industry, but they did? What if they knew more than you? Would you want to do business with someone like that? Highly unlikely.

The reason why the law of averages doesn't matter to the outperforming elite sales leaders of the world is because they don't want to wait for the average time frame it'll take to get a sale. They want the next opportunity to become a sale. Is that super obvious? Salespeople want more sales. I'm sure you're shocked to hear or read that, right? LOL.

I wrote this book to give you the tools you need to become one of the elite. It just requires effort. You can read this book. You can read other books. You can listen to podcasts (preferably mine), you can go to masterminds, trainings on a product or service you offer, but IF YOU DON'T TRULY understand and implement what you're learning, you're wasting your time and not creating the highest and best use of your time. I don't care if you have to read or listen to this book 38 times to constantly remind you of the process that'll guarantee your success, DO IT!

Remember, WHO YOU ARE as a person is equally as important as WHO YOU ARE as a salesperson. How you present yourself. How you dress. How you speak. All that is part of credibility. I've taken people I grew up with in the streets to high-level earnings and positions they've fought for, but it didn't come without some serious life changes and moves they were willing to make to become more credible. For instance, let's say you meet me face to face, and I show up to earn your business on a $30 million commercial real estate project with a sleeveless shirt on and I have tattoo sleeves on both my arms. I have a pair of gym shorts on and a tank top revealing the rest of my tattoos. What do you think the odds are that that high-end prospect will do business with me? Will they judge me? A lot of you are gonna say, "They shouldn't!" But they do and will. Your credibility is out the window if you won't even clean yourself up enough to present yourself in a credible way.

Two people could say the exact same things and the one who presents themselves as more credible will be the one a prospect will choose to work with. It may suck, but it's just the way the world works. Presenting yourself professionally is necessary and if you think otherwise, then you better get your shit together and fast. A prospect owes you nothing. You have to earn their respect, their loyalty, their confidence that you're the obvious individual to do business with.

I want you to challenge yourself to be better than you were yesterday. I'm sure you've heard the saying, "You're your only competition," right? I mean, I can buy into that as it targets specific areas of self-improvement, BUT when you're in a field working with others that you're in direct competition with, challenge yourself to know more than the most knowledgeable person. Push yourself to work harder than the hardest worker. This will get you to the top of your industry and fast. Yep, I said it. Compete with them all. Someone has set the bar; it's your job to raise it!

When you do everything in this chapter, you'll not only dominate your field, but create a brand that spews confidence, knowledge, and the willingness to crush your competition. Word will spread to your competition and to your prospects. You will be the undeniable choice. You will have credibility like no one else, which is one of the most important aspects of your career.

Credibility is crucial to your business success and overall success in life. Having strong character, loyalty, good judgment, being likeable, open to learning, having good listening skills, communicating effectively, having integrity, being the example for others, and ALWAYS working in the best interest of others are all relevant when creating who you are to prove how credible you are. Don't take this chapter lightly. It's never too early to start or too late to rebuild. You can be the go-to person. All you have to do is believe and start.

CHAPTER 7

SERVING VS SELLING: THE MSGA WAY

This chapter is what made me. I need you to dig deep, listen, read, highlight, and take notes. Do whatever you need to do in order to ingrain this information into your brain. THIS is the moment. THIS is the information that is needed so badly in today's world. It's what will separate the elite from the mediocre. It's what will either elevate you or force stagnancy in your life. Pay close attention. These next two chapters alone can, simply put, MAKE SALES GREAT AGAIN and it all starts with one powerful word: "serving."

So much is predicated on this hardcore closer lifestyle. The ego mindset that you can close the uncloseable. How about serving? Doesn't sound as sexy, does it? The world has been brainwashed into believing that in order to be a great closer, you have to learn tactics and strategies to get to the cash. It has really left a horrible imprint on the world today. It has forced phrases like:

- "Don't close me."

- "Just tell me the truth."

- "Would you sell this to your mom?"

- "Is there anything else I should know so I'm not surprised later?"

The list goes on and on, but this was spawned from weak, untrained, unethical people who call themselves sales individuals.

Then you have your trainers out there trying to teach people to be the hardcore closers, who aren't serving, they're forcing people into deals. So many good people are being taken advantage of these days because of persistent selling tactics and crafty words from strong-speaking people convincing others to do business with them, rather than serving them and doing what's best for them. So selling, having to be the "hardcore" closer, isn't necessary at all.

I'm not implying that you give up when someone says no. You should always continue to serve your prospect by asking good questions to find out if you can serve them properly. Selling has become pushy, whether deliberately or not, and it's now the downfall of so many people who just need to learn how to serve better.

This is where selling has become aggressive, while serving is being informative and listening to what matters to the prospect. In some cases, serving means being truthful even if what you're offering isn't for them. Selling to survive is a real thing. I've seen it in all sorts of industries where people manipulate and lie their way into the pockets of good people. It's a pathetic way to make a living. Most of the time they use scare tactics or get aggressive to force someone into a deal.

Here are a few examples of pushy or hardcore closer techniques and the results:

- You could be pitching or selling to a passive person who doesn't have the guts to say no. Good for you! You got the sale, but you can rest assured there will be no referrals or future business from this person ever. You lose.

- You could be presenting your product or service to a hard-headed, strong person who is argumentative. Let me be clear. Getting combative with a prospect is never a way to make the sale. A lot of times they're prone to making scenes and causing the entire sales environment to suffer, based on you being too aggressive. You never win this way, ever.

- What you're offering could be amazing, but if you're using cheesy sales lines and they don't like you, you've already lost the sale. People buy people.

- If you're aggressive or pushy or lie or use sales tactics, your reputation will precede you. An unhappy prospect will tell the world about you. Especially these days with so much access to social media reach. Pushy, aggressive people who say they're salespeople are everywhere online. Don't be one of them.

The point is, don't be so salesly, but instead, serve. So how do you serve properly? Compassion, clarity, integrity, honesty, and concentrating on what matters most to your prospects.

Here are a few tips for serving:

- Seek permission to ask anything that might be a sensitive subject. By asking permission, the level of respect from serving, instead of just asking a sensitive question without their permission, means the world to everyone.

- Talk less and listen more. Untrained salespeople talk way too much. Be an active listener so you don't waste their time by offering something that means nothing to them. If you ask the right questions, they will tell you how to serve them. Most untrained salespeople just throw out the features and benefits until one hits a hot button for their client. It's the wrong way to be a sales professional.

- If your prospect isn't engaging or their body language tells you they don't seem interested in what you're offering, stop and ask them what they think so far. At this point, be quiet, let them speak, but when this is done properly, you have actually stopped selling and you have proved that the sale is irrelevant if there's no value for your prospect. Pausing and having a conversation about that saves time but comes from a servant mindset.

Matthew 20:26 "Whoever wishes to become great among you shall be your servant."

It's very difficult for ego-based, arrogant people to live a servant lifestyle. Serving is selling. There's no question about it. So are you just serving or are you just selling? If you serve properly, you're doing both. A lot of people need to be guided into making good decisions for themselves. This would be you serving and selling something that adds value to their life, but in an intentionally ethical and compassionate way.

If you're not doing both, leading from a servant mindset always, you're losing money and a ton of future business.

Here are a few ways to level up when serving:

- Provide unexpected value. Make sure they know you'll be there before, during, and after the sale. Your goal is to provide ongoing support. They don't just get the product or service, they get you. That's the biggest win.

- Always offer solutions to problems they might have. When they know you're there, you'll be the one they come to for help. You have to be the solution or at least the go-to person they trust for guidance.

- Give them your time. Your cell. Your email. Connect on social media. Prove to them that you're a real person and they can always find you somewhere, somehow. In today's world, the only time someone doesn't want to provide that type of information is if they're doing something shady and don't want to be found.

- Stay very consistent contacting your customer. Always being there is one of the largest differences in serving vs. selling. Most salespeople never follow up with a prospect after they get their money. It's horrible. That's selling without serving.

How do you know if you're serving or selling? I found out by reaching out to several people I've done business with and asked them if there was anything they wish I would've done to better serve them. The best way to grow is to go the prospects. Not co-workers, family, or friends who will pat you on the back and say, "You're doing great!" NO! Go to the real people who have sat through one of your presentations and ask them to be brutally honest with you, because you're trying to be the best version of you. You will be surprised at how many people are willing to help, and the powerhouse information they give you will take your career to new levels from a servant mindset.

You can do this even if you don't have previous clients. If you're pitching a client or prospect and their answer is yes or no, ask why? If yes, why did they choose to do business with you? If no, what could you have done differently to earn their business or better your presentation? In both cases, ask for raw and real feedback because it's important for your self-growth. This process of client feedback is one I teach, suggesting that everyone from salesperson to CEO use it in order to grow properly.

Most people say they hate "being sold" these days. Most salespeople try to plant the hook and reel you in. Servant-based sales is solely derived from asking questions that elicit a response to pinpoint what matters most to the client.

No one is less important than any transaction. Put the people before the paycheck. Please don't ask someone for the heat, the sauce, or the pitch that they're using. The weakest way to sell is having to create something to say to get others interested in what you're offering. Be informative, be quiet, and listen, and you'll get all the information you need to know whether you can serve that person or not.

Just don't forget that you are part of a financial choice, an emotional decision, that could impact a family's life in a good or bad way forever. If you're the cause of someone getting sold something, forcing them into something that they don't need or might not get value out of, and you know that to be the case and still close them, you're just a good thief, not a good sales professional.

Serving is showing humility, getting personally involved, and caring about your prospect. Servants know when to be quiet, and are great listeners who speak less and listen more. Always serve first and sell later. Be kind. Be honest. Be grateful you have the luxury and opportunity to serve. You will sell people who aren't even potential clients because you're constantly serving. Serving makes you the obvious choice. Selling without a servant mindset just makes you another salesperson selling to survive. When you seek to understand how you can help, doing whatever it takes to provide solutions, this creates a pipeline of clients and referrals that the hardcore closer could never have. It's way more profitable in your pocket and in your soul when you implement the servant selling and servant leadership mindset. I recommend if you aren't already, that you start now. It'll be the best move you've ever made.

CHAPTER 8

THE DEATH OF THE ALPHABET

The days of just Always Be Closing (ABC) are long gone. It's not just "closing" anymore; it's more "informing." The customer cares how much you know, but won't care how much you know until they know how much you care.

People are tired of the ABC days, feeling like all you care about is the commission. Trust me, they're not only more educated about the product or service you're offering before you pitch them, but they also get educated on ways you'll try to close them! We can thank the internet for that and I mean it, not sarcastically, but I'm so glad that there's information out there to help prospects distinguish the difference between an asshole, "all I care about is your money" salesperson… and the "I care about what's best for you and the commission will be a byproduct of our relationship" salesperson.

Not only are they prepared before your pitch, but they're prepared during it! When you want the deal that bad, they can see it and hear it. Your demeanor is different. Your voice inflection is different. You'll be more defensive and aggressive if they say no. Instead of informing, listening until your ears hurt, and knowing how to ask the right questions that will seamlessly transition to the close, you'll be spewing features and benefits that probably aren't even the main reason they'd buy from you anyway. You'll waste valuable time running your mouth so much, like most "closers" living by the old ABC rule do, that they won't even get a chance to speak.

Closing and informing are two different things. Yes, you need to be able to do both, but the best salespeople transition into the close by informing the prospect why they need what you're offering. That starts with listening and asking the right questions and utilizing that information to help earn their business. Information is key, when closing used to be defined as "forcing" the client to say yes whether they needed what you're offering or not. I can't tell you how many times I've heard a sales rep come to me and say, "I got 'em! I closed the hell out of them. You would've loved it. They said no several times and I talked them into doing it when they were dead set on not buying from me." Let me say this, "talking" someone into the sale is almost twisting and leading. If you provide valid information that solves a problem for your client, then you won't have to talk them into anything! That's selling.

The core of any great salesperson is to be an expert on your product and most importantly know how it can help your client. Now what does this really mean? I'm going to say this, and once you read it, you might need to go back and read it again. The best salespeople in the world inform their client on what the product "won't" do for them rather than what it will. Yep, I said it. The most powerful salespeople in the world are confident enough to talk about what the product won't do for them, rather than what it will. Let me explain.

In sales, a lot of trainers want you to preach about all the positives of what they're offering and how it will solve all the client's problems, when you and I both know there's no perfect service or product. I've built sales teams for years by teaching people to use the negatives in sales presentations, rather than throwing out how perfect what they're offering is for the client.

People don't expect that! They appreciate the honesty. They want the real. They want the truth. They don't want to find out later that it doesn't do everything.

A simple statement like this is more powerful than you'll ever know:

> *"I'm sure every person you've talked to who has tried to sell you something in the past mentions all the good, all the features and benefits, saying that what they're offering is a perfect fit for you, right? Not me. I want you to know what it will do and what it won't do to see if the good adds enough value to do business with me today. Fair?"*

There's rarely a perfect fit. Is it possible? I'm sure, but you don't see it often. I want to build such a relationship of truth with my prospect that I'm the **obvious choice** to do business with. People will choose honesty over a product that might do a tad bit more than what you're selling them, because of YOU! They'll buy that. They'll buy you. They want integrity when you're offering your product or service.

People buy people. Brad Lea said, "Relationships are the new currency." When you're brutally honest, even if it means what you're selling isn't the right fit for someone, tell them! Try something like this:

> *"I want to be very honest with you. What I'm offering isn't going to solve your problem. It means more to me to help you than for me to just sell you something that won't add value to you. So, let's see if I can find the right person and product to do just that."*

OOOF! You may not get that sale at that moment, but guess what you will get… their respect, referrals, future business when they need you, and you'll be the first person they call because YOU WERE HONEST WITH THEM.

I've made more money by telling people what my product **won't do**, rather than what it will. Let that sink in! Salespeople are SO SCARED that it's going to eliminate an opportunity to close. Again, you may not get the deal right then, but the upside will build a long-term and very profitable relationship.

If you want a strong piece of advice and want to master sales, be comfortable informing people of what your product "won't" do, as much as you are telling them what it "will do." Be that strong and know your product that well!

Studies actually show that if you give a customer three positives and one negative, they're more likely to buy from you. It proves that you're willing to admit your vulnerability. That's the difference between closing and informing. Be a master informer, even more than a master closer!

CHAPTER 9

BE DIRECT

How many of you love to be sold? NO ONE really enjoys being sold, if we're being honest with one another. Being direct doesn't mean turn and burn opportunities (meaning rush the process through prejudging and moving on to the next one). It means, get to the point. The sales tactics, so-called slick pitches, corny phrases, and bad jokes will turn a prospect off fast! Being direct with a client is so important. Don't waste time on something that's of no interest to them.

Average salespeople beat around the bush. Master salespeople do not. They cut to the chase by not wasting time with the bullshit. They dive into what matters most to the client. There are no circles. It's a beeline to the heart of the problem, and if they're the solution, they'll be able to prove why.

The no-nonsense style is the most effective. When you're selling anything, the client must trust you. Unfortunately for the less educated sales individuals, they spend so much time breaking the wall down, or the "barrier to the real" as I like to call it, that time becomes limited. You have a very short window to build trust and trust is built through the real.

For instance, many sales trainers will tell you to take your time, ask the prospect about their family, talk about anything other than the sale, because rapport is the most lucrative way to thrive in sales. It is definitely needed and I am NOT telling you to sit down and not build rapport. The truth is, learning how to introduce yourself and mastering the art of building a quick rapport will help you cut to the chase in a fraction of the time! People just want you to talk to them, but directly.

Do you think people know you're trying to sell them something? Do you think they know you're in sales? I've literally heard weak salespeople say, "I don't work on commission" or "I'm not in sales" or "I'm just a customer service agent and don't care whether you do this or not," thinking it's going to break down their "wall." BUT IT INSTANTLY becomes stronger, almost eliminating the opportunity to close because you've presented yourself as something you're not. NEWS FLASH! They know you're in sales and they know you're going to earn something if they buy from you. People aren't stupid. Don't question their intelligence; instead be direct. When you start out lying, the probability of you selling them becomes virtually nil.

Get to the point! The idea of "selling" someone is still very real, but it's way harder in today's market. I'm sure you've noticed. Don't be pushy, but try something like this:

> *"Look… I know that you know that I'm in sales, and I also know that you know that I'd love to sell you something. But can we just be direct and have a conversation? Because if what I'm offering adds value to you, then great, let's do business. If it doesn't, let's not and I'll try to find someone who can help you get what you need. Deal?"*

Sales is simply having a conversation. That's it. No fluff. No creative sales tactics. Just honesty. Your prospect will appreciate the real and be way more open to listening. When you do that, the wall is instantly demolished. You'll get more time to listen and see if you have the solution to their problem and if you do… you'll be the obvious choice to do business with. People want real. They want the professional raw. Wouldn't you?

I'm going to tell you what every client and prospect wants the moment they shake your hand. NO BULLSHIT! Just be direct. The more honest you are, the more relationships will form, which inherently means more money.

If you're in phone sales, the first 5 seconds of the conversation will set the tone on whether or not they stay on the phone. If you're knocking on doors, the first sentence will make them keep the door open or shut it in your face. If you're face to face doing a presentation, from the moment you shake their hand and introduce yourself, you need to be brutally honest about your intentions. If you're not, they'll be there, but they won't be listening.

The prospects are smarter these days. They've heard all the corny sales lines. They're waiting for the bullshit tie downs like the "if I could… would you …?" old school nonsense. I mean, don't get me wrong, a lot of those sales tips are still good today, but remember it's not what you say, its HOW you say it. The best salespeople in the world have morphed all the corny bullshit or old school sales tactics into real ways to close.

You know that cheesy salesperson you never want to be like? Well, if you're not being direct with your prospect, that's how they'll see you! Don't do that. Be OK with being bold. Be OK with getting to the point, because ultimately, it's massive respect for their time and their intelligence.

DIRECT, TRUTH, INTEGRITY & DRIVING SALES THROUGH SOLUTION-BASED PROBLEM SOLVING = long-term and consistent growth. That's the key, my friends.

Being direct not only builds credibility in your ability to negotiate and present solutions, but gives your prospect a better understanding that in dealing with you, they are dealing with a sales professional whose intention is strictly service based. Too, it will minimize the chance of your hearing the statements we hate to hear most at the end of your presentation.

Phrases like:

"Do you have a business card?"

"We like your numbers; what's the best way to get back to you?"

"We have to think about it."

These phrases are very common when you're not fully authentic in what your product or service offers, or maybe you just skipped steps and didn't educate them enough. When you're extremely direct on how you can serve them, this eliminates many of the phrases you just read.

Remember what we talked about in the last chapter. You can and will earn more business by being direct about what your product or service won't do for your client, over what it will. BE DIRECT! No product is perfect, so tell them!

An undertrained sales representative literally throws out all the features and benefits which allows a prospect to wonder, "What aren't they telling me? I know they want my business, but this sounds too good to be true." BE DIRECT! Tell them the bad. Tell them the limitations of what you're offering. It's OK, I promise. The trust you will build by doing this is unmatched. It's one of the guaranteed ways to earn long-term business with prospects for years to come.

Most sales individuals are afraid to do this because they just don't want to hear "NO" or they don't know how to flip what the limitations are into a massive positive for the client. It's simple really; there is no perfect offering. Not one in the world. So be truthful about that. Prove to them why staying in your lane is what you're good at. Prove to them why you're the BEST at what you provide, because you've mastered what you're offering will do and are conscious of what it won't, which is equally important.

If you're offering tech sales and not good at marketing that tech product, don't fake it. Tell them something like this:

"I'm very transparent and need you to know that I'm not great at marketing, nor is my product we are offering you. We have built extraordinary tech software and have mastered that, which is why we stay in our lane. It's what WE ARE good at. We serve clients at what we're best at. We are not a marketing firm and don't want you to think we are, but we know someone who's tremendous in that arena and I'll connect you so you can get the value you deserve."

Another way to be direct is not to offer timelines if you can't meet those deadlines. Here's a life nugget that I just happen to use in sales. Have you ever heard "Under Promise Over Deliver"? When setting expectations for your client or prospect, don't say things that may or may not happen. Be specific. Master sales professionals will never promise an unrealistic timeline. If you know something usually takes two weeks and you've seen it take longer, TELL THE PROSPECT THAT. Something like this:

"I know it says we can get this completed in 14 business days, but I want to be very honest. I've seen it take longer. The last thing I want to do is promise you a timeframe and not mean it. So let's just say 21 business days and, hey, if it's completed before that, we both win, but if takes those 21 days, I just don't want you to be disappointed in me wondering what happened. I know if I were you, I'd want full transparency, which I'm hoping you respect."

Now **THAT** is the way to gain trust, be direct, and eliminate expectation issues in the future. Again, JUST BE HONEST! Now here's the gold in this, if that sales professional completes what was promised in 21 days, in 13, he or she becomes a superhero for getting it done early. If it takes 18 days, it's still early and within the timeline presented, and you're still a champion in the eyes of that prospect. Why? Because you told them that it says it'll be completed in 14 days, but you told them 21 days to be safe. Knocking it out in 18 is still early from the timeline promised.

That being said, let's say you went with the 14-day timeline, KNOWING that it can and does usually take longer. If it takes 18 days, they'll be blowing you up wondering what's going on and why you're late. Now you look less professional and less punctual when serving a prospect. Not a good look.

Another HUGE mistake less trained sale individuals make is promising something they're not completely sure of. They have this disease called the "what's coming disease," presenting something as if it's happening, when in reality, it may never happen at all.

This usually comes from a customer asking if the product comes with something that the sales representative may not be sure of or they're sure it doesn't, but the rep tells the client it's "coming soon" to try and secure the sale now.

Making false promises about your product will **guarantee**:

1. To eliminate any possibility of doing future business with that prospect.

2. To make you a liar, not a sales professional.

3. To prove that you care more about you than the prospect.

This is PURE WEAKNESS. It's not selling, it's lying, and there are way too many people doing this these days. Master the art of serving and adding value to someone and then you'll become that master sales professional. Anything less makes you a master liar.

AGAIN, BE DIRECT! Be up front with expectations. Such as what your product offers and what it won't. What your role serving them will be and what it won't.

We'll get into more detail on how to handle objections from being more direct later in the book, but for now, practice pure intentional honesty when serving. What you'll find is you'll actually not have to sell or convince prospects to do business with you. They'll just want to.

A habit is a product of practice. You have to practice how to be direct. I don't mean be aggressive. I don't mean say things like "That's just the way it is." Your job is to assist the prospect in making a decision. It is NOT to convince them to do business with you by forcing features and benefits that may not be the right fit for them. You don't need to "sound smart." You need to "be smart." Are features and benefits important? Of course they are, but people buy people more than they do a product or service. I've seen clients who LOVE a product or service but who have chosen not to do business with someone because they were unsure about the person, not the product.

Think about it. If you thought you were just being sold rather than served, you DEFINITELY would not do business with that person. The prospect doesn't know you, period. They hate changing the way they do things and yes, price matters. It's always an objection, I don't care who tells you otherwise. Help them first by being direct in every single aspect we just spoke of.

Everything is easier when they trust you. Price, Product/Service Limitations, The Value you present and more.

There's also a time component here that's beneficial for both the prospect and the person serving them. Being direct, asking the hard questions, presenting the hard truths will eliminate less synergistic relationships in a timely manner. Simply put, you waste less time and move on to someone you can serve. The prospect respects your honesty, saves time because you were honest, and is then either guided to someone who can serve them or finds someone on their own.

You'd be floored at the amount of business I've earned from a prospect when what I was offering was NOT the right fit for them. They trusted and respected my honesty and referred me tons of business. I was direct. I didn't try to sell them; I continued to serve even though the fit was perfect for us at that moment. It doesn't mean never and the amount of business I added from that relationship helped my company scale rapidly.

When you're direct with everything and being completely honest with a prospect, it almost feels "to good to be true" how much business you'll begin to earn and how easy the transition to the close is. Try and see. I dare you.

CHAPTER 10

THERE'S ONLY ONE FIRST IMPRESSION

Does your appearance matter? How you speak? Your posture when serving/selling? Sales is more than just having the knowledge. It's more than having the tools to succeed. It's more than having the best product or service that you're offering. It's also about getting a good feeling that you're the person the prospect feels is a good fit to do business with. UNFORTUNATELY in today's world, most salespeople don't set the standard that they should throughout the sales process.

If I can be candid, people prejudge. They prejudge you. You prejudge them and although we'd wish this didn't happen, it does. Their initial opinion of you, your debut if you will, is so important. It's far beyond a firm handshake, and in this chapter, we're going to dive into what the top sales professionals in the world do to set themselves apart from the rest!

How you introduce yourself matters!

Harvard Law did a study on how long it takes for a salesperson to gain the appropriate attention it takes to give yourself the best chance at getting the sales, along with the percentage increased on deals closed. The study found that a positive introduction, including how you dressed, making eye contact, speaking with confidence, and your posture, increased sales by 87% for sales professionals who had all of the above attributes. The study also showed that if you were good in only half the areas, the sales increased still, but only by 21%. Not a bad percentage increase, but why not master them all and 4x your closing possibilities?

The study also showed that the time you had to gain the proper attention from the moment you meet was 7 seconds. WOW! I bet you expected more time to build value in who you are as a person, right? Well, don't worry, this doesn't mean you won't close deals, but in this chapter I'm going to show you how you can and WILL close more deals by being an expert at your debut!

The first impression is everything. There are a few questions people ask themselves when they first meet you. First, "Am I going to be able to trust this person?" Second, "Am I going to be able to respect this person?" And finally, "Will they have the knowledge I need to do business with them?" Let's break down each of these.

It has been statistically proven that the moment they've decided who they "think" you are (yes, prejudging you), it's 5 times harder to get them to work with you if you made an initial negative impression. The crazy thing is, the same Harvard study showed that whoever they perceive you to be in the first few seconds was just as on point as who they'd perceive you to be in first 7 minutes. The two impressions (first 7 seconds and the first seven minutes) are not the same, but the studies weren't far off, if the first few seconds weren't in your favor from the start.

MAKE SURE YOU KNOW WHO YOU'RE TALKING TO:

I know this may seem elementary to some, but the truth is salespeople get robotic in how they approach potential clients. It's the same routine day in and day out. Prospects want to feel special. They want you to introduce yourself as such.

In some industries, if there's information about the client before you spend time with them, find out everything about them you can. When you do this and bring up stuff intentionally to let them know you've done your homework on them, it's a great initial feeling.

Then there are some industries where the sales representatives abuse information they have of their potential client to figure out ways to sell them, instead of serve them. If you're in an industry like that and you're a leader or even an experienced sales professional, challenge yourself and go beyond what you see in their file and do deep discoveries to find better ways to serve them. This is also a great feeling for a prospect because you are proving to them that they matter. This eliminates most possibilities to "pitch" someone based on knowledge that could be used to direct someone maliciously.

If there have been past interactions, make sure you bring them up. Good or bad, it shows you've done your research when you have that information. If you don't have that information, it's always good to ask if your company has served them in the past. Knowing this, reading their body language or just simply by their response whether they've worked with your company or not, gives you a good idea of what they think about the company as a whole.

SELL YOURSELF, NOT THE PRODUCT:

At the introduction, everyone has their opinions on talk time. The first time a conversation ignites, let them speak a minimum of 75% of the time. Confirm that you're listening by keeping eye contact, nodding your head, smiling, just so they know you care. Far too many sales representatives use the introduction as their resume time. This is not the place for it. Remember, it's all about them. MAKE THEM FEEL THAT and mean it when you do!

BE DIRECT:

I know we just spoke about this, but I wanted to reiterate how important this is at the introduction as well. In my opinion, this is THE MOST IMPORTANT time to be direct. Be sure they know: Who you are. Why they're speaking with you. What your reach/capability is. What you're offering. All of these things should be initially addressed so you both are prepared on how the process will flow throughout your time together.

BE REAL (DON'T SOUND SCRIPTED):

I've written many "scripts" for multiple different sales organizations and the truth is, I tell them to memorize them, but never use them word for word. When you sound scripted, you sound robotic. You don't want to sound like someone taught you how to speak to them so you can get their money. The sole reason scripts are created is to know the process, but to make it your own. One personality doesn't sound the same or speak the same as another. When you're introducing yourself, hit the key points in the script, but intentionally make it your own intro.

Get to know their goals and what they're looking to achieve. What do people love to talk about most? Themselves. You know it to be true because you have a story. Good or bad, most of the time people love sharing it. You must know what makes them tic. What matters to them most? What made them connect with you? All needed, relevant information that will help cater your presentation to their specific needs.

There are many things that don't create the best introduction you should be conscious of in business and sales:

- **Not dressing the part**
    - o Dressing professional doesn't always mean a suit. Professional wear is important, but it can also mean business casual. More so:

- Ironed clothes
- Clean (no visible stains)
- Presentable shoes

- **Hygiene**
    - I think this speaks for itself, but there are many who get up, rush to work without taking a shower, and just aren't prepared professionally with their hygiene.
        - Deodorant
        - Brushed hair
        - Mints, Gum (the breath check)

- **Too much cologne or perfume**
    - Everyone wants to smell good, but don't lay it on thick where people physically find it hard to be around the strong smell. A big no-no at the introduction and equally if they're going to spend some time with you.

- **Limp handshake**
    - Let's be honest, no one likes a weak handshake. Have a firm one ready, but don't squeeze the hell out of their hand like a lot of men do for masculinity purposes. Don't do that.

- **Too cocky**
    - I'll tell you this. There is NOT ONE PERSON who likes an arrogant, cocky, I-know-everything, "you're lucky to be with me" salesperson. You need to be humble and be thankful you have the luxury of being with them. Now don't get me wrong. Confidence is needed when meeting someone and they should feel lucky to have you as well based on your introduction, but don't be arrogant. It never helps and it's a consistent uphill battle.

- **No eye contact**
    - No side eyes. No looking the other direction. When you meet someone make sure you're looking them square in the

eye. This is a respect factor that most miss from the start. I know way too many people who, when having a conversation, just can't look people in the eyes. It's the biggest turn off in general, but without a doubt, diminishes any chance for trustworthiness from the start.

- **Too passive**
    - o You never ever want to seem too passive. Meaning, be excited, grateful, humbled that the prospect is giving you their time. Make them feel that way, because when they do, the business relationship starts right and will stay the course when serving them in future business.

- **Bad mouth**
    - o Don't curse. Watch how you speak to people as you don't know what will offend them or not. It's important to always have the same professionalism, especially when first meeting someone.

- **Hand them your card first**
    - o Business cards aren't my favorite, but aren't the worst thing in the world. Just don't meet someone and hand them your business card. Let them get to know you first.

- **No religion, no politics**
    - o Never talk about religion or politics. Your opinion is yours and theirs is theirs. They don't have to be one and the same, but limiting this conversation is imperative from the first meeting.

- **Name-drop someone of authority or title**
    - o It doesn't matter who you know. It doesn't matter what your title is. What matters is what their opinion is of you and who you really are. Don't name-drop or title-drop at the beginning. They'll get to know you and your status throughout the presentation.

- **Selling from the start**
    - Don't ever start selling when you first meet someone. Talk about anything other than the product or service. Ask them about themselves, as people love to tell you their stories and who they are. There's a time and a place for sales and it's never the first introduction.

Where do the top three initial traits, Trust, Respect, Product Knowledge, stack up against one another? Respect is at the top of the charts in most studies, but my personal belief after decades of initial interactions is that most prospects want to be able to look at you, speak to you, and feel some level of trustworthiness right out of the gate. Let's dig deeper into the initial trust factor and how it plays a giant role in your overall success.

Let me start by saying, in 2023 people expect salespeople to be dishonest. Beginning your introduction with things like this will negatively impact your chances of doing business with your prospect:

- **"I'm not in sales."**
    - Whether it's phone sales, door knocking, timeshare, real estate, any type of sales, DO NOT say you're not in sales if you are.

For instance, you talk to someone and say, "Oh, don't worry, I'm not in sales. Just here to offer information." Not good. The worst way to start is by lying! You're in sales. They know it. Be honest.

- **"I'm not here to sell you anything."**
    - You are here to sell them something. You are here to serve them. Again, be honest. They know you're in sales.

- **"I don't want to waste your time."**
    - This phrase simply oozes, "All I want is your money." Do some discovery. They might not even know that what you're offering could be something to help them. They might want it. Don't assume you're wasting their time. When you say

this, in their minds they're thinking, "This salesperson doesn't want to waste THEIR time." Not the other way around.

- **"To be honest with you."**
    - o People don't know you well enough to know if you're honest or not. You might be intentional and truly honest, but today in sales, when you say it, it seems more dishonest than honest, unfortunately.
- **"You look like the decision maker."**
    - o You don't know them yet. You don't know who the decision maker is. Whether it's one person or two people or a group, don't assume that one person is the decision maker and the other one isn't.

The list can go on of the corny, dishonest, very salesy ways of eliminating any opportunity at all to gain the most important feature at your debut: trust.

What about if you're in a sales environment like retail. You approach a prospect, they know you're coming, you ask, "Can I help you?" and they reply with, "I'm just looking." Most of the time they're actually looking for something, but because of the question you asked when you first approached them, you gave them a way out.

Let's name some easy ways to start conversations by assuming they've come into your environment looking to buy. Instead of saying, "How can I help you?", how about something like this:

Home Depot: "What project are you working on that I can help you with?"

Clothing Store: "What occasion are you shopping for?"

Coffee Shop: "What can we start getting ready for you?"

Solar Company: "What's the reason you're considering solar?"

Roofing: "What's your favorite style of roof and how important is the durability to you?"

Timeshare: "What's your dream vacation and what's stopped you from taking it?"

Insurance: "What type of coverage is most important to you?"
"What's the main reason you're getting coverage?"

Car Sales: "What features of a car are the most important to you?"

There are many ways to start a conversation. Many of today's top sales professionals use assumptive conversations starters like these. They assume that the prospect is speaking with them, came in today, called them, because they're considering purchasing your offer or service. Saying things like this lets them know what matters to them, matters to you. It's all about the prospect. They want to feel wanted and appreciated that they took the time to speak with you. And let's be honest, that is a gift.

Initial questions help you answer key factors on how the presentation will proceed. Here are a few of the most important things you should figure out when you're serving someone:

1. DO THEY EVEN NEED WHAT YOU'RE OFFERING?

Being honest and intentional in finding out if what you're offering your prospect is even in their best interest is integrity-based and will save you TIME! It also respects the prospect's time equally. Salespeople aren't doing that these days. They're forcing what they're offering on good people who don't need it. This is the worst way to sell. When you're honest, they might know one or more people who might be a good fit for what you're offering them. They respect that you've respected their time and most importantly that your honesty will prove to them you'll be honest with whomever they refer you to work with. It's one of the best ways to get referrals.

2. IS THIS AFFORDABLE FOR THEM?

Some sales trainers will say "affordability" or "the price" doesn't matter. Well, they're wrong. They may want what you're offering. They may need what you're offering, but the timing to purchase based on credit or availability of funds plays a huge role in whether they can afford what you're presenting.

Yes, many will find a way to pay for it, but this isn't only about the sale and getting paid. As someone serving someone, the integrity part is also very important here.

Is it worth finding a way to pay for it for them?

Is it in their best interest to take a loan out now?

Many sales representatives won't consider the best interest of the prospect. Make sure YOU DO! The amount of future business depends on how you serve them at this very moment.

Now if it is the solution they need and they can afford or have options to pay for your offering and it'll give them enough value to move forward, then you're good to go and are handling things the right way. It's always good to have an idea of what their available funds are, not for you to forecast how much you can possibly make with this client, but for ALWAYS finding the best options that best suit their needs.

3. KNOWING HOW THEY SPEND THEIR MONEY AND HOW THEY WOULD SPEND THEIR MONEY.

This is a great way during your debut to see how to guide your prospect best. Asking them what they're currently doing or what they'd like to do moving forward gives you a great way to cater your presentation to them. This also saves a lot of time if you're offering something that has multiple layers, when some layers might not be as important to focus on as others.

All 3 above have imperative information so you're not wasting their time or yours. Unfortunately, untrained sales representatives waste tons of time presenting a product or service, only to find out the prospect wasn't interested in what you were offering at all.

If you can master these 3 steps to sales success, you'll be very efficient in your growth. The phrase "time is money" is a very real thing. For you and your prospect.

Does posture matter? YES! Sales posture is very important.

It's 2023 and it seems like posture is becoming less and less important. Not just in sales, but in the world. BUT having correct posture shows respect, that you care, that you're listening. Posture can show how you feel about something, whether good or bad. Is the prospect's time important or not? So much goes into making sure you're ready and able to send the right signals to the people you have the luxury of spending time with.

Every high achiever in sales understands this and has mastered their movement to show their client the most respect. You can literally lose deals when you lack this. You can serve them to the highest degree, offer the best possible product, the best prices, it ALL makes sense, but how you were sitting didn't show them their time mattered to you. Your posture spoke of boredom or like you didn't you care. Result: deals are lost.

The definition of posture: the position in which someone holds their body while standing or sitting and a particular way of dealing with or considering something; an approach or attitude.

It's all communication and how you're reflecting it to the prospect.

People send messages in many different ways: what we say, our body language, the tone we use and when we use it, but when you use all of the above with a positive attitude, it makes for a much smoother way to serve your prospect.

Cornell University did a study on posture and they found that there were 3 main language components when it comes to posture:

1. SUPREME:

This posture language was defined as someone who felt above or better than the prospect. The way they communicated makes the client feel like they're inferior to the salesperson. A lot of times this would include talking down to them, or facial expressions that indicate a lack of excitement in meeting with the prospect. Most of the conversation is run by the salesperson in an aggressive fashion, has a low tolerance for other people's opinion, big talkers with loud mouths that don't net many results.

2. MATCHING:

This is by far the best posture to have. You'll see this a lot with high performers. No one is better than the other. Their body language shows they are grateful to have the time with the prospect. It proves confidence and gratitude to the prospect. It also shows that both are willing and open to hearing each other's opinion for the most productive outcome together. This posture reciprocates respect, care, authority, and develops a level of urgency to serve each other equally.

All parties work together to solve issues with the utmost confidence, regardless of how easy or hard the issue may be.

3. SUBSTANDARD:

Statistically and unfortunately, this is where most of the salespeople in the world fall. In 2021, Cornell proved that 81% of all sales representatives fell into the substandard posture sector of its study. This allows the prospect to take total control of a sales presentation, not allowing the salesperson to guide it efficiently. The prospect usually doesn't allow the substandard representative to speak or take any type of leadership role during the sales process at all. Frequently, this allows prospects to get out of presentations quickly, minimizing any chance of the salesperson's ability to serve them. Long story short, salesperson = no control, prospect = all the control.

To sum up the posture portion of your debut: always communicate equality. You're grateful for the time with them and they're happy they're with you, a competent, professional person. This allows for the best outcome in any presentation.

Communication is key. From the way you introduce yourself, to what you wear, your facial expressions, your movement, your posture—it all plays a vital role in your overall success. It's also adjusted by the people you meet and their specific characteristics to make you relatable and to feel a sense of trust from the start.

The moral of your debut is to make it intentional. Have a process that's yours. Don't skip any steps. Short cuts never work! Keep it real always and sell yourself! Take time to role play each of the steps in this chapter.

It's easier than you think to start off your time with your prospect because there are too many people doing it wrong. Don't let it be you.

CHAPTER 11

STRATEGIC TONALITY: USING YOUR VOICE AS A TOOL

Have you ever heard yourself speak? Not when you speak, but actually recorded yourself in a conversation or during a sales presentation? How do you know that the way you're speaking is the most effective? Have you ever heard the phrase, "It's not what you say, but how you say it"? Well, that's what this chapter is about. We're going to dive into how voice inflection matters!

As a speaker, I'm constantly looking for ways to bring people deeper into my story, the speech, so they can really FEEL what I'm saying. When I'm on stage, training, or having a one-on-one conversation, I don't want anyone to lose interest. Unfortunately, for many people when they go to events with not-so-trained speakers, it puts a bad taste in their mouths and they tell others about it and they don't go to events anymore.

Well, the same thing happens in sales presentations. To the ones who don't understand how important this is, it doesn't matter how hard you try, the prospect never retains anything you're telling them. This usually leads to having to repeat yourself, the same questions get asked over and over again, because your listeners are not engaged. They don't feel what you're saying. They're not interested in what you're saying and the truth is, you could have a product or service with amazing value, but if presented with insufficient voice inflection, it could be undervalued just because of how you speak. Your tone could be a very serious issue. If you don't fix it and pay attention, your tone and voice inflection could limit your success in sales.

There are grammatical pathways when dealing with clients, either on the phone or in person, such as: tone, pitch, volume, and the speed with which you talk. These inherently affect your ability to serve your prospect.

The minute you meet someone, the minute they answer the phone, there are two ways to communicate. In person, you have verbal and non-verbal communication, because they can see you. When you're on the phone, you lose the non-verbal side.

When you're on the phone with a potential client or even a previous client, voice inflection is SO IMPORTANT and plays a major role in the decision-making process. Here are a few examples:

- Zero excitement in your voice. Very monotone, you seem extremely boring and not interested in what you're offering or in your prospects.

- If you're talking super slow, it makes you seem like you don't care or have a down, miserable attitude.

Keeping a good pace of speech makes you seem more engaged and interested in what you're offering and in your prospects, which means a much higher probability of serving them. When you speak confidently, a large part of that is using tones in a low pitch; some call them down tones. On the contrary, up tones, ending conversations in a high pitch, makes you seem less confident. Also, when you end in low tones, it projects that you have great problem-solving skills.

I know this may sound weird, but I want you to try this the next time you're on the phone with a prospect. Try smiling the entire time you speak. It literally forces you to sound happier and more confident, eliminating the chance of a meek or monotone conversation from you.

When you smile, yes, even fake smile, it releases endorphins in your body that make you happy. There's some gold for ya right there! Having a bad day? Fake smile. Just try it, I dare you. We all have bad days and this actually works, both on the phone and personally, to help you through those trying days. Subconsciously, you're empowering your tone to be more confident. I challenge you to try it. If you fake smile and you don't feel better for that moment, if you can fake smile and sound boring, I'll give you 5 of these books personally shipped to you and signed by me!

Speaking confidently means you have to be conscious of what you say and how you say it. A lot of people have problems with the words "um" or "uh" as they speak. This can do a few things:

- Make it seem like you don't know what you're saying.

- That pause with the words "um" or "uh" eliminates a smooth tone pattern, almost having to start over.

- Is like a mental disconnect for a prospect or even someone listening to you as a speaker.

Don't get me wrong, breaks and pauses when you're on a presentation or speaking in a morning meeting or on stage are AMAZING to use, pulling people in and out of your story line or about what you're offering.

You don't want to sound like you're unsure when you speak unless you really are. Then the BEST WAY to handle that is just say these magic words, "I don't know." Those are the best words to use when you use the proper tone and inflection. It proves that you're trustworthy and don't want to give them a fluff answer you may not know to be true, like many untrained salespeople these days.

As a leader, you need to know how to speak. Know how to speak and master it for every situation. Your job is to handle things accordingly. For instance, if there's a heated argument and you're intervening, you'd lower your voice and speak calmer. Subconsciously, the people arguing will lower their voices as well. If you want the volume to go up and get people to engage with high energy, you'd raise your voice with the proper tone and watch the crowd go wild.

If you're in a corporate environment, a leader of any kind, in sales on any level, in management, it's imperative that you learn the art of down tones. It gives you the image and truth from an authoritative level.

There was a study done at Berkley which researched the number of tones that the human ear can distinguish as different. The study found that an average IQ human can notice 1391 different tones and voice inflections. The study went on to prove that high IQ level humans can notice 1832 different tones and voice inflections. Remember hearing is 9 times more sensitive than seeing.

Berkley's study also proved that HOW YOU SAY THINGS is 6 times more important than WHAT you say. So what does that mean to salespeople? Voice inflection is an ESSENTIAL TOOL we all must master.

Very few people sound the same in sales. We all have our own voice inflection. Especially when on the phone, when you're serving a prospect, voice inflection is the separator between the average and the elite. Prospects can't see you. They can only hear you. So there's no judgment on what you look like. They make their decisions on how you speak, trickled in with a little of what you say.

Let's get into the two most important types of inflection:

1. UPWARD INFLECTION:

This is when you're speaking low and travel upward in sound and tonality within a word you're trying to put meaning behind. A lot of times—well, in my opinion, most of the time—this shows prospects that you're not sure of what you're saying, not confident, not being real. This is a bad inflection to use if you're trying to verify a fact or something to be true.

2. DOWNWARD INFLECTION:

Different from the upward inflection, this is where you're starting higher and transition into a lower inflection within a specific word or power statement, fact, or timed portion of your presentation. This is the way to go! Studies have shown that when using a downward inflection, you have an 81.9% better chance of getting the deal, because a downward inflection demonstrates confidence, sincerity, and power. You want to use this in every moment that you'd like to make your prospect remember. The power moments. I will tell you, this is one of the most difficult to master. It should be practiced.

There are places to use both, but my advice is to make you sound sincere when you do. There's nothing that will ruin an opportunity to earn a sale, when sounding like you were waiting for the right moment to use either.

Now let's talk about speed. If you talk fast, you're already being looked at as dishonest. I'm a New Yorker. A fast talker. Every single time I'm in a conversation, especially when people know who I am, I get this statement: "Todd, you're not gonna close me!" When I really wasn't even trying to. Because of how I used to talk—fast, cutting people off—I lost the ability to connect.

There are several things talking fast does:

1. Means you usually interrupt people when they're speaking (among the top 3 no-no's in sales).
2. Means you're just trying to sell your client, not serve them. (You just want their money.)

3. Means that there might be dishonest statements made. And finally…..

4. Means that what you're about to say doesn't have much weight (not that important).

All of these limit your ability to be successful in sales, so if you're like me, a New Yorker fast talker, my advice is to SLOW DOWN!

This is one of the best lessons I've ever learned. When I slowed down, it showed my prospect I cared about what they had to say, that what I was saying was important, that I cared enough to concentrate and take my time with them, giving them my full attention. This makes you sound confident and your prospect feels more confident working with you.

Even speaking softly can help a lot. Slowing down doesn't always mean speaking softly, but there's definitely a need for it. When you bring down the volume of your voice, it makes people feel way more comfortable and will give them more reason and time to pay attention more.

I use this when I'm going over something hard to understand. I used to assume that people understood what I was saying when I spoke fast. I thought that the faster I spoke, not wasting their time, would be good for them, so we can speed up the length of the presentation. But all it did was prolong it. When I didn't speak softly in complex explanations, they'd stop me at the end of my speed rant and say, "Whoa, you went through that so fast. Can you explain that again slower please?"

This happened far too often, so I consciously stopped and forced myself to take a deep breath and slow it way down. This helped me avoid saying things like:

1. "Does that make sense?"

2. "Do you get it?"

3. "Understand?"

I hate those statements. Cornell did a study with 40,000 people in the coaching, sales, leadership, and consulting world. An astounding 73.1% of people felt insulted when someone used the statements above or similar. They felt like you were questioning their intelligence. Not a good way to brand yourself or speak to a client, right?

When you speak softly, people understand more and when you combine that with a smooth speed, it gives them the ability to ask you questions they have, not having to wait till the end because you won't give them the opportunity to speak.

When you're in tele-sales, you have a VERY short window to make a first impression. The moment someone answers, you're on stage. Your time to shine is within a 15-second window. You have to make sure that your ability to communicate properly, using the right tone and inflection, gives them a reason to keep listening. The WHOLE MESSAGE on the phone is your tone. How you say it, not what you have to say.

Here are some things I like to teach on mastering the art of voice inflection:

1. Record yourself. Listen to yourself and see how fast or slow you may be speaking.

2. Count the "ums" and "uhs" during a presentation or speech.

3. Count how many times you cut someone off when they're trying to communicate with you.

4. Listen for when you have an upward tone and when you have a downward tone.

5. Practice in the mirror over and over again. Watch yourself and your expressions.

6. Be conscious of certain power statements in your presentation and make sure you're using a downward tone rather than an upward tone. Or are you even emphasizing those important times at all?

7. Take deep breaths before you start your presentation. Breath control is real and helps control the speed at which you speak.

8. Constantly practice how fast you speak. When you do this, you'll be able to notice when and where you need to fix it.

You have to take the time to dig deep and keep practicing these steps. It took me years to understand and master this voice movement. Don't wait as long as I did. I'm giving you the tools right now. USE THEM!

Your voice matters. Your tone matters, but unfortunately sales trainers, corporate trainers, never go into the importance of this skill. As a matter of fact, most don't even think about it or use it during their trainings and most salespeople don't use it properly when trying to serve a prospect.

For instance, using pauses before a power statement or an important word, or using pauses to take people in and out of your story are necessary strength moves when speaking in any capacity. I was on Victor Antonio's Sales Influence Podcast as a guest, and after the interview was over, he was helping me understand when speaking on stage, how important the pause is. He talked about having people in the story, they're engaged and then he pauses, looks up and almost becomes the narrator to his own speech. He paused to take them in and out of the story, which makes them want more. It helps them better understand what he's saying. If you haven't seen him speak, you need to and soon. You'll see these pauses often. He gives the audience time to absorb the information. Also, pausing minimizes the "ums" and the "uhs" we were talking about earlier. That old saying, "Think before you speak" is real.

Victor also emphasizes key moments and words when he speaks using voice inflection to the fullest. For example, if you used the phrase "and then what happened was," there are many different meanings using the same words based on HOW you say it.

- "and then what happened was" monotone, meaning nothing special happened; just normal
- "and then what happened was!!!" louder voice, meaning get excited something big happened
- "and then what happened was?" monotone, basically saying, "tell me what happened"

You get the drift, I'm sure. All of these statements are the exact same words, but with much different meanings because of how we say them. The voice inflection changed in each.

The tone in each is essentially communicating what each of those phrases mean when you say them as well. Are you bored? Are you annoyed? Are you excited? Are you confident? Are you unsure? Knowing what you want to say is only half the battle. You must also know HOW you're going to say what you want to say.

For instance, if I write: "That's cool" and I end that statement with an ! or … or just a period, or a question mark, this will change the entire meaning of what "that's cool" is trying to communicate. It's the same when you say it.

You always have to be fully aware of your tone.

- Is it a soft tone?
- Is it energetic?
- Is it strong?
- Is it happy?
- Is it angry?
- Is it boring?
- Is it emotional?

I can't reiterate this enough. Your voice has to match the words you use. The voice you use has literally hundreds of different meanings to the human ear as the studies have proven.

To be a sales professional, you have to master how you speak. You have to master your tone, when to use what type of tone and inflection. Role play with someone you know and try each of the different ways we've spoken about in this chapter. You be the presenter and someone else the receiver of the words and then switch it up. Make sure to record yourselves. When you hear it played back and you feel how it feels to be spoken to with each tone and voice inflection, it'll give you a better understanding of when to use which and why.

Remember, your voice matters!

Here are some great tools and role-playing activities to get better with tonality that you can implement and start using right away!

1. COLD CALLING AND INITIAL PITCH:

Scenario: Your company has developed a new cloud-based project management tool specifically designed for small businesses. You are a sales representative tasked with making a cold call to a potential client, Mr. & Mrs. Smith, who owns a small graphic design agency.

Role-Playing:
- Salesperson A (Sales Rep): Initiates the cold call and introduces themselves and the company.
- Salesperson B (Mr. & Mrs. Smith - Potential Client): Responds as the potential client, expressing mild interest but also hesitance due to her busy schedule.
- Salesperson A: Delivers a concise pitch, highlighting the tool's time-saving features, collaboration capabilities, and ease of use.
- Salesperson B: Asks questions and raises concerns about the learning curve and integration with their existing tools.
- Salesperson A: Addresses concerns by sharing success stories of similar businesses and offers to set up a quick online demo to showcase the tool's benefits.

- Salesperson B: Agrees to the demo and provides contact information for follow-up.

2. HANDLING OBJECTIONS AND CLOSING:

Scenario: Your company, World Class Travel Company, is offering a premium vacation package to an exclusive island resort. You are a sales representative trying to sell this package to a potential client, Todd Speciale, who is concerned about the price and lack of amenities on the island.

Role-Playing:
- Salesperson A (Sales Rep): Opens the conversation by introducing the luxury island retreat and its unique features.
- Salesperson B (Todd Speciale - Potential Client): Responds skeptically, expressing concerns about the price and limited conveniences.
- Salesperson A: Acknowledges the concerns, then paints a vivid picture of the breathtaking natural surroundings, personalized service, and off-the-grid relaxation.
- Salesperson B: Raises specific concerns about internet access and medical facilities.
- Salesperson A: Assures that while the resort is secluded, it provides high-speed satellite internet and has a medical center staffed by qualified professionals.
- Salesperson B: Still unsure, but intrigued, asks about any special offers or discounts.
- Salesperson A: Offers a limited-time discount and emphasizes the exclusivity of the experience.
- Salesperson B: Expresses interest in the offer and asks about booking details, signaling readiness to proceed with the purchase.

3. PRODUCT PRESENTATION AND CONSULTATIVE SELLING:

Scenario: Your company, MedSuite Solutions, has developed a state-of-the-art diagnostic imaging system for hospitals. You are a sales representative giving a presentation to Dr. Brandon Biskie, the head of the radiology department at a leading hospital.

Role-Playing:

- Salesperson A (Sales Rep): Begins the presentation by introducing the innovative imaging system and its potential impact on diagnostic accuracy and efficiency.

- Salesperson B (Dr. Brandon Biskie - Potential Client): Engages with questions about the system's capabilities and how it could integrate into their current workflow.

- Salesperson A: Presents detailed information about the system's advanced imaging modalities, ease of integration with existing systems, and compatibility with electronic health records (EHR).

- Salesperson B: Expresses concerns about training staff to use the new system and asks about ongoing technical support.

- Salesperson A: Outlines the comprehensive training program offered, along with 24/7 technical support to ensure a smooth transition and operation.

- Salesperson B: Inquires about costs and payment options.

- Salesperson A: Provides a transparent breakdown of costs and emphasizes the long-term cost savings through improved diagnostics.

- Salesperson B: Expresses interest in a trial period to evaluate the system's effectiveness.

- Salesperson A: Proposes a customized trial period to Dr. Biskie's specifications, scheduling, and department's needs.

Remember each role-playing scenario should be customized to your specific business, but if you're not tied to one particular brand or company, it's always a great way to train on how you'd handle scenarios if you were in a different industry.

Mastering tonality and role playing will have you prepared to do anything! It's one of the best tools to have in life, but you MUST train constantly with people who will give you constructive feedback to help you grow. KEEP TRAINING!

CHAPTER 12

MASTERING THE ART OF MIRRORING

Have you ever been out with some friends and you look at your watch and then someone sees you do it and then what do they do? They look at their watch. Maybe they yawn and then you instantly yawn when you weren't even tired. When you see someone cry, you feel it. Some cry too; some just feel it. There are a ton of different examples I can share with you here, but they're all mirroring! You've done it and have been doing it your whole life. Now it's time to make it a skill to serve your prospects in the best way, optimizing your ability to get more deals.

Mirroring is an extremely powerful tool to master in life. It's a psychological concept used in negotiations, sales, debates, politics, arguments, and more. If you can control how you mirror, you can come out on top in the majority of your conversations.

So what's the actual definition? "When one person emulates another person's behavior, either verbal or non-verbal." This isn't just doing the exact same thing they do, the exact same way.

There have been a ton of scientific studies done on mirroring in sales specifically. There are many studies on the "Psychological Implications On Mirroring." Now I won't act like I know the scientific measurability and the details of what all that means, but what I can tell you is that there were 17 different studies that proved to be similar in their results. So similar, that there was just a 3% difference in their results.

The studies proved that mirroring was directly connected to behaviors, abilities, learning limitations, facial expressions, and mostly, INFLUENCE! Mirroring is a universal language of communication. If you go someplace and you don't speak their language and you point at something you want, what does the person who speaks the other language do? They point at the same thing to confirm that's what you want. There was no talking. This is another non-verbal way of communicating in this example.

Monkeys have been known to have a high level of something called "mirror neurons" as well. That's why their level of intelligence and communication ability thrives compared to some other species. Now it's yet to be proven that the human race has these, but some think we do.

The cool thing about all this scientific stuff is that there are two proven functions of mirroring:

1. The understanding of the actions of others.
    - This process turns visual observations into information about the client or prospect or person you're speaking with.
2. Learning to do something observing others.
    - "Watch and learn" is a thing and this is where it's derived from neurologically.

In sales, mirroring is the simple process of a sales professional mimicking a prospect's verbal or non-verbal communication cues. It can involve tone as well, as in the previous chapter. You can mirror just about anything and the main reason for it is to prove understanding, build rapport, and establish a strong foundation of trust so the prospect knows they matter.

The one who uses this most is anyone who negotiates on any level. It's a great skill that can be used in business and life. You're taking the movement or words of someone to determine how they feel about something and then doing what they do back to show them you understand.

Have you ever looked at someone when you wanted them to agree with you and you started nodding your head? What happened? They nodded their head too. You want them to agree, you nod your head up and down. You want them to disagree you nod from right to left. It's intentionally replicating the movement or words of others.

I know what you're thinking. Someone will see that coming a mile away. Well, for one, you don't use this as a tactic, more a skill and a process that shows you're listening and agree or understand what they're trying to communicate. But the reality is, if you practice this, it's virtually impossible for someone to think, "Oh, they're using that mirroring thing…" This is just a practice that gets both parties on the same page in sales. One understands the other. And if you watch carefully, your prospects do this to you unintentionally all the time.

When you use this in sales properly, the prospect feels that you feel them and you're more alike than they might've thought. It helps with building rapport instantly too. The emotional aspect of mirroring helps you make more sales than any other sales tool used.

There are also many different styles of mirroring that can be used with one another or separately.

The first style is Body Language.

For example, if a prospect leans in and is looking at your sales material, lean in with them and show them that what matters to them matters to you. Give them their personal space, of course … LOL … but mimicking this movement shows that you're acknowledging that this is important to them, so it's important to you.

If you're on the phone with someone and they say, "Wow, that's cool," you can respond with, "Yeah, its very cool," confirming you've heard them, you know they like that about what you're offering, and you've taken the time to prove that to them.

Both of these send a subliminal message to your prospect that you heard them loud and clear even if they didn't use words. The power of that message being conveyed properly to your potential client is one of the most valuable tools you can learn in sales and just communication in general. Giving someone the respect of your full attention gives you a 5x higher chance of closing the sale.

Another verbal example of mirroring is in the speed someone speaks. Again, a fast talker from New York is usually more relatable to someone who speaks as fast and has a similar accent. It's proven that if someone mimics a speed pattern or accent, the client feels more comfortable doing business with them.

There are three key benefits to mirroring in the sales process:

1. Creates trust
   - It helps bring sales resistance down, as mirroring makes your prospect feel like you understand what matters to them, which in turns makes them feel like they can trust you more.

2. Trust is easier to build
   - It just helps a customer feel more comfortable when you use this technique properly. In today's world of "hard core closers," it makes people feel way more at ease when working with you.

3. The focus is on them
   - In order to be effective using this technique, you have to listen, be attentive to their movement and their responses. This automatically makes the prospect respect you more. All eyes on them.

Obviously a prospect is not going to buy from you just from mirroring, but it does make a large impact on whether or not they buy from you.

A few popular techniques in sales mirroring are:

1. Resembling tones
   - Sometimes the way you speak could scare a customer off before you even have the chance to serve them. You could be loud; they could be soft spoken. Try resembling their tone. The commonality opens wider for a potential opportunity.

2. Gestures
   - A lot of people don't recognize this of themselves, but they have consistent patterns in how they move. Such as, waves, how they shake hands, head nods, facial gestures, and more. If you can find out the common gestures of your prospect, you can mimic them and it instantaneously boosts morale and the willingness to work with you.

3. Communication in the details
   - Some people love to talk about every tiny little detail in the sales offering. They want to read every single line, very analytical. Others want to know "how much is it and what do I get for it" – simple, quick, and easy. Recognizing this and mirroring how they communicate earns huge points with most buyers these days, because untrained sales reps just make the same robotic moves without taking this into consideration.

4. Body language
   - Some are chill. Some are serious. Some are nervous. Some are excited. Some are bored. Some are annoyed. All are fine and all can turn into sales. The important thing here is that you find out which of these is your client the fastest way possible. Recognize it and then address it. Your body pos-

ture can send the message, without you ever having to say anything, that you and your client are on the same page.

Some of the simpler psychological styles are:
- They sit up straight, you sit up straight.
- They lean forward, you lean forward.
- They cross their legs, you cross your legs.
- They move slow, you move slow.
- They use hand gestures, you use them.

Volume and Speed
- They talk fast, speed up.
- They talk slow, slow down.
- They are loud, get louder. (Don't yell … LOL … don't do that.)
- They are more soft spoken, you should be too.

You get the idea. Mirroring is a simple way to add value to you as a sales professional and is very effective when it's done right. BUT beware: when it's done wrong it can can instantly kill your opportunity.

Here are some of the biggest mistake people make when trying to mirror.

Don't mirror people's:
- Disabilities
- Unique attributes they may have
    - Dialect
    - Speech imperfections/impediments
    - Expressions
- Mistakes they make
    - In speech
    - In movement (physical)
        - Looking away if they do

- Crossing your arms because they are upset
- Rolling your eyes

Now I know a lot of that seemed like common sense, but I've trained huge companies that didn't teach this properly and it was a disaster in their overall efficiency.

Remember, this technique is only effective when the prospect doesn't understand you're copying them and doing it on purpose. If they feel like you are, it'll be considered mocking them and the odds of closing that deal will go way down.

So the question is, is the risk worth the reward? IT ABSOLUTELY IS! Once again, work on this through role playing and mastering this art with someone who's as motivated as you are to learn!

One last piece of advice. This is usually much more effective in a one-on-one or a one-on-two type of environment. Mimicking during meetings or in group settings isn't an optimal use of this technique. I don't recommend it at all in group settings.

Familiarize your team with the technique of mirroring in sales conversations to build rapport and trust.

The only way you do that is by training! Here are some great role-playing exercises for your team.

SCENARIO 1: IN-STORE PURCHASE

Setting: An electronics store where a customer is looking to buy a new laptop.

Role Play:

Customer: "I'm trying to find a laptop that's good for both work and some light gaming."

Salesperson (mirroring tone and content): "So, you're in need of a laptop that balances work tasks and light gaming. Let's see what we have that fits that description."

Breakdown:

1. The salesperson mirrored the customer's words by using "balances" to reflect the dual needs and repeated the core components of the customer's statement.

2. This subtly signals to the customer that they are understood.

SCENARIO 2: OVER THE PHONE SERVICE INQUIRY

Setting: Customer calls a travel agency looking for a relaxing vacation package.

Role Play:

Customer: "I've been so stressed lately. I need a vacation where I can just unwind and not think about anything."

Salesperson (mirroring emotion and content): "It sounds like you've had quite a hectic time. You're really looking for a getaway where you can just relax and switch off. I can certainly help with that."

Breakdown:

1. The salesperson mirrored the emotion behind the customer's words, acknowledging the stress.

2. By repeating the need to "relax and switch off," the salesperson reinforces understanding.

SCENARIO 3: BUSINESS TO BUSINESS SALES MEETING

Setting: A conference room where a salesperson is pitching a software solution to a company executive.

Role Play:

Executive: "We've had issues with our current software being too complex. Our team spends so much time just trying to navigate it."

Salesperson (mirroring the problem): "Complexity issues can be a real time-drain. So, you're looking for something more intuitive where your team can spend less time navigating and more time being productive?"

Breakdown:
1. The salesperson mirrors back the problem to show understanding and to reinforce the pain point.
2. The question at the end encourages the executive to engage and further explain their needs, already feeling like they are on the same page with the salesperson.

After each scenario, have the team discuss each scenario:
1. What did they notice about the salesperson's mirroring technique?
2. How might the customer feel after the salesperson's response?
3. Any improvements or alternatives in how mirroring can be applied?

Practice mirroring in conversations to become more adept at it. Remember, the key to effective mirroring is subtlety. Overdoing it can come across as insincere or can feel like mocking.

If you don't train, you won't get better.

CHAPTER 13

PLAY THE PERSON, NOT THE CARDS

I was excited to write this chapter because I grew up in a pool hall gambling. I used to sit in the pool hall for hours upon hours, just watching all the different negotiations going on, the hustling, the winning, but keeping it close so the person who lost would keep trying to win. Then to the card players, playing games like Gin, Tonk, Pinochle, Cribbage and more. Where they held the cards, the facial expressions, the intentional movements that favored a victory for them. Then years later I ran poker games for a living. You have to really master the art of reading people. Do they have the winning hand or not? Their betting patterns and more.

I took what I learned in the streets and transferred it to the real world. This skill I spent years mastering, in my opinion, was without a doubt the separating factor of me scaling above the rest.

In card games we look for specific habits, physical movements, certain behaviors that'll give me an idea of how to proceed with the hand. Being able to read people gave me a huge advantage in the streets and in the corporate world. In my interviews, in a sales presentation, speaking at events, my personal life. I usually knew the outcome or how someone feels before most, which gives me the ability to pivot properly to realign towards getting the sale.

When you have a fair idea of what your prospects are thinking and how they're feeling, you can react accordingly. This process will take you from ELITE to an anomaly in your life. Not many people take the time to master this, but they should.

The best of the best read body language, facial expressions, breathing patterns. They read how couples communicate through eye contact and more.

As we've already spoken about in previous chapters there are two ways in which we all communicate—verbal and non-verbal. How you speak matters, as we know, but you're constantly meeting people with different incomes, backgrounds, levels in their careers, age differences—all of which make it challenging to determine the best way to navigate to the close.

For instance, the easiest tell in a person for me is when they're intentionally not paying attention. Have you ever been presenting your product or service and the person(s) you're presenting to are on their phone(s) the entire time? That's not a hard read or tell to understand. They're just not into you or what you're offering. So what do you do?

- Ask them a question.

- Touch them to get their attention (simple professional touch).

- Stop talking to see if they notice, if not one of the two above.

- If they're on the phone say: "Oh, my apologies, I'll wait till you're off. Sorry to interrupt you."

There are many ways to control the conversation, but if you see someone not paying attention, you have to regain control. Many salespeople will read someone, see this easy-to-see tell, and just keep pitching. If you want to be a professional, you need to stop and regain interest.

During most presentations it's easy to see if a prospect is receptive to what you're saying, is defensive or frustrated, is not showing interest, has affordability issues, disagrees with you and so on. If you don't pick up on this and get back on track, you'll get major resistance on the backend. Many prospects will actually use non-verbal communication, expecting you to pick up on it and get mad that you didn't when it's time to ask for the money.

What do we look for in tells and reading people?

- Eye movement
- Head movements
- Hand gestures
- Posture (how they're sitting)
- Arm gestures
- Facial expressions
- How they're breathing
- Leg/feet movement (getting anxious)

It's simpler than you think to notice this stuff too. You've actually been doing it your whole life. When you were a kid and you wanted candy, you saw the look on your parents' face when you wanted it even after they said no, so you changed your face, put your lip out, and begged some more. MOST of the time, parents would give in because they couldn't handle that little face. You read your parents at that young age!!!

Noticing the eye movement with your prospects to observe their feelings about you or what you're offering is one of the top things to pay attention to when reading people. The eyes give away a lot.

I actually studied the eyes when I was younger. It was important for me in cards and in the pool hall to understand what I was seeing. There are so many studies done on this and they all seem to have similar results on how the eyes give you away, such as:

EYE SHIFTING

When you're talking to someone, mainly when asking a question, see if their eyes go up. If they look up, studies have shown they're buying time to think of an answer to give you. The interesting part of this, is that in men and women equally, if they look up and to the right, scientists have proven that their studies proved 87% of all people who looked up and to the right, failed the lie detector test or admittedly said they were lying. That's the bad news. The good news is that if they look up and to the left, the same study proved that 91% we're telling the truth!

When you're shifting your eyes it can definitely vary per person, but statistically if you look down you're emotional, if you look up and around, not in one specific direction, it usually means you're just processing information.

BLINKING

People blink more in stressful scenarios. So if you see someone blinking more, usually their stress levels are high. Blinking a lot can also mean a person is lying more times than not. A CIA strategist proved that out of 100 interrogations, when a suspect blinked at a rate higher than normal, they proved to be lying 72.7% of the time. The average blinks per minute is between 8 and 12 total. This doesn't mean everyone blinking fast is a liar, as environmental conditions also play a factor, but it's something to consider when combined with other tells.

RUBBING YOUR EYES MUCH?

Studies have shown that if you ask a question and someone rubs their eyes right after answering, it means they feel comfortable or fully agree with what you asked. So men, next time the wifey asks you to get her that expensive bag and you say yes and rub your eyes, you know why! We do this subconsciously. You don't even have to rub your eyes, you can look down for a long period of time with your eyelids down too. One doctor even said a blind child will rub their eyes or cover them when they don't feel comfortable with what you've requested or stated.

DOES SIZE MATTER?

Pupil size does for sure. You might be the best facial-expression person out there, but if you meet someone who knows how to read your pupils, it has a strong possibility of giving you away! Studies have shown that if you like what you see visually, your pupils grow in size. If you don't like what you see, they shrink. An FBI counterintelligence officer also said that stress and frustration reduce pupil size as well.

DO YOU SEE ME?

Eye contact is the most obvious of all. Just because someone looks you dead in the eyes, doesn't necessarily mean they're telling the truth. The same FBI officer said that contrary to what most believe, society knows this and have learned to engage more with eye contact instead of looking away even if they are not telling the truth. He went on to say, when you feel comfortable and at ease, you don't have to look them in the eye, and more so than not, means you're telling the truth. Fun fact: in the United States you have 2 seconds to look at someone in the eyes before it gets uncomfortable. Be careful! But throughout the presentation it's a proven fact that you should stay connected with eye contact 60-70% of the time. Don't be looking down the entire time at your "pitch material," as there's no emotion in that.

There are many other tells such as watery or glazed eyes, raised brows, narrowed eyes when annoyed, and so many more. In sales, try giving your prospect three options. You might notice they look at one longer than the other two. That's a tell. If they look at one and instantly put it to the side, that's a tell.

Studies have also proven that people tend to look much longer at things they're drawn too. Use this in the sales process to see what's most important to your prospect.

How much do you like feet? If you like them, you're going to love this info. If you don't, get to loving them, because this is going to save you time and make you money. Feet and leg movement tell us a lot and many have neglected this tell for far too long.

Your feet can tell when you're nervous, flustered, happy, sad, excited, and so much more.

Some of the most common tells from the feet and legs are:

- Crossing your legs
    - Maybe it's sitting down or standing with our legs crossed, but if something or someone makes us feel uncomfortable, we subconsciously uncross our legs to give us the best chance at protecting ourselves or running away.
    - It can mean someone feels superior to you.
    - It can also mean someone is intrigued by what you're saying.
- Facial expressions
    - Someone agreeing usually smiles, nods their head, and seems engaged.
        - When they don't agree, you'll see:
            1. Clenched muscles in the jaw
            2. Not looking directly at you
            3. Head slightly turned from where you're presenting
            4. Lips pursed
            5. Tense face
            6. Narrow brows

- The Lean in
    - The shoulders and abdominal section mean a lot. The more someone agrees with you and the more engaged they are, the more they'll lean in to see what you're saying. A good way to test this is to take a pen or your finger and point to something, getting them to engage. If they lean forward, they're usually interested; if they don't lean forward and just kind of look from afar, it means you need to stop and start asking questions to get the prospect to re-engage.
- Gestures – there's meaning behind them all
    - If a prospect seems tight, arms not crossed but hands clinched, they're less receptive than if they were sitting with their arms open and hands free. How excited are they at the introduction to be spending time with you? Do they seem like they don't want to be there? Are they excited? When they answer the phone, do they sound busy, glad you called or not so much? People who aren't happy or who are argumentative may fold their arms as a sign of protection or frustration, they might make fists, bowed chest, etc.
    - Once you're in the sales process more towards the middle or end, the hand and arm movement is the best for tells and reading your client to see where they stand. Are their hands open and resting on the table? Are they pointing at or looking at pricing or the product or service offered? If the prospect isn't engaging and the hands and arms are anywhere but a part of the sales process, crossed, on the phone, pointing outside…. Then it proves less interest and minimal opportunity to close the deal.
- Do you love feet? You should when you're reading people in the sales process!
    - If a prospect's sitting upright and the feet are flat on the ground, it usually means they're ready to go.

- o If they stand up while you're presenting options. Bad sign.
- o Your prospect's brain has a limbic system, we all do actually, which tells our legs what the probability is that you run or stand firm. This is good to know in the sales process.
- o The best feet and leg combination is if the feet and legs are extended and the feet are crossed. This gesture is a positive one and means they're interested and in no hurry to leave. They're comfortable and open to hearing more and spending time with you.

Reading people, noticing tells, is a great sales tool to have. Trust yourself. Trust your instincts. If you're wrong, you're wrong, but you've got to start someplace. The more you notice these things, the more prepared you'll be to guide yourself to the best possible outcome. There are tons of free YouTube videos out there where you can learn how to read people better.

Remember, you've been doing this your entire life; why stop now when you can make it profitable, right? But the only way to do that is to make sure you fully understand how to correctly interpret body language and why it's crucial in sales. It provides insights into a customer's feelings, doubts, and intentions, allowing you to adapt your approach in real-time.

I've put together 3 trainings that will help you, not only get better at it but actually understand how to read body language cues:

SCENARIO 1: THE NERVOUS BUYER

Setting: You're selling a high-end software solution to a potential client.

Body Language Cues:
- Avoiding direct eye contact
- Rubbing the back of the neck
- Fidgeting with hands or items on the table

- Rapid breathing or shallow breaths

Role Play Breakdown:
1. Recognize the nervous cues.
2. Address the concern indirectly. Ask open-ended questions to gauge the root of their nervousness.
3. Offer reassurance. Highlight the benefits of your product and share testimonials.
4. Encourage questions. Make them feel comfortable seeking clarity.

SCENARIO 2: THE SKEPTICAL BUYER

Setting: You're presenting a new product to a long-term client.

Body Language Cues:
- Raised eyebrows or furrowed brow
- Crossed arms
- Leaning back in their chair
- Tight-lipped smile or pursed lips

Role Play Breakdown:
1. Notice the defensive or skeptical posture.
2. Engage directly. "I notice you seem hesitant. Do you have concerns about this feature?"
3. Provide evidence. This could be in the form of data, case studies, or customer feedback.
4. Encourage a dialogue. Instead of a monologue, turn the conversation into a two-way street. Ask for their thoughts and feedback.

SCENARIO 3: THE INTERESTED BUT HESITANT BUYER

Setting: You're at a trade show booth, and an attendee has been examining your product for a while.

Body Language Cues:
- Leaning in closer to the product or information board
- Touching or holding the product frequently
- Quick nods while reading or listening to product details
- Glancing towards the salesperson intermittently, perhaps hoping for interaction

Role Play Breakdown:
1. Recognize their interest. Approach with a friendly demeanor.
2. Open with a soft question: "What caught your eye about our product?"
3. Address potential hesitations. They might be waiting for a special deal, more information, or just a push to make the decision.
4. Offer something extra. It might be a discount, a trial period, or additional support to make them feel secure in their choice.

Some Implementable Action Steps:
1. Practice Observation: Dedicate time every day to observing body language in different settings. This will hone your skills and help you pick up on subtle cues.
2. Seek Feedback: After a sales meeting, ask a colleague for feedback on how well you responded to body language cues.
3. Stay Updated: Body language reading is an evolving field. Attend workshops, read books, or take courses to stay updated.

Remember, the key to using body language effectively in sales isn't just about recognizing signals but also responding to them in a way that builds trust and rapport. Once again, you've been doing this your entire life and the only difference here is how much more you can achieve in life and accelerate your careers by mastering this skill!

CHAPTER 14

SHUT UP AND SELL

What makes salespeople amazing? What makes them the elite? How do they close so many deals? Is it their fast, smooth talking? Somewhat, but the best sale professionals in the world master the art of listening. Whether face to face or over the phone, untrained salespeople just talk right past the close, they talk right past the moments the prospect wants to hear more, but because salespeople do what they love to do, run our mouths, we miss crucial moments where the prospect tells us how to sell them.

Selling is more about active listening. Not mastering the "pitch." Not the "features and benefits." Not the intellect of the person. It's always been about listening, but too many corporations don't teach reps how to listen; they just teach them how to sell, sort of.

The hardcore closing days are gone. People want to be informed. They want to be served. They want to be heard.

There are several things that go into active listening.

Let them speak. The most important rule in sales is: talk less, listen more. Salespeople in today's world get "creative" on how they enter a conversation with potential clients, when all you have to do is let them talk about themselves. You'll find out:

- What drives them
- What they're interested in most
- What concerns they have
- What their needs are

If you're speaking more than 30% of the time, it's too much. Most of the time you can't learn this information because you're too busy spewing stuff that may have zero impact on the prospect's decision to buy. Throwing it up against the wall and hoping it sticks is a weak sales process too many companies are accepting these days.

You want to reduce rescission? Listen more. Talk less.

How do you know what to talk about? How do you know how they feel about you or your company? Do you know if they even want to speak to you? Ask good questions, then listen to the responses. (We get more into good questions to ask later in the book.)

The problem is, corporate training usually tends to teach the features and benefits of a product, and how to handle objections, rather than diving into the psychological aspect of what really drives production: listening.

By the way, if you talk too much, it sends a message to the prospect that you can't answer questions they may have. Although that may not be true, Cornell's study on influencing the sale proved that out of 1,000 sales closed with 11 different products and services, the customers said–anonymously, I might add—that the product and offering were great, but feeling heard was the number 1 reason they decided to move forward.

Salespeople, with a click of a button, can be caught in a lie or proven wrong. Information is at the fingertips of every person they have the luxury of serving. All this means credibility is harder than ever. So how can they trust if you're telling them how great what you're offering is the entire presentation? They don't. Trust is earned, but it's earned more easily when the focus is truly on them. How do we do that? Listen more.

This is harder than I'm making it sound, though. Sounds easy, but so many of you can NOT WAIT to speak. You're drooling at the mouth to prove them wrong. It's like a contest to you of who's right and who knows more. You want to handle an objection rather than using it as a tool to close the deal. You want to elevate your team above the rest. Put out a contest to see who talks the least and has the most deals. Spiff them on staying quiet, not just closing deals.

When you listen carefully it gives you the ability to repeat back what's important to them, and this:

- Confirms you've heard them.

- Assures them you know what's important to them.

- Gives you a chance to ask questions that are about what means the most to them.

Listening saves you an incredible amount of time. Time is money. This isn't something new. Many studies prove that sales representatives waste ample time on prospects who've made it very clear they'd rather not move forward with you, but you keep fighting. The grit is cool and admirable and by no means am I telling you to just give up, BUT there's an end and you need to listen to know when that end is. The longer you spend with someone who clearly doesn't want what you're offering, the less likely you can pull referrals off of them by just keeping it real and respecting them. (We get into referrals later in the book. You don't want to miss a word in that chapter.)

I want you to really test yourself. Be honest. How much time do you speak during your sales process? I bet if you timed yourself, you'd be shocked by how much you speak compared to your prospect. Some of the top sales trainers in the world say your speaking/listening ratio needs to be 30/70 or 20/80, depending on what you're offering. If we average it, that's 25/75.

In 2022, Harvard Law wanted to see how much a seasoned sales professional spoke compared to the prospect when influencing them to buy. The study showed that a top salesperson spoke only 18% of the time!! The same study showed an average performer spoke 65% of the time and a new salesperson spoke almost 83% of the time! WOW!

The study also proved that the newer the salesperson, the sooner they spoke and the later they listened. By the time they start listening, it's too late. They've already lost time with the customer; they've lost the chance to prove that what matters to them matters to you. Just an all-around mess and one that is easily avoidable. Just hire someone (preferably us ☺) who can come in and get your team on track or hire someone who can start every training class with how important it is to listen, rather than to speak.

When you talk more than you listen, you are actually telling your client:

- Helping them solve their problem or fixing their issues doesn't matter to you.
- You just want their money.
- You're trying to rush through the sales process to go home or finish your day.
- You matter more than they do.

The truth is they're right. Once again, if you just flip the script and do it the right way:

- You would actually save more time by listening instead of rushing and forcing information on them.
- You're proving they matter.
- What matters to them matters to you.

- They tell other people how you treated them, due to your patience and listening.
- The objections won't feel so much like objections. They'll ask for your opinion rather than form it as an objection.
- Most of all, proves that serving them matters more than the money.

When you're listening, take notes, some mental, some written. It gives you a way to circle back, digging deeper into the underlying meaning.

There are many ways to get your prospect to talk more so you can listen better and talk less. Asking questions and using them to elicit a response will trigger them to have to respond. When they do, just let the information flow!

There are several ways to get them to talk more and you talk less.

1. THE TIMED QUESTION

For instance, if you're in the life insurance business and you say something like this:

"Family seems to be very important to you. I love that covering them means the world to you."

This confirms you've heard them, but you need more details of emotion to drive the sale. You want to know more in depth why they feel the way they do. Or maybe they didn't respond to your liking and you misunderstood them. You see a facial expression or something that doesn't seem to match how you thought they felt… Just end the statement with a question like this:

"I love that covering your family means the world to you. It seems like _____. Is that correct?"

Then just let them answer.

Here's another one. Let's say you're in the vacation industry and you meet a prospect and want to know more about how they like to travel. You can elicit a response to get them to talk more with a statement like:

"A lot of people don't travel because they either don't know how to make it affordable or they don't have time. It looks like you _____ say whatever pertains to them). Is that about right?"

The insert could be:

- "want to travel more, but need to find the time."
- "love spending time with family; we just need to show you how to get to the places you'd love to see."

There are several ways to get them to speak, but you get my drift. Ending statements with questions is an easy way to get you to stop talking and then just listen. Take good notes, and the information they'll give you will guide you to the best probable outcome to serve them.

This usually works best when it drives emotion. Like you're speaking about something that means something deeper to them. Time with family, something special for a loved one, doing something their parents could never do for them, financially setting up their kids' futures, buying their dream home, and so much more.

Just make a statement that drives emotion and end it with a question. Maybe one of these:

- *"It seems like you _____. Is that right?"*
- *"Great, so it sounds like you _____, just so I understand what matters most to you?"*
- *"So I can better understand, it looks like you or you've _____ , right?"*

You can also elicit a response to get them to speak more when you've hit a hot button. Something that you can tell has hit a nerve. They can agree or disagree, but you know you need more context. You can say something like:

"I can see you agree with me on that one. It seems like you've experienced something similar to this in the past. What kind of issues have you had?"

BOOM! Then shut up and let them tell you their pain points. Your job is to serve. You can't serve if all you're doing is talking. Let them speak. Even if they don't agree with something you've said, stop and say something like this:

"I just want to be sure I'm helping in the best way and it doesn't look like you agree with what I just said. So I can better understand, what's different about your process?"

Then let them speak.

Again, your job as a sales professional is to actually practice talking less to get more information by letting the prospect talk more. It is by far the most effective way to own the highest level of performance in a career in sales.

2. THE GUT PUNCH

This is another easy way to get them to speak. You should already have been listening by now and all you have to do is put into words what they've been feeling. You're proving, YOU GET IT! You know what they're going through and you're going to confirm it like this:

"I've found that most companies are so focused on sales quotas and hitting goals that they forget how important culture is. If they're happy, the opportunity is there and they know they have

the right leaders in place, which is the biggest pitfall for the masses, then they can drive results much easier."

Then just let them agree. They might say, "That's exactly right … " (let them keep going). They might say "We don't have that problem, we … " (let them keep going). Which brings me to the next way to force them to talk more.

3. THE AWKWARD STOP

You'd be surprised at how much more people have to say if you just wait. Just be patient. Just pause. There's so much gold in the add-on. So what do I mean by that?

If someone says: *"Yeah, I'm looking for a 3-bedroom 2-bath house with two stories."*

If you just wait, you'll hear: *"Oh, and a fireplace and a pool."*

The problem is, most salespeople take the limiting information and run with it. Yes, you can ask better questions to get more information, but what if you just waited? Just stopped dead in your tracks to where it was almost awkward?

I have a rule here. The first person who speaks, loses. Try practicing this. It's a great way to get great information that will help you help your prospect more. The information will just come right out with the right pause at the right time.

Finally, and my favorite way is …

4. THE CONFIRMATION QUESTION

This is an easy but VERY effective tool. People want to know that you've heard them and understand what matters to them. If you simply ask them a question confirming how they feel, you might be right and you might not be. Either way, you're going to get valuable information.

For instance:

"So what you're saying is that you've had a hard time retaining people because there's a gap in leadership training. It seems like if we provided the proper training, production levels would increase across the board and people would be happier. Am I missing anything?"

See, easy. And trust me, they'll tell you whether you're right or wrong and guess what, BOTH will get you the information you're looking for and let them SPEAK MORE and you speak less.

We'll get into asking the right questions later in the book, but these are some great ways to force yourself to give them the stage!

Listening is also tied directly to all the previous chapters, mainly the body language, reading people's tells, and more. When they speak, you can see what's exciting to them. If it's phone sales you can hear it. Make a note of this and make sure you're consciously repeating the important notes you took at those moments when it's your time to speak. Your credibility will skyrocket.

By the way, when you talk more than you listen, in many industries these days, it 100% means you've created some sort of tactic or pitch you're trying to get them to believe. Lying. If this is you, shame on you and the name you're giving to the sales world. Any award you've received for deceiving people isn't an award for great salesmanship, it's a constant reminder that you weren't capable of doing the right thing and helping someone, so you had to lie to fill your pockets. Don't worry, that exposure is more real than ever. We will Make Sales Great Again by sharing *The Ultimate Sales Bible* with as many people you know and rebuild something that used to have a good name.

THE REAL with all of this is that the Zigs of the world have all said this well before me. Nothing I'm saying here is all mine. I'm just hoping how I'm saying it hits the core moral values of those wanting to serve others.

The more people you serve, listen to, get what's important to them, the easier it'll be for you to reach your goals and guess what, YOU'LL FEEL GOOD DOING IT!

I'd like to give a way to equip you and your salespeople with the skills to effectively communicate by focusing on listening more than speaking in order to understand the prospect's needs, concerns, and desires, which will lead to a successful sale.

So I've added 3 different scenarios that you can role play to start mastering the art of listening.

SCENARIO 1: HEALTH INSURANCE

Scenario: A prospect walks into your office, looking for health insurance coverage for her family. She seems anxious.

Wrong Approach: Salesperson: "We have a fantastic premium plan that covers X, Y, and Z. It's one of our best and offers a wide range of benefits. We also have discounts available for new sign-ups."

Right Approach: Salesperson: "I'm here to help you find the best coverage for your family. Can you tell me a bit about your primary concerns or needs?" Prospect: "Yes, my husband was recently diagnosed with a condition and we want to make sure his treatments are covered. We also have two kids, one with asthma."

Breakdown: By allowing the prospect to share her concerns, the salesperson can tailor the options and present a plan that covers the husband's treatments and pediatric asthma care. This approach makes the prospect feel heard and understood.

SCENARIO 2: CAR SALES

Scenario: A couple walks into a car dealership, glancing around the showroom, showing interest in the SUVs.

Wrong Approach: Salesperson: "This latest SUV model is packed with top-of-the-line features! It's got a sunroof, leather seats, and a cutting-edge infotainment system."

Right Approach: Salesperson: "I see you're interested in our SUVs. Can I ask what's important to you in a new vehicle?" Couple: "We have a growing family and need something spacious. Safety is our top priority."

Breakdown: Instead of overwhelming the couple with features they might not need, by listening, the salesperson can focus on showing SUV models with the best safety ratings and adequate space.

SCENARIO 3: VACATION SALES

Scenario: A man calls into a travel agency wanting to book a vacation but seems undecided.

Wrong Approach: Salesperson: "Our tropical island getaway is on sale this month! It's an all-inclusive package with beachfront resorts and water activities."

Right Approach: Salesperson: "I'd love to help you find the perfect vacation. What kind of experiences or destinations are you thinking about?" Man: "I've been so stressed at work. I just need a quiet place to relax, maybe some nature."

Breakdown: By listening, the salesperson realizes that a bustling beach resort might not be ideal. Instead, they can suggest a quiet cabin in the mountains or a serene countryside retreat.

Below are some key takeaways from each of these scenarios. If I were you, I'd make sure you and your team start doing this daily and listing your own takeaways to make sure everyone can see, hear, and feel what others do when you're training this skill.

KEY TAKEAWAYS:

1. **Ask Open-ended Questions**: Instead of making assumptions, encourage the prospect to share their needs and desires by asking questions.

2. **Active Listening**: Truly pay attention to the prospect's responses. This shows respect and allows for a better understanding of their needs.

3. **Tailor Your Pitch**: Use the information gathered from listening to provide solutions that address the prospect's unique concerns or desires.

As this chapter lists out, by listening more than you speak, you empower the prospect to guide the conversation, making them feel valued and increasing the likelihood of a successful sale. If you don't spend time training this, you'll only hold you and your team back from the success you all deserve!

CHAPTER 15

SOLUTION-DRIVEN SALES

Do problems really drive sales? Are sales professionals really solution finders? Or are we just people looking to sell someone something and convince them they need it? Well, if you've read this far into the book or listened this long to the audio book, you know the answer to all three of those questions. Yes, Yes and NO!

If you're looking to be a sales professional, like truly looking to master the art of sales, then you MUST be willing to serve the prospect or client and focus on what matters to them. What problems are they facing? Asking the right questions to get to the heart of what they need to make the value of what you're offering almost priceless.

There are many ways to do this but the best way I've taught for years is a three-step process.

1. Ask good questions.

2. Find the real problem.

3. Offer a solution (if, and only if, you actually have the solution).

If you don't have the solution, remember, be honest and tell them that what you're offering isn't the right fit. Because guess what, it might be in the future and they'll remember how you treated them, plus it's always a great way to get referrals when you're that honest.

Let's start with number one: Ask Good Questions.

Some think it's hard to get to the root of what a customer's buying motives or pain points might be, but it's as simple as asking questions like this:

- What's been going on?
- How's everything been going for you?
- What's been great and what do you think needs help the most?
- How long has that been going on?
- How long have you had that problem?
- If you had to guess, how much time or money do you think it's costing you? (Be very, very real when you ask this. This isn't a push to sell. This is a genuinely caring question. You need to make sure they know you are there to help.)

There are a ton of additional questions that you can customize for your specific industry, but make it simple. Don't ask in-depth questions early on. Just keep it very simple, getting them to open up and just have a conversation with you. Let them know you're there to help, whether it's you helping them directly or you referring them to someone who can.

Most sales representatives miss this. They are so hungry for the sale, they start pitching before they know what matters most. They also start guessing what the customer's needs are, rather than actually knowing. This wastes a TON of time.

Asking good, simple, and real questions, proving that what matters to them most matters to you most, is crucial. Mastering this is essential to your growth as well, but when asking, be compassionate and authentic, and make sure they know that this is ALL about serving them. Once you get the information, it's time to move on to step number 2.

STEP #2: FIND THE REAL PROBLEM

You do know that there are two parties selling during a sales presentation, right? The salesperson AND the person you're trying to sell. You're trying to get them to buy whatever you're offering and they're trying to sell you on why they don't need it. So when you're finding the real problem, make sure it's the REAL PROBLEM and not some smokescreen to get you to think they don't need what you're offering.

A lot of sales trainers will tell you to ask leading questions, which I love, but once again lead them with authenticity. Don't lead them for the money. Lead them to serve. When your prospect feels that you want to serve them, they're more open to being real with you.

OK, so now we've asked good questions. We have some great information, but now we have to isolate what the biggest problems are. Many sales representatives spend way too much time solving small problems and missing the big ones. When in reality, when the big problems are solved, the smaller ones usually fall into the mix, getting fixed too. The time you have with your prospect is important. Get down to their biggest pain points.

For example, if a prospect says something like:

"The last time we did something similar to this, the value wasn't worth the money. The product didn't do what we thought it would."

Here's how you should reply:

"So just to be clear so I can serve you best, you're saying the last product you purchased you were unpleased with because the cost didn't live up to what you thought it would do, correct?"

Andddddddddddddddddddd PAUSE. Don't say a word. The first person to speak, loses. Once they answer, take notes, write their issues down. This proves that what they're saying really matters to you and that you're paying close attention to them. DO NOT miss that part. Far too many untrained sales representatives don't do this. The prospect is usually left wondering:

- How do they even remember everything I just said?
- Did they really hear me?
- Are they actually listening or do they just want the sale?

You can eliminate anything like that by taking notes, not mental ones, ACTUAL ones to prove what matters to them is a TOP PRIORITY to you.

Then when they are finished, ask them another question, such as:

"I understand and can see how that's an issue."

(Say that first, confirming you've not only written down what they've said, but you're confirming you feel them and agree how troubling that might be.)

Then follow up right after that statement with:

"Is there anything else that bothers you about (insert service or product) that you wish would be different or at least more efficient?"

When I tell you this is probably the biggest missed power follow-up question in the sales industry, it really is. Usually if they're trained and top sales professionals, they won't miss that follow up. DO NOT leave this follow up out. You have to understand the importance of this. If you just use the first question, you'll be missing so many more pain points that they will use to get out of the sale on the back end because you didn't ask.

Our job is to find the pain points, verify them, ask what the others are, and offer a solution so they can't say at the close:

"Well, I also have this problem and I'm really looking for something that can help with all of it."

That won't happen to a badass sales professional. They will ask and ask and ask until the prospect knows they've touched on everything that they need a solution for. Then, it's time to offer the solution in step 3.

STEP #3: OFFER A SOLUTION

Now remember, you just spent all that time taking notes, listening, verifying every problem or pain point you've extracted from your prospect, so don't waste this final step by offering a solution to the minimal problems. Offer the solution to THE BIG BAD BOY of problems that will most likely solve the little ones.

Before you offer the solution, verify one more time what the MAIN PROBLEMS are. Be 100000% sure they agree that you're about to offer a solution to the real mac daddy problems. Make them speak it. When they speak it, they own it.

When this is done, offer your solution, if and only if you have one. If what you're offering can add value to them and fix their problems, the sale should literally be mutually agreed upon and go down with ease.

If what you're offering won't solve their problem fully or at all, just be honest. I've closed millions in sales, when what I was offering wasn't a full solution, but fixed a few of the larger areas of concern so they moved forward with me anyway. But I was honest about it. If I lie, like the weakest thieves in the world do just to get a paycheck, it'll ruin a relationship forever and will eliminate any possibility of repeat business.

Weak people lie to earn. Strong, trained sales professionals earn with ease, as their prospects stay with them and give them referrals, because they know they'll always get the real from you.

So if it doesn't fully solve their problem but can help them in some cases, say something like this:

"I've heard you and understand your needs here, but what I'm offering won't solve all the issues. I'm not going to sit here and tell you it will. BUT what it will solve is ..."

And go into how you can help. Harvard University did another study on the honesty of a salesperson on the back end, when trying to close a deal. The study was done on over 4,300 sales presentations. It proved that when a salesperson was honest and identified where they could serve and WHERE THEY COULDN'T serve a prospect, the closing ratio was 47% higher than those who said they could help with all the prospect's issues, but truthfully couldn't.

How crazy is that!!!? Would you want to add a 47% increase to your closing percentage? When all you have to do is just tell the truth? Not worrying that your product won't solve all the problems, but it will solve some? How cool is that?

Consultative selling has been talked about for decades, yet hardly ANYONE trains their team how to do it properly. It's crazy to me that all these companies out there spend so much time teaching about the product or service they're offering, but never take the time to actually teach their reps actual serving sales skills.

Most salespeople who work for companies like this can't get past pitching the features and benefits. They spew the luxuries of what they're offering, but they don't even know if what they're offering helps or matters to their prospect.

There are CEOs, CROs (Chief Revenue Officers), or CSOs (Chief Sales Officers) that have plateaued in their sales growth wondering why. They think by adding more salespeople, it'll add more sales. There's so much underlying costs that go into that and the company ends up spending more money, time and resources working harder, rather than properly training, minimizing those cost, and sitting back and enjoying the luxury of a more profitable company based on exercising the proper practices in training up their current talent.

Most sales practices taught these days concentrate on "the hardcore closer" method. They seek the pushy, never let up, aggressive salespeople. This is an inefficient and outdated way to scale, with minimal and capped results. There's no real connection between the salesperson and the prospect. No relationship. No compassion. No real connection.

Contrary to that outdated method of training and sales, a consultative approach puts the needs of the prospect first. It teaches the salesperson to seek and determine the actual value that their product or service will add to their customer's world. They dial in to the larger problems and help solve them. And if we are being completely honest, the prospect unfortunately doesn't expect sales professionals to care that much these days, which is why I'm going to Make Sales Great Again!

Concentrate on what the most important needs of the customer are, then position what you're offering to fit into their business or lifestyle. When you do this, you're effectively putting what you're offering into their world, solving their problems. In other words, offering a solution to eliminate their problems.

Now I know this sounds easy, but it takes training from people who know what they're doing. When I consult for small- to nine-figure companies, I always always always tell them to let us train the trainers first. If you don't know how to teach people solution-based, consultative selling, you're going to find yourself back in the same problems and inefficiency in sales growth as you've always been.

When I'm on stage speaking at events, I am shocked at the amount of untrained people who still swear by sales being solely driven by motivation, great personalities, customer service, and drive. Although those are key elements to the success of some sales professionals and that all must have a little of each, it's definitely far from how to create an integrity-based, trained sales beast!

Learning the consultative sales approach is ever changing, but the foundation was the strongest many years ago, when you shook a hand

and your word was your bond. Trust was real and not questioned, for the most part. Then fast forward to today in the 2020's when trust is never expected and prospects are finding it harder and harder to find a real person who cares more about them than they do their money.

So how do you teach yourself or your team or your company and where do you start? First, evaluate your team and make sure that your leadership understand how to use this process and teach this process to others. Most companies have people training their sales teams that are less talented and less knowledgeable than the people they're training. This is VERY common in today's sales world.

Most of the time, when I go to a company to train leadership and sales, the leaders don't have a clue how to do this properly. Which means one of two things: 1. The company hasn't taken the time or allocated the funds they need to hire someone to train the leaders properly, or 2. They have trained them, but ego creates a world of "don't do it that way, do it my way," which trickles through your sales organization like a poison looking for its next victim.

So what's the solution, right? It's MSGA! Haha! But really, it's hiring someone from the outside to train properly or add additional new value to you or your team. Way too many companies think because they have an in-house training team that they've got it all figured out. Your sales team is hungry for something new, a different perspective, a different voice, a new way to add value to how they create a living for their families.

So the real question is: How long are you going to believe that you, your company, or your sales team has it all figured out? How much money are you going to lose by letting your pride or ego get in the way of exponential growth possibility?

There are many ways and good people out there to teach this process; you just need to realize the value and importance of it.

Stop pressuring your team to sell more sell more sell more, because you need that percentage increase in revenue. You're trying to force growth rather than teach them a way to best serve your prospects and have increased revenue bursts by providing the tools they need to excel, not stay stagnant. Don't miss this chapter. It will change your world. Learn this process. Teach this process and thank me later.

We don't find the problems in sales. We do offer solutions in sales and we do SERVE when we actually care about who you're offering your product or service to.

If you'd like to keep training on solution-based sales—as you SHOULD!—I've created 3 different scenarios below for you and your team to train from. ENJOY!

SCENARIO 1: DOOR-TO-DOOR SOLAR SALES

1. Ask Good Questions:
- "Have you ever considered the benefits of solar energy for your home?"
- "How much do you currently spend on your electricity bills each month?"
- "Are you aware of the tax benefits and incentives available for solar panel installations?"

2. Find the Real Problem:
- Potential problem: High electricity bills.
- Uncovering the issue: "It sounds like your electricity bills can get quite high during summer months. Have you noticed any particular patterns or concerns with your current energy consumption?"

3. Offer a Solution:
- "With solar panels, you could potentially save up to XX% on your electricity bills. Plus, the government offers tax rebates for homeowners who install solar panels, which can further offset the costs. We also provide a flexible payment plan."

SCENARIO 2: CALL CENTER SALES

1. Ask Good Questions:
- "How did you first hear about our product/service?"
- "What challenges are you currently facing that led you to consider our solution?"
- "Have you used similar products or services in the past?"

2. Find the Real Problem:
- Potential problem: Dissatisfaction with a competitor's product.
- Uncovering the issue: "You mentioned that the previous service you tried was inconsistent. Can you share more about what aspects were inconsistent or problematic for you?"

3. Offer a Solution:
- "I understand your concerns. Our product has a proven track record of reliability and high customer satisfaction ratings. Additionally, we offer 24/7 customer support to address any issues you might face."

SCENARIO 3: REAL ESTATE SALES

1. Ask Good Questions:
- "What are the most important features you're looking for in a new home?"
- "Is there a particular neighborhood or school district you're interested in?"
- "How soon are you hoping to move?"

2. Find the Real Problem:
- Potential problem: Need more space due to a growing family.
- Uncovering the issue: "You mentioned wanting an extra bedroom and proximity to schools. Is this because you're planning

for a growing family and need to be near quality educational facilities?"

3. Offer a Solution:
- "I have a few listings in mind that fit your criteria perfectly. They're in top-rated school districts and offer the space you need. I can schedule viewings for you this week."

Now that you have some different scenarios and training methods, I'd create your own. Whether you're a sales team or an individual, understanding and mastering solution-based sales will give you an edge over the rest!

CHAPTER 16

ELEVATING EQUITY: THE PATHWAY TO BUILDING VALUE

Value. Is there? Or isn't there? It's easy to sell when there's value, but can you sell when there isn't value for every prospect? The answer is yes and in this chapter I'm going to teach you what most salespeople miss.

You're in sales and the main objective for most is to close the deal, but it doesn't have to be. Creating value should be the goal always. Does it have to be in what you're offering? Or can you add value even if what you're offering doesn't meet the needs of your prospect? That answer is also yes and is one of the biggest misconceptions in sales today. I've made more money off of "NOT" selling someone, than I have off of selling someone.

You're probably thinking, "What is he talking about?" LOL … I get it, so allow me to explain. In this chapter I'm going to teach you how to create value in what you're offering and create value in what you don't have to offer. Be prepared though, because if you're one of those weak liars who steals from people, you might as well not read this chapter. To do this, you have to be fully integrity based. You have to be honest and it's entirely about serving at its full capacity.

When you're using a value-based approach in selling, you ALWAYS put the needs of your prospect first. The entire presentation should be tailored to them. What matters to them, their company, their team, the most. When you do this and create value, the transition to the close is easy, but what about when what you're offering doesn't add value to your prospect. What do you do then? You.................................. TELL THEM IT DOESN'T! Yes, I just yelled that.

I'm beyond upset, actually appalled, at the lack of salesmanship these days, in that so many companies are letting their sales teams lie just to hit goals or budget. Equally for the salespeople who are doing it and stealing from good people. The truth is, most companies know it's happening, but know if they stop it, it'll result in less income to them.

The solution is easier than ever, though. When what you're selling doesn't add value, help them find someone or the right product or service that will help them. Most untrained salespeople are fine saying:

"I'm sorry we couldn't help you."

And just ending the presentation and moving on to the next opportunity. It's just wrong and what you don't realize is that you're costing yourself so much money.

When what you're offering doesn't serve your prospect, help them find something that will. You've spent time with them. They've spent time with you. Time is money, so if possible, let's help one another. When you can help someone, moving past just trying to get that sale right then and there, it can result in a massive number of referrals and future business when what you're offering might suit them.

Try saying something like this when you can't add value to your client during your presentation:

"First off, I'm so sorry that I couldn't help you today, but I'd like to connect you with someone who can. Our time to do business may not be now, but I'd like to stay in touch just in case it will in the future. I'd also like to be a resource for you, even if that means connecting you with someone who's better suited to serve you. Do you mind if I get you with someone I know can help you?"

BAM! Try that one time, I dare you! Like I've said multiple times, honesty sells. Sales is about relationships, not just for now, but potentially long term! But I'm not done yet. Pause, wait for their answer, because they'll definitely agree to let you find someone to help them, but say this after they agree:

"Awesome. So just to be clear, what do you think our product/service doesn't have that's most important to you so I can guide you properly to who can help?"

I'm smirking writing this because you HAVE TO KNOW where I'm going here. Most salespeople just give up when the prospect says no. WHAT IF… you ask that second question and throughout the presentation they missed something you said and didn't realize that what you offered ACTUALLY has what they want?

This happens all the time in presentations. They might start listing off value they need that you might've forgotten to show them or they just didn't understand fully too, right? It happens ALL THE TIME!

Finally, if you've exhausted all available value opportunities and you truly can't serve them, do what you said you were going to do. Find them someone who can. Even if it's hours, days, or weeks later. HELP THEM. SERVE THEM. When you do this and follow through with your promise, they're not stupid. They know you're not making anything and you're just a great sales professional serving, and they'll never forget it. Some people ended up finding ways to use what I was offering when I helped them and bought what I was offering just because I actually did what I said I was going to do and put them first.

This is another really good way to get referrals. When you're honest, just ask them if they know anyone else whom you can serve or add value to through your product. You'll be surprised at how just being honest, not selling them, will result in so much business that most salespeople never get the chance to earn. Learn this, practice it, and watch how well NOT selling someone allows you to scale.

Now let's get into the proper process to build value.

If you're selling something where you have a chance to do research on your prospect before you meet with them, do your research on them or their company. When they meet you and you know about them and their company, it shows how vested you are in being an additional component to their world. People love to talk about themselves and they equally love it when other people know about what they do. Especially when you might have to meet them a few times to actually close the deal.

You also never want to jump straight into a pitch. I see this mistake all too often and it's usually the result of training that's dependent on product knowledge, rather than on how to serve someone. Jumping straight into a sales pitch turns almost everyone off. Be personable, get to them more.

Value comes from teaching them how your product or service works, while tying it into their needs. Constantly adding value at every power point your service or product offers. Use third-party stories, which we'll talk about later, on how other customers have benefited by what you've served them with. This is a real easy way to let them tell you if it will also add value to them.

Just remember, they're usually with you for a reason. If they didn't have a problem that needs a solution, they wouldn't be meeting with you. Now there are circumstances where people are bribed to be with you, like timeshare, where a prospect is usually gifted to sit with you. But for the most part, prospects are with you for a reason. It's our job to provide value and teach them why what you have to offer would make sense for them to have.

Value to me is defined as: "offering something that a prospect can't obtain on their own."

Here are 5 guaranteed ways to set yourself ahead of the pack.

1. KNOW WHAT YOU'RE SELLING.

How many times have you been in a situation where someone seemed as if they were making up answers or they just didn't seem knowledgeable about what they were offering? Unfortunately a lot in the sales world today. You need to be the expert and if you're not, it's OK, just eventually it's better to be than not.

People want to work with a bad ass. They want to know that who they're working with will always have the solution or guide them to who will.

Speak with ABSOLUTE conviction. Don't stumble on your words. When you're sure of your knowledge, you don't fumble. You're always ready to run right into the endzone. That confidence builds massive value.

Salespeople do NOT work hard enough or spend enough time mastering what they sell.

2. KNOW YOUR COMPETITION.

Knowing what you sell isn't enough. How do you stack up against the competition? Do you know what your competitors are offering? Do you know the differences between what they lack and you don't, or what you lack and they don't?

How about your cost verses theirs and why that difference is? Are you prepared to authentically answer questions that challenge your cost?

Knowing your competition is an invaluable piece of your sales master puzzle.

3. KNOW WHAT YOUR CUSTOMERS CARE ABOUT.

I'm not the only sales and leadership trainer in the world who helps companies scale. I'm constantly listening to podcasts, reading reviews, watching customer testimonials, as well as customer complaints within my company and others to see what the customers care about most.

Rarely do I have a client where I'm not sure about the problems they face. I have solutions, proven credibility and offer a value that's integrity based, which makes most gravitate towards working with me. But what if I wasn't as educated on what matters most to them? I could still earn their business, sure, but not nearly as easily as if they knew they were working with a professional who understands what helps them thrive.

Do you know how they feel? Have you felt that pain or worked with others who have felt their pain? When you know what it feels like to not have the solution to their problems and the pain that comes with that… it gives you a relatability most other salespeople don't have.

4. ASK OPEN-ENDED QUESTIONS.

You need to learn to ask questions that elicit a response that gives you the information that gives you the best possible outcome to add value to your prospect.

Sales representatives these days dive right into the pitch and start telling prospects how what they offer can add value to them, rather than asking them what matters to them most.

This process saves you so much time. Asking good questions is quite possibility the top sales trait you can have, when you know how to verify that their answers are real.

5. QUALITY OF WHO YOU WORK WITH.

A lot of companies are on this "sell anyone and everything" phase. Although revenue and sales are great, cancellations suck.

Your prospects should know you working with them is an honor, but then working with you is equally important. The privilege should be two-sided.

When you're honest with a prospect when the product isn't a good fit for them or you truly believe it's not the right time for them to buy from you, people sometimes believe this is a take-away (a sales tool to make them think you don't want their business, when you really do) when the reality is, you're just being honest.

You need to make it very clear that you are selective about who you work with as well and that you don't mean any disrespect, but that who you serve matters and you want your product or service to be in the best hands at all times.

This actually makes the people you do work with feel amazing. It makes them feel important and it should. I have turned down working with a lot of people that would've given my family and me a large pay day, just because I didn't think they were a good fit for me or what I was offering.

Working with people who will always serve you and get you business as you will always serve them and provide value in their lives allows you to make a great living working smarter, rather than playing the numbers game.

There's value in quality business and quality people. Never forget that.

There's no one perfect way to create value because everyone's different, and what's valuable to one might not be to another. There's different motivation to do business with you. Our job is to find out what those motivations are. What's most important to your prospect? The easiest way to do that is to "LISTEN." Ask good questions and then shut up. Let them speak. They'll tell you all you need to know if you let them.

Another mistake salespeople make is selling the prospect on the best part of what they're offering first. Explain what your product does or your service offers, but don't just give away the gold from jump. It literally minimizes anything else after. Have some build up. Some sales foreplay, if you will. Slowly and intentionally get to the good stuff that will blow them away.

Another great way to add value is adding a little extra value that you surprise them with. This isn't the old "but WAIT, there's more" method. It's like adding a topping to the cake when you've confirmed interest. Knowing they're interested and "under promising and over delivering" is a sure way to please your prospect.

Finally, the BEST AND SURE WAY TO ADD VALUE is being 100% truthful and always proving that you will be. They need to know they can trust you when it makes you money and when it might not. You are the authority in their world when you're the one they're working with. Trust is earned. Be available. Answer the phone. Answer the text. Do what you say you will always.

There are so many great ways to build value, but mastering this chapter will give you the life you've always wanted in sales. Lucrative, knowledgeable, honest, and serving.

That's value that is currently not readily available in today's sales world. Be different. Most importantly, as in the majority of my chapters, KEEP TRAINING! Below I've added a few different scenarios on how to build value. Practice them each until you and/or your team feels confident in how to present value in the right and most powerful way.

Building value is essential for any sales process. The key lies in understanding the unique pain points, needs, and desires of your customer, then positioning your product or service as the ideal solution. Let's delve into three different industries to understand how to build value effectively.

SCENARIO 1: ROOFING SALES

Scenario: A homeowner, Mr. Anderson, complains about frequent leaks and drafts in his home. He's unsure if he needs a new roof or just a few repairs.

Steps to Build Value:

1. Identify Pain Points: Engage in a conversation to understand the challenges. "Mr. Anderson, how often have you noticed these leaks?"

2. Educate: Share knowledge about the lifespan of roofs and how wear and tear can affect energy costs and property value.

3. Offer a Free Inspection: By physically assessing the situation, you provide immediate value and gain trust.

4. Present the Solution: If a new roof is needed, explain the benefits - energy savings, increased property value, peace of mind, warranty, etc.

5. Share Testimonials: Offer references or before-and-after photos from previous projects.

SCENARIO 2: LIFE INSURANCE SALES

Scenario: A young couple, Jay and Carrie, recently had a baby and are considering life insurance, but they see it as an unnecessary expense.

Steps to Build Value

1. Understand Their Priorities: Ask questions about their long-term goals and their child's future.

2. Highlight the Importance: "Imagine if one of you were to suddenly pass away. How would that financial strain impact the surviving partner and your child's future?"

3. Customize Solutions: Propose a policy that fits within their budget but covers essential needs.

4. Position as an Investment: Talk about the cash value accumulation in some life insurance policies, which can serve as a savings mechanism.

5. Address Concerns: Clarify misconceptions and provide statistics on the likelihood of young parents needing life insurance.

SCENARIO 3: GYM EQUIPMENT SALES

Scenario: Stacey, a 40-year-old woman, is looking to set up a home gym. She's overwhelmed by the options and isn't sure what equipment to invest in.

Steps to Build Value:

1. Understand Her Goals: "Stacey, what's driving you to set up a home gym? Is it weight loss, strength training, flexibility, or something else?"

2. Recommend Based on Goals: If she's into weight loss, maybe a treadmill or elliptical is ideal. For strength training, weight sets or resistance machines might be more suitable.

3. Offer a Package Deal: Bundling items can make the purchase more appealing. "We have a 'weight loss package' that includes an elliptical, resistance bands, and a few free training sessions to get you started."

4. Discuss Long-term Savings: Compare the one-time investment in gym equipment with monthly gym memberships over the years.

5. Offer Post-Purchase Support: Provide resources on workouts, maintenance tips, and perhaps a helpline she can call if she has questions.

CONCLUSION:

While each industry has its intricacies, the principles of building value remain consistent:

1. Understand the customer's needs.
2. Educate and provide solutions tailored to those needs.
3. Present the benefits, addressing both immediate and long-term value.
4. Position your product or service as an indispensable tool for achieving their goals.

With these principles in mind, salespeople can confidently navigate any industry and consistently deliver value to their clients. Never forget to ALWAYS BE HONEST and that you can equally build value by selling from the negatives as well.

What your product or service "won't" do is equally, if not MORE, important than what it "will" do. Keep training and create real-world scenarios for you and your team to work on together!

CHAPTER 17

HOW KAFFEE GOT JESSUP: HOW TO ASK THE BEST QUESTIONS!

Lemme guess. "Todd, what's that title even mean?"
In the movie *A Few Good Men*, Lieutenant Daniel Kaffee, a young and inexperienced lawyer in the United States Navy, defends two Marines accused of the murder of a fellow Marine. Throughout the trial, Colonel Nathan Jessup, who's a tough guy played by Jack Nicholson, who is known for not giving up information and being strategic on how he answers questions, gives Kaffee nothing to work with.

Kaffee is trying to figure out how to get what he needs, so he spends hours the night prior to prepare for his final direct examination of the Colonel, creating questions that will force the Colonel to give him the information he needs to win the case. The following day during the trial, he goes in hard on the Colonel with basic general questioning, but he fails and as Colonel Jessup starts walking off the stand, believing he's stumped Lieutenant Kaffee, he's stopped by Kaffee and told to get back on the stand because he's not done with his examination. This was planned by Kaffee beforehand to get what he needed out of Jessup.

When Jessup gets back on the stand, Kaffee uses the responses from the general questions to ask more intentional questions that get the Colonel flustered. The questions were so specific, using what the Colonel previously stated as ammo to uncover the real truth.

At the end of that scene, Tom Cruise (Lt. Kaffee) screams, "I want the truth!" and then Jack Nicholson screams back, "You can't handle the truth!" So frustrated with emotion, he pours out the answers Kaffee was looking for. The Colonel admitted he ordered a "Code Red," which was the death of the Marine whom the other two Marines were accused of killing, and the Colonel was arrested immediately and the two Marines were set free! The point is this: good questions get you vague answers; exceptional questions get you the answers you need to close the deal.

Great questions build paths to great deals that save time. Whether you want to admit this or not, many of you lose sales by not mastering the art of asking the right questions. When I say many, I mean MOST! You won't admit it, but a huge problem with salespeople, that's been going on for years, is that you don't know how to be quiet long enough after you've asked a question to let your prospect guide you to the close. A good rule of thumb to live by is talk about 30% of the time, which should include asking intentional questions, and listen about 70% of the time to get the knowledge you need to ask questions that will lead to the sale.

I'm going to make up a statistic here, BUT I bet I'm close. I bet that 99.99% of all prospects absolutely hate when all you do is run your mouth's during a sales presentation of ANY KIND. It's like a college lecture where you're falling asleep. You're constantly talking about all the features and benefits of your product/service and the worst part is, you don't even know if what you're talking about even matters to your prospect! You do it in the hope that if you just keep talking about all the good stuff you're offering, eventually you MIGHT come across something they like. I wish I could hit a red buzzer right now and it'd make that screeching annoying noise letting you know how wrong you are if this is you. It's OK if it is because we're going to fix that during this chapter. This style, or horrendous way of presenting, is costing you so much money it's not even funny.

In this chapter, I'm going to teach you how to ask the right questions and let your prospect TELL YOU what's important to them and ultimately, they'll tell you how to sell them. This chapter is a simplistic lesson in the art of saving time, which makes you money and helps you make more sales, and your prospects will love you for it! When this is done right, the prospect sells themselves.

There are different questions you can ask. Let's dive into them and really add skills that will help you reach higher efficiencies for years to come.

So what types of questions are there in a sales process:

1. OPEN-ENDED QUESTIONS

Wikipedia's definition is: An open-ended question is a question that cannot be answered with a "yes" or "no" response, or with a static response. Open-ended questions are phrased as a statement which requires a longer response. The response can be compared to information that is already known to the questioner.

Every internet sales forum defines open-ended questions as: Questions that allow someone to give a free-form answer other than Yes or No.

In a sales presentation, asking open-ended questions is crucial to finding out what matters most to your prospect. Getting deeper into what matters to them. This allows you to save a ton of time. When executed properly, you won't waste valuable moments with your prospect on things that don't interest them.

Tons of untrained sales representatives haven't really been trained properly on this, so they start going over every single feature and benefit of what they're offering, HOPING something will sound great and the prospect will respond.

Remember, you want to be speaking less and listening more.

Let's get into Open-Ended Questions:

Is the prospect a right fit for the product or service you're offering?

Some of you might say yes without even diving into the prospect's needs, which is a huge mistake and a waste of your time and theirs. The only way to find that out is by asking open-ended questions that will give you those details that matter most to them. Also remember that it's OK if what you're offering doesn't suit the prospect's needs. The number of referrals you can get by just TELLING THE TRUTH about how what you're offering won't add value to them, is insane. Just be HONEST!

Knowing the IMPORTANT POINTS or HOT BUTTONS that matter most to your prospect helps you become laser focused on time and tailoring your presentation to their needs.

In sales, way too often, undertrained sales individuals waste their time on the wrong prospects and waste their prospect's time as well. It's better to find out, by asking great questions, if what you're offering is truly the right fit for them. The number of referrals you can get from people by not trying to force close them, embellishing, or twisting the way your product or service works is insane.

People want honesty. They want the truth. They want you to tell them, "This just isn't for you," but hardly anyone does that these days. The undertrained and greedy sales folks out there, who are selling to survive rather than selling to serve, are ruining the name of this industry by taking advantage of those who allow it.

One of the biggest and most profitable moves I've ever made in this business is saying this, "I promised complete honesty and I just don't think this is for you."

CAN YOU IMAGINE? I told the truth! The looks on the prospects' faces are always the best when you do this. They are in complete SHOCK that you aren't going to try and figure out a way to close them. You're actually doing the RIGHT THING and guess what...? You instantly earn their respect and trust when you do. Do you think it's easier to get referrals when you do this? Without a doubt! They're usually so surprised that they'll do just about anything to get you connected with people who can add value to their world with what you're offering.

Asking great open-ended questions, finding out what's important to them, their "hot buttons," allows you to fine-tune your pitch.

Have you ever been in a sales presentation and said this, "Well, why didn't you lead with that? We could've saved a lot of time!" LOL. Identifying what's important to your prospect is extremely important. Time is money, right? Yep. For them and you.

Taking the time to ask the right questions to find out what matters most will move you closer to the close more efficiently. No one wants to sit there and listen to features and benefits that aren't features and benefits to them. We all want what matters to us, not what doesn't.

When you're spending time mastering the art of asking the right questions, be sure to hone in on their needs. Remember, this isn't about you. Spewing everything and hoping you'll say something that triggers their interest is a straight path to efficiency.

Let the prospects talk when you ask questions. Don't cut them off. Hold your questions until they're done speaking because eventually they'll not only tell you how to sell them, but people love to talk about themselves. This gives them a great reason to do so. Let it all come out. The good. The bad and the ugly.

Have you ever been serving a prospect and the husband or wife says something they know might open the door for a salesperson and they kick each other under the table or stumble over the next few words trying to cover up the "salesperson's opportunity to dive in"? LOL. This happens all the time when you let them speak. Untrained sales individuals cut people off, asking additional questions right in the middle of their prospect's answers. DON'T DO THAT! Just let them keep going.

They'll get more comfortable as you let them speak. The sales resistance will go down and they'll most likely let information slip they never wanted to tell you in the first place. Huge win for a trained sales professional.

Let's get into some good questions. They're not all a perfect fit, but there are some extremely great examples of a very good place to start learning. I always encourage anyone I train to ask questions as if YOU are asking them, NOT sounding scripted. You have to make sure they feel the empathy and that it's real, but most importantly, that it's authentically you and not some "sales tactic" that you learned to ask. Remember, when you're done asking your questions, let them speak. They'll move into "it's all about me" mode and start talking. Let them, because it truly is all about them.

Buying-history questions are always a great way to learn about what's good and bad about how your prospect's been doing business. Sometimes you'll find similarities in what you're offering. Sometimes you'll learn the mistakes they've made in the past and use that information, providing a solution through your product or service.

Long story short. The more you know about their business, the better. Listening to them gives you a real good idea of how their mind works, what their routines are, what their dislikes and likes are about their previous buying experiences. Their opinion of salespeople will come flowing out of them, along with the value they're looking for.

BUYING-HISTORY QUESTIONS:

What have you purchased or have you done business with us before?

This is one of the most underrated questions people forget to ask or are scared to ask. Gathering this information is HUGE in understanding how they felt about whether your company helped them or not.

Most people are afraid to talk about the bad. Some actually enjoy it and think it'll push a salesperson to get through the presentation faster. But PROFESSIONAL sales individuals use the information to solve a previous problem the client had when doing business with your company and instantly prove how they can help.

That may mean getting the sale. That may mean NOT getting the sale and just adding value to them, so in the future, you're the go-to person when they have problems to solve.

Too many untrained sales individuals don't do this properly and at the end of their presentation, the client says, "It all sounded great, but we've had a bad experience with your company in the past." OOF! It's like a dagger to the heart of any salesperson who has spent a ton of time trying to get the deal.

The only way to really get better at this is to just do it. Ask this question, learn the most common responses. Listen fully and show the prospect that their experiences matter to you. Good or bad. It'll add so much respect and integrity for you and it's a fantastic way to build a solid foundation with your prospect.

What do you know about our company?

This is another question salespeople are afraid to ask. They don't want to hear all the bad stuff or start off negative with a client. When the truth is, you need to know this information so they can't use this as a way out on the back end.

Ask the hard questions. Get the hard answers. Supply the proper solutions. When you solve a previous issue, explain how things have changed or simply why they're going to be different working with you. When done properly, you gain a really great starting advantage that most salespeople don't get, because they don't do this!

Listening to what they've heard. Explaining the bad they've found online. Truly caring about stuff that has shifted them in one direction or another, is a testament to your ability to not just listen, but understand why they feel the way they do.

People need to know they matter. They need to know what they think matters. They need to know, whether right or wrong, that you're willing to explain to them why the information is out there that they've seen, felt, or found.

Another extremely good way to start your discovery process. Master this, master being comfortable hearing the bad and you'll be leaps and bounds ahead of most people in this industry.

Have you ever bought something similar to what this (insert product or service) offers?

Find out what they know. Find out what they "think" they know. Just because they've bought similar products doesn't mean those products are the same as what you're offering.

Other companies will diminish the value of their competitors when asking this question. DON'T DO THAT! Worst mistake ever. Bashing your competition NEVER EVER helps you close a deal. Let me repeat. TALKING BAD ABOUT YOUR COMPETITION NEVER HELPS YOU CLOSE A DEAL! Ever.

You have to understand that, like you, there are several other organizations and people trying to earn this prospect's business. So why you? Do you think they'd rather work with someone who bashes the competition, or someone who listens to understand what's important to them and explains how they can get better service or a better product with you?

People want to be served, not sold. Educating is key these days. You're going to help MAKE SALES GREAT AGAIN if you start mastering the art of caring. It's that simple. If they've bought something similar and they're in front of you, it's for a reason. They're seeking something different. Could be to save money. Could be that they're looking for different benefits or value adds. It could be simply just a good person to serve them, rather than the normal salesperson who never follows up with their client once they've been paid.

Asking this question and responding with empathy and understanding will gain you massive kudos. And guess what? The prospect doesn't expect people to care these days. They think everyone is in it to get paid and, although you do make money selling, when you prove you're there to serve, it'll be a swift injection of real that today's sales world is missing immensely. Be different.

Asking what experiences they've had—good or bad—with a similar product or service in the past can help you fine tune your presentation to what matters to them most. It saves you time. It saves the prospect time and it shows you've been listening to what matters to them most. Now just offer a solution and boooooom... the transition to the close becomes seamless, because you are serving, not selling.

If the answer is no, they haven't bought anything similar to what you're offering, you should ask this:

So if you don't mind me asking, because I'm truly grateful you're allowing me time with you, but why us?

They're in front of you for a reason. It could be creative marketing. They could have seen or heard of business you or your companies have done before adding value to others. There are tons of ways a prospect gets in front of you, but knowing WHY they are there is extremely important to understanding their buying motives.

People gravitate towards things they see might solve problems for them or create opportunities for them. Which one are you? Or are you both? How do you know unless you ask, "Why us?"

Listening, letting them completely finish telling why, can offer a road map that's created specifically for your prospect. No more wasting time on what you think matters to them, but now you get to prove why they chose your company.

Remember, they don't know you yet. If you spend enough time serving them, they'll get the solutions your company offers and a prospect service from you that's unmatched. This is a guaranteed combo for infinite success.

Have you tried anything like this before to solve the problems you're currently facing or just simply to become more efficient? And if so, what problems are you still facing? Or if you're still looking, what are you looking for our product or service to do that the current one may be lacking?

Yes. This is a lot, I know. But these questions will give you all you need to slay the sales game. So stop reading, pause a moment, get with your team or someone you can role play with, and become an expert in asking and responding to these questions.

The sales elite don't mind going up against their competitors, but they've mastered how to ask this sequence of questions, to limit risk in presenting the wrong or same thing they might already be doing.

Remember, the prospect is there for a reason. They definitely see or are curious to see if what you're offering can increase efficiency in their lives or add value to their business that they currently don't have.

Asking "Have you tried anything like this before?" gets to what they like about similar products or services and, equally as important, what they DO NOT like about similar products or services. Again, you're gathering intel to fine tune your presentation to what matters to them most. Most salespeople don't do this or ask this question, so they ramble on, hoping they might spew a value-add that interests them. WHY WAIT? Why not just find out right away? If you ask, they'll just tell you.

If they've tried something similar to what you're offering, then what's it lacking? Let's be real. If what they're using did everything and they got it for the cost they wanted, they wouldn't be with you now, would they?

Don't let the prospect fool you. Again, they were either marketed to come to you or saw something of interest that brought them to you. Either way, it's an opportunity. You just have to find out what's important to them. Mastering this process of questions will allow you to do just that.

Use these examples as a template, but if you really want to step up your ability to serve others, while maximizing your growth on all levels, tailor similar buying history questions to be more industry specific to you. Role play like crazy and get to what will give you the best guideline and road map that matters most to your client. This will save you a ton of time throughout your presentation and you won't waste any time on things that don't matter to them.

DISCOVERING PURCHASE-SPECIFIC QUESTIONS

Although similar to the buying-history questions, these are more purchase specific to help relate to a prospect's needs or wants. If you can constantly drop seeds to value-adds your product or service offers that is client specific, you'll never have a wasted moment in a sales presentation. You're designing your pitch around them. THAT, my friends, isn't done enough and I personally believe this is diminishing the value of a servant-based sales process that we need to get back to.

When you can ask client-specific questions and tailor your presentation to them, there's nothing that needs convincing. The prospect closes themselves because you've offered solutions to their problems. Cost, when the value-add is there, becomes a minimalistic issue.

Let's start with some of the most important client-specific questions:

So what brought you here today?
Don't waste time. Let's get to the point. Let's clarify why they're with you when they didn't have to be. They're there for a reason. Don't get it twisted. Don't let them tell you otherwise. They don't have to be there. So why not find out why?

Did someone force them to be there? It could be. Maybe someone suggested you or your company. Maybe it was a gift they received to be there. Something they saw the value in receiving for taking the time to listen to you. Maybe they are just curious about what you're offering. There are so many reasons someone chose you and gave up their valuable time to be with you, so let's find out why.

No time wasted. No sugar coating. Let's acknowledge why they're there so you can custom your pitch to what they see as value.

Speaking about what matters to them and asking this question gives you that opportunity. No more wasted words. No more pitching something that doesn't mean anything to them. Getting down to the real gives both of you the chance to provide and receive information to see if there's synergy to do business together.

What are you looking for most? What qualities matter most to you in (insert product or service)? I know we just met, but I won't waste your time or mine. Because if what I'm offering adds value, great. Then I want to be the one to serve you. BUT if it doesn't, I'm also going to be the person to tell you it won't.

Let's be very clear on one thing if you're reading this book. I DON'T AND WILL NEVER teach anyone how to MANIPULATE someone to do business with you. Providing a service or product by educating your prospect is how every salesperson should be serving. Selling has slipped through the cracks, because social media wants the world to think it's cool being the "hard-core closers." Why does it have to be hard core? Do you have to force someone? Convince them? Or does it mean just never giving up? That I can deal with. But if you're trying to be the person who pushes people into deals, you're not a closer, you're a manipulator.

Serving a client can only be done when you know what they're looking for. Why you? Why your company? What about your product or service brought them to be with you?

Gathering this information is huge. This knowledge, once again, saves time. Shows the prospect that the only thing that matters to you during your time together is what matters to them.

If they're unsure, move on to this next question.

Everyone wants a perfect product or service and, although there are plenty of great fits, rarely is the "perfect" found. **Knowing that, what are the top three things that matter most to you?**

Man, this is the gold. This is the fire. This is a question that may seem repetitive, but it is for a reason. The more we can get a prospect or client to be honest and real about what's most important to them, the quicker we can determine if we have what they're looking for.

Remember, it's OK if you don't. It's OK if your product isn't the right fit. Please do the right thing and tell them it's not. In the referral section of this book, I'll explain why doing this early is so important. Being honest with a prospect from jump is the way to net a 10x return with someone, rather than doing what most untrained salespeople do and forcing the close. Treat them as you'd like to be treated.

If their top 3 is doable, great. If only one is, great. If a couple are, great. If none are possible, also great. You can net a ton of business either way, but the only way you figure this out is by ASKING!

Everyone wants to get the most value for their dollar. I promise I get that because I do too. **But what type of budget do you have for this so we can guide you properly?**

This is another question that a lot of salespeople avoid. They'll get responses like: "You tell me what it costs and I'll tell you if I can afford it" or "I'm not really sure"… They don't know how to use this to their advantage. If you're getting push back, you can respond accordingly. Such as saying, "Not a big deal at all. I just want to stay within your budget and add the most value," and then moving on.

Often, the prospect will just tell you what their budget is. This gives you a good guideline, but it DOES NOT mean you have to stick to what they're spending. Remember, you have cost they're spending. It doesn't mean they won't spend more if the ROI (return on investment) is there. Always offer more in a 3-choice offer. As the great Victor Antonio says, "In life, don't ask for what you want. Ask for more than what you want, so you GET what you want." Being strong enough and talented enough to ask this question can be a huge tool in the overall decision-making process.

Who else is involved in the purchasing decision?

Ding. Ding. Ding. Ding. We've hit the jackpot! This question, again, is a seriously underrated question that untrained sales professionals don't ask. How often have you been pitching, you think it's going so well, and then at the end of the presentation your client looks at you, smirks and says, "I love it, but I can't do anything without my wife's (boss's, partner's, sister's, cousin's, dad's, you get the point) approval."

Wouldn't it be nice to know this from the beginning? You could even ask it like this, "If everything is a great fit for you today, are you able to make this decision on your own to move forward today?" Leave it at that. Wait for the response and when they say "yes" you respond with, "Awesome, I figured as much, but just to clarify. If what I present to you today adds the value that you're looking for, you won't tell me you have to talk to anyone else on the back end of this presentation before you can move forward, right?"

You might be thinking … "Does he really ask that?" and the answer is… YES! Look, there are too many sites that tell people how to get out of sales presentations. What to say to stump your salesperson. How to be nice, but let your salesperson know you won't be making a decision today. Blah blah blah. They're prepared, so we need to be prepared.

Be strong enough to verify what they say is true. If they speak it, they own it. Especially if they speak it twice. Does this mean they won't say it on the back end? No, but it sure as hell minimizes the chances to close to zero.

It's imperative that you get used to addressing this up front. If they say yes there will be others involved in the decision, offer to get them on the phone to answer any questions the other decision maker may have before you get started. This shows both the prospect and the other person who's not there that they matter and you care enough to make them a part of this process.

You really do have to just keep it real. Be straight with them. If they absolutely keep insisting that they can't move forward without speaking to someone else, tell them what's most likely going to happen.

"Look, if you loved everything we went over today, truly feel this is a good fit, and believe I'm the best person to handle your account, there's no way, without being a part of this, that your partner (other person they need to speak to) will get the same experience and 99% of the time, they'll just try to talk you out of spending additional funds. So let me help you make a decision today that's going to truly take you to the next level."

It's honesty that's lacking with sales individuals today. 99% of the people in the world would agree. Salespeople are just known as liars and con people who force you into buying something you may not need. The truth: real salespeople use honesty as their biggest asset yet.

In this situation, they might be open, and some cases they won't. If they're totally closed off, I always ask to reschedule a time to have all the decision makers present. I know, not ideal, but if you don't, you'll be saying the same thing twice and presenting everything over again. It's better to get all buy-in fully from all parties so the sale is solidified.

That being said, asking this question up front can save you time, and limit back-end objections that may exclude you from closing a deal today!

RAPPORT-BUILDING QUESTIONS

What do people love to talk about most? Yep, themselves. So let them do it! The more they speak, the more you learn, the better the odds of building rapport. You'll start to educate yourself on what makes them tick. What information will be most valuable to them. It'll also help you eliminate their dislikes so you are able to cater your product or service directly to them.

What do you do for a living?
Simple yes. But getting to know how they earn a living is important in so many ways. How much do they work? What do they love most about what they do? Does it give them time to spend with people they love? What is their role and what do they love most about it?

All these things are important to find out who you're dealing with. If there's more than one person, make sure you spend EQUAL time getting to know each. This is an extremely important move that a lot of salespeople miss and it lets them know you care about who they are.

If you know what they do, more B2B (business to business) stuff, then ask similar questions like this:

What's your role with the company and how long have you been there?
Again, let them speak. Don't interrupt. Studies have shown that at any point of a sales presentation, when the salesperson cuts the prospect off while they're speaking, they miss approximately 64% of what the prospect was going to say. WOW! Imagine, if you just let them talk, keeping your mouth shut, they'd tell you things that are very important to help you get to know them better.

Another study showed that when the salesperson cuts the prospect off while speaking, the prospect gets offended 71% of the time and closes back up, making it harder for a salesperson to close the sale. Ooof! I don't want to be that salesperson and I'll teach you not to be.

Moral of the story, ask them about them. Let them speak about them until they're done. This information is key to building rapport and helps the transition to the close seem easy.

Asking question about personal items, being aware of what someone is wearing, or pictures, furniture in their office, a watch they're wearing, etc… shows you are paying attention to the details of their lives. This shows them that they matter to you.

I always teach my students to be conscious of all of this and ask non-sales-related questions that build personal rapport. You should do this, because it really should matter to you, but also because your prospect needs to KNOW it really does matter to you.

Most untrained salespeople don't do this. Everything they speak of is about the sale. Every question they ask is about the sale. What about the person? Do they matter? I mean, they're the one making the decision to do business with you. I guess I've never understood how sales trainers don't spend more time on this.

So ask questions like this:

If they have a nice watch on…

- Are you a watch person? … Let the convo begin.

If they have a cool picture in their office…

- You like art? That picture is amazing … Let the convo begin.

Nice shoes on…

- Shoe person, I see… What's your favorite pair? (wait for answer) Oh yeah, nice… How come? … let the convo begin.

If you see pictures of family…

- How long have you been married?
- How old are your kids?
- What grades are they in?

Pictures of a dog/pets….
- Dog lover, huh?

Or how about if they came to you. It's important to have personal items of your own out in the office, like the above mentioned, to spark conversation. I can't tell you how many times I've had my book out or a picture of my family and someone says "Beautiful family" and that gives me a way in to ask about theirs and talk about what's important to me equally.

Another great rapport-building question is this:

In a perfect world, what do you want this product or service to do for you?

- Again, why are we not asking this question!?!? I'll tell you why. Because you have too many people leading or training other salespeople who don't have a clue what real salesmanship is. That's the hard truth.

Asking this question will give you more information to dial in on what matters to them. Don't forget. This presentation is ABOUT THEM, not you.

GET CLEAR AT ASKING GOOD QUESTIONS THAT GET YOU CLEAR ANSWERS

If I ask someone a question, I need a full response. I'm not looking for half an answer and too many salespeople accept half the information they need, which can lead to a half-ass presentation.

It's important that you fully understand what your prospect or client is telling you. If you're not fully clear on what they mean, ask questions like this so that you can serve them at your best:

- That makes sense, but I'd like to fully understand what you mean so I can best serve you. Tell me more about that.

- That's great. Knowing all that, how did it affect you or your company's performance?
- So I can understand completely, can you give me an example of what you mean?

Sometimes it's as easy as this:
- Can you be a little more specific so I can dial in the best possible service for you?

You don't have to make it confusing. Don't ask them what color pen they like best or what their favorite shirt is when they purchase options for their company, but understanding what their needs are fully is essential in serving your prospect best.

Master the art of asking clarification questions so they know you care and most importantly that you can offer something that's customized to what's most important to them.

OBJECTION-BLOCKING/SURFACING QUESTIONS

Let's all be on the same page here. Every single successful sales professional surfaces objections before their prospects or clients. They don't wait for them to pop up. They don't wait till the back end of the sales presentation to handle the objections. They surface them at the beginning and middle to LIMIT the possibly of a prospect using an objection on the back end.

If you're the expert in your field you say you are, then you already know the most common objections that are going to come up anyway. So let's go over a few ways to surface objections by asking questions that will allow you to handle these objections, so you have the smoothest transition to the close on the back end.

By the way, when you actually follow this process, it builds massive credibility and shows that you care about what their doubts and concerns are and that you're there to help solve their problems. Prospects love this.

The only people who don't do this are afraid to surface an objection that might never come up. WRONG WRONG WRONG! When you master this process, it'll reduce rescission and help you retain your business much higher than salespeople who don't. If you somehow get through a sales presentation, then close the deal without certain objections surfacing that you know normally do, you better believe the objections will surface when the client leaves and buyer's remorse begins to set in.

When you bring out all the possibilities of objections they may have, you increase your retention of business by 87%. This was a national study done by Harvard University with over 365,000 sales presentations used as a trial source. They also found that 79% of all prospects won't surface objections on their own, because they don't want to be mean. Think about that. Imagine if you can get back or save 87% of the business you've lost, would you? Welp. Here's a few good questions to ask to do just that. Customize them to be your own and make sure you trickle in some generic ones and industry-specific ones.

Here are some great ones to know:

- I know we've gone over a lot of information. What are your thoughts so far?
- You've asked some great questions. Is there anything that would stop you from moving forward today that we should discuss?
- What else should we go over to make sure this is the best fit for you?

Those are some common strong objection-surfacing questions, but this one, for some reason, less trained salespeople are afraid to ask:

- It seems like it's a great fit so far. I want to make sure you're getting everything out of this you can. What other concerns do you have? Let's make sure we go over them before you move forward today.

I'm clarifying that we've had a great start to the presentation. That there's been a lot of good, but I want my prospect or client to know I care about what they're concerned about. When you get really good at asking this question the right way, your client's respect goes way up.

Sometimes prospects won't tell you what's bothering them. What their concerns are. Sometimes they just make a facial expression that you have to notice and stop the presentation to find out what that's about.

The worst move you can make is to disregard their feelings. Don't move past an objection or concern when it surfaces until they're fully satisfied with your answer.

Here are some of my top questions to ask in a sales presentation:

- You have some pretty high goals. Why do you think you haven't met them yet?
- Best case scenario, what expectations do you have by purchasing this (insert product or service) today?
- We all want the perfect solution, but what are your top priorities?
- How often do you make purchases like this?
    o And if they do it often…
    - "Honored that you're here with me, but why aren't you looking for solutions with the person you're already doing business with?"
- I want to better understand your short- and long-term goals. What's the top 3 for each in order?

These questions are really great discovery questions that can take your sales career to a whole new level. Stop shortchanging the questions you ask, because usually, to a prospect, it will result in you shortchanging their time with you. GET INFORMATION by asking BETTER QUESTIONS!

Learn when to ask the right questions and it'll lead to much higher results, short- and long-term, in building an unmatched rapport with your clients. You'll find out their concerns, what matters most to them, putting yourself in their shoes to add the most value to your prospect or business you're trying to serve.

Great questions matter most. They allow you to prove that their concerns are yours, and that you're going to be the person to help solve the problems other people they've spoken to in the past didn't take time to fully understand.

Here's the real issue, though. The majority of salespeople who just don't get the training they need, don't know how to ask questions properly. They sound scripted. They sound robotic and they have zero sequence. All that does is irritate their prospects. It's the reason why EVERY SINGLE COMPANY should hire outside trainers in sales and leadership, so they get a new perspective on how to scale their teams. Most companies don't, due to ego or thinking the extra cost isn't warranted. They're wrong.

When a prospect feels like they're getting questioned, rather than served, the wall builds back up, the sales barrier gets stronger between the sales representative and their client, which is the reason why most don't learn this process properly. When you do it properly, trust builds through the roof!

Master how to ask questions WITH rhyme and reason and you, your team, and your company will see a huge increase in efficiency. You won't have to close anything if you ask questions properly. Provide solutions to the questions they have. Then the sale will close itself.

Just make sure when you're asking questions, your main job here is to understand what they're saying. Not just gather information, but truly understand what they mean.

When I first got into sales many years ago, I was too quick to tell prospects, "I got you," or "Yep I can do that," when they had a concern. I didn't dig deep enough to understand what they meant. I rushed the yes. I didn't stop and think about what it would take to fulfill their request. Soon I found out that doing this, although it sounded great, was the worst thing I could do. I may have closed the sale right then and there, but I also saw cancellations instantly when I couldn't do what they asked me to do.

Mostly this happens when you just see the commission check, rather than trying to serve your prospect. You rush to the yes, saying anything they need to hear to get to the close, and don't think about back-end repercussions. Don't learn the hard way like I did. Don't close deals for applause. Close deals to serve.

The prospects I sold never had faith in me again. They didn't refer any business to me because I couldn't do what I told them I would. Be the person your clients know they can count on, not the person who's just trying to make the sale. That comes with FULLY understanding what matters to them.

Don't rush the yes. Ask questions to get to know your clients personally and financially. This matters most. I learned a hard costly lesson in sales my first couple years and I'm hoping you learn the process in the book so I can save you time and money from making the same mistakes I did.

Asking the right questions also calls out the liars. I'm sure you've heard the phrase "buyers are liars" and it's true. People will try to get out of presentations because they just hate to be sold. No one likes being sold, but some won't even give you the chance to learn about what you're offering.

Asking proper questions will weed out the liars. The ones who tell you one thing, but mean another. If you ask direct, informational-based discovery questions, you make the opportunity to wiggle out a limited one.

Keep your questions simple too. When you try to sound smart, or say things that might challenge the intelligence of your prospect, it never goes over well. Simple, to the point questions are the best.

Don't ask questions to confuse someone or distract them from an objection or lack of what your product can do for them. Just be honest. No games, just questions that serve them.

The old "If I could… would you…" days are gone. Ask questions that serve your client to a seamless back-end transition to doing business together, not to "hard core close them."

Remember, this is hopefully the start of a long-term business relationship you're building. Whether it's a business or a person, there's one word that will do that: CARE. I know, I know. It seems way too easy, right? Well, unfortunately, the unprofessional salespeople in today's world have ruined the handshake days of trust. They're expecting you to be all about you and your pocket. Help MAKE SALES GREAT AGAIN with me and I promise you the best sales career of your life and the best way to do that is to train!

Below I've added some real-life scenarios for a few different industries to give you some examples of how to train and master this skill!

SCENARIO 1: RETAIL BUSINESS – SELLING A SUIT

Background:

A customer enters a retail clothing store, seemingly interested in buying a suit for an upcoming event.

Role Play:
- Salesperson: "Hello! How can I assist you today?"
- Customer: "I'm looking for a suit."
- Salesperson: "Great! What's the occasion?"
- Customer: "A business conference."

Questions to Ask:
1. "What kind of look are you going for: conservative, modern, or something in between?"

2. "How do you usually feel in a suit? What's been your experience with previous suits?"
3. "Are there specific colors or patterns you have in mind?"

Breakdown:
These questions help in:
1. Understanding the specific requirements.
2. Identifying past pain points.
3. Tailoring the offerings to the customer's preferences.

SCENARIO 2: JEWELRY BUSINESS – SELLING AN ANNIVERSARY GIFT

Background:
A gentleman seems lost in a jewelry store, trying to find the perfect anniversary gift for his wife.

Role Play:
- Salesperson: "Hello, sir. Are you looking for something special?"
- Customer: "Yes, it's our anniversary soon."
- Salesperson: "Congratulations! What kind of jewelry does your wife typically wear?"

Questions to Ask:
1. "Is there a particular gemstone or metal she loves?"
2. "Has she mentioned anything she wished she had in her jewelry collection?"
3. "Would you consider something personalized, like jewelry with her birthstone or an engraving?"

Breakdown:
The questions are designed to:
1. Navigate through the vast options.
2. Connect with the customer's emotional journey.
3. Offer something unique and memorable.

SCENARIO 3: CONSTRUCTION SALES – SELLING HOME RENOVATION SERVICES

Background:

A couple is considering home renovation and approaches a construction company.

Role Play:

- Salesperson: "Hello! How can I help bring your home renovation dreams to life?"
- Customer: "We're thinking about renovating our living room."
- Salesperson: "Sounds exciting! What inspired you to consider a renovation now?"

Questions to Ask:

1. "What's your main goal with this renovation? More space, modern aesthetics, or functionality?"
2. "Are there specific designs or features you've seen elsewhere and loved?"
3. "What's your desired timeline for the project?"

Breakdown:

These questions aim to:

1. Grasp the vision of the customer.
2. Suggest design elements fitting their preferences.
3. Align the services with their schedule.

Mastering the art of questioning can and WILL guide the sales process the most efficiently. I stand by many of my posts and trainings that highlight how important it is to master this skill. It allows the salesperson to truly understand and cater to the customer's needs. As you practice in these scenarios, remember: the quality of your sales process is often determined by the quality of your questions. For that alone, I'd advise you to get with your friends or leaders and re-create the scenarios above to cater to your specific industry.

Most importantly, have FUN when you're training!

CHAPTER 18

SECURING THE WIN: TIE DOWNS & TRIAL CLOSES

People have a misconception about what a tie down really is. Do you know what one is? When to use it? How to use it? It's OK if you don't. Some will say, "Its asking questions they can't say no to." Or "Boxing them in," meaning there's nothing they can do but agree to the sale. Others will even say, they're stuck and they can't get out. Well, look, there's some unfortunate truth to all of those if not used with integrity, but HOW you use tie downs is more important than the result, in my humble opinion.

Don't use this method dishonestly! Use it the right way. I know I'm going to sound like a broken record, but there are some shady assholes who use this when they're blatantly lying. Like offering something that's not real because they know it'll get the deal. They're using tie downs as a way to forcefully influence someone who may not be leaning towards the sale. NOT GOOD! It's wrong and anyone reading this book should be using these sales tools the right way. So please do that!

Let's get into how the world defines tie downs. TIE DOWNS ARE DEFINED AS: short questions you add to statements throughout your presentation to get your prospective customer to start saying yes long before you go for the close. You want to engage your customers and get them used to saying yes. You should be asking little questions along the way and pay attention. Ask the question, then shut up and listen! Tie downs can help guide you to the close, but most importantly help guide your clients to the close. They help you confirm that your prospect understands what you're putting down. When they say yes or agree after a tie down, you know it's OK to move on with the presentation.

Making a statement and following it up with a question, verifying the statement you just made is truly what a tie down is. You need to have conversations that create patterns of agreements, which may not always get you a "yes." You may not know it, but that's gold too! It immediately helps you surface a problem and solve it now rather than waiting until the back end. We'll get into that later, but tie downs are super powerful when you get a yes or a no!

They're also known as trial closes. They aren't always questions you ask at the end of a statement, which elicit a response from your prospect to say "yes." That's definitely been proven to be a little aggressive these days and if not perfected… your entire sale could backfire on you. You also have to master this tool to use it correctly. People are smarter and can see tie downs or trial closes coming from a mile away.

There are uneducated sales individuals trying to use tie downs, unmastered, which turns a client or prospect right off. They can see it. They can feel it and they know exactly what you're trying to do. Again, it should be used as a tactic, but it should be used with authenticity utilizing the information you gain from asking the right questions to get the true response from someone who may or may not be a little tougher to do business with.

By the way, don't push too hard to get the answer you want. Respect your client and yourself enough to know when it's not going to work.

THE BIGGEST mistake you can make is to fight to get the answer you want, if a prospect doesn't give it to you right away. WORST IDEA EVER! It'll ruin the odds of you closing the deal. Don't get defensive. Don't get arrogant. Watch your facial expressions. Just accept the fact that the tie down didn't work and move on with your presentation.

Next, do NOT try to use multiple tie downs or trial closes back to back. It's way too salesy and way too much pressure on the person you're trying to do business with. Just seems pushy. Time them throughout the sales process. No, I'm not telling you to do it every 15 minutes exactly. I'm saying use them when you see there's an opportunity to solidify value. Notice I didn't say an opportunity to close them, but SOLIDIFY VALUE. If you use them too early, you also risk losing the sale from the start. It makes you seem like that person who just wants the cash and doesn't care about what matters to them. Tie downs are used properly when you are allowing the client an opportunity to confirm what they know to be true or you see that they like something you've said or presented. Confirming the information they've heard actually solves a problem for them. Using the same one over and over like, "That make sense?" can annoy people and they will begin to view you as not caring about them and just wanting the sale.

By getting your customers to agree with you in small steps along the way, you have a better chance of reaching agreement when it's time to do business. You want to use them to end statements of value to the customer, literally as simple as:

- "You know what I mean?"
- "I'm sure that makes sense?"
- "Would you agree with that?"
- "Am I right when I say that?"
- "Absolutely, right?"
- "It definitely should, right?"

- "Isn't it?"
- "That would obviously make sense, right?"
- "Won't they?"
- "Does that help?"
- "Now that you visually see what I mean, do you see how it can help you?"

You can also use some much more humble tie downs if the more direct ones don't suit your personality, like:

- "I hope I've explained that so it makes complete sense to you. Have I?"
- "Sometimes I move too fast and I want to make sure you fully see the value in this."
- "I really hope this helps you. Did it?"
- "The worst thing I can ever do is present something in a way that doesn't make sense to you. I personally believe it makes sense to do business together. Is there anything I didn't explain thoroughly or do you fully understand how this will help you?"
- "All I care about is that we can add value and you see it. Obviously, if it's a no brainer and helps you convert more sales, it'd make sense to do business, right?"
- "What matters to you is most important to me. This is about you. If I look at what we spoke of earlier, you said that you like our company and all you really needed was the interest rate and the payment to make sense to you, and we can get this ball rolling, right?"
- "So if I redirected the same money you're already spending, not more, but the same or less, with more value… we both can agree it's a no brainer to move forward, right?"

See, you don't have to be Mr. or Mrs. CLOSER! You can use tie downs nicely, so it's not aggressive in any way and it shows how much you care that they've received the information you're giving them and they see the value in it. When you recite what's important back to them, things that they've said throughout the presentation that they've fully agreed with, getting the final yes is very easy and becomes a fluent part of your sales process. Remember, they've already said yes. The hard-core closers of the world call it ammo. Some people, no matter what you say or do, just hate being sold. They'll say no, just to say no. All genders, when feeling threatened by a strong sales individual, whether it be their skill or perceived cockiness or maybe they're good looking, will create a "the salesperson vs. me" contest or war, to prove to their other half that they're stronger. Using micro, soft tie downs throughout the presentation gives you ammo to use on the back end, knowing they're going to say no. That being said, it's really hard to say no to something they've already said yes to throughout your pitch and you can convert a lot of them if you just use the tie downs gently and give them control if what you're serving them adds value to their lives.

Tie downs should be the norm during your presentation. They have to come off naturally, not scripted. You have to know how to use them, when to use them, and most importantly how to express them verbally.

If you're selling over the phone and don't have the visual cues you do when you're in person, you have to use some kind of check-in statement to see how the conversation is going. The key to successfully checking in with your prospect is to ask a tie down that engages your prospect and gets you some kind of response.

Tie downs can be insulting. If you use it the wrong way, you can turn off a prospect in no time. For instance, let's say you were pitching me and you arrogantly said, *"Obviously, what I'm saying makes sense, Todd, right?"* What if it didn't? What if I didn't see the value? Yes, it's good to find that information now so you can help me to understand, but if you say it in a way that makes me feel stupid or if you're smirking while you speak, it'd turn me off instantly!

Your tie down can't be confrontational, sound rude, threatening, argumentative, or like you're questioning someone's intelligence. Make sure you switch them up with repeat clients. I've been secretly practicing on my wife for years and my tie downs used to work if I wanted to talk her into doing something, but now she laughs, smiles at me, and says, "Don't try to close me. It ain't working!" You ladies know too much! You're too smart and so are clients these days. Knowing that, you need to role play tie downs daily. Let your co-worker be hard on you. Who cares if you get embarrassed in front of others, because if you keep going, you'll master them in every scenario.

The problem is if you're not trained properly, you'll become that cheesy sales individual out there who isn't serving their clients because you're using the weakest tie downs or using the good ones incorrectly.

Here's a list of old school, played-out tie downs that can build the wall higher between you and your prospect if you're not careful how you present them:

- "You with me?"
- "I know you like that feature, don't you?"
- "You seem smart. You get it, right?"
- "Obviously that would be great. Wouldn't it?

There are tons of other lame tie downs that are so obvious, using them makes you sound like a horrible used ANYTHING salesperson. Yes, it is about asking questions to get a bunch of micro agreements, but don't get frustrated if they don't work. This is about transferring belief, but only doing so if your prospect actually believes in what you're offering. Remember, if they speak it, they own it! When you say it, you own it! I can't tell you how many times I've trained large groups of sales professionals and get them to use a tie down pitching the services that I offer, and they say something like this:

- "Todd, I believe the best part of what we're offering is that you will learn so much about sales from one of today's top experts, right?"

Truth. You may not believe that Todd's one of today's experts. Their reply could be:

- "I really don't know that. I've never taken one of his courses and I'm not opposed to it, but he may not be the fit for me."

What if you set up the tie down like this and asked questions that forced them to resurface what matters most to them before you went in for the agreement.

- "Earlier you said that the area of your sales process you wanted to master the most was handling objections and that you loved how Todd's course gave you one-on-one time for some Q & A. Why do you believe that one-on-one time will help you excel?"

They reply:
- "Having one-on-one time means he's dedicated solely to my growth, which is how I know I will elevate the most."

My reply:
- "That makes complete sense and so many other people feel the same way. The results are proven. So, if I could get you some one-on-one dedicated time with Todd that was affordable to you (nodding my head), you'd be ready to master the handling objections course and get signed up, right?"

The setup has to be real, though! REMEMBER, WHEN THEY SPEAK IT, THEY OWN IT! When they say what matters most to them, there's true value. When you say something you "think" adds value, you're just taking a shot. A guess, if you will. The elite in sales don't guess. They set up their tie downs and use them to convert.

In order to be different, you have to be real. You have to be authentic. Everything you say and how you present has to come from a sincere place of honesty. Using a tie down can seem very tactical and shady and if used incorrectly, it can kill your deal and fast. People automatically assume salespeople are slick, fast talking, in-it-for-themselves type of people and WE HAVE TO CHANGE THAT and Make Sales Great Again. This only comes from good intentions created through serving, not trying to "close" people.

If you're taking notes like YOU SHOULD BE, you probably recognized some of the tie downs we went over in this chapter and know when used properly they'll add massive value to your career in sales, right? Nod your head if you agree. PSSSSS. I just used a tie down on you. See how easy it is?

Remember what your purpose is in using tie downs: to take the pulse of your prospect to see if you're losing them or if they're with you, or if they're bored or engaged, or if they have a question, etc.

This is where the tie down sales technique was born; it allows you to make a statement, and then turn it into a question at the end to help transition into the sale smoothly.

Once again, it's easy to reword the worn-out tie downs and update them to better ones… for example:

Instead of using, "That's a nice feature, isn't it?" you can ask:

"This will save you a lot of time based on the way you're doing business now. I know time is money.... so out of curiosity, what would you do with the extra time this will save you?"

Instead of saying, "Would that make you feel better?" you can ask:

"I'm sure we both agree this service would save you money; you think that'd go over well with the boss? LOL."

Instead of saying, "Are you with me so far?" you can ask:

"I've shared a lot of information with you; what do you think is the best feature that you'd use the most and how would it impact you positively?"

Instead of saying, "And you'd like that, wouldn't you?" you can ask:

"Everybody obviously likes to save money (less work, save time, more time, more money, etc.). How have you been able to save in this area this year, and knowing what you know now about our service, both agreeing it'll save in several areas, how much more do you think it'd impact that savings next year?"

THE POINT is to ask questions (tie downs) that encourage your prospects to reveal information that you can learn from. Then you can use that information to truly educate yourself on whether what you're offering the prospect will add value to them or not. If you're listening carefully, then you'll be surprised by the buying motives, and they'll literally tell you how to sell them.

Everything we've just gone over is more related to "tie downs" than to "trial closes." At times, they are one and the same, but often they're not. A tie down is not always a trial close. If you don't understand and master the trial close, you might as well look for another career right now. This is going to be hard for some of you to hear, but the truth is without the trial close, you'll never be a top salesperson.

I need you to think of a time you were being pitched and the salesperson never shut up until they asked for the cash. Think hard about whether you bought or not. I know I've been there and I didn't buy what they were selling either!

The step-by-step breakdown is like this for the client. The salesperson starts the presentation. You come to a point where you have a question. You want to ask, but you can't get a word in because the salesperson won't shut up. You internally realize that you don't agree or feel as if what they're offering makes sense for you to purchase. They keep talking. You keep listening.

When they're finally done running their mouth, never once asking a trial close or your thoughts on what they're presenting, you realize you have 1000 objections and questions, but were never asked how you felt about what they were pitching. Then guess what happens next? They ask you to buy, and you go, "Dude, I've been sitting here listening to you run your mouth for the past hour and never once did you ask me my thoughts or my opinion on what you're trying to sell me. The answer is NO!"

This happens way more often than you probably know. What your prospect thinks is the only thing that matters when you have the luxury of them listening to you pitch your product or service. Never forget that. Their opinion is the game changer. Their opinion is the best direction to doing business with them. The only way you fully understand what's important to them is asking trial closes.

However, when used properly, the trial close will keep you from being THAT salesperson. You know the one I just mentioned who talks more than listens. Who tries to convince, rather than serve. Talk to your prospect. Have a simple conversation with them. Stop trying to sell! Serve them, stopping after every major point and asking questions to see what matters most to them. Yes, them, not YOU! When they have questions or need clarity on something that may be an objection, immediately stop your sales pitch and address their concerns. Make sure they fully understand what you've said, and then they'll be completely satisfied to move forward with your presentation.

The best thing about this process is it provides necessary information to help get to the close. You'll reveal obstacles that might stop you from closing the deal early, giving you a chance to handle them, when most untrained sales individuals don't get a chance to.

The trial close reveals opportunities. Opportunities can be objections and/or obstacles as well. A prospect could love everything but one tiny little thing that most sales individuals miss. Use this process and you won't miss what the majority does. It can also take a smaller deal and turn it into a bigger one, hence opportunity. A lot of untrained sales individuals in the world miss an opportunity to upsell and using this process makes it easier than ever. If you use a trial close and it seems like what you're offering isn't enough to the prospect, offer more reasons why it is, and get them to agree that the new offer is right for them using a trial close.

For example, let's say you're selling me a bag of "The Ultlimate Sales Bible" customized golf tees. You proceed to tell me about the quality, what it can do for my branding, but then tell me the quantity. A trial close would be a something like this:

> *Knowing the tees are durable and great for your brand, I'd recommend purchasing in bulk around 100+ tees. But knowing that you sponsor a lot of events, do you think that'd be a good place to start or should we see what the bigger options look like?"*

My goal here is to use a trial close as an opportunity to upsell where they tell me they should, rather than having to convince them.

Trial closes also show your prospect you care. When you stop when something seems off or they don't seem to agree with what you're presenting and you show them you're listening and you care, this builds relationships and trust. You're proving their opinion matters when you stop and let them tell you their opinion. Asking questions demonstrates your ability and full intention to actually serve someone, rather than selling them.

Let's just call it what it is. Trial closes actually increase your likelihood of getting the yes we all are seeking. The more trial closes you use and the more they agree with you and the more you prove that their opinion matters, you will undoubtedly MAKE MORE SALES, simply put, finally helping me, help the world, to MAKE SALES GREAT AGAIN!

Many sales professionals also use the trial close to temperature-check the prospect. Meaning, how interested are they? How much are they actually listening to you? Some even use this technique to see if the prospect is listening to them. For example, if I'm speaking to a family and they're looking down at their phones, I might use a trial close to see if they're truly listening to what I'm saying.

Example: I look up at a family and can see they're not paying attention, so I'd say something like this:

"OK, well, Mr. and Mrs. Smith, it seems as though you understand everything fully, so how will you be paying for this?"

LOL! Trust me, that trial close will never work in that scenario, but it'll get them listening again. There are key points in the presentation that you MUST make sure your prospect is listening to, so mastering the art of WHEN to use these is equally as important as mastering HOW to use a trial close. The proper timing is usually before you're about to drop some serious gold for them. If you know when to use them and when to close the sale, the timing of this duo can be very useful.

For instance, if I asked someone a simple trial close like:

"Based off everything that matters to you, I think we'd both agree, if the numbers made sense, this would be a no-brainer, right?"

Shut up and listen after that statement! If they say yes, there's no reason to keep pitching. CLOSE. THE. DEAL. Do it right now and right there, reconfirming everything they know adds value to them.

Master trial closes. Use them and understand them fully. They can be respectful, and they can also be fun to gain the attention of your prospect that you need to fully build value in what you're offering.

Most sales individuals are scared to use the trial close in its truest form, because they haven't been trained how to. It's not only extremely effective, but there are so many ways to use this process to simply determine the mood of your buyer. A trial close determines the level of interest in what you're offering. It's that simple. Are they interested or are they NOT interested? That's the goal.

When using trial closes, you're using specific words like if, when, I'm sure, we'd agree, etc… assuming the buyer has already said yes to buying what you're offering. You're basically painting a picture of closure in the prospect's mind. Like the presentation is over. Assuming the sale. You're in the driver's seat when trial closes are used properly, guiding them to make a decision to do business with you.

There are three things I usually train sales professionals to look for when using a trial close:

1. Prospect agrees with you, so you're ready to close.

2. Prospect isn't all in yet. They don't fully agree and have questions. They're not all the way out yet either. This is the "in limbo" portion most presentations fall into. So figure out the issue, clear it up, and then move on.

3. Prospect doesn't agree with you at all. At this point you need to stop the entire presentation and ask some hard, polite questions, figuring out why they feel the way they do or what went wrong before you offer one more tiny piece of information about your product or service.

Here's another hard truth. If you don't master this process and when to use the trial close, you'll never know if the prospect had a question or concern 3-4 points back in your presentation. It's the easiest way to guarantee a "NO" on the back end and never know why. You can prevent that by diving deep into understanding and learning the trial close.

One of the best things about a trial close is that even if it doesn't close the sale, it'll still help surface mainstream objections that you need to get out anyway. Trial closes don't need to be hidden. Honesty and directness is the best avenue always. So, when using this process, it's OK and still massively beneficial to get an objection out early, to give you time to handle it.

Don't forget to control timing as well. Nothing I'm telling you here is new. I want you to use them:

- at every major selling point during your presentation

- immediately after you answer a question your prospect asks

- after you handle any objection they have
- right before the close

You're reconfirming, making them speak and say how they feel and when they agree, again, THEY OWN IT WHEN THEY SPEAK IT!

This guarantees:

- They hear you.
- You hear them.
- They agree that the benefits of what you're offering benefit them.
- You're invested in what matters most to them.
- You've handled their objections and/or obstacles.
- They have a chance to ask any more questions or concerns they may have.
- That the buyer is ready to close the sale.

Most of the inexperienced sales individuals get so caught up in following the proper steps of the presentation that they forget to be real, to listen and make sure they're serving their prospect fully. They forget to use this absolutely necessary skill to help their efficiency rise.

A trial close isn't there to just get a "yes, I agree" and move on. It's there to truly respect and understand the opinion of your prospect. You can best serve them by letting them know you are fully committed to providing a service or product that will guarantee their money is being used properly and at its highest value.

Here are a few of the most common trial close examples:

- Does this make sense to you? (Make sure you use this one right. Sometimes, if used wrong, it can come across as you questioning their intelligence.)
- I know it's been a lot of information, but what stood out to you most?

- There's no perfect solution, but knowing what we've gone over, what would you change or add to this product or service if you could?
- How do you feel about what we've gone over so far?
- How do you think this product or service can benefit you most?
- How's everything sound to you so far?

OK, so here's another tool I want to impact the sales world with. There are so many "cookie cutter" sales individuals being trained in today's world and ZERO emotion behind the questions they ask. So here's some of the same trial close examples with a little MSGA REAL added in:

- Does this make sense to you? (Make sure you use this one right. Sometimes, if used wrong, it can come across as you questioning their intelligence.)
    - o Re-worded MSGA style:
        - "I know you get everything I'm saying, but I always like to make sure I'm explaining it properly. Does everything make sense so far?"

I just feel this eliminates any thought or feeling that the salesperson is questioning their ability to understand. Remember, it's not just what you say, but it's also how you say it.

- I know it's been a lot of information, but what stood out to you most?
    - o Re-worded MSGA style:
        - "We've gone over a lot so far, but what's most important to me is what stood out to you the most. What'd you like best?"

Confirms I care about what matters to them. You must ALWAYS serve clients. Not "make them feel as if," but making sure they're 100% sure you have their best interest in mind.

- There's no perfect solution, but knowing what we've gone over, what would you change or add to this product or service if you could?
    - o Re-worded MSGA style:
        - "Most people in sales talk so much they forget to listen. I know there's no perfect product or service in the world and the only way we learn is by listening to the ones we're trying to serve. That being said, if you could add or change anything at all, what would you change?"

A confirming statement that their input is crucial to the success of your company even BEFORE you're doing business with anyone proves that you aren't with them just to "close the deal," but that you care about growth and constructive criticism. This type of preset right before you ask the trial close will get you better information than just asking the question itself.

To be truly effective using trial closes, you have to cater them to what you're offering. You have to role play daily and know exactly how you want to word them. The best way to do that is to find someone to brainstorm with. I know every time I've sat at a conference table with others, the result of multiple minds was greater than my own.

Here are a few catered to the time and process using trial closes:

- Right before you close the sale you might ask:
    - o "From what we've discussed and what you've told me, it sounds like this product can really serve you and increase your overall efficiency. Do you agree?
- When you handle any objection you might say:
    - o "I'm so glad we talked about that because I want you completely comfortable in understanding what we just went over. Does that solution help?"
- If you just answered a question they had:

> o "I hope I've answered your question. I'm here to serve you and want to make sure I've handled any concerns you have. Did I answer your question fully?"

I want you to listen or read this very carefully. YOU WILL LOSE OPPORTUNITIES if all you're doing is spewing the features and benefits of what you're offering without finding out if they add value to your prospect. The way you do that is through trial closes.

Statistically, those who master this skill and use it have a 67% higher chance converting prospects into buyers. Do you like those odds? I do.

By the way, if you're a sales manager, this is a great exercise for a meeting.

Get all your reps together and make a list of the worn-out tie downs they are using now, and then brainstorm new ones that are open ended and that engage people.

Your team will not only make more sales, but prospects will enjoy talking to them as well.

Remember, deliver tie downs and trial closes properly, with integrity. These processes are just the act of having a conversation with a person, learning about their pain points, finding out how they define value, using that information to confirm that what you're offering adds value or a solution that the prospect will see as something they need, rather than being unsure.

I'll say this again, don't trick, force, or convince someone to do business with you.

You're not looking for just the yes. You're looking for the agreement which will lead to the yes.

When a prospect speaks it, they own it, which means it's their belief too.

There's a ton of gold for a real, authentic, honest sales professional to use. Study, role play every day, and keep mastering the art of these two sales techniques, always putting the client first. It'll make a massive difference in you and your organization.

1. REAL ESTATE SALES

Scenario: Jessica, a real estate agent, is showing a young couple, Tom and Linda, around a beautiful suburban home that's close to local amenities and in their preferred school district.

Jessica: "You mentioned wanting a home in a quiet neighborhood yet close to schools for your kids, right?"

Tom: "Yes, that's right."

Jessica: "This house is just a five-minute walk to the best elementary school in the district. Imagine your kids being able to walk to school every morning. How would that feel?"

Linda: "That would be amazing."

Jessica: "And with this beautiful garden, there's plenty of space for them to play. Can you see your family spending weekends here?"

Tom: "Definitely. It looks lovely."

Jessica: "Would securing this house in the next week help ensure your kids start the school year in their new school?"

Linda: "Yes, that would be ideal."

Breakdown:
- Jessica used tie downs ("right?") to reaffirm the couple's needs.
- She then painted a picture of the benefits directly relating to their wants and used trial closes ("How would that feel?", "Can you see your family spending weekends here?") to gauge their interest.

2. MORTGAGE SALES

Scenario: Mike, a mortgage broker, is discussing loan options with a first-time homebuyer, Rachel.

Mike: "Rachel, you mentioned wanting a mortgage plan that offers flexibility since you're a freelancer, correct?"

Rachel: "Yes, that's a primary concern for me."

Mike: "We have an adjustable-rate mortgage that allows for greater flexibility during its initial period. With your unpredictable income, having lower initial payments might be beneficial. Does that sound like a good starting point for you?"

Rachel: "It does sound interesting."

Mike: "And if we could lock in a competitive interest rate for that initial period to save you money, would you consider moving forward with the application process?"

Rachel: "If the rate's good, absolutely."

Breakdown:

- Mike used tie downs ("correct?") to confirm Rachel's needs.
- He presented a solution that aligns with her needs and used trial closes ("Does that sound like a good starting point for you?", "Would you consider moving forward with the application process?") to gauge her interest.

3. HEALTH INSURANCE

Scenario: Karen, a health insurance advisor, is assisting Steve, a middle-aged man looking for comprehensive health coverage.

Karen: "Steve, from our earlier conversation, you're primarily concerned about having coverage for major medical events and hospitalizations, right?"

Steve: "Yes, especially since my family has a history of heart conditions."

Karen: "I understand. We have a plan that offers extensive coverage for hospitalizations, surgeries, and even provides access to a network of specialized cardiologists. Imagine having that peace of mind knowing you're covered. Would that be the kind of security you're seeking?"

Steve: "Absolutely, that's what I need."

Karen: "Great! And if we can offer you this coverage at a reasonable monthly premium, would you be interested in finalizing this plan?"

Steve: "If it fits within my budget, yes."

Breakdown:
- Karen used tie downs ("right?") to reiterate Steve's primary concerns.
- She presented a tailored solution and painted a picture of the benefits. Karen then used trial closes ("Would that be the kind of security you're seeking?", "Would you be interested in finalizing this plan?") to measure Steve's interest.

In all these scenarios, the sales professionals use tie downs to validate the customer's needs and concerns. Trial closes are then employed to test how close the customer is to making a decision. Both techniques can be powerful tools in a salesperson's arsenal, helping them lead the conversation and gauge the customer's readiness to close the deal.

Don't feel like you need to use the tie downs or trial closes in these scenarios. These are just a few examples of how to build great trainings for you and your team. The key is, you have to do it! Here's my promise. Once you learn how to master this, it'll double your sales volume instantly!

CHAPTER 19

THE TAKEAWAY: PEOPLE WANT WHAT THEY CAN'T HAVE

Human psychology is interesting to me: The more you tell somebody they can't or shouldn't have something, the more they want it.

Don't believe me? Why do you think girls want the disinterested guys? The ones who act like they don't care at all. It's like a drug. They immediately wonder why you don't want them. The insecurity sets in bad. Guys, you know I'm right. The harder you try to get the girl the less they want you. Be honest.

I remember when I was single and there was this stunning girl standing at the bar. I watched guy after guy after guy try to hit on her with these cheesy moves, trying to buy her a drink and most likely some corny ass lines too. She crushed each of their souls by rolling her eyes or turning them down. So a buddy of mine made a bet that I couldn't get her to come over and talk to me. Well, as I'm sure you're aware, I happily accepted.

So I walked up to the bar right next to her. She looked at me, I looked at her and she gave me the "Jesus, not another one" look. LOL. I quickly ordered a vodka soda and 6 shots. When the bartender got done making the drink and shots, I purposely had a hard time picking all the drinks up by myself. She saw me and started laughing. So I looked at her and said, "I'm honored my lack of drink holding skills is what made you smile tonight. LOL. That being said, since it's so funny at my expense, can you PLEASE PLEASE grab some of those shots and help me bring them to my friends?" She replied while laughing, "Sure, I can do that."

We started walking towards the guys and I could see their surprise. When we get to them, I handed them the drinks I had in my hands. Then I grabbed the drinks out of her hand and said, "Guys, this is _____ oh shit sorry didn't even get your name. Sorry." She replied, "Its Amber." I said "Well, thank you, Amber. I appreciate your help. Have a good night," and turned my back to her like our time was over. That move, the "our time is over back turn," was takeaway #1.

She tapped me on the shoulder and said, "That's it? You're just gonna let me walk away?" I said, "I'm not sure I'm the guy for you." (Takeaway #2) She laughed again and said, "Oh really, why's that?" I said, "You tell me," and the conversation went on and I got the girl.

I didn't seem thirsty. I didn't approach her in a way that was overwhelming or aggressive. Then she wanted me because I seemed disinterested in something that everyone else wanted, which in turn, made her want me.

This happens in sales a ton. The thirsty aggressive sales individuals who make prospects feel like they're the target are never as effective as the trained sales pros. If a prospect is hesitant or you feel like the presentation isn't going anywhere, there are a few moves you can do that are extremely effective. These include acting as if you don't want to proceed with the sales process:

- Fold your pitchbook and move it to the side.

- Turn the monitor off that you're using for the presentation.
- Start packing your briefcase.

All of these are body language takeaways when combined with, in a very sincere and serious, yet soft voice, "I'm not sure this is right for you." The key is "soft voice." You have to seem like you're upset that what you're presenting matters to you and it feels as if it doesn't matter to them.

If you do this right, your prospect will usually say, "Wait, hold on," and most of the time ask you to continue while paying way closer attention to what you're saying. They will engage more after this and it's the best opportunity to get them to listen to what you have to say.

Let me sum up what a sales takeaway is in two sentences:

1. People want what they can't have or what you say they shouldn't have.

2. People want what others want.

It's literally one of the strongest ways to close deals when used properly, and equally one of the strongest psychological triggers in the sales process ever.

Before we get into this chapter, I'd like to clarify how a "takeaway" seems to be interpreted in today's sales world. A takeaway is real, is very good when used and taught properly and can be taught in a way that doesn't demean or make a prospect feel less than worthy of doing business with you. Too many ego-based sales individuals today use it incorrectly, thinking they're "closing" someone, never "serving" them, but actually tricking them into buying the product or service they're offering. That is NOT what a takeaway is. It's not a trick or tactic, and ultimately has helped play a huge role, unfortunately, in the negativity having a sales title gets these days. Let's first look at how it's being perceived. If you searched "what is a sales takeaway" online right now, like literally put this book down or pause this audio book, you'd see this: "The sales takeaway is a sales tactic where you take away or disqualify the prospect for what you are trying to sell. The way to use this type of technique is to only use it at a particular time and that would be when the prospect appears to be 'on the fence.'"

So let's break that paragraph down. The first sentence says a few things that have tarnished the sales industry for years that immediately need to be redefined, retaught, or completely eliminated from how we teach others to serve clients.

First, I see two words used side by side that I personally don't like. The words "sales tactic." You shouldn't have to use "sales tactics" when serving prospects. Using a "tactic" is when you're only worried about "selling" prospects. So let's see how Google defines these two words: "A sales tactic is any action you take to put your sales strategy into action. It is how you deliver your message to consumers. For example, creating business brochures or a website and generating leads are tactics. Whereas strategy explains your purpose, tactics show the process you use to move forward."

The Consumer Expenditure Survey, a department that collects information on the buying habits of U.S. consumers through the BLS (Bureau of Labor Statistics), surveyed 2.6 million consumers and has proven that 92.3% of all consumers that participated in the study saw the word "tactic" as slimy and displeasing.

Common synonyms are: scheme, maneuver, stunt, dodge, trick, play, game, and shift, just to name a few. The definition of tactic is an action or strategy carefully planned to achieve a specific end. Another definition is: the art of disposing armed forces in order of battle and of organizing operations, especially during contact with an enemy.

Can you see why I hate the word tactic? I'd also bet you can see how a consumer doesn't like that it's associated with the sales process at all.

As a matter of fact, the actual statistic reads like this: "The Bureau of Labor Statistics have proven that 92.3% of all consumers feel that the word 'tactic' is a less than flattering word associated with the sales industry at any level." Most consumers define a takeaway as a tactic, and the way most sales individuals are using it, they'd be correct. They see it coming anyway! I've been in the sales industry for 30 years and it's been the most fun, lucrative, and intellectually stimulating skill set I've used to scale multiple businesses and still continue to learn and use daily. That being said, selling someone today isn't the same as it was in the early 90s, as it wasn't the same in the 90s as it was in the 60s and 70s. Consumers evolve, get smarter, and have the internet with all the information they need right at their fingertips to google away and see if there's something "not right" about what you're offering.

The takeaway has made its rounds throughout the years as well. In my father's many years in sales, he told me a man's word used to be his bond. Trust was expected. Getting lied to or swindled wasn't as easy and people weren't pitched, they were served. So a takeaway wasn't really needed as much. People did what they said they were going to do.

Then as times got tough, when the economy wasn't the best and sales individuals began to sell to survive, rather than sell to serve, they started embellishing more, lying, and using a takeaway as a tactic to make consumers feel they weren't worthy or couldn't afford their product or service to close deals. Over the years, this has made it very easy for prospects to enter a sales presentation with a bigger and stronger wall built up than they've ever had before and with good reason.

So let's help Make Sales Great Again, redefine the takeaway, and get back to serving consumers rather than concentrating on selling them.

Every time I've taught and helped others apply this principle thoughtfully, intentionally, through integrity-based practices, putting the prospect first always, the exceptional elevation of income was simply a byproduct of doing it right.

In leadership, when sales is taught by amateurs who are more interested in SUPERVISING salespeople instead of actually going out and closing deals themselves, proving how it's done, this has a negative effect on the sales industry. This is a real reason why the sales industry is slipping.

If you're reading this and it's you, you're forgiven if you've made this rookie mistake. It's not your fault. You didn't have this book to help yet. But promise me, yourself, and the people you lead/work with that it stops today.

The bottom 96% of salespeople in any industry concentrate on talking people into buying what they're offering. A "takeaway," when not used properly, almost pushes people away. When you look like you need the sale or want the sale, it's statistically proven that the buy rate is less than one-third as productive than if a consumer understands you're there to serve them, but don't want them to do business with you unless it's the right fit for them. In short, you don't "need" them to work with you, you want them to "want" to.

You should also only want to do business with prospects who are worthy of your time, as you're vying for a spot with them as well. I know what you're thinking. What does that actually mean, Todd? It's simple. When a prospect is in a presentation with you, they have walls up, barriers if you will, that require time, trust, and care to bring down. Why should that be any different with you? The consumer should be fighting for that spot to work with you equally.

It's not every day they get you! It's an interview with one another, an application process, if you will. As you work for the right to do business with them, they should do the same for you. Have your walls up, your barriers. Don't make it so easy to work with you. That's the ultimate takeaway, when done without ego or arrogance. PLEASE, FOR THE LOVE OF GOD, lose the arrogance and ego; it'll work with few and not with most, which will cost you millions!

The best salespeople make a consumer go through a maze to do business with them, jump through hoops, if you will. And guess what? This takeaway works flawlessly. I know I know, it seems completely opposite of what you're trying to do, which is make the sale, but it's how you will make the sale when you're taught this and you utilize this properly.

In today's world, people prejudge instantly during a sales process. During the first words you speak, the first hand you shake, the first pitch sheet or sales tools you use at presentation. Yep, it sucks, but it's very true. You're probably saying, "They don't know me, Todd," and you're right, they don't. People will hate you, judge you, and not believe you during your time together when you are offering anything that has a price tag, whether you like it or not. That's just the facts. They're going to think you're just like every other average, less educated, less integrity-based salesperson in the world today. I know it sucks, I get it, but that's the world that master liars rather than master closers have created. This is another reason we, together, will do what's right, implementing integrity-based practices in this industry as a whole to Make Sales Great Again! How do we break down their wall? By equally forcing their effort to break down ours as well.

We have to prove our willingness to serve, build trust, and have a product that adds value to their lives, yes, but not everyone has the luxury and I mean that LUXURY to work with someone like you either. The consumer will feel that, if proposed as an equal opportunity.

So, let's simplify a takeaway. I'll use my daughters Averigh, Addyson, and Abriella as examples. They're very beautiful, powerful, and individually different young ladies, but when they were kids, one thing they had in common was their stubbornness to eat ONLY when they wanted to eat! I remember I'd put chicken nuggets in front of them that they begged to have for dinner, and then they would eat one bite.

I used to get upset and this is how the convo would go:
The girls: "I want chicken nuggets."
Us: "You promise you're going to eat them all?"
The girls: "Yes."
(We make the nuggets. Then 5 minutes later…)
The girls: "Mommy, Daddy, I'm done."
Us: "You only ate one nugget"
The girls: "I'm not hungry anymore."

Us: "You promised you'd eat them. You're gonna eat them all." (Obviously mad.)

The girls: "No, I'm done!" (Throws tantrum and then parenting styles differ so I'll leave the next move in this example up to you. LOL.)

After a few times of this, a different move had to be made. A takeaway if you will. When I did this, a whole different result came to fruition. Some call it reverse psychology, if you'd like.

The girls: "I want chicken nuggets."

Us: "You got it."

(Then 5 minutes later...)

The girls: "Mommy, Daddy, I'm done."

Us: "You better not eat those chicken nuggets. They're mine."

Suddenly they shove all the chicken nuggets left in their mouth at once.

Isn't it funny how that works? When we want something so bad and they know we want something to happen, it doesn't. BUT, when we act like we don't care or want what they might want, they end up wanting it.

The takeaway is powerful, but again, it should never be sleezy or misleading.

There is a plethora of ways to do a sales takeaway. Let's discuss a few.

YOU CAN EXPRESS DOUBT

Express doubt that the prospect needs what you sell or is the right person to work with or utilize the product or service that you're offering.

You can say something like:

- "I'm not sure you really need what we provide."
- "I'm not sure this is the right time for you to make this move or purchase."

- "I'm not sure you're truly ready for this type of service."
- "I'm not really sure you're going to be able to utilize all the benefits this has to offer."
- "This might do more than you and your company needs, to be honest."
- "I'm honestly not sure we can help you at the same level we've helped others."

These are just a few that plant that seed of doubt in the prospect's mind. When you're a well-trained sales individual, you have NO PROBLEM using the sales takeaway like this. It immediately injects this question into a prospect's mind: "Why?" When "why" is planted, they start wondering more about why you're "not" selling them, since most sales individuals are always trying TO sell them. That curiosity breathes new life into the presentation and allows you to measure their level of interest easily.

Another great option for a takeaway is when a client or prospect doesn't seem too interested in what you're presenting. It's a perfect time to tell the truth! Most salespeople will start spewing more features and benefits, which usually just annoys a prospect. But what if you called them out on it?

Try something like this:

"To be honest, it sounds like you guys have done an amazing job connecting all the pieces in accomplishing your goals. Maybe it doesn't make sense for me to go into much more detail."

This even works when you have that prospect who seemed interested in meeting with you, but changed quickly and seemed very disinterested. Maybe they stopped paying attention or started acting as if anything you're saying doesn't have much value.

Try something like this:

"I'm gonna do something most salespeople wouldn't and be extremely honest here. You seemed pretty interested in the beginning, but after speaking with you for some time now, it seems like you've got a system in place that works for you. Knowing that, the last thing I wanna do is waste your time on something that might be a tad out of your range, since it's a big step from what you're currently working with."

Now I know what you're thinking. You're thinking, "Oof, that's aggressive, Todd!" Well, it can be, if you're not careful how you deliver it. Remember, the delivery of a sales takeaway is equally as important as what you say.

You don't want to offend someone. I know there's probably a few trainers who say it's OK to piss people off; it's just not my cup of tea. And I know for a fact that conversion when people are happy and interested is much higher than when they're pissed off and feel as if they're being called out the wrong way.

TIMING OF THE TAKEAWAY

I've sold a ton of different things in my sales career and have had the luxury of consulting for many different companies over the last 3 decades, teaching when to use the takeaway and the truth is, it depends. You can implement it anywhere, at any time, depending on the prospect's level of interest to meet with you.

A pre-set appointment in the timeshare industry is usually set by offering someone a free gift to meet with you for 60-90 minutes. That's the deal. That's the price they paid to get their gift(s). They're usually not happy, quick to get it over with, and will gladly express to the sales rep their level of discomfort and that they're only there to get what they were promised.

Their walls are up and ready to crush you with so many no's that it can limit someone's excitement to be in that industry quickly.

In this case, a lot of the most successful and well-trained sales individuals use a takeaway the moment after they shake their prospect's hand. Yep, that's right. At the very beginning. Let me give you an example after the representative introduces themselves.

Prospect: *"Listen, Todd, I'm not buying anything today. I don't care what you say or what you're offering, you're wasting your time. Just get this over with so I can get what I was promised."*

Insert Takeaway: *"I understand and hear you loud and clear and completely respect that. Here's the best news. You don't have to buy anything and you're still going to get your gift as promised. This club is only for a select few anyway. So, now I know that you're not gonna buy anything, you may not qualify anyway, so let's just smile, have some fun, make the best of it, and I'll get through this presentation as quickly as possibly for ya, deal?"*

Again, you might say, "That's too aggressive, Todd." I say, it's direct and piques interest. Yeah, I could've schmoozed them and stroked their ego, but I want them to know that I hear them first, release any pressure closes they think might be coming second, that this isn't for everyone third, and finally, that it's something you have to qualify to own. All very true, by the way. Remember, people want something they can't be a part of or what others think they can't be a part of.

The takeaway in this case was from the start. You'll be able to measure their interest levels quickly at the beginning and fine tune how the process of the presentation will go moving forward. This type of takeaway needs to be practiced and presented from a non-ego based, non-arrogant way or you could lose them instantly. All in the delivery.

How about radio stations these days? I was listening to the radio the other day, a song ends and then a big loud voice comes on and goes, "DON'T BUY A CAR TODAY!" Which was weird to hear, because we're usually told to buy something, not be told NOT to buy something. Then the pause ends and he says, "YES, YOU HEARD

ME RIGHT! Don't buy a car today! Wait till Saturday for your $2,500 off sale." It was different. It was a takeaway at the very first sentence, but I guarantee it was one of their most successful radio ads ever.

For those of you in lead generation. Change the verbiage from "For more information" to "Find out if you qualify." I bet a lot of you are thinking that verbiage change isn't a big deal, right? The U.S. Bureau of Labor Statistics has proven that an overwhelming 78% of all Americans wants to know they "qualify" for something offered that requires the need to qualify for.

Remember, like I told you before, people want something they can't have or think they can't have or get.

I have a nationally syndicated podcast called Gutcheck Uncut with my co-host Brandon Biskie. When we first started with zero episodes, we would try and book potential guests on the show. We would never allow them to say, "Let me check my schedule." We'd take control and say, "We can probably squeeze you in on Saturday at noon." We never once alluded to the fact we had a wide-open schedule and that we could do it now if they wanted to, because it seems way too desperate.

It's the same in relationships, isn't it? We all know the "hard to get" ones are the ones we all want! How about when you see they've texted you, but you purposely don't reply back and know it drives them nuts. Maybe if you're an iPhone user and you "leave them on read." LOL. You know what I'm talking about. You purposely wait for them to call you, rather than you call them first. These are all takeaways and we've all done it. If I'm being 100% honest, these dating takeaways are unreal to use in business as well when dealing with a difficult to close prospect. I dare you to try it. You'll thank me later.

The takeaways work. It might be simple psychology. It might be greed. It might be to prove some can have what you or others say or think they can't. There are a ton of theories on "why" they work, but one thing is for sure. They do.

Remember, some may call it a sales "tactic," but in my opinion, it's a sales strategy. Maybe it just sounds better to me. You have to master the takeaway and I end this chapter by giving you three true positions for takeaways.

When they're positive - Interested: They're super interested, but you want to find out how much. Perfect time to use a soft takeaway.

When they're indecisive or neutral - On the Fence: The prospect can't decide. Not sure you're the person to work with or the product or service you're offering is right for them.

When they're negative - Not Interested: Their body language is bad. They're not engaging. Showing no interest in buying what you're selling. Sometimes, not responding at all, which is where a hard takeaway works very well.

Master these three spots in your sales presentation to use this tool. It'll help trigger that psychological aspect of your prospect and help you get them back in the game!

P.S. No, this doesn't work every time. There isn't a sales strategy that does, but mastering the art of sales in all aspects will give you extremely high efficiency, netting you results some never reach. This is one of those strategies you want to know like the back of your hand, and the way to do that is what? You guessed it…. TRAINING! So let's dive into 3 ways to use the "takeaway" using a limited offer approach.

SCENARIO 1: TIMESHARE SALES - "THE LIMITED OFFER"

Context: A couple is at a timeshare presentation at a beautiful resort. The sales representative has just given them a tour and highlighted all the benefits of investing in the timeshare.

Role Play:
- Sales Rep: "I can see you both loved the place! We actually have a limited promotion where we're offering a 10% discount for any commitments made today. However, I just got word this morning that there are only two slots left for this offer."

- Couple: "Well, we really like it, but we need to think it over and discuss it with our family."
- Sales Rep: "I completely understand. However, given the limited nature of this offer, it's unlikely it will still be available after today. It's a rare opportunity, especially for such a prime location."

Breakdown:
- Use the scarcity principle to encourage immediate action.
- Focus on the benefits the customers showed interest in during the tour.
- Be understanding and patient, but also highlight the urgency.

SCENARIO 2: PROPERTY MANAGEMENT - "SWITCHING COSTS"

Context: A property owner with multiple properties is considering hiring a property management company. They are meeting with a representative from a property management firm.

Role Play:
- Property Manager: "You've managed your properties on your own for so long. May I ask what's prompting you to consider a property management company now?"
- Property Owner: "I'm finding it harder to manage all the responsibilities. But I'm concerned about the costs of hiring a company like yours."
- Property Manager: "It's a valid concern. However, think about the time and stress you'll save, not to mention potential costly mistakes or vacancies. By not taking on a trusted property management company, there might be a lot of unseen costs. And for this month only, we're offering a discount for new clients like you."

Breakdown:
- Understand the customer's pain points and challenges.

- Highlight the potential "costs" of not using the service, both financial and emotional.
- Provide an immediate incentive to reduce the perceived barrier to entry.

SCENARIO 3: COMMERCIAL REAL ESTATE - "THE UPCOMING DEVELOPMENT"

Context: A business owner is considering leasing a commercial space for expansion. The real estate agent knows about an upcoming development that could increase the value of properties in the area.

Role Play:
- Real Estate Agent: "This space seems perfect for your requirements. Plus, there's an upcoming development in this area – a new transit hub that will make this spot even more desirable and accessible."
- Business Owner: "The location is good, but the rent is at the higher end of my budget."
- Real Estate Agent: "I understand your concern. But with the new development, the commercial real estate value here is expected to skyrocket. Locking in a lease now could save you significantly in the long run, given the potential rise in rents in the near future."

Breakdown:
- Provide valuable insights or information the customer might not be aware of.
- Emphasize the long-term benefits and potential savings.
- Address budget concerns by highlighting the potential ROI and the cost of waiting.

In each scenario, the "takeaway" approach is applied by presenting limited offers, highlighting potential unseen costs, or offering unique insights. This creates urgency and provides additional value, nudging the customer towards a positive decision. Notice I said "nudging," not PUSHING!

The takeaway isn't to make people feel less of themselves, it's to simply move along the sales process, nudging them to make a decision faster ONLY if what you're offering adds value to their lives.

I'd suggest you get with a friend or your sales team and list the top 5 takeaways you use for your business. Dial them in, train on them and you'll, simply put, make WAY more sales!

CHAPTER 20

OBJECTIONS: BLOCK FIRST, HANDLE LATER

One of the hardest things to master in a sales presentation is blocking and handling objections. When I was coming up in the sales world, I realized that ego got in the way of so many talented sales individual's growth. They were afraid of looking stupid to their colleagues and their prospects. No, I don't want to look like I don't know what I'm talking about either, but the way you learn is through trial and error. In this chapter I want to eliminate as much of that as possible for you guys. I want to teach you the right way to block and handle objections, once again with honesty and integrity at the forefront.

What do most people think of salespeople? Be honest. They think we're all fast talkers only concerned about getting their money and the unfortunate truth is that recently, in today's world, they'd be right. It's one of the main reasons I titled this book *The Ultimate Sales Bible*, and a big reason the sales industry has become so slimy is because of how sales individuals handle objections.

There's been a ton of data and studies done on this and we're going to dive into it all in this chapter. Let's talk about "Handling Objections" and then we'll get into "Blocking Objections."

Most prospects will object for a few different reasons:

1. They don't believe in you or the product or service you're offering.

2. They don't see the value in the cost or in the product or service as a whole.

3. They might see the value, but they want to negotiate cost.

What you don't realize is that all three of these points give you the best opportunity to keep the sales process and conversation moving in the right direction. Let's be honest here. You, me, the prospect and/or business wants you to either offer and prove a solution to their problem or provide something of value they believe will add value to themselves or the company. They don't care how good of a talker you are. Just don't lie; instead, let the honesty behind what you're offering prove to them why they need it.

When handling objections you need to follow these steps:

STEP 1: PAUSE

Take longer than most. This isn't the time to be a fast talker. Most salespeople start running their mouth the minute they hear an objection or no. It's important to think before you speak and assess the situation.

STEP 2: SLOW DOWN

Although you think this may be the same thing as pausing, it isn't. As stated in step one, MOST salespeople actually increase their speed of talking, getting nervous that they're going to lose the sale. Harvard Law did a study that when an objection arises in a sales presentation, the salesperson increased their speed of talking to 188 words per minute, from the average speed while presenting of 167 words per minute.

When you stay calm, you earn respect. When they see that their objection doesn't faze you, it proves your professionalism and willingness to understand their concerns. Speaking slower, being sincere, showing you care, but with authority, will create the "I'm here to serve, but I know my shit" mutual respect moving forward.

STEP 3: SHUT UP AND LISTEN

TALK LESS! Most untrained salespeople, when presented with an objection from their prospect, will start rambling about reasons why they should want what you're offering. A sales study done by Cornell University that tested 51,238 sales presentations proved that when a salesperson gets an objection, 51% of salespeople cut the buyer off by trying to handle the objection before the buyer is done speaking. The study also showed that the salespeople who instantly responded without pause spoke for an average of 23.7 seconds before letting their prospect explain more about why they feel the way they do. THIS IS CRAZY!

If you just shut up and listen, they will guide you to what's most important to them, which will guide you to the sale.

STEP 4: ASK A QUESTION WHEN AN OBJECTION ARISES

I'll go into more detail throughout this chapter, but historically, multiple studies show that when a prospect surfaces an objection, asking them a question proves you hear them and care enough to find out the root of why they feel the way they do.

For instance:

Prospect: *"I don't think this is a good fit for me."*

Salesperson: *"Just so I can understand fully, when you say it's not a good fit for me, what do you mean?"*

One of the main studies on this was done by the U.S. Bureau of Labor Statistics, which showed that less than 11% of all sales professionals counter an objection with a question, but the ones who do have a 71% higher conversion rate. WOW! Now that's proven results!

Finally,

STEP 5: MAKE SURE THEY KNOW YOU KNOW AND CARE

People want to be heard. They want to feel understood. They want to know that you know why they feel the way they do.

Examples:

"I get it completely, so here's my thoughts _____."

"That makes complete sense, so let me make sure I understand you fully. What you're saying is _____."

"I understand exactly how you feel. Other people I've spoken to have felt the same way, so what you're saying is _____(insert objection)_____. So what if I told you I had a solution for that?"

These skills separate top sales representatives from mediocre ones. One of the biggest misconceptions about objections is that most think it's the reason most sales don't close, which is true if not trained properly, but I'm going to change your way of thinking that an objection is the reason you "lost" a sale, to being excited when you or the prospect surfaces them and how to use them to help transition to the close.

What the statistics show is that the top 10% of the best sales individuals in the world RESPOND to objections by clarifying with questions of their own, when average performers don't do it near as often. Most lower performing sales representatives are just less trained on why it's important to clarify and how to do it through asking the right questions. That's the first step in a nutshell. Clarify by asking questions.

Most clients surface a concern (objection) and then the salesperson goes on a rant of high-speed chatter that reeks of insecurity, without actually clarifying what the customer's true concern was. This does a few things. Most of the time it will raise the level of tension. They know you want the sale and you know they know that. Let's call it what it is. Prospects are not only smarter, but they have information at the tip of their fingers, just by hopping on Google to see if what you're saying is true. A lot of salespeople are scared of that when not prepared.

When a customer has a valid concern, just remember this rule. The faster and more you talk, the faster you lose the sale.

There's a concept called mirroring that a ton of sales gurus claim to have created. Now, I can't tell you who did, but I can tell you it wasn't me. This process is extremely effective and probably the least talked about sales tools and one of the most underrated ones as well. I personally believe mastering this will absolutely take your sales skills to the next level!

Mirroring is just repeating a few words of the buyer's objection with an upward tonality/inflection (question tone) that gets them to tell you more or elaborate on their objection, such as:

Buyer: "The price seems way too high for me to do business with you."

Salesperson: "The price is too high?"

Now this sounds easy and it is, but the hardest part for most salespeople is the move after. The minute you ask the mirroring question back, pause and let them explain what they mean. Don't keep going. Don't keep talking. Don't try to use some fancy response. Just shut up and listen, letting them explain.

YOU MUST PAUSE, otherwise the buyer won't respond. Literally count to three, and by then they will respond. I know this is hard for you sales talkers, but being quiet is another skill that'll separate you from the pack and help you rise to the top. I talk about mirroring more in depth in another chapter, but for objection handling it's very effective.

Oh, and since we're on the topic of asking questions, which is in another chapter, let me remind you never to ask the question, "Why?" It doesn't clarify anything, except the validity of the buyer's objection. It more often than not makes the buyer feel like their objection doesn't matter to you and puts them in a defensive mode. Asking "clarifying questions" is the only route for any sales professional.

Try replacing "why" with:

"Can you help me understand what's causing that concern?"

First, I'm asking if they can help me. Almost as if I don't know what they mean with their objection, whether I do or not. It's better to fully understand what the heart of the objection is. When you say it this way, you're almost asking them to teach you and it allows them to be in more of a control status. It also shows you care about what matters to them. You can tailor this to any situation, but I'm sure you get what I mean.

There are also several layers to objections:

- Surface level
- Symptom
- Getting Closer
- Root Cause

Your job as a sales professional is to get to the root cause. Some objections are smoke screens, some are to throw you off your game, some are to protect the buyer's wall because they know they're buyers, and some are actually real. Every salesperson should treat them all as if they are real concerns. Validate the sincerity and truth behind each and follow this first step, which will get you to the root cause of their concerns.

The second step to handling objections is truly validating their concerns. Let me be very clear here, THEY MUST KNOW YOU CARE! Most people just want to be heard. Just shutting up and listening to someone will get them to do business with you. You don't have to know shit about the sales process. For example, I was brand new in the timeshare industry many many years ago. Now I knew about sales, but what I didn't know was ANYTHING about the product and even when you learn in training, you get nervous your first time presenting and forget it all anyway. LOL. I closed the first 8 opportunities out of training class and when asked how I was doing it, my response was, "I don't know." My average tour was 4 hours, which in the timeshare business is about 3 hours longer than what it was supposed to be. Now that was then, but many many years later I realized why I broke every record in that industry. Now I teach people to do the same thing I did when I first started and that was just this: get to know your prospect.

Crazy, I know, right! All I did was have a conversation with them and listened. I rarely even got to pitching because we would spend most of the time talking about them. I remember I'd be 3 hours in and I hadn't even mentioned a word about the product I was selling yet. LOL. By the time I did, the client had such a different experience with me, meaning I didn't just try to pitch them the entire time, that deals would fall down as they trusted me. They knew I truly listened to what mattered most to them.

My point is this in reference to handling objections, most people just want to be heard. Most people are denied the gift of being understood. Showing them you understand them will accelerate trust and it will validate to your buyer that you truly care. Believe it or not, most people just want to be understood by another human being and as crazy as that sounds, it's directly related to handling objections.

It's rare to get that principle right, but it's easier than you think just by using this phrase:

> "That's a really valid concern. Based on what you just said it seems like _____ (insert the clarification of their objection)."

I'm not gonna lie. You get this phrase down, it's literally the super empathy tool jacked on steroids that will build rapport like you've never seen before.

The next thing you need to do is ISOLATE THE OBJECTION and its authenticity.

There are a ton of objections a prospect will bring up that aren't real at all. There are multiple reasons why they do, and for some I don't blame them at all.

Do you know that you can google what to say to get out of a sales presentation in any industry? I'm not kidding. The dishonest people who lie to prospects in many different industries have led to a backlash of YouTube videos, blogs, and articles that teach consumers how to surface an objection that most salespeople won't be able to handle, and that will get them out of any presentation. Crazy, right? I don't think so. The dishonest liars, not the sale professionals of the world, made it happen. I feel bad for those swindled by those types of individuals and it's THE MAIN REASON I created Make Sales Great Again as a consulting company and THE MAIN REASON I wrote this book. What I teach has sharpened the skills of the elite who serve prospects at a high empathetic level by doing what's right, hopefully fading out the riffraff who have unfortunately scaled over the last decade.

Isolating the real objection is important. You need to determine what's true and the objection that needs a solution in order to do business with your prospect.

I'm going to give you the easiest way to handle smoke screen objections.

Example:

Prospect: *"This is way too expensive for me."*

Me: *"So you're saying if this made sense financially to you, we can sign the deal?"*

Most salespeople wouldn't respond this way. They'd start spewing the features and benefits of their product, trying to convince the prospect why they should pay what the price is. WRONG! Hint: price is only an objection if they don't see the value in what you're offering.

When you start running your mouth, the prospect wall you've been trying to break down just rises even higher and higher. As a matter of fact, there are people who love to watch salespeople squirm. They'll do things like smirk when they give you an objection, or say things like, "I know what you're trying to do here and it's not going to work," just to get you agitated. Handling objections has many mental levels on both sides as well. But here's the good news: the good, honest, integrity-based sales leaders of the world rarely have this problem because the prospect can feel it.

Here's a good follow up to the first two steps of the handling objection process. When isolating, you need to make sure that objection is the decision-making objection and is the only one.

I teach my students to say something like this:

"If we can figure out a way to solve that completely... what other concerns or obstacles would we have to address before doing business together?"

Once again, you can customize and tailor the verbiage to your specific industry. It works with them all, but how you present this and the words you use is different from one sales professional to another. You don't have to use the exact words I do, but at least this gives you an understanding of isolating questions.

A lot of undertrained salespeople and trainers will read or listen to this and say, "You're opening the door for them to give you another objection. Don't do that." To whomever is reading or listening to this book, if you are being taught by anyone who tells you NOT TO surface an objection, bring it up before they do, or not to mention something that might keep you from closing the deal...... RUN AS FAST AS YOU CAN!

The top-tier sales professionals of the world aren't afraid of objections. As a matter of fact, they can't wait to surface them, so they can use the real information to get to the close sooner. It's exciting when you're equipped with the proper process in handling objections.

You must determine what is truly holding them back from doing business with you. When you ask questions like we just went over, if they bring up more than the objection they spoke of, more than likely, that first objection isn't the reason they're not moving forward. Not always, but it happens often.

Now if they don't have any other concerns or obstacles, then you've isolated the objection. Do you see what I mean now about surfacing the objections as quickly as possible? Don't be afraid. Because if you don't ask, "What other concerns or obstacles would we have to address before doing business together?" then you're giving them a way out on the back of the sale that the professionals never get.

Once you've isolated the objection(s), step four is gaining permission to overcome them or to create a solution to their concerns. Oh, and do me a favor. DO NOT SAY "Can I make a suggestion?" This question triggers massive amounts of defensiveness due to the way untrained sales individuals present it. It's almost like you're saying you're smarter than they are. So, can I make a suggestion? LOL. I'm kidding. Just had to mess with you for a second.

I use: "Can I bounce a few thoughts off you?" It's less threatening and the buyers are more receptive to a solution you're about to present.

There are 5 types of objections:

1. SMOKE SCREEN

a. This objection is the easiest, but finding the real issue comes by simply using what we went over already, which is: "If we can figure out a way to solve that completely… what other concerns or obstacles would we have to address before doing business together?"

2. CONCERNS

a. This is usually an emotional concern that a buyer has before they say yes. They're almost sold, but they just want to clarify a few things before they move forward. For instance, let's say you're selling a client a pool and they love the design and everything you've offered. Their only concern is the time it's going to take to get a permit. You were honest about a realistic time frame, as you should be, and told them the city was backed up. So, the solution would be to use a customer testimonial or refer them to someone you've built for so they can verify how good you were keeping in touch with the timeline and that you fully understand time is a priority to them.

The idea is to just prove to them through real, authentic proof that their concern is unfounded. Now, if their concern is something that is a real concern you don't have a solution for, be honest and tell them that. Don't lie. Don't bullshit your way through it.

You will get a ton of business referrals from people you may not be the right fit for, by just telling the truth. I've built my business on not being the right fit for some people and telling them I wasn't. Sounds weird, right? It's the right thing to do for one, but two, it'll spread the word about how honest you are which will take your referral game to another level.

3. REAL OBJECTIONS

I want you to listen to this word carefully called "reframe." Let me define it for you.

Reframe: *An insight that changes how your customer thinks and feels about an objection, problem, or opportunity.*

It helps your prospect see things through a new angle. Here's an example:

FRAME - CLIENT: *"I'd rather not buy your sales training right now because it's the end of the year, which is the worst time to train due to year-end close outs."*

REFRAME - YOU: *"The lessons and techniques your team will learn are going to increase efficiency on a much higher level. It's important to get them trained, adding volume to the 4th quarter, and being fully trained is imperative before the new year begins. Right now is the time to schedule you in before the year end."*

I reframed the objection. I added enough value so the timing was perfect to get us in before the end of the 4th quarter. I spoke of efficiency and money, both of which are real and factual ways to reframe the objection.

There are ways to determine a chance to reframe an objection:
Is the objection:

- A problem that can be turned into an opportunity?
- A weakness that can be turned into a strength?

- A timing issue that can be turned into the right time?

A good way to start reframing objections is to make a list of the most common objections you get and put them through this process, determining how to reframe them, and then role play daily with the reframed solutions.

4. SPECIFIC CONDITIONS

These really aren't objections. They're just problems that need to be solved and sometimes you can't solve them. For instance, say you're selling real estate and the home you're showing has 2 bedrooms, but the client, who loves the house and said they were originally OK with 2 bedrooms, now wants you to add a third bedroom or the deal is off. This would be considered a "specific condition."

There are only a few solutions:

1. Build another bedroom, which we all know most likely won't happen.
2. Find another home with 3 bedrooms in another area.

Or the solution I like the most—be honest with them and say something like this:

"So you need a third bedroom?"

(pause 3 second mirroring method)
If they say yes, then reply with this:

"I understand. You've told me that the home, the lot, and the area are a perfect fit for what you were looking for and that originally you only needed two bedrooms, right?"

"Great. Well, we can do one of two things. 1. I'd be happy to serve you and find a 3-bedroom home in this area but they might not meet your original standards and it would definitely take more time or 2. this home checked off all your boxes and you said its *location is perfect, right? So why don't we see what an addition would cost since the lot has room for it and see if I can negotiate a better deal on your behalf to help with the cost of the addition, so we don't lose this dream location. From what you've told me, I think we can both agree that would be an acceptable solution, don't you?"*

You're not always going to have a perfect solution for a prospect, but again, just be honest with the real solutions you have. If you can make the deal work serving your prospect, then great. But if you can't make the deal work, be honest and guide them to someone who can.

Or how about if they don't have the cash to do business with you. You can't make cash appear, but you can start with something they can afford. This would also be a condition. Conditions, like concerns, are usually not true objections. They're sold on what you're offering with a few tweaks needed.

5. COMPLACENCY – THE HARDEST SELLING PROBLEM FOR MOST TO OVERCOME

Notice I didn't say this is an objection, because it's really not, but it can potentially stop someone from moving forward with you.

Most of the time this is someone who just doesn't do business on the same day. They are the "think about it" clients or the ones who need to do their research on you and the product first.

The reason I like talking about "complacency" is because it ties directly into blocking objections. You correct this early in the sales process. High-end sales professionals can easily determine this type of prospect pretty quickly, and only time will allow you to do that. I don't mean pre-judge at all. I mean through proper discovery questions early on.

Let's get into the second part of this chapter, BLOCKING OBJECTIONS, which is one of my favorite parts of training salespeople. This skill is about as powerful as it gets. The strongest top tier and most successful sales individuals in the world have this process mastered and use it every time they speak. In general conversation and when trying to close a deal.

Blocking objections is more valuable than handling objections. Say this with me: "If they speak it, they own it." When they speak it, they own their objection and it's way harder to overcome that objection. They're basically protective of it and if you try to convince them otherwise, the presentation can become combative or argumentative because you're trying to overcome or solve their problem and they're defending why they said what they feel to be true or the reason why they won't do business with you. They will literally make stuff up just to be right. But if you bring it up, you own it! The prospect is more likely to listen to the solution you're offering and more open to conversation about it. Less defense and more listening to understand. Knowing and understanding the mindset of your prospect is the first step in mastering the art of blocking.

Here's my promise to you. If you truly dig deep and learn this skill, it'll not only increase efficiency on all levels, but it will help your prospects make easier, educated decisions that will trim down your presentation time.

When you're prepared to handle any objection at any time, that's another great skill, but most salespeople make the mistake of waiting until the prospect brings the objection up, which leads to a longer presentation. They're playing defense and now you have to start "convincing" them why what you're offering is the solution to their problem. Blocking can eliminate that completely.

Here's a tip before we get into the steps of blocking objections. Most sales professionals know what the top 5 objections are when presenting their offer to a client. Knowing how to handle them is important but knowing how to surface them and present a solution, proving to them your solution works, then asking them the right questions in order to receive a response supporting your solution, will have them tying down themselves and eliminate that objection from popping up on the back end.

Get those top 5 objections and then role play using this technique on how to handle them at the beginning of this chapter and then know how to block them, which we will learn now.

There are a few steps to blocking objections. You first have to surface the objection, meaning you bring it up before they do, so you own it. Then you have to present a solution. Then you have to prove to them your solution will solve their problem and then, as stated above, tie them down on that solution by asking questions so the objection doesn't resurface.

Let me be clear, when I say, "tie them down," I don't mean go for the jugular. LOL. I don't mean close the deal. I mean that your prospect has full clarity on what you've suggested and agrees, so you can continue with the presentation. Answer all questions and do not move past what you've surfaced until they agree that this is no longer a problem for them.

Before we break down the steps of blocking, I just want to give you a piece of advice. DO NOT USE THIS SALES TOOL unless you are fully confident in your ability to block an objection. I say this because if you try and don't know what you're doing, you'll lose the opportunity with your prospect almost instantly. It can backfire if you don't master what you're surfacing.

Let's talk about step 1 & 2, *How to Surface the Objection & Offer a Solution:*

Surfacing an objection that you know is a common objection in your field builds trust and confidence that you're the right person to do business with. When I go to buy something and a sales professional surfaces an objection I was already thinking about, I know that they are in the higher standards in sales and have been trained properly. Now I know that because I'm a sales trainer, but what if you weren't?

The U.S. Bureau of Labor Statistics says that surfacing an objection to a client offers a 57% increase in the client trusting your knowledge as a salesperson in a third of the time it would take if you didn't surface the objection. A study by Harvard University also proved that asking for permission to solve a problem or offer a solution during a sales presentation reduces resistance from your prospect, shows that you respect their authority in their role, and will yield a much higher chance of them allowing you to move forward with your solution, instead of just diving in without asking for their permission to do so.

WOW! I'm good with numbers, but even if I wasn't, I'll take faster trust building and faster credibility in my field any day of the week. What does this really mean? It means they're just more impressed with your knowledge and professionalism, proving you're the most likely candidate to solve the problems.

Here's an example of how to surface an objection:

Sales Rep: *"Mr. Prospect, most of our clients are under the assumption that our _____ (insert product or service) is difficult to use and I can understand that if it wasn't presented properly. But since I have the luxury of your time, I'd like to show you why that's just not the case and let you be the judge, if you'd give me an opportunity to do so."*

Most of the time, if you've framed the surfacing properly, meaning 99% of the time, the prospect will allow you to show them how it's not difficult to use. You just surfaced the objection and offered a solution.

So let's talk about that for a moment. I know, since I've trained myself on how to block and surface the top 5 objections in my field, that this is a common problem or objection that gets in the way of transitioning to the close. Surfacing this objection and following the next steps in the chapter will give me a high probability of this objection not re-surfacing, blocking me from earning their business on the back end.

Now most of you reading or listening to this book are probably thinking that it's better to not surface this objection, as it might not even come up. But what if I were able to prove to you that knowing it's one of the top 5 reasons people don't do business with you, I'm sure you'd like to at least hear how I can offer a solution that will immediately impact your efficiency in a positive way, right?

Yep, I just surfaced something most sales individuals say to me when I'm training on how to block objections. I spoke it, which means I own it, I offered a solution, and you're more open to listening to what I have to say now, right? I earned your permission, if you're still reading or listening to my book and now, I'll demonstrate how this is one of the best tools to learn in your sales career.

Surfacing objections is probably the most undertrained and undervalued sales skill in the world today.

Robert Graves said, "A genius not only diagnoses the situation, but supplies the answers."

Top salespeople can anticipate objections. They know what's going to come up before it does. When you understand the most common objections in the sales world, you can handle them before they're brought up. This creates massive credibility and trust that you're the person a prospect wants to do business with. It clarifies that you understand the most common concerns of the consumer. That is a valuable trait for a salesperson to have. Most salespeople don't know how to create that trust or are afraid to try because of how the customer may reply.

Are you ready for a shocking statistic? According to a Harvard study of over 36,000 sales presentations, 94% of the objections came down to these top 7:

1. "NOT INTERESTED" OR "I DON'T NEED IT"

This is usually due to lack of value or lack of interest that the client or prospect sees in the product or service you're offering. They're basically telling you that this isn't for them, not the right fit, won't work for them based on the information you've presented.

Ask some open-ended short questions to better evaluate the client's needs. This objection is an opportunity to give more information about what your product or service offers, which will in turn get you information that's imperative for them to consider doing business with you.

Responses:

A. *"I completely understand. Our product or service isn't for everyone, but if you don't mind me asking… why is it not for you? Just so I can learn and make it better next time I run into someone who feels the way you do."*

A couple of things that are important to understand here. First, you're confirming and acknowledging how they feel. Second, you're asking a question seeking their advice on why what you're offering doesn't create need for them. By them responding, they'll feel as if they're doing you a service (which they are whether the sale goes down or not) which when they explain why there's no need, you can fine tune value to their specific needs to create urgency to do business with you.

B. *"A lot of people felt the same way at first, until I dove deep into how I can help them. What matters most to you when looking for a product or service like this?"*

Most of the time, the "I don't need it" doesn't mean they don't need it. It means they don't have enough information on what you're offering them can do for them. This response confirms that you've heard them, but then guides them to a place of releasing information that will help you find out what their most important "needs" are, so you switch the "I don't need it," to "now I'm curious." When they become curious, it's amazing to feel that you've revived your prospect's interest in working with you.

C. "I get it, I really do. How about this. Give me 10 minutes to understand your needs fully and if what I'm offering doesn't make sense for us to do business together, I'll tell you first. That being said, if what I'm offering does add value to you or your business, I think we both agree it was worth the time, right?"

Again, confirmation is key. When you offer something like this statement with sincerity, most people will give you the time to prove to them how you can either solve their problem or add tremendous value to them or their business. It's only 10 minutes, right? But be prepared to produce value in whatever time frame you get them to agree on. This type of value add creates long-lasting business relationships for years to come.

You have to keep in mind that when people say the words "I don't need it" or "I'm not interested," it's usually because you as the salesperson haven't or didn't build enough value for them to be interested in doing business with you. It doesn't mean that what you're offering doesn't fit their needs. Don't get frustrated. Ask intelligent questions, find out what matters most to your prospect, and then get the buy in from them to allow you to prove why what you're offering makes sense for their needs.

2. "IT'S TOO EXPENSIVE" (LACK OF BUDGET)

This was the most common objection from the 2022 Harvard sales objection study. The study showed that purchases having even a minimum level of financial risk tend to be the easiest opportunity for a client or prospect to close up, raise sales resistance, and lean towards not working with you. This is VALUE on all levels.

Many sales trainers say that price should never be an objection if the value is presented properly. I mean, look, that sounds good, but it's just not true. There are plenty of things I wanted to do because I knew the value was there, but financially I just couldn't afford it.

For example, I wanted to market my brand nationwide and run ads to build my brand. After reaching out to several marketing firms and realizing "cost," I determined that I couldn't afford that level of marketing. So how we define "too expensive" is completely based on the person's capacity to pay. What's expensive for one isn't always expensive for another.

The ultimate truth: PRICE DOES MATTER. Building value is CRUCIAL, but all of the so-called sales gurus that say price should never be an objection are wrong. Studies prove that. Now it's just understanding what's NOT too expensive for your client or prospect and build value from that. This means building your presentation to what's valuable to them, where it substantially reduces risk to them, not you.

When you do this, you start to show them how the solution you're presenting adds massive value, based on the dollars they have available to spend.

Be committed to listening when you ask the questions that lead to giving you the proper information that SERVES THEM, not you.

When a prospect says, "It's too expensive," you need to find out what they mean by that. Are they comparing you to a competitor? If so, you need to find out the details of the other product or service so you're comparing something similar, rather than something that's completely different that could be causing the cost difference.

Here are some common responses to this objection you can learn from and make your own. Remember, what you learn should never be scripted. Teach yourself to respond the way you would. So make these you! They need to sound like you and be extremely natural in the delivery.

Responses:

A. "I completely get it. The products that add the most value, the best products, are usually more expensive."

This just confirms you stand strong on what you're offering. We'll get into negotiation later, but make sure they know that you're passionate about the value of what you're presenting.

B. "When you say expensive, how are you coming to that conclusion?"

You're simply getting your prospect to explain in detail why they believe what you're offering is "too expensive." You'll learn how they think and what triggers them to believe this. This is common when they hear the price for the first time.

C. "How much will it cost to do nothing?"

This is a power response and it can't come off cocky. You have to be sincere in your tonality, so when you ask this question, it makes them truly think.

D. "Is it a cash flow issue or is it a budget issue?"

The two are NOT the same. Budget usually means they want a discount or are looking for a cheaper overall route, which in most cases does NOT mean better. Cash flow issues are normally tied directly to a payment term. Once you find this out, you can usually solve the price objection by creating a monetary solution to their specific needs.

E. "Let's say money wasn't an issue. How do you think our product or service would solve your problem?"

This an intentional question that makes your prospect start targeting specifics in the value on what your product or service can offer them. Remember, when they speak it, they own it. This is a great question that leads back to value, which in turn can create buying motives they speak, that they themselves will eliminate this objection. You just sit back and watch the magic happen.

F. "I completely respect that, but if you were to break down what this product will do for you in the short and long term, how much value do you think it would add by month, quarter, and year?"

Another power question. Note, do NOT ask this question unless you can personally show them the savings over the month, quarter, and year. When you ask this question, you're getting their insight and thoughts on the value they believe your product or service will add to them personally or business-wise. After they reply, use this information to guide them on what's most important to them.

G. "How soon would you need to see an ROI on this, realistically? And please don't tell me in a week (laugh) but realistically."

Two things here. One, I'm asking them to be "realistic" on a time frame and, two, I've suggested a time frame that's NOT realistic, to bring some humor to the objection, but most importantly to make them give me a real answer on when they'd expect to get an ROI on their investment in your product or service. This question gives you a better idea of how to navigate what you're offering them to get them into that time frame, which will help you get their buy in the long term.

H. "You think it costs too much?"

Notice all the responses are questions. When you ask someone this question, most of the time they start telling you "why" it's too expensive. This is an exceptional way to get down to the reasons they feel the way they do. Confirm them. Address them and then use your new knowledge, combined with what you're offering to get your prospect to fully understand why it's a good idea for them to do business with you.

I. "Is it the value you don't see?"

Here's the thing. People buy what they desire or see the value in. They'll figure out how to pay for something when they want it bad enough. For instance, if you wanted a Rolls Royce SUV and you knew the price was $500k, most people can't afford it, so they don't even try to figure out how to find the money even though they want it bad enough. Now, let's say the EXACT SAME (nothing wrong with it) identical Rolls Royce, a billionaire was selling for $40k because he wants others to get a taste of the luxury lifestyle, how FAST would someone find the money, whether they had it or not? It's the INSTANT DESIRE based on a cost they can attain.

If they don't see the value, you'll find out why, which will give you an opportunity and knowledge to guide them to the close. Getting information and understanding why they feel the way they do is extremely important.

J. "What's 'too expensive?'"

This is another power question that will lead to them spewing why your product or service is too expensive, so be ready for that. BUT the good news is, they will explain their meaning of expensive.

K. Pure Silence

The first person to speak loses. In some cases, the prospect will almost feel obligated to explain why they feel the way they do when you say nothing after their objection.

There are plenty of other responses, but these are just a few.

3. "I HAVE TO THINK ABOUT IT."

Every sales professional in the world would rather hear an absolute stone-cold NO, instead of hearing, "I have to think about it." Believe me. This objection, stall tactic, excuse, whatever you believe it to be, is simply due to how bad indecision has set in in the world today. People just can't make a choice. They either don't have the money, don't want to hurt your feelings, want to do their own research, or need to consult someone else because they aren't the decision maker.

Let's be honest, there are plenty of studies that prove more than 85% of the people who say they need to "think about it" don't go home and think about anything at all other than what's for dinner that night.

Most of the time this is a stalling tactic, but it can mean that they truly just aren't sure if what you're offering is for them. It could also mean that they want to see competitors' pricing to consider other options. It could also mean they aren't comfortable in a buying conversation or sales atmosphere, or it could mean they're just happy where they're at.

To me, it usually means there are unanswered questions or concerns the potential prospect has before they move forward, ultimately guiding them to the "think about it" objection.

You have to be conscious of a prospect's needs. Usually during the sales presentation, the salesperson talks right past a crucial moment that could've led to the close, but they either didn't ask the right question or shut up enough for their potential client to give them the proper information about what's important to them. Long story short, they're just not sold on you or the product or service you're offering.

If the client sees that there's enormous value and they clearly see the return on their investment, this objection won't come up.

One of the easiest ways to make sure this objection doesn't arise is to clearly diagnose what's important to the prospect and be thorough on what you're pitching offers to them so they see the ROI (return on their investment) fully. That's the key.

I'm gonna tell you a little secret. "I need to think about it" isn't a real objection to begin with, anyway. It's a smoke screen, as we spoke about earlier. It's just something that takes the place of the true objection that they either don't want to tell you or haven't surfaced yet.

Most of the time, this smoke screen is directly related to cost. As a matter of fact, the U.S. Bureau of Labor Statistics said this: when a prospect says "I need to think about it," cost was determined to be the true underlying factor that guided them one way or another.

What does this tell us? THE MONEY MATTERS! Get better at asking questions that will allow them to see the value, that will in turn eliminate this smoke screen so the ROI is clear, concise, and direct.

One of the best ways to get rid of this altogether is being very clear on what it will cost a prospect NOT to do business with you today. When they understand the loss that accompanies inaction, when you've listened and confirmed their concerns and offered solutions to their pain points, it usually solves this issue.

There are several ways to reduce the number of times you hear this, by surfacing the most common reasons people would respond with "I need to think about it," and mastering how to determine what matters most to them and using that information to create the urgency they need to move ahead.

Responses:

A. "I get it and respect it. A lot of people feel the same way. Knowing that the likelihood of you doing business with me today is slim, what specifically is it about what I'm offering that you need to think about, so I can be prepared next time we speak?"

This is a real easy way to act as if the sales presentation is concluded, and in some cases it will be, but for MANY sales pros this just re-opens the opportunity to do business today. The pressure of "having to do business with you right now" goes aways completely or reduces significantly. This allows your prospect to open up more. If presented properly, you can get down to the exact reason why they don't want to do business today and give yourself the best chance to address their concern and still close the deal today!

B. "Which part do you need to think about?"

Although direct, it's a very good question to ask when you hear this stall tactic. You can diagnose what the problem is and prove how you can solve this problem now and there's nothing left to think about. Most of the time you end up finding out what the real objection is by asking this question and the majority of the time, the objection, the real one, has nothing to do with thinking about anything.

C. "I know you said you need to think about it, so I'm assuming there's something you're unsure of and that's OK. But what about this product or service do you like and how can you see it impacting you or your company is a positive way?"

This is a very strategic confirmation and question. You're allowing them to bring up what they love about what you're offering, which you can use to redirect their positives into what their main concerns are with something like this:

"That's awesome. Well, I'm definitely glad you see so much value, so let's focus on what you don't see value in now. What specifically is holding you back? And it's completely OK that we most likely won't do business today, but what matters to you, matters to me. So what is it?"

This again is a smooth transition from a positive to determining what's stopping them from doing business with you. The REAL objection. Don't let this stall tactic stall you. They want to do business with you; they just need you to guide them to know that.

D. "Usually when someone says they need to 'think about it,' one of three things is going on. One: they're thinking about other options and want to get the best fit for them. Two: What they see isn't the right fit for them. Or three: The cost doesn't match the value. To be honest, I'm OK with any of these because they all help me or my product/service get better.... So if you don't mind me asking, which one is it?"

This is basically a choice close for information. Even if you don't get the EXACT reason they're "thinking about it," you'll get the range they're in and can do more digging with whichever they choose to get you closer to the sale.

Let's break this response down:

a. "Usually when someone says…"
- o This is a soft way to say I know, what you know, what you think, I don't know. LOL. Yep, I've been doing this long enough to know that the majority of the time a prospect thinks like this. Using the word "usually" isn't as direct and aggressive and it also means that you know you could be wrong.

b. "One of three things is going on"
- o You're asking them to choose between three options here. It's a choice close for information, narrowing down why they feel like they need to wait to do business with you.
- o They might choose two or all three or not even one here, but in the process you're eliminating objections or dialing in the problems they're facing in order to offer solutions to get the deal, if it's mutually beneficial.

c. "thinking about other options"
      - Some trainers may tell you NOT to say this, because why plant the seed that there might be other options out there? Simple. Those trainers don't know how to train you to be intelligent, competent sales professionals who can surface any and all objections, knowing you have the confidence that they will choose you because you are the most educated and business-like fit for your prospect's needs.
      - This also lets them know that it's OK to talk about other options. (Hint: don't ever bash the competition if they say they're looking at a competitor. You lose the deal instantly.)
   d. "it's not the right fit for them"
      - This is a power statement. Most sales reps don't understand that it's OK to hear, "No, this isn't a good fit for me." All you have to do is find out WHY they feel that way and then, IF and ONLY IF you have a solution for them, you can help them better understand why they should do business with you.
   e. "The cost doesn't meet the value"
      - It's important when saying this you don't use the words "can't afford" or anything like that, as it may seem insulting.
      - This statement has to be made with ease, but very transparently, that if "cost" is an issue, it's OK to discuss that.

      Don't be afraid to talk about money. But you don't know what's offensive to a prospect or what isn't. Make sure you're not too hardcore like some of the weaker sales trainers of the world tell you to be. Again, being direct is one thing, but compassionate transparency is another and also the right way to net the highest efficiency per prospect you meet.
   f. "to be honest, I'm OK with any of these"

- o Another permission statement that gives them the OK to just be honest and tell you what the real issue is here.

g. "they all help me or my product/service get better"
- o Just clarifying HOW the information they're about to give you can help you and your company get better.
- o Gives the prospect a sense of ease that the presentation is almost over and you're just asking for their help, which gives them freedom to teach, which gives you information you need to move forward or not.

h. "If you don't mind me asking, which one is it?"
- o Getting permission from them shows a great amount of respect for the prospect. Asking them, instead of telling them what you think, is a much better way to diagnose the true objections.
- o Asking them "which one is it" is asking them to choose. They might choose one or all of them or even say none of the above, but the majority of the time the prospect will tell you the reasons they're not moving forward when you ask them for help in understanding. This is a great question to get to know your prospect better and what's important to them.

Be empathetic. Be understanding. Be conscious of the fact that this smoke screen usually means they want to do business, but need our help to see why. And you already know they're not gonna say that. LOL.

4. "I HAVE TO TALK TO MY SPOUSE/ BOSS/SOMEONE ABOUT IT"

This is a common objection that can either be a smoke screen or it might actually mean you're not speaking to the decision maker. This objection is usually a prospect's favorite one, because if they aren't with their spouse or boss, they're challenging you to test their loyalty to make a decision without them present. If you go there, you need to be prepared and I'm going to show you how.

There's an easy way to find this out early in the presentation where top salespeople recognize and ask if there's anything that would stop their prospect from doing business with them today. They literally say something like this:

> "Before we get started, if what we talk about adds value to you or your company, would there be any reason at all that you couldn't make the decision to move forward with me today?"

This question is POWERFUL! But don't let them just say no. If they say "no just me", then follow up with something like this:

> "I'm glad to hear that because the ROI on what we're going to go over is going to be huge for you, so it's always nice dealing with the decision maker. It just saves us both time when there's not someone else's approval needed before making a decision like this. For that I thank you."

See what I did there? I'm simply reconfirming so they hear me. I'm also complimenting them as the "decision maker" and I'm clarifying once again that they're telling me they don't need anyone else's approval before we move forward.

Now what if they say, "*Yes, I need to speak to my spouse/boss before I can move forward*"?

Respond with something like this:

> "Totally understand and I respect that very much. So who other than yourself needs to give their approval before you move forward with me today?"

Additional questions to consider depending on the person and circumstances would be:

a. How much influence do they have in making decisions like this?

b. When you've brought stuff like this to them in the past, what's their common response?

c. Based on what you know about what we're going over, what do you think they'd like the most?

d. What do you think they'd like the least?

There are obviously different times that you ask these questions, but another powerful question when they've seen the value in what you're offering would be:

"Now that you see the value in what we went over, what do you think they'd say about doing business with us. Your honest opinion?"

Gaining clarity and allowing them to speak it is a crucial part of the sales process. Their clarity can be good or bad. If it's good, you have an optimal chance to serve this client throughout the rest of this process. If it's bad, it's a great time to address what's most important to your client and find a mutual place where you're solving any issue(s) they might have before you proceed any further.

Responses:

A. "I don't blame you at all. What question(s) do you think your ___(spouse or boss)____ will have about what we covered today?"

If they say they think their spouse/boss would say, "I think it is perfectly fine," then you're dealing with a sales objection or condition that you haven't uncovered yet or maybe you have and they're just afraid to pull the trigger, so you have 2 choices here:

- Get the spouse or boss on the phone now or

- Set a confirmed appointment creating urgency to get them together.

This is gonna be your call. Either decision you make will be the right one. You're either going to get in touch with the person and get the deal or find out why they don't want to do business with you and build off of that.

Either way, the sale is far from lost. This process just gets to the real objection faster to work on, or it gets you right to the close, wasting no time.

What this question does is allow the prospect to start talking about what they think their spouse/boss would think about doing business with you. Their opinion. This is such a crucial tool in transitioning past this objection and getting right to close.

B. *"Totally get it. I know what you've loved about the product today, but before you talk to your ____(spouse/boss)____ what do you think they'd like the most about this….? And what do you think their biggest concern would be?"*

5. "IT'S NOT THE RIGHT TIME."

There are so many objections that specifically relate to timing. I'm sure you've heard them all, but here are a few to get to know very well.

- We'll think about it.
- I'll need to talk to someone before making a decision. (like #4 above)
- It's just not the best time for us.
- Email me the info and I'll review it.
- Next quarter would be a better time to connect.

The list could go on and on, but I'm sure you see a common factor here…. There is NO URGENCY! We dive deeper into urgency in another chapter, so let's talk about how to handle this objection when urgency just isn't there.

There are several ways to tackle this objection, but once again, in today's day and age, you really need to be direct in your responses. Your prospect will respect this much more than the fluff or trying to "talk them into" doing business with you.

Empathy should always be relevant and a part of the objection handling process. No matter what the prospect says, you don't know what they're going through. You don't know how serious it is. You don't have the details of why they're responding as they are. Your tonality is very important here. If you speak or sound as if their concern, objection, or even if it's a smoke screen isn't important to you, you've lost them.

This objection sucks. It doesn't feel good to get it, but don't be thrown off your game by it. Less trained sales representatives will give up and ask to get back with them. DON'T DO THAT!

You should constantly role play the responses below and MAKE THEM YOUR OWN! There is not a script to memorize. Each person is going to have their own unique way of responding, BUT these are some extremely good foundational starting points.

As always, make sure you're teaching yourself to handle ANY and ALL objections as they surface. DO NOT LISTEN TO THE LESS TRAINED TRAINERS! Don't push an objection off. Don't act like it doesn't exist. Stay committed to mastering this and the results will speak for themselves. Like any other objection, this one is no different, as it is usually the smoke screen to what's TRULY holding them back from moving forward today.

Here are some responses that will create a conversation that will help you transition into the close seamlessly.

Responses:

A. "I completely understand that right now might not be the time and I respect the fact you're not ready. Knowing that we're most like-

ly not going to do business today, if this were a perfect scenario for you, I mean a REALISTIC ONE... and don't tell me if it were free you'd do it (and chuckle)... but honestly, if what I'm offering made complete sense to do business today, what would that have looked like?"

There are a number of things I did here I'd like you to understand fully.

- First, I acknowledged their concern about today not being the "right time."
    - o This shows I'm listening to what they're saying and that it matters to me. That beginning line will create instantaneous respect for you and they will appreciate you not losing your shit like most untrained sales individuals.
- Second, my statement "knowing that we're most likely not going to do business today" brings buyers resistance down.
    - o It makes them feel as if the "sales process" is over or coming to an end. It's a huge sense of relief for the prospect and usually allows them to be more open in their response.
- Third, I am asking them to be "realistic" when creating a scenario to do business with us today.
    - o This makes them think about an ACTUAL REALISTIC scenario where this might make sense to them to move forward today.
    - o This also gives me a chance to see if I can accommodate them, either fully or to a high degree, on what they need to do business with us. A lot of the time you'll see that what they want really isn't too far out of the question at all. BUT you have to ask this way to find those details out.
- Fourth, after asking them to be realistic, I'm blocking an objection by stating a crazy scenario such as, "don't tell me... if it was FREE you'd do it."

- o What if they said, "Yeah, I'd do it for free" – then we know it is about the money, or they don't agree that the cost equals the value of what you're offering. They're basically saying, in other words, "It's not worth what you're asking."
- o Again, this is still GREAT INFORMATION to dive deeper into to see if we might be able to offer additional services, or maybe we truly didn't explain in enough detail what we're offering, or maybe they didn't fully understand it.
- o This is a great time to find out what's important to them, which leads to the fifth part of this response.
- Fifth, I asked them to create a perfect case scenario of how they'd do business with us today and what that would look like.
  - o What if they said something completely absurd? So what! Laugh with them and then bring it back to a real conversation. Reconfirm with something like this, "HAHA, yeah, that'd be nice. Like I said, I know we're most likely not doing business today because I most likely can't give you what you need anyway, but truly… if I could what would it look like?"

This response has so many great parts to it. This isn't a tactic, this is extracting information to see if we can SERVE (not sell) the prospect, where it makes complete sense to them. Most of the time, less-trained sales individuals lose deals specifically by not knowing how to communicate properly. ALL THIS IS…. IS COMMUNICATION!

B. "I totally get it and respect that very much. So, let's get you guys outta here. But real quick, before you go, do you mind helping with something? Your input is crucial to my personal growth and the company, and we love to learn how to be better. We know why people do business with us and that's important to know, but I personally believe it's equally as important, if not MORE important, to find out the reasons people DON'T do business with us. It's the only way we learn and the best way to do that is from great people like you….

so we always make it a point to ask because your HARD TRUTH is what we need to hear. So what can we do differently in the future that could've possibly earned your business today?"

You may think this is a long response, but it's meant to be. Let's break down why. Here are some important things to learn when using this response.

- "I totally get that and respect it"
    - o I may sound like a broken record, but confirming that you've HEARD them and respect how they feel is very important and needs to be in the majority of responses, in my opinion.
- "So let's get you guys outta here"
    - o Yes, I meant to say "outta." LOL. Speaking TOO PROPER can seem extremely disingenuous. I like to be very raw, real, and authentic when I'm serving someone or training. I even write scripts to learn from with stuff like "gonna" in it, because it's just how most people speak. Keep it real. It goes a long way when it doesn't sound like a robot is speaking to them reading a script.
    - o I'm also pretty much saying, "The presentation is done. You can leave now"... once again allowing them to feel a sense of relief and most importantly RELEASED from the jaws of us crazy sales folk. LOL. In their mind, they're done and more open to give us some much-needed advice we're about to ask for so we can get better.
- "do you mind helping me with something?"
    - o Now that they feel the presentation is over, you're asking for help is usually a guarantee (i.e., they will give the "help" that you have asked for which continues the sales presentation and gives you an opportunity for a sale) if you ask it meaningfully with compassion to truly want to learn.
    - o Most prospects LOVE to tell you how they feel, but most sale individuals DON'T ASK! Whether or not you close

this deal, you can learn way more from people who DON'T BUY than from those who do. Once you find out all the reasons people don't buy from you, it'll help you with future prospects and make what you're offering more valuable to the next client.

- "your input is CRUCIAL to my personal growth and the company"
    - o Ooooof. I love this one. Because it's so true. IT IS CRUCIAL to growth on any level.
    - o I said "your input is crucial," which proves that their opinion MATTERS TO YOU, which almost forces them to answer. It shows that you genuinely value the reason they DIDN'T buy and they'll usually spew the reasons, which you can use to transition into the close by finding out the real reasons they didn't buy and just maybe, you can offer solutions RIGHT NOW to help them see why you're actually the right fit to do business with.
    - o Stating that we love to get better proves we are willing to grow and we know we're not perfect.
- Restating that we know why people buy from us, but that it's just as important, if not more important, to find out why people don't buy... really gets people to open up and let us know how we can get better. Again, solidifying access to the REAL reasons they didn't buy. This is KEY INFORMATION most sales individuals aren't trained to ask and they should be.
- "because your HARD TRUTH is exactly what we need to hear"
    - o THE HARD TRUTH! In other words, WHAT'S THE REAL REASON you're not doing business with me today? Spit it out. We can take it! Keeps it real and basically tells them... "Let it out! All the bad... we want to know!" If you emphasize this properly, like use the right tone and make it fun... the "LET ME HAVE IT" mentality, this statement will get you more deals than you can ever imagine. Because when

they LET YOU HAVE IT, they're truly LETTING YOU HAVE ALL THE REASONS THAT MATTER TO THEM WHY THEY DON'T WANT TO MOVE FORWARD TODAY! They're giving you the gold you couldn't extract through the presentation.
- "so what would've earned your business today"
    - o This is asking them to paint the picture, give me the deets on what would've given me the opportunity to earn your business. Again, this information is the gold you need to transition back into the close.

Remember, that verbiage in my response DOES NOT and SHOULD NOT be the way you say it. Make it your own, but the process and the information I'm giving you on how I respond is what you need to master. Make it your own always!

Just remember, this response gives you the information you need to get them back into the sale. When you can get them to tell you what's important to them and you now have that information, they have no choice but to listen because they SPOKE what means the most to them (which means they own it). So it's the old "if I could… would you…" scenario that's old and played out, but when reworded, it can get a bunch of no's due to the "it's not the right time" objection to turn into immediate yes's!

C. "If you don't mind me asking, just give it to me real. What's holding you back from doing business with me today?"

This is a very direct way of finding out the real reason someone's not doing business with you. It's a no bullshit, no fluff, direct approach to getting the prospect to stop selling you or giving you a fluff response to why they're not moving forward with you. You have to phrase it from a very respect-driven question, meaning tell them it's OK to be completely blunt and honest about what's missing. It becomes an equal business respect that cuts through all the negotiation, all the dodging and weaving in the sales process on both sides and forces one another to face the hard dead on.

The sales professional who masters this short but effective response to this objection really takes their careers to another height. It's getting down to the nitty gritty. Do we make a deal or don't we?

A couple of things to make sure of:

- I asked, "If you don't mind me asking…" I'm seeking permission out of respect to get a real and authentic response to why they've decided not to do business with me today. In return, if they comply, you should always be INTEGRITY based, whether you can help them or not, once they give you the real of what they'd need to have in order to do business with you.

- "Give it to me real…" I just want to get down to the MAIN REASON(s) the prospect is choosing to "think about it." Like, let's cut the shit, professionally of course. If I can provide them with what they need, what makes sense to do them, the value their honest response needs, then are we doing business or not?
    o "What's holding you back?" Same thing… make sure your tonality is respectful, but they need to know you're a professional who respects their time, but YOUR TIME is equally as valuable.

- I said, "do business with me today…" not tomorrow. Not the day after. Not the week after. Not the month after, but TODAY!

Also remember, confidence and arrogance can elicit two totally different responses from a prospect. It's important that being direct with confidence doesn't get confused with arrogance, as though your time is more important than theirs.

It's also true that when a prospect speaks to someone of authority when being direct, there is almost an immediate semi-submissive moment that happens in the sales professional's favor. For instance, Grant Cardone…. The Marketing Genius he is, constantly posts

YouTube videos of how he takes a cold call and flips it into a sale. I think we all can agree that if Zig Ziglar, Grant or Elena Cardone, Brian Tracy, Deb Calvert, Dale Carnegie, Tom Hopkins, Jeffrey Gitomer, Danelle Delgado, Victor Antonio, Jill Konrath, Brad Lea…..etc….. were to grab the phone while you were on the other end or walk up and sit down and ask you to buy, you're most likely going to be more persuaded. If you say you wouldn't, you'd be lying.

I love watching Grant's videos. So direct. So bold. He even tells people sometimes to "cut the shit, you wanna do business with me man or not?" BOOOOOOOOM. You see him get the deal while the prospect is on speaker phone in complete shock they just got closed after Grant took over the phone call. Shocker the deal went down, right? I think not. You were talking to GRANT CARDONE, a billionaire household name. Then he trains others to BE DIRECT like he was. I don't disagree, but when someone's on the other end of the line trying to sell you Cardone University that's someone you've never heard of, who most of the time, won't even give you their last name….. rather than GRANT CARDONE ….. the odds of being THAT direct and the deal going down are WAY LESS than if it was Grant or any of the extraordinary humans/sales trainers I've named above.

I'll give you another example of being direct as an authoritative figure.

I had Brad Lea on my Podcast, Gutcheck Uncut Season 1. Brad's an awesome dude. Hilarious. Great at sales and just enjoys helping people. That being said, Brad owns Lightspeed VT, which is a virtual interactive training system that helps people truly learn from video-based online training platforms. His company is also extremely powerful in marketing and has packages that help people really scale themselves and their companies to extreme heights.

Now I'm a sales guy. I personally believe I can not only hang with all the above named, but truly compete with them as one of the top trainers in the world. Call that cocky, arrogant, or conceited all you want… I call it confidence. I know what I'm good at and I know what

I'm not. I'm not good at marketing and didn't, at the time, have tools to create an online training platform like Brad offered. Which is the reason I reached out to him after the show and said,

> **Todd**: *"Hey, Brad, I'm ready to scale, man, and I've heard your platform is the way to do it."*

As sales individuals, we love to run our mouths, I know, which is why I don't talk much when serving/selling anything, because people will tell you how to sell them. But this time, I *PURPOSELY* kept talking and talking and talking after he told me he can help anyone make money. I wanted to see what his response would be when I *purposely* said I don't have the money really to invest in his Lightspeed. His response was short and sweet.

He mirrored what I said:

> **Brad Lea**: *"So you're telling me you don't have the money to invest but want to do a rev share with me based on results, right?"*

> **Todd**: *"Yes sir"*

> **Brad Lea**: *"OK, well, I've got the 30k, the 60k, and the 90k package. Which one suits you?"*

LOL. So wait, I'm speaking to Brad Lea. A champion businessman. A rockstar sales trainer. The guy was in a movie, for God's sake. I'm a fan and he knows that because I asked him to be on my podcast and he just completely disregarded the fact I said, "I don't have the money to invest in your program," and asked for huge numbers… and guess what… I was considering it.

I was going to invest because of WHO HE WAS, not because of his sales ability. He's a social media genius and has helped many people grow like crazy. He's GOT THE RESUME. He's GOT THE RESULTS. He's proven what he can do multiple times over, but I was ALSO speaking directly to him. It wasn't someone pitching it for him.

Had one of his call centers sales reps jumped on the phone and tried to do that after I said I can't afford it, I would probably have reexplained my position passionately, LOL, so they understood what I just said. But since it was Brad Lea himself who asked me... I just shut up and thought about it and I wasn't even mad.

I didn't do the deal. Not because of money, but I wanted to test how he handled the objection and possibly working with someone who wouldn't shut up.

He still wanted the deal.

He still pitched me ever so briefly.

He still gave me a 3-choice close, which most choose the middle.

He never wavered from value, but he understands the leverage of authority when asking for a deal now that he's earned that right.

Being direct is OK. It's a timesaver and a really great tool to use, when perfected.

So does having an authoritative figure help when being direct? Absolutely. It's OK to bring someone of authority over and have them sit and help you or have them take over the call.

Just be careful is all I'm saying when you're being direct. There are many factors that go into either being productive or falling flat on your face when doing so.

D. "I get it and I respect it. The question that I always ask is, 'How much money do you think this this will cost you by not making a decision to work together today?' Because if you don't move forward, you're losing immediate success. If this helped you get 10 more deals a week, what does that look like in net revenue to you?"

- I know you see it. "I get it and I respect it."
    - o Again, respecting your prospect. Get used to this. Active listening is WAY more important than active running of the mouth.
- "How much will it cost you NOT to make this decision now?"

- o Getting them to think of how much the product or service will make them if they move forward. Basically, what are the possibilities if they do?
- Make a decision when? TODAY!
  - o I want to let it be known I want to do business today.
- If you don't, you're losing instant dollars. (A little poke and creatively getting them thinking "what if?".)
- Let's talk about the actual dollar amount this will cost you daily, weekly, monthly, quarterly, and more.

6. "JUST SEND ME THE INFO AND I'LL GET BACK TO YOU."

The less trained, insecure, or less seasoned sales individuals most likely feel that if they just send the prospect the information they've requested, it JUST MIGHT be seen by the prospect and then the prospect JUST MIGHT call them back and ask to do business with them, giving them that incorrect feeling of hope. So the problem is they keep doing it and efficiency suffers tremendously because of it. Maybe, just maybe, you feel that in sales this is the right way to approach people, nudging them, instead of leading them to the close in a more trained process to get the deal.

This is DEFINTELY positive thinking at its finest moment. The problem is the real world doesn't work this way at all.

When you just send them information on your product or service, you're not building relationships. You don't even know if they're qualified to do business with you. You don't know what's important to them. You don't know what problems your product or service may or may not be able to solve. So the question is: HOW DO YOU KNOW WHAT TO SEND THEM THAT WILL ADD VALUE TO THEM SPECIFICALLY? The answer: you don't.

You're starting off the relationship in the dark and throwing shit against the wall to see if it will stick. This is NOT the way to do business.

Do you know that the average response rate to an email is less than 1% if you're not specific to a prospect's needs? That means that if you send 10,000 emails out like this, you'll get 100 responses and out of those 100 responses, you'll get 1% of those willing to work with you. Which is 1. The bad news is your efficiency is horrible. The good news is it can be fixed. Sending your prospect information that's tailored to their needs will net you your biggest results.

This objection is very common. More so in call center sales, but it's used widely among prospects as the "easy way out" method due to the lack of training in so many sales organizations.

Most of the time, you're dealing with nice people who don't want to tell you no. They're basically saying, "I'm not interested in what you're offering me. I have no desire whatsoever to continue to talk about it." A sales professional will handle this objection with the information we're about to go over, but if they can't, they set up a time to go over it again right then and there. Which we talk about in another chapter training on FOLLOW-UP, but don't let that prospect get off without confirming the date and time to reconnect.

Make sure you're asking them good questions. When someone is just trying to get off the phone, you'll find that if you ask them specifically about themselves, it will turn into the longest call ever. Why? Because people LOVE TO TALK ABOUT THEMSELVES MOST. This allows you to fine tune what you think will best suit them. I've had many sales calls where a prospect tried to get rid of me by asking for more information, but when I used the technique I just went over with you, I closed them on that same call. It happens all the time.

Yes, they might also say they don't have time for this. That's also OK… just follow the response below and you'll win them over more often than not.

By the way, DO NOT, I repeat… DO NOT say, "Sure, what's a good email to send you some info?" Oftentimes a prospect is testing your perseverance and wants to work with rock stars. When you give up that easy, the only thing you're closing is the door to work with that prospect. Let's go over how to help you win when this happens.

Response:

A. "You got it! Anything you need, I'll make sure you have it. What are the main things you need to know about, so I don't bore you with random stuff?"

Let's break down this response.

- "You got it!"
    - o You have to say this with a smile and enthusiasm. They need to feel that you're "OK" with them getting back to you. It reduces sales resistance and they'll feel as if they've accomplished their goal in ending your presentation. When that resistance is down, it'll be way easier for you to get the information you need to possibly solve their problem now, rather than getting back to them.
- "I'll make sure you have it."
    - o This is letting them know you're here to SERVE THEM with anything they need and agreeing you're going to do just that.
    - o This also gives them peace of mind if they TRULY want to get back to you, that you're willing to do what it takes on their terms to earn their business.
- "What are the main things you need to know about?"
    - o This is a great follow-up IMMEDIATELY after you agree to get them what they need. You've AGREED to do something for them, now it's their turn. It's easier to get something from them when you've done something FOR them.
    - o When asking this question, make sure you're asking them for the SPECIFIC things they want "to get back to you"

about. This information can usually be handled right then and there to see if this is the real objection or not. When asked properly and answered properly, it gives you a very high probability of transitioning into the close when this is the true objection. What does that mean? It means, you get the deal NOW rather than getting back to them.

- o "I don't want to 'bore you' with random stuff." In other words, you're asking them for the SPECIFICS! Let's get to what's important to you. As a sales professional, you're basically saying, "Let's not waste each other's time. Give me the REAL things you need to make your decisions to do business with me or not." Even if it does turn into a follow up, you're not wasting their time with information they don't want or need to receive. Get them what's relevant to them.

When this objection surfaces, you want to get the information you need to see if:

a. This is a REAL objection. When handling it like this, you'll be able to diagnose the real reason they aren't ready to move forward.

b. You'll find out if they're just trying to be nice and can't just say "no."

c. You're able to show them that what's important to them matters to you and you're willing to do what it takes to earn their business.

d. Solidify a follow-up time, confirmed and set in calendar by both parties if you can't earn their business that day.

e. You get the details, the information you need to help transition into the close. Removing fluff.

When you can go into detail handling this objection, you will immediately be able to determine if this is a deal now, later, or maybe not ever. When you can't close the deal the day of and they're not willing to set in stone a time to reconnect, then you've assessed the prospect fully. If there's no opportunity for a deal, get referrals by being the ONE SALES PROFESSIONAL who doesn't throw fits when they don't close the deal. I've said this before and I'll say this again, I've earned more business from people I've NOT done business with when there wasn't synergy to work together. If you treat them well and respect their decisions, they'll refer you to tons of business opportunities for being a class-act salesperson. This process is explained in detail in the referral portion of this book.

Moral of the story, don't be a jerk, ever.

7. NO TRUST. "I DON'T KNOW ENOUGH ABOUT YOU OR THE PRODUCT TO MOVE FORWARD."

TRUST. How important is it? It's damn near everything. People have tried to argue this with me forever and have lost EVERY SINGLE TIME. It doesn't matter what you're offering, how much value they may see in it. If they don't trust you, they're not doing business with you.

You have a great product or service. Everyone seems to want it and you can literally prove it, but people still don't buy what you're offering. You even take it a step further and break down the numbers and logically prove they should do business with you on paper, but yet, they still don't buy.

The issue is, there's an enormous amount of doubt. They may be scared it's the wrong move. What if they make a mistake? No one wants to be wrong. Everyone wants to make the right decision.

The numbers make sense. There's nothing that looks wrong, but if they pull the trigger and something goes wrong, guess whose fault it is? Guess who gets to hear the "I told you so"s.

The real question here is, why risk anything at all? Most people won't make a move because it's easier to stay safe. No risk. No grief. No wrong choices to be made. Just continue doing what they normally do. They know there's a problem that needs a solution, but they'll spend more time justifying why NOT to make a move than taking a risk that could potentially add massive value to their lives. It's just EASIER!

I know what you're thinking. "Todd, I get it, so what's the solution? How do I help someone who's that scared to do anything?" Well, let's talk about what NOT TO DO first.

If you're working with a client who for some reason doesn't trust you or the process, or is scared to make a potential personal or business move, you can NOT try to convince them that what they're thinking is wrong. All that does is make them defensive and they'll start to make up other objections that aren't even real just to prove that how they feel is valid. They'll fight to prove that they're right and confrontation NEVER EVER helps you get a deal. It's a fight you can't win in sales ever.

Here's a breakdown of how I handle this objection.

There are three things that are crucial to minimize this objection from surfacing. If done correctly, you'll start transitioning potential losses into huge wins.

First, you have to obviously have a great product or service that you're offering.

Second, you have to sell yourself. Again, when the smartest graduates in Harvard history asked Warren Buffet, "What skill do we need most to be successful in the real world?", Warren said, "Learn how to sell."

I guarantee the entire class looked at each other in shock. Probably saying, "We didn't graduate at the top of our class in salesmanship. What's he mean?" Don't get me started on my rant about how this skill should be taught in high school and up, but he means SELL YOURSELF! You can be the smartest person in the room on paper, but there are others who have your level of intelligence. So what sets you apart? Why choose you? You HAVE TO MASTER the art of selling you!

Third and finally, you have to SELL THE COMPANY as the stable, growing, efficient company that it is and they'd be wrong to choose not to work with you and the company. They want to know the company's not going anywhere and that the future is bright.

Companies spend millions on testimonial videos, social media proof, branding, and more to make sure people know their name and that it's important for the world to see who they are.

Customer testimonials ARE SO important in building trust. It's one thing to say your product or service works. It's ABSOLUTELY COMPLETELY DIFFERENT when someone who has used what you're offering says how amazing it is to work with you and how the product or service has added massive value in their lives.

To be honest, I've never been a product person. What's that mean? It means that there are tons of great products out there that do the exact same thing for the most part. So how do I decide who to work with? The person. It's that simple. If the company is stable, the product is good and does what I need it to do… I'm choosing WHO I want to create a business relationship with.

Step 1: BLOCK THIS OBJECTION. SURFACE IT BEFORE THEY DO.

We talk about blocking in this chapter and now's the time to do it. When you bring this up, it creates instant credibility. There are several ways to do that. Let's look at a good way to do it.

Remember, my suggestion on how to surface objections doesn't have to be exactly the way you say it, nor should it be. But something like this is usually very effective:

> "I know what you're probably thinking, and I don't blame you one bit. You're skeptical. Does this really work? How can I trust him or the company? And that can make it hard to move forward.

A lot of my clients felt the same way when we first started doing business together. So how about this. Tell me what worries you most. What scares you? Be honest. In return, I'll also be 100% real with you whether what I'm offering can help you or not. If I can, I'll prove it. If I can't, I'll guide you to someone who can. Deal?"

Let's break this down:

a. "I know what you're probably thinking, and I don't blame you one bit."

It's always better to address this issue that you know already exists but giving them the OK to feel that way is equally powerful.

Your prospect needs to know that you're smart enough to know the concerns upfront. What most people feel when making a decision like this. It creates credibility in your ability to do business.

When you're basically telling them, "It's OK to feel the way you do. I know that you feel that way, so let's talk about it," it's a huge weight off their shoulders and they feel much more comfortable talking to you about their concerns.

b. "You're skeptical. Does this really work? How can I trust him or the company?"

- At this point you're calling out what they're thinking.
- You're also planting seeds about certain things like, "Does this really work? How do I trust him or the company?"

Everyone's skeptical. Let's just call it like it is. In today's world, with social media and the scams out there, it's hard to trust anything or anyone. Make sure your prospect knows that you know that. When you do that, they'll start verbalizing how they feel, either agreeing with you or disagreeing with you. Either way, that communication is so crucial to moving the relationship along.

c. "and that can make it hard to move forward"

- You're saying "I get it. I understand you."

People need to know that you know that without fully believing in you and the company, anyone would find it hard to do business.

d. "A lot of my clients felt the same way when we first started doing business together"

- People love knowing they're not the only ones who feel that way. SO TELL THEM ITS OK!

Stating this makes them realize that you're fully aware how people feel, BUT notice the next words: "when we first started doing business together."

You're confirming that they felt like you, BUT they still did business with me. That's very important for the prospect to hear.

e. "So how about this. Tell me what worries you most. What scares you? Be honest."

You want prospects to be honest. You want them to know that what matters to them, matters to you. You want them to list what scares them, so you can truly see if what you're offering makes sense to move forward with.

When asking them to be honest, it doesn't mean you're calling them liars, but let's not create any fluff here. You're saying… Let's get right to the point. Tell me all the BAD, so we can both figure out what that next move is.

When you say this right, as in compassionately caring what's best for them, they'll engage more and it builds the trust they're seeking.

f. "In return, I'll also be 100% real with you whether what I'm offering can help you or not."

If you'll be honest, I'll be honest. You're making a pact of no bullshit here. Let's both be honest so we can both benefit from this relationship. You tell me the things that concern you and I'll tell you if I can help! It's that simple. It's that easy.

g. "If I can, I'll prove it. If I can't, I'll guide you to someone who can."

Time to prove what you say to be true to help, but only if you can.

If you can't, say that too! It's OK not to get this one deal and people will respect you for saying, "This isn't the right fit for you." And as I've said before, you'll get WAY MORE BUSINESS long term with honesty and integrity! Remember, great liars get the one deal. Integrity-based sales professionals get a lifetime relationship that nets multiple deals.

If you can't help them, guide them to someone who can, but only to someone you know to be equally as honest as you. Never refer anyone to someone you're unsure of.

If you do this the right way, their no will turn into future yes's for you, both from them and people they refer to you!

h. "Deal?"

Once you ask this and they say yes, you've just bonded and agreed to consider the opportunity to work with one another. If they say "no," stay connected and ask the right questions about why they don't feel comfortable to do so.

In the end, when handling this objection, you're truly just extracting information so both of you can make an intelligent decision whether it makes sense to do business together or not.

A great tool is to ask skeptical prospects if they remember a time they might have been unsure of moving forward with something or someone, but chose to do so and it worked out. Every single one of us has been there and they know it and so do we. It's a great reminder of how they took a chance and it worked out.

Harvard Law did a study about "Lack of Trust" in the sales process, and what they found after 21,000+ surveys with prospects and business owners is that TRUST IS THE SINGLE MOST IMPORTANT FACTOR WHEN PURCHASING PRODUCTS OR SERVICES. 81% of all the surveys chose TRUST as the most important factor for personal prospects and 63% of all the surveys chose the same thing as a business or organization.

If there's no confidence in you or the business, if there's no trust, people just DO NOT commit. They will literally make things up to get out of the presentation, if you don't know how to handle this objection properly. The crazy part is… it doesn't take much to fix this and start helping you win.

A lot of people like to say stuff I've listed here that does NOT give you the best possible outcome when handling multiple objections, like:

1. **"Obviously, there's something that doesn't make sense to you."**
   - Basically you're implying that YOU ARE CERTAIN (obviously) that they are stupid or don't get what you're telling them, which is insulting to most.

2. **"Procrastinating won't help you or make this decision any easier."**
   - Although true for the most part and being direct is awesome when it's done respectfully… to me, it sounds like you just called me a procrastinator and I don't know how to make decisions and you as the sales individual are taking zero responsibility in why I'm not buying. Nor do you care about anything other than the sale, because you're not asking me the reason I'm not buying. You're calling me an indecisive person. LOL. When the truth just may be that you're not asking the right questions. It's your job to get to the reason they're not buying. Possibly insulting someone won't help you in that process.

3. **They might say, "What proof do I need to give you that proves this will work for you?" THINKING this is the right way to ask, but it isn't.**
   - It implies that you just need to know what you need to know to get the sale, in my opinion. It shows zero compassion, in my opinion, and compassion is what opens your prospect up to what's truly important to them. Instead you could've

said, *"What are the things you like most about what I'm offering and what do you wish it had that would allow you to feel more confident to do business with me?"*

Rephrasing that question might get you the answer you don't want to hear. They might say "nothing" but that allows you to transition to defining what "nothing" means so we can learn for the next client or prospect, which will give you the information you need to serve your prospect better and get the deal.

4. "When someone tells me they need to think about it, it usually means the price isn't where they'd like it to be. Is that true?"

- Just so we're clear, I threw up a little as I typed that horrid response that's being taught on the internet for sales individuals to learn from.

- You're basically saying one of two things.
    - o You can't afford it.
    - o If it was cheaper would you buy it?
    - o You're saying you know that's the reason they're not buying and just want to clarify that.

- Now let me explain this. A lot of sales trainers will tell you… "Todd, if they say you're wrong and it's not about the price, then that eliminates that objection so you can find the real one." UMMMMMMMMMMMM….. NOPE. IT DEFINETELY DOES NOT. They may think you're saying they can't afford it, which may be, but you pissed them off now and the sales wall is built back up so they're not gonna tell you anyway now!

- Less trained sales trainers will also say, "Todd, if you ask the question 'is that true?' at the end, you're not insinuating…" Yes, you are. You can use the words "usually means" but that means "most of the time." This is a better phrase to use when speaking to your prospect and it leads them to respond to your assumption, which helps you find out the real objection.

- You're implying that you know what they're thinking, which spews arrogance, NOT confidence, and potential prospects hate that. Oh, and if you're wrong and that's not what they're thinking, you look like an idiot.

- Don't ask the question that way ever. Use the price objection responses to choose from in this book, to find a way to surface that objection properly, please!

5. **When price is a true objection, another top favorite throw up "sales assumptive" supposed close that I hate is, "Well, Todd, you get what you pay for with this and then some, so let's go ahead and get started today so you can see the massive value it's going to add with all the benefits we've gone over that'll be at your fingertips."**

- If you just read that or listened to it on my audio book, please pause, go directly to your bathroom and vomit for me instantly. Please and thank you.
    - o Listen carefully, THIS IS NOT A TIME TO ASSUME THE CLOSE! They have to see the value first. They have to know the money they are spending is being put towards something worthwhile. If you're trying to get the deal at this point, you're wasting your time.
    - o Most of the deals that go down using this close have an enormous cancellation rate. They just don't stick!

6. **"If there was one thing that would get you to say YES today, what would it be?"**

- I know to some, this might work. Yes, it does get them to say things like "if it was FREE" and stuff like that, but this is a real salesy question and turns most prospects off almost instantly.

- o You're asking them to tell you something you should've already found out in your discovery process.
- o This question makes you seem like you're reaching in desperation to see if they'd be "kind enough" to just give you the gold that will get them to say yes to you.
- o Now I'll tell you, very very very seasoned sales professionals can ask this question in a light and humorous way in getting the information they need to help close the deal, but it's not even in my top 15 ways to get to close.

7. **"There's no downside here. I've shown you all the numbers to prove this makes financial sense. So just start with the basic package and go from there."**
    - "No downside"? How do you know? If you haven't really found the actual objection, you can't really say that. There might be additional factors you know nothing about. Saying this is insulting to most and makes prospects feel you don't want, nor care, to take the time to see if there is a downside.
    - You may have shown financially how this makes sense, but that's just one factor of most prospect's buying motives.
    - "Start with the BASIC package" or "entry level" or "smaller program"… No one wants to be basic, entry level, or small… let's be honest. LOL. If you're going to start someone out in a package, product, or service less than what you've been offering, make sure you explain the benefits properly that actually add value to them. Then give them a real scalable action plan to grow and tell them your job is to prove how having you is the most valuable tool they'll need and you're

willing to do what it takes before asking them to invest any more of their time or money.

8. "If money and resources were no object, would you be willing to move forward with me today?"

This has got to be one the worst objection responses EVER! So wait, lemme get this straight. If you had enough money to do whatever you want and all the resources you'd ever need at your fingertips, you'd be willing to try this to see if it adds value? COME ON! Of course they would! Don't ask questions that question the intelligence of your prospects. This response does just that.

- It's insulting, due to the fact that if they saw ANY value in what you're offering, they'd be stupid not to if money didn't matter.
- If you had all the resources to add something to your business or life, of course you'd use them.

Most untrained sales representatives think this response will help them when it absolutely does the opposite. You're asking a question trying to lead your prospect and that's the old A.B.C. (always be closing) method. That's far from the way the world works today. Again, people want to be served and helped, not closed or forced into a deal.

It's incredible what I hear people being taught during training these days. The things sales individuals say are crazy. Things that if said to me might warrant an immediate ending of the presentation or quick smack for some of the things they think are OK to say, such as:

- "Is making/saving money not a priority to you?"
- "Is it really worth losing your goals for not moving forward with me today?"
- "You know waiting is just going to cost you money."
- "Do you understand value?"
- "Where would the price have to be for us to make a deal?"

- "Did I do something wrong?"
- "Is there anything I can do that will change your mind?" (desperation at its best)

Some of these are smack worthy. Others are just guaranteed to never get the deal with your prospect ever.

Handling objections is an art that just HAS TO BE mastered if you truly want to be a sales pro. Just be very very careful about the advice you take from so-called sales trainers on HOW TO master this art. You've got to make sure that every move you make comes from a PROSPECT-FIRST, CARING way. A.B.C. is now A.B.S. (Always Be Serving). I hate when I hear sales individuals and even worse, sales so-called trainers, teaching this the wrong way.

If you learn the wrong way, it'll most likely have you looking for another career sooner than later. Please role play the above consistently. Don't EVER let anyone teach you a scripted way to handle an objection. Make it your own. As long as you do it with honesty, integrity, and for the purpose of the client, never being cocky, arrogant, or inconsiderate to what matters most to them, then your sales efficiency will be extraordinary.

BONUS OBJECTION INFORMATION:

Many of you reached out to me asking about email rejections. Here's how I do it and train my top sales professionals to do it as well.

There are 4 rules to live by when responding.

1. BE NICE!

People are going to reject you. Personally and in business forever. LOL. It's just a fact of life and, depending on how you respond to it, it'll change the course of your life in either a positive way or a negative way. That's why my NUMBER 1 RULE is to JUST BE NICE!

Sales individuals, at least the untrained ones, seem to take rejection personally when most of the time, it's not because of them at all. ESPECIALLY in an email. If you don't get the response you want, you lose it. Then if you respond incorrectly, you've really lost it. And what I mean by "lost it" is, you've lost the deal forever!

Rejection is a fact of life, but it can still be hard not to take it personally. If you don't receive the response you're looking for via email, don't bite back, be snide, or act unprofessionally when you respond.

Remember, just because they're not on board now doesn't mean they can't be farther down the line. You want to keep the possibility of a future relationship open — that starts with remaining respectful in your follow-up.

2. WHEN YOU GET REJECTED, ACKNOWLEDGE IT!

Think about this for a minute. Someone's trying to sell you something and you tell them no. How would you feel if they disregarded what you just said and continued to spew more features and benefits on you? You'd hate it and it'd most likely piss you off. Acknowledge that your prospect told you no, EVERY SINGLE TIME. Show that you've heard them and want to understand more clearly where they're coming from and ALWAYS RESPECT what they're saying.

Remember, you don't have to agree with them, but not respecting how they feel won't get you anywhere. Once you prove to them that their opinion matters, they'll be more open to your opinion, which gives you the chance to transition back into a possible sale. This process works in person, in an email, over the phone, or in any circumstance.

3. ASK THEIR OPINION TO OFFER MORE CONTEXT.

When you send emails, it's hard to legitimize the product or service you're offering. You can't expect the prospect to know if what you're offering is going to add value to them now, later, or even at all, just by reading some verbiage they got in an email. So the easiest thing for the prospect to do is to not respond at all, or if they're nice, LOL, respond that they're not interested.

If this happens, ask their opinion so you can offer more context. I'd respond by asking questions about why they think what you're offering isn't a good fit. Something like this:

"I totally get it. Our product/service isn't for everyone. If you don't mind me asking, because we always love hearing new ways to add more value to what we're offering, what would this product/service have to have for us to do business?"

This is a discovery question. You're finding out what matters most to them, basically just asking for their opinion, because it matters. The truth is, whether they buy or not, you win if they respond. If you transition them into a sale, you win. If you don't but you hear some great things about how you can better what you're offering, you win.

Some trainers will tell you to offer new information about your product/service, but I hate that response, especially in an email. It seems WAY TO SALESY and if you're dealing with an intelligent prospect, it might seem as though you don't care about why they're saying no if you don't acknowledge and ask about it.

If you do this well and you do a great job in genuinely making your prospect feel that their opinion matters, it's a great way to get them to re-engage.

4. DON'T THROW UP.

Look, they've already said NO. If you ramble on with a 20-paragraph response, the odds of them replying, or EVEN READING it, are virtually nil. They're already not interested and have basically written off doing business with you.

Keep the response short and sweet. With something like this:

"Totally respect that. Quick question, I know we're not doing business right now, but I'd love to know what we missed so we can get better and your opinion is important to me. I have some free time tomorrow at 2pm or the following day at 1pm. Which is better to catch up?"

Short. Sweet and right to the point. You're telling them that it's OK you're not doing business right now, but also telling them how important it is to hear why you lost the opportunity, so you don't lose future opportunities. All this does is get them to engage. It's an authentic way to gain value and respect, to possibly do business with this prospect in the future. You weren't pushy. You didn't puke on them. You didn't get mad. You kept it short and, worst-case scenario, built a relationship where the odds are definitely in your favor to work together in the future.

Finally, be respectful, empathetic, and effective in how you reply.

Unfortunately, let me say that again, UNFORTUNATELY, salespeople today suck and it's not entirely their fault. Yes, some are just thieves who are good liars, but others are just being taught the wrong way. One of the reasons I wrote this book, *The Ultimate Sales Bible*, was because people are more concerned with their pay, rather than with serving people, NOT REALIZING that when you ACTUALLY CARE and do the right thing…the money comes BIGGER AND BETTER!

Because the majority of salespeople are in it for themselves, prospects don't even want to speak to us. EVEN THE GOOD ONES! You have to be REAL, AUTHENTIC, and RESPECTFUL, ESPECIALLY when responding in an email. Take every opportunity to show how flexible you are, how understanding you can be, and how empathetic you will always be with others. People want to work WITH good people. When you respond this way, prospects will keep you around whether it's to do business now or later.

By the way, if they still seem uninterested again over email, DON'T ASK an open-ended question if you can schedule a time to reconnect. Give them a choice option by acknowledging they still said no.

Something like this:

"I understand and I can't thank you enough for your reply. I have a few quick questions on what you do. I've got Wednesday at 1pm and Friday at 3:30 available to catch up. Which day is better for you?"

Untrained sales individuals will ASK something like this: *"I'd love to show a little more about what my product offers. CAN I set up a time to talk more about it with you?"* You most likely won't even get a reply and if you do it'll be something like them telling you they'll get back to you when they have time. DON'T DO THIS! Be strong in your presence and make sure they know your time is valuable too.

Oh yeah, and if they say they're still not interested even after you responded in the best way, acknowledge it and give it a rest. Don't blow them up. The worst thing you can do is bombard and annoy people. Being persistent doesn't mean be annoying. Some larger call centers will tell their teams to call them, text them, and email them until they block you. HORRIBLE ADVICE. You risk not just losing them as a client, but anyone that they told how annoying of a person you are. LOL. It's not worth it.

Although this chapter is by far the longest, I felt it necessary to add a few training scenarios for you and your team to work on together. Remember, when you go through these, it's always good to practice using industries that aren't your own, but when you've concluded these 3 scenarios I've created for you, then make your own and tailor them to your industry.

1. REAL ESTATE: SELLING A HOME NEAR A RAILWAY LINE

Objection Anticipated: "The noise from the railway line will be disruptive."

Proactive Approach: Before the potential buyer mentions the nearby railway, the sales representative says, "Many of our residents have found that proximity to the railway is quite convenient for commuting. Plus, these homes are designed with noise-reducing materials and double-pane windows to ensure a peaceful living environment. Many residents even say they hardly notice it after a week or two!"

2. AUTOMOTIVE SALES: SELLING A CAR WITH A NEW TECHNOLOGY FEATURE

Objection Anticipated: "This new technology seems too complicated. I prefer something simpler."

Proactive Approach: As the sales representative introduces the car and its features, they might say, "This model comes with our latest infotainment system, which might look different from what you're used to. However, most of our customers find it intuitive after a quick walkthrough. Let me show you some of its key features, and I'll also mention that the dealership offers free technology training sessions for the first month after your purchase."

3. SOFTWARE SALES: INTRODUCING A NEW SOFTWARE SUBSCRIPTION MODEL

Objection Anticipated: "I'm not interested in ongoing subscription fees. I prefer a one-time purchase."

Proactive Approach: When introducing the software pricing, the sales representative could lead with, "Our latest software now comes in a subscription model, which has been incredibly beneficial for our users. Instead of a large upfront cost, you get continuous updates, ensuring you always have the latest features and security patches. Plus, it offers flexibility; you can scale up or down based on your needs. It's like ensuring your software grows and adapts with your business."

In each scenario, the sales representative uses proactive strategies to address potential objections head-on, alleviating concerns before they even arise in the conversation. Which, by the way, is the easiest way to help build credibility. They'll trust you more and they'll be more apt to give you referral business and work with you more in the future.

PRACTICE! PRACTICE! PRACTICE!

Remember, you should always know two things in sales in your specific industry.

- The top 5 most common objections – to master how to block them.

And

- The top 10 objections in your industry – so you can know exactly how to handle them if they were to arise.

Knowing these things will give you a huge edge against your competition! So get to work!

CHAPTER 21

LOGIC AND EMOTION: THE BALANCING ACT

Here's a good start to this chapter. If you were to ask 50 people in sales this question:

"Which drives sales more, logic or emotion?", what do you think the answer would be? Well, Harvard Business School did another study and they wanted to answer this question in depth. What they found was that 96% of our buying decisions are made subconsciously. The study worked with over 17 different neuroscientists, and they all agreed that the research proved that rationalism plays a very minimalistic part in the decision-making process.

To add to that, in 2001'ish a guy by the name of Nelson Cowan did a study that proved that a human can only process up to 4 pieces of information at one time. Hence, the common saying that if you hear something without recording it or writing it down, you won't remember most of it and what you do remember will be mostly wrong. So what's that mean? Long-term memory, your subconscious, plays a huge role in why we buy.

When we buy on emotion, it seems to net the highest probability for rescission (cancelled business). Why? You know you've done it. You buy something on emotion and then you start to think things like:

- "Should I have really spent the money on that?"
- "I didn't really need this right now."
- "I could've used that money on something more important."

Etc... Etc... Etc... Buyer's remorse, right?! So let's break down the specifics on both, because they both have value to your prospects differently and it also depends on what you're selling.

Let's start with Emotion first.

The definition of emotion is: a natural instinctive state of mind deriving from one's circumstances, mood, or relationships with others.

When we're talking about an emotional buying decision, it's literally a decision made on how the customer feels about you or the product or service you're offering. Usually a salesperson can bring out emotion through their product, service, themselves, pitchbooks, third-party stories, and more.

In most sales environments, you'll find the bulk of emotion-based sales being made through fear of missing out, fear of loss, like a sale that's going away soon that could save them money. Then you have those ego-based buyers who just want the "new thing" and they want to be the first to have it. They really want to be seen as the person who gets what everyone else wants first. That's an emotional buy.

Have you ever seen a marketing ad that uses a small child, a sad story, tears, a story of how what they're selling has impacted lives, maybe a vacation someone's always wanted to go on, and with your product they can make it happen affordably.

Personally, I feel like I'm a mix of both emotion and logic when I buy. More logic as I get older, but I'll tell you a story of how I was the easiest sell at a car dealership one time. So my daughter turns 16 in a couple weeks and I'm car shopping. I go to a dealership that has a beautiful Honda Accord that would be perfect for a brand-new driver. My daughter is my world, so as I'm walking towards the car, the salesman was complimenting me on being a great dad and he pulls out his phone to show me another father who bought a Mercedes for his daughter. It was her first car too. The video shows her seeing her father pull up in this beautiful Mercedes, beeping the horn with a huge red bow on it.

The daughter runs full speed as her dad gets out of the car, smiling from ear to ear, and she leaps into his arms, bawling her eyes out. She saw the car, but couldn't let go of her dad. Her friends jumped out of the bushes and their eyes were wide open as they were in awe of this beautiful Mercedes. At the end of the video, the girl is telling her father that she has the best dad in the world and he will always, always, always, be her first true love. That it had nothing to do with the car, but the fact he just cared about her happiness.

OK, I know what you're thinking. LOL. Yes, I'M A SUCKER! I'm not totally sure if the sales guy was genuinely just showing me a similar scenario or used it AS EMOTION to get me to look at a car that was $6000 more than what I wanted to spend. Nevertheless, I bought a Mercedes that day. LOL. Zero regrets. Same red bow. Same pull into the driveway. Same tears and it was worth EVERY SINGLE CENT!

That being said, had this guy not shown me such an emotional video, I would've walked out with a very nice Honda Accord, but I just put myself in that picture as the amazing dad, my daughter leaping into my arms, crying and holding me. ZERO chance I wasn't getting her that Mercedes. So does emotion drive sales more in some scenarios than others? Yes, it does.

People buy when it "feels right." They use the emotional sales-driven buy and then justify their decision later. EVEN IF they know they shouldn't have purchased something when it's way out of their price range. You need to sell driving emotion and use logic to make it make sense to limit buyer's remorse later. Mastering the use and when to use both are very important.

Anything you're presenting as a benefit should have an emotional hook. This should start immediately. The prospect needs to know why you're the person they should work with, rather than you just shoving the product or service's features and benefits down their throat. They don't care about any of that until they know why you're the person they should be doing business with. To believe in what you're selling, they need to believe in you first.

1. Explain the risk of not buying (Fear).

2. Describe what they will get (Greed).

3. Point out how you make them better (Jealousy).

4. Explain how their decision can help others (Altruism).

5. Highlight the consequence of missing out (Shame).

6. Emphasize ways you help reach goals (Pride).

But the truth is to sell anything you must understand all the facts about the product or service you're offering. Master everything. Take time to know the good and bad facts, because the bad facts matter just as much, if not more, than the good ones. Your offering might be great at one thing, but not so good at another. Be honest about it. Rarely is there a perfect fit, but you can use the truth/facts about what it won't do to build trust. Therefore, when you offer the good facts, they believe that they are real. VERY few sales reps do this, but they should.

All the facts, good or bad, are directly attached to the emotion of the sale and inevitably will be a part of why they do business with you or don't. Too many salespeople spew the good and don't understand that being honest about what the product or service won't do will have a huge impact on how the prospect feels about you and their purchase.

Now the cost of the product has a direct role in how the hard logic can affect the buying process. For instance, if it's a lower-cost item, rather than a high-ticket offering, being instantly direct about the facts is a better approach. If it's a higher-ticket offering, you have to present the logic, but gradually do it throughout your presentation as the logic can get more intricate with each fact of what you're offering.

Most of your lower-ticket products or services have more familiarity. Don't assume this without confirming, but usually the prospect understands or is more familiar with what you're offering. People use facts to buy more in this instance than emotion. The only thing you really need to tell them is:

- How much
- When will they see the value
- Is it easy to use
- The quality
- How fast can they use it

Etc…

These are usually in bulk purchases or simple-use items or services. The stats are easy to understand when the value is fully understood. It's a faster purchase when a buy-now type of sale with zero to very little follow-up needed. Direct, straight to the point:

This is the offer. This is what it will do. These are the stats on durability, life expectancy, value, and customer opinions on the product or service.

Facts are also extremely important when you're dealing with an analytical buyer. They're more stat-based buyers. They want to know the numbers on mostly everything. Remember to make sure that you can somewhat determine what type of buyer you're dealing with. If you know they're an analytical buyer, you should tailor your presentation to that specific type of buyer.

The decision-making process is completely different when you know this. Data-driven sales are usually weighed more towards a buyer who needs to see the data on the value that's related to their cost to purchase your product or service.

For instance, if I'm selling pots and pans, an emotional buyer might love the color and how it looks more than how long it will last and the quality of the product. My wife would buy them because they match the colors in her kitchen. Whereas I want to know the cost, how long they last, are they non-stick products, and the overall quality of the product. If you're speaking to a doctor, the conversation is different than if you're speaking to a college kid looking for pots and pans.

Another thing you always want to make sure of when using more fact-based logic is that you are appeasing the decision maker. The person who can make or break the sale. You should be able to know who that person is throughout the process. Using the example of my wife and I above, if my wife loved the color because it matched her kitchen, I could talk her out of it if I don't see the quality and value of the purchase.

FACT OR LOGIC-BASTED APPROACHES TO CLOSE THE SALE

There are good things and not so good things about fact-based presentations.

The benefits are that your prospect knows everything they need to know about what you're offering, but that's not always going to get you the sale.

Some of the good things would be:

- **Direct**
    - o When you're direct, it usually gains respect from your prospect, because you're not wasting their time or they don't feel like you're trying to just talk them into buying

something without understanding fully what the benefits are.

- **Saves time**
    - o When you're direct and go straight to the point, small talk can become nonexistent. Present the facts. Present the price. Make a logical buy based off both.
- **Decisions are easier**
    - o They either want it or they don't. The facts are presented. They like them or they don't, so decisions are usually made without having to "pitch" as much.

Some of the not-so-good things would be:

- **Too many facts, too soon.**
    - o You have to remember that the prospect doesn't know the product or service like you do, so when you're direct and go straight to the facts, using the logic, it can be too much information in too little time. It gets confusing, with too many moving parts, and they don't understand how to best use what you're offering. Which leads to indecision and that usually results in not closing the sale.
- **There's no relationship.**
    - o When all you do is offer the facts and concentrate on the logic, it may make your prospect feel like they don't matter, which means the wall comes back up and they feel like you just want their money.
- **Minimal Understanding**
    - o What you're offering might not be what they want, but because you're being direct, you spend little time finding out if what you're offering even adds value to them. The result? Another deal lost.

USING EMOTIONS TO CLOSE THE SALE

When using emotions to drive sales, it takes time, care, and understanding of your prospect. This is usually, but not always, when you're selling something harder to explain, with tons of moving parts, or a higher-ticket item, where cost drives the emotion of the sale. Value has to be there, but putting the prospect in the picture and being conscious of how they'll feel when they make the purchase matters tremendously.

Emotional sales are also very useful when a prospect is getting multiple offers, with others trying to sell them something similar to the product or service you're trying to sell them. Why should they buy from you? Too many people miss the value of care, of relationship building, and of fully being aware of what matters most to the buyer, rather than just trying to make the sale and get paid. It's the easiest way to lose a sale.

I know you know what I'm talking about. We've all bought something from someone just because we've liked them so much, they were honest with us, we had a better conversation, they spent more time with us. The question I always ask salespeople I'm training is: why buy from you? If you can't answer that, you're just another salesperson. BUT if you can and there's actual emotion that can drive a purchase by SERVING someone, prospects will be way more inclined to buy from you.

Emotional sales are exactly that, emotion driven. The facts and data and specifics about the product you're offering matter less than how you make them feel, how the product will make them feel, how it will help them, proving the outcome will solve their problem.

Have you ever heard the phrase: "Emotions Drive Sales"? Well, it's true, both for the salesperson and the prospect or client.

There are usually a number of emotions that are directly related to a buyer's problems, such as:

- Complacent due to lack of money

- Can't figure out how to solve the problem
- Frustration due to not being able to fix the problem
- Embarrassed they haven't already fixed the problem
- Stressed out because they have a problem to solve
- Want to find the answer, but too afraid to ask for help

These are EXACTLY the issues we run into with Make Sales Great Again business consulting, sales training, and leadership training. Ego, pride, not being open to listening to the opinion of others—all this is emotion-based and drives performance, sales efficiency, and overall business success. The salesperson's emotions, ego, pride, etc., attached to this could lead to questions or comments they have like:

- Why should I spend the money for consulting?
- Why should I pay for sales and leadership training?
- I'd never pay someone to mentor me.
- Are you sure buying this will help me?
- How will the product or service do what you say it will?
- Are you sure this will help?

Prospects, people in general, are commonly looking for validation or assurance that the move they're about to make makes sense and is the right move. They won't admit it, but it's very common for most.

With expensive purchases, they need to emotionally be bought in, rather than needing every little detail or analytics. Things like:

- How will they feel when they buy _____?
- How will this make my family happier?
- How will my team feel if we give them this tool?

All the "feels," if you will. Why? Because most higher dollar purchases have to mean something to someone and the outcomes need to emotionally be attached to their happiness or success in the end.

Complex, problem-solving situations are extraordinary for emotion-driven sales presentations.

Also in an emotion-driven purchase, the prospect likes some sort of human accountability and will say things like:

- Do I get you if we move forward?
- Are you going to be there to help us always?
- If you're not here, who will help us?
- What level of support will we have with this purchase?
- If I have a problem, can I contact you?

All this matters so much in an emotional sale. The prospect needs to FEEL! They need to know you will BE THERE! When you accomplish this, you need to do WHAT YOU SAY and be there always. When you do, the relationship becomes long-term and everlasting.

Again, this is big with other companies reaching out to your prospects offering something of similar value that may solve similar problems, but when they know you and you do what you say, always there to SERVE, competition becomes irrelevant. Saving a few bucks to lose someone good isn't worth it to most people.

This also helps when most logic-based salespeople miss the emotion. Information overload becomes easier to navigate through, as they know they can ask you and you will serve them. You'll take your time, so they FEEL the care to provide a value others won't so they can better understand the information most just spew on them.

An emotion-driven presentation has two things that matter most.

1. Explain how they will feel when they have what you're offering. How they will feel as the owners, how employees will feel, how it will affect their family, the business as a whole, or whomever will be affected by their purchase.

Mention how they will feel when they've finally found a solution.

2. Give them the validation they need to know they're making the right decision so they feel confident. Tie in how you're the best fit for them to work with. How working together, you will assist them in eliminating future problems they might have or continue to have if they don't have you and what you're offering.

Those two things alone are beyond strength in a sales presentation. They will change the game for your success and most importantly add value to the people you have the luxury of serving.

Like the logic- or fact-driven sales process, there are good and not-so-good things about an emotion-based process as well.

Some of the good things would be:

- Close more sales
    - When you do this right, you don't have to "close the sale;" it just happens organically without pressure.
- Long-term business
    - Emotion-based sales processes drive repeat business where your prospect will choose you first always, which usually results in additional business for you in the future.
- You know one another better
    - This builds a relationship where you get to know one another from a business standpoint and on a personal level. This helps you with referral business and trust is greater than just a logic-based sale.

Some of the not-so-good things would be:

- You can miss facts through logic that matter
    - Emotion-based salespeople tend to concentrate so much on getting to know the client that they forget to go over facts that could result in a sale that matters most to the prospect.
- Know your audience

- o All too often, emotion-based sales presentations are used with highly analytical prospects which will result in less conversion.
- Some don't like caring approach
  - o Look, prospects aren't stupid. If you're not completely genuine about who you are, that you actually care, it can turn a client off immediately when you seem fake to them. Results... huge wall that's hard to bring down. They need to know you're genuine or the emotional sales process can backfire on you and fast.

So the real question is: How do you know when to use an emotion- or logic-based sales process? The truth? There's really no way to ever be 100% sure, but a good way to find out is through storytelling. When you use personal or third-party stories of yourself or someone you've served, you will get a pretty good idea if they're more of an emotion-based prospect or just want to get down to the numbers.

PERSONAL OR THIRD-PARTY STORIES

Have you ever told a story? I'm sure you have, but have you noticed that most are emotion driven? It's usually a memory that meant something to you in some capacity. It could've been finance driven or impact driven. Long story short, about money or how someone felt.

When using storytelling, it should put the customer in the picture, almost as if they can picture themselves in the story to prove how they'd feel if they moved forward with you or if they had what you're offering. This is a POWERFUL tool that most untrained sales professionals don't train themselves on or forget to do.

You can usually find out how they feel by just asking.

"How would you feel if you had this option and it made life easier?"

Their response can give you some context on how to better serve them. The non-emotional person is going to respond way differently than someone who answers more in-depth and answers in a way where they explain how they FEEL.

PERSONAL STORIES

Your story matters. Talk about personal things in your life that have been affected by the product or service that you're offering. For instance, if you're selling vacations, talk about your favorite vacations. The smiles on your kids' faces when they saw something cool. How it made you feel that you could take them to a place you only dreamed of as a child. Show them the happiness, such as videos and pictures of the good times.

They want to put themselves in the picture, but if they see the raw, real, and honest emotion in how what you're offering them affected you, many would like to feel the same when they're driven by emotion.

Just be honest. Don't make up stories and mislead people. They need to see how you feel, and to feel that from you. If you haven't been affected by the value of what you're offering, use third-party stories.

THIRD-PARTY STORIES

In this day and age the use of technology is a must. Many companies will show commercials or videos of people smiling or laughing while making money using their product or service. When you walk into a lobby you see this. That's intentional, obviously. It makes people wonder, "If I had that, would I feel the same or get the same results?" Then curiosity sets in, opportunity opens, and they're more open to what you're offering.

Having people tell you how they were affected by a product or service adds massive credibility. People want to FEEL. They need to FEEL. The more your story affects them, the more personable you can be and have a quicker emotional connection with your prospect.

There are a few things you need to be able to answer before you start telling stories.
- Do you know why you're telling the story?
    - There has to be substance and a reason you're telling the story. Your product or service may have affected a previous client, family, or business in such a way that data may not really paint the best picture. The story has to have impact and value related to a better outcome for your prospect without having to tell them directly.
- Is it important to tell a real story vs a made up one?
    - I've seen it done both ways over the past three decades and I can tell you that real vs made up... It's not even a competition when presenting one vs the other. When presenting a real story, emotion is evident. You can see and feel the emotion. Whereas with a made-up story, you have to be a good actor, who's also OK with lying. So just tell real stories. It's ethical and it'll work better always.
- How will the story affect your prospect or client?
    - Your stories should be intentional. There should be a reason you're telling your prospect that specific story. Have an arsenal of authentic stories so you can use the right one for the right client that actually has purpose.
- Will the story help you find the EBM (Emotional Buying Motive, not the DBM "Dominant Buying Motive")?
    - Be intentional about what your stories set out to do. You should use them to reveal the EMOTIONAL buying motive. What's driving them emotionally to do business with you?
- Will the story help solve a problem?
    - Does your story prove how it solved a similar problem for a previous or current client of yours? You should make sure

it's relevant. Not just another story to tell, but a story that ties into how you can help them.

- Will the story block an objection that you know usually surfaces?
    - o Many third-party stories can be used to block objections and are purposely driven to block common objections. Many highly trained sales professionals do this to prevent objections they know are common. The story allows you to handle the objection indirectly.
- Are you presenting it in a timely manner, not dragging it on?
    - o Make sure your stories are told in a timely manner, getting to the point of why you're telling the story. If the story is too long and loses the intention and the attention of the prospect, it can lead to less conversion.
- Are you finishing with a power statement that drives the reason behind the story?
    - o Finish with a strong statement such as:
    "They really loved that because it helped them with x, y, z. It led to better, x, y, z and continues to add value daily."

This is a recap of the story, the Cliffs Notes version, confirming that they've heard you and understand how you've added value to the prospect you've served and/or are currently serving.

There are 2 things that matter most when telling stories, personal or third party.

1. They have to be REAL!

Yes, I know, you can make up stories to create emotion, but to me that's the weakest way to sell. Document REAL stories with REAL people. When they're real, they're presented better and your prospect can see it and feel the difference. You should also never want to mislead anyone and making something up doesn't prove that what you're offering adds real value to the lives of others.

2. The story should be intentional.

There should be a reason for every third-party story. You need to have an arsenal, so based on the situation, you can tailor your presentation to your client's needs.

- Why does this story matter for this specific prospect?
- How will it impact them emotionally and logically when I tell it?
- Will it solve an issue they have?
- Will it give them an idea of how having you there for them will make life easier?
- Will the story give them an idea of how it will serve their business needs, people around them, family members?

Every time you tell a story it must be purpose driven. There should be a reason why you're telling it and you should have another story ready to go when you need to use one. It's a really good way to get a point across without being pushy. When you're intentional and you tell a real story, a real example of how you and/or your product or service has helped others, it gives your prospect a really good way to put themselves in that same picture.

Third-party stories crush objections too, without sounding like you're trying to. It's a great technique to master and makes the customer feel OK letting you make your point, because you're not arguing, getting combative or trying to prove your point directly. You're indirectly allowing them to yield without making them feel embarrassed or hurting their ego when you're right.

It can also help you not look like a lion trying to pounce on its prey. You're helping them realize how you can solve a problem by using another prospect's example of how you've helped them. You're basically guiding your prospect to understand better how what you're offering can add massive value to them, without directly disagreeing with them.

Just remember to keep your stories human. Your prospect has to connect with the story. Sharing a personal story is really good for this. There's a time to be vulnerable. When they feel your truth and emotion, it becomes transferable and puts the prospect in a completely different mindset. Keep your stories simple. Don't get too technical. Keep them short, fun, and authentic. Meaning: "I had a client who had the same issue and here's what they found." That's it. You're not writing a book or at a storytelling convention. KEEP IT SIMPLE!

Another good way to tell your stories is to let them tell theirs. Ask them to give you an example of the problem you're trying to solve. Ask them to tell you a story. It's a great way to transition into your own story to give them more context on how you can help them.

I also recommend letting people you've worked with in the past tell their stories. Get the testimonials! Video testimonials are amazing, but even written are fine. People will believe a prospect and their success way more than they'll trust a salesperson. Remember, these can be social media posts, videos, postcards, written testimonials, case studies, or data offering proof of before and after you served someone. Just any highlight that you can tie to someone you've helped.

The good news is, ANYONE can do this and you don't need to do it like anyone else but YOURSELF. The way I tell a story will be different from the way you tell the story. Be you. Use your gifts. Just make sure when you tell the story it's something that will make them THINK and FEEL!

I recommend every salesperson master the ability to use logic to close deals, to use emotion to close deals, to tell their own story to close deals, and use third-party stories to close deals. Role play and have fun with it. Know when to use one or all of them, but when you master them, you'll be prepared to use them the right way at the right time and you'll serve people properly while making a ton of money. Win-win!

Here are 3 different ways to train using logic only, emotion only, and then a combination of both.

1. LOGIC-DRIVEN CLOSE: SOLAR BUSINESS

Scenario: You're presenting a solar panel system to a homeowner.

Salesperson: "Based on your last 12 months of utility bills, you're currently paying an average of $150 per month. With our solar system, the projected monthly cost would be around $100. That's a saving of $50 every month or $600 annually. Over the 25-year lifespan of the solar panels, you'll save approximately $15,000. Plus, our system comes with a 10-year warranty. It's a smart financial move to switch."

Explanation: This approach is purely logical. It breaks down the financial benefits, focusing on clear savings and long-term advantages. In industries like solar, quantifiable benefits can often be persuasive, as the primary barrier to entry is typically the initial cost.

2. EMOTION-DRIVEN CLOSE: VACATION BUSINESS

Scenario: You're offering a tropical vacation package to a couple.

Salesperson: "Imagine waking up to the soothing sound of waves crashing on the shore. You step out onto your balcony, feeling the warm sun on your face and walking out onto the beach, the soft sand between your toes. This is a chance for you both to truly disconnect, reignite your passions, and create memories that'll last a lifetime. Don't you both deserve this getaway?"

Explanation: This approach is emotionally charged. It paints a vivid picture of the experience, tapping into the couple's desires for relaxation, connection, and escape. The travel industry often capitalizes on emotion, as vacations are seen as treats or escapes from routine.

3. COMBINED LOGIC AND EMOTION CLOSE: REAL ESTATE BUSINESS

Scenario: You're selling a family home to a young couple expecting their first child.

Salesperson: "This home is located in one of the top school districts in the city, ensuring a solid education for your child. Not only that, but its value has been consistently increasing at 5% annually, making it a sound investment for your family's future. Picture celebrating birthdays in this spacious living room and watching your child play in the safe and friendly neighborhood park just a block away. It's the perfect blend of a smart financial move and a loving environment to raise your child."

Explanation: This strategy balances both logic (school district, property appreciation) and emotion (family memories, safety). Real estate sales often require both components because purchasing a home is both a significant financial decision and a deeply personal one. Combining these aspects can be a potent way to persuade potential buyers.

IMPORTANCE OF EACH APPROACH:

1. **Logic-Driven:** This method is vital when targeting customers who prioritize numbers, metrics, and tangible results. Some decisions are made based on cost-benefit analyses, and in such cases, a logical argument can be highly effective.

2. **Emotion-Driven:** Emotional appeals can be powerful, especially when selling experiences, aspirational products, or when there's a personal aspect to the decision-making process. Emotion often drives impulse buying and can create a sense of urgency.

3. **Combined:** Some decisions, like buying a home, require a blend of heart and head. In these scenarios, a sales approach that incorporates both logic and emotion can resonate on multiple levels, addressing both practical and emotional concerns. This dual approach increases the chances of closing a sale.

The MSGA way is this: Understanding your customer and the product or service you're selling is crucial to your overall success. The best salespeople can gauge which approach will be most effective and tailor their pitch accordingly.

Some are all emotion. Some are all logic, but most are a combination of both. Create some real-life scenarios for you and your team to role play using both logic and emotion, and then another two just using one or the other. This is how you will become a rockstar sales professional and it's also how you'll build the strongest sales team ever!

CHAPTER 22

THE CHOICE CLOSE

Prospects need options, folks! This works and it doesn't matter what you're selling. It could be a very expensive product/service or it could be a small-ticket item used to upsell, but when you learn how to use this properly, it'll change the game for you.

So what exactly is "The Choice Close"?

Simply put, you're just offering more than one option for them to choose from. In this chapter, I'm going to explain how to use this to help you get bigger deals, get the prospect down to a buying decision more easily, and so much more.

When you use this technique properly, it's one of the most powerful closing tools you'll love to use. It can and most likely will completely eliminate the word "no" from the prospect's vocabulary.

If you were to ask me, "Todd, do you want to go to dinner or not?", I could easily say, "No." But if you said, "If you had to choose a restaurant to eat at tonight, would it be Ruth's Chris or Morton's Steakhouse?", I can't say just "No." I'm forced to choose one OR give you a reason why I don't want to go to dinner, which is also good, because I'm surfacing the objection. Finding the problem is easy when you use a choice close.

There are times to use 2 and there are times to use 3 choices.

When you use 2 options, it's usually you trying to narrow down the choice you want them to lean towards. When you use three, most prospects choose the middle-cost item.

The great Victor Antonio talks about this a lot on stage. In his professional opinion, he dives into how fast-food companies usually have three options and that the most profitable option is usually the one in the middle.

He spoke about people being hungry in a drive-through and being indecisive. They pull up, they look at the combos, and they say:

"I'm hungry, but maybe a small isn't enough, but the large might be too much.... So I'll just take the one in the middle."

You know, he's right! LOL. When I heard him say this, I was like, "Man, I do that all the time! He's right!" We consciously try to pick the safest route.

This is very common. When presented with three options, the prospect usually will choose the one in the middle. They don't want to spend too much money going for the most expensive one, they don't want to buy the small as it might not be enough, so the majority choose the one in the middle. This is a great way to get a client to make a buying decision.

Here are some examples of a choice close using 2 and 3 options:

"Todd, I know we both agree you see the value in the consulting services. Do you prefer the 3-day deep dive or the weekly accountability calls?"

"Rob, we have the elite package that has everything you want and more. We have the Gold package that solves the problems we spoke of, and we have the starter package that will get you

onboard where you can always upgrade to the other two options in the future. Which one do you think is the best one for you to start with?

"I completely understand, Brandon, so do you think the yellow jacket or the all-black one better suits you?"

"Makes total sense, Tristan. Knowing that matters to you, do you think the black SUV with the third row is the best fit or the Explorer with more storage space in the back?"

"That's perfect, Averigh, so which clubs fit you better, the cavity backs or the blades?"

"I know what matters to you most now; thank you for sharing. So we have 3 options for you. The house with everything you want that extends your budget a bit, the house you really like that's a bit smaller but makes more sense financially, and then the fixer upper. Which do you think is best for you and your family right now?"

"I get it and I want to make sure this works for you. I have tomorrow at 1pm available and 6:30pm. What time works best for you?"

"I know finding time to meet in person can be hard, so would you rather use Zoom or Google Meets for our follow-up appointment?"

Not so hard, right? Offer some options and ask them which they'd prefer. Easy-peasy, but salespeople sometimes go for the kill and push one product and one price, trying to pitch them on why they need it. It's rarely ever a good way to work with someone and quite frankly the only thing you're guaranteed to close in that case is their minds from being open to working with you any longer.

When you use the choice close the right way, it gives you a foolproof way to get a commitment from your prospect without the option for them to back out without giving you a reason, which would then give you a reason to handle any issue they may have. This doesn't mean they're going to buy, but it'll narrow down the information you need to better serve them.

Offering more than one option is a way to ask for the sale and then redirect your presentation from the answer they give you. Sometimes it allows you to transition to the close very easily. You're asking or assuming the sale non-aggressively. It's not pushy. It's their opinion on what they think best suits their needs and usually lets you know how ready they are to make a buying decision.

One very important note. The best of the best never lead their prospect to an option offered. A lot of untrained salespeople will start out the right way but mess up the entire process by saying something like:

"I understand, Abriella, I have the option with everything you want and then a really good starting package. If I were you I'd just do it all, because whether you think you need it or not, you're going to eventually want what that package has."

Your pushing them to one choice or another could turn the prospect off, and their decision might be they don't want to do business at all with you. Some would say to offer them to start with the smaller package, so they can grow into the bigger one. But all you're doing there is eliminating the opportunity to buy the bigger package.

The best move in the choice close is to offer it, shut up, and let them speak. When they do, you'll know how to move forward based on their answer.

The choice close is one of the best tools to have on the back end. Offering more than one option gives you the ability to ask for the close softly and also upsell them on a potential bigger option without being salesy or pushy. Get used to offering more than one option; it'll definitely lead to a much higher conversion rate.

The only way to get a much higher conversion rate is to train and master the choice close! Here are a few different scenarios to help you and your team master this process.

1. CAR SALES:

Scenario: A customer, Linda, has been examining two different models of cars on the showroom floor: a sedan and a hatchback. She's expressed interest in both but seems indecisive.

Choice Close: The salesperson says, "Linda, both cars are fantastic choices. If you had to drive one home today, which one do you see yourself in? The sleek sedan or the versatile hatchback?"

Why this works: In car sales, the choice close is effective because it gives the prospect a feeling of control while guiding them towards making a decision. Instead of asking if Linda wants to buy a car (a yes or no question), the salesperson asks which car she would prefer. This narrows down her options and makes it more likely she'll make a decision.

2. DOOR TO DOOR SALES (E.G., HOME SECURITY SYSTEMS):

Scenario: A homeowner, Mr. Thompson, has been listening to the salesperson explain the benefits of two different home security packages: a basic package and a premium package with extra features.

Choice Close: The salesperson says, "Mr. Thompson, I genuinely believe a security system can provide peace of mind for your family. Based on our discussion, which package do you feel would best suit your needs: the basic package that covers all essential areas or the premium package with those extra surveillance features?"

Why this works: In door-to-door sales, you're intruding on someone's personal space, so it's vital to ensure the prospect feels in control. The choice close here not only guides Mr. Thompson towards a purchase but also reassures him that he's making the decision based on his family's needs.

3. LIFE INSURANCE:

Scenario: A young couple, Jake and Melissa, are considering life insurance. The salesperson has shown them two plans: one with higher monthly premiums but a larger payout, and another with lower premiums but a smaller payout.

Choice Close: The salesperson says, "Jake, Melissa, both of these plans offer great value and security for your family. Do you see yourselves preferring the plan with the larger payout to ensure more extensive coverage for your family, or the one with smaller premiums to balance your current budget?"

Why this works: Life insurance is a sensitive subject, revolving around the well-being of loved ones. The choice close here subtly reinforces the importance of having life insurance. By presenting two beneficial options, it centers the discussion on how to protect their family, not whether to protect them.

IMPORTANCE OF THE CHOICE CLOSE:

The choice close is crucial because:

1. **Reduces indecision:** By presenting limited options, it helps prospects overcome indecision.
2. **Empowers the prospect:** It allows them to feel in control of the decision, rather than feeling pressured.
3. **Guides the conversation:** It shifts the conversation from "Should I buy?" to "Which one should I buy?"
4. **Builds a relationship:** It shows the salesperson is listening to the prospect's needs and offering tailored options.

In every one of these scenarios, the end goal is to help the prospect make the best decision for their needs. Serving them, not just selling them. The choice close is a tool that facilitates this while making the process feel collaborative and customer centric. It takes a ton of pressure off of them and, to be honest, it makes your job way easier.

As always, keep working on this and dial it in to your specific industry. Make a list of choice closes and when and how to implement them and watch your efficiencies grow like crazy!

CHAPTER 23

DON'T TALK $H!T

Never ever, ever, ever, ever, ever, ever bash the competition. Whether it's C2C, B2C, B2B, whatever sales environment you're in, just don't do it! It may seem like an easy way to steer people away from the competition, but it's far from that. It actually works more against you than helps you. It's also one of the weakest sales "tactics" that I don't teach ever. If you have to bash the competition to get the sale, then you have way more work to do on your sales game. This is not how you get deals.

There are a bunch of reasons why this is a bad thing. Let's jump into them so you can stay away from doing this or teaching this to your business or team in the future.

1. YOU'RE OPENING THE DOOR.

Bashing the competition surfaces their name. When you're talking about them and their inadequacies, the prospect may wonder if what you're saying is true, tell you they'd like to verify what you're saying is true, and then they will get back to you. You're opening the door for them to talk to the competitors and not do business with you today.

2. WHAT IF WHAT YOU'RE SAYING IS WRONG OR UNTRUE?

Your competitors are always making moves too. You might say something about them that isn't true anymore, or maybe you've just received the wrong information about them. If your prospect finds that out, all of your credibility is out the window and you just look like a shit talker. A lot of slick talkers like to say things about other companies and call them facts. But if you're wrong, the buyer's trust is gone.

3. IT'S NOT TIME WELL SPENT.

Look, you know just as well as I do that you only have a short window of time to be present with your prospect. Do you think spending time bashing the competition is the best way to earn their business? The answer is No! but If you said yes, stop reading at this point and go back to the beginning of the book and start all over again please. Thank you.

Spend time serving, helping, solving your prospect's problems, and offering solutions. Don't waste time on this.

4. WHAT IF THE CUSTOMER KNOWS MORE THAN YOU DO?

Unfortunately you see this happen a lot these days. By the click or swipe of a finger the prospect can find out more information about someone or something almost instantly. So what's that mean for someone bashing the competition? What if the buyer steps away, pulls information about your competitor, and finds conflicting information from what you've just said? What now?

Either you spend time trying to convince them you're right, or they conclude you're wrong and they see you differently. Plus, they could just actually know more than you do.

A lot of times, the prospect might get insulted if they know something about the competition and you're talking to them as if they don't. Be very careful not to offend them or question their intelligence. You will lose the sale instantly.

5. WHAT IF THEY'RE WORKING WITH THE COMPETITOR YOU'RE BASHING OR HAVE WORKED WITH THEM?

Many salespeople forget that they're not the only option out there. We may not have been their first choice or the first person they've worked with in your space.

It's pretty common for an untrained salesperson to bash a competitor and the prospect is either working with that competitor or considering it. The prospect gets turned off instantly.

6. WHAT IF YOUR COMPETITOR DOESN'T BASH YOU?

You might answer this question by saying, "We are far superior; that's why they don't bash us!" Or it could be that they're just really good salespeople. Would you want to work with someone who talks trash about others or someone whose main focus is serving you? Don't get caught up in that game. It's a loser every time.

7. YOU'LL SCARE THEM AWAY!

Listen, they've just met you. Do you think they should trust you? You might say yes, but trust is earned, so the answer is, they shouldn't. They will verify what you say. But another reason bashing the competition is always bad is because you could be scaring the prospect away from what your competition is offering which, let's remember, is similar to what YOU are offering. It might just make them scared to work with anyone at all.

8. YOUR CHARACTER WILL BE IN QUESTION.

When you talk bad about others or your competition, do you think buyers look at you as a person of good character (which I'm sure you are)? But they don't know that. Their impression of you is that you take the competition down so it builds value in what you're offering. How about building value in what you're offering and be the obvious choice. Build your character. You're not just tearing down the competition, you're tearing down who they think you are.

The top 8 reasons not to bash the competition, as given above, all usually result in something like this on the back end of a sales presentation:

"Thanks, Todd, but we'd like to verify everything you said and get some other quotes."

It happens almost every time. There's no trust in bashing. There's trust in serving. Be the good and the obvious choice for them to do business with.

Competition is very normal and it's OK to be competitive with another company or person and it can and is very fun when done with integrity. The way we compete, what we say, our facial expressions, our body language all matter when approaching the time to distinguish the difference between you and a competitor.

Remember, weak salespeople, dishonest salespeople, bash the competition because they aren't skilled enough to just be the right choice through serving or their ego won't allow them to "not" be the right choice at times. It proves that the salesperson bashing the competitor is insecure and doesn't know how to do business in a way that a prospect ends up asking them to work with them or help them.

You will get judged when you judge.

You will lose credibility when you trash someone else.

You will lose trust when you talk bad about a company someone else is working with.

The prospect is looking for someone they can have a long-term relationship with, someone they can trust and count on, someone who is just a good person. They are more influenced by you, the person, than they are by the product or service you're offering. There are tons of competition out there; bashing the competition won't get you the deal. Being a good person, solving their problems, and giving them massive value makes you the right person with the right product!

Here are some alternatives to master if they ask you how you compare to other companies.

1. SURFACE THE COMPETITION EARLY

Block the "How are you compared to your competition?" question right away. I like to bring this up very early in the sales process. It shows strength and that you're not afraid to talk about it in an integrity-based way.

You're always going to have competition in everything in life. Many prospects might even try to sell you on the fact that you're the only one they're considering. If you believe that, you should let them train you. They're closing you, just as much as you're trying to close them, believe me.

2. HIGHLIGHT YOUR DIFFERENCE (HYD)

You should know exactly how your company differs from competitors. Emphasize what sets your company apart and explain how it can benefit the prospect. Now, DO NOT spew features and benefits only.

Talk about how YOU, yourself, are different and what you do that will specifically impact them in a positive way.

Discuss your strengths and how those strengths compare to the competition. Provide examples of how your company excels in certain areas and why this is important to the prospect.

3. HONESTY IS KEY

Don't discredit the competition or exaggerate your strengths. It's important to be honest about your company's capabilities and limitations. When you highlight what you're not good at or what the product or service "won't" do is equally, if not more important, than what it will do. This builds trust instantly and TRUST is exactly what you need to serve your prospects better.

4. YOUR REPUTATION MATTERS

If your company has a good reputation in the industry, mention this and explain why it's important. If the reputation isn't all that good, explain why, being honest, and talk about the direction your company is going in to recreate who you are to better serve your clients.

A reputation is earned and it's OK to talk about, without arrogance, but as a tool to prove why they should do business with you.

5. TALK ABOUT YOUR CLIENTS – LEVERAGE TESTIMONIALS

If you have clients who have worked with you for a while and love what you do and how you serve them, mention them and explain how they have benefited from working with YOU and your company. This establishes credibility and demonstrates who you are and your company's expertise based on the opinion of others who have worked with you in the past.

Using testimonials is a powerful way to increase credibility and trust with potential customers, which can ultimately lead to increased sales. Testimonials provide social proof that your product or service has been successful for others, and they can help to address common objections or concerns that prospective buyers may have.

Here are a few reasons why leveraging testimonials can be beneficial when selling:

Testimonials can help establish trust with potential customers, especially if they are from people or businesses that the prospect knows or trusts. Testimonials provide social proof that your product or service is effective and that others have had a positive experience with it.

Prospective customers also might have objections or concerns that hold them up from doing business with you. Testimonials can help to address these objections or concerns by providing evidence that you and your product or service have solved for them.

Testimonials also highlight the value that your product or service provides to others, putting them into the picture on how it might be able to help or serve them as well. Basically proving from a third party of what your company can serve them with.

They help to differentiate your product or service from competitors by showing the unique, specific benefits that it and you provide. They can also help to position you and or your business as a trusted and reliable partner to work with.

Overall, leveraging testimonials can be an effective way to build trust, overcome objections, demonstrate value, and differentiate from competitors when selling.

The goal is not to disparage other companies but rather to focus on what sets your company apart and why you are the best choice for the prospect's needs.

Just speak good about your competitors or don't say anything about them at all unless the prospect asks questions. When and if they do, be prepared to be nice and talk nice about other companies. Talking bad won't ever help you. When you speak about other people or companies with respect, this says everything about you. Prospects are listening to you and judging you, believe that.

Remember, don't be a part of, don't engage with, don't be around anyone speaking badly about anyone or any business. It will NEVER EVER EVER help you get a deal. That's a promise.

CHAPTER 24

YOUR NEGOTIATION ARSENAL

You've been negotiating your entire lives. When you were a kid and you wanted something from your mom and dad, maybe a new toy, baseball glove, clothes, and you said to them, "I'll give you a kiss, Daddy, if you do this for me"—that's negotiation! Maybe when you just got your license and you went to Mom and Dad and said, "If you let me borrow the car Friday night, I'll clean both of your cars all day Saturday." See, NEGOTIATION AGAIN!

This is a natural skill that we've all used for years, yet as we get older, unless it's a tool that you use daily, it's a hard one to keep working the way you'd like it to. Also, it's harder to negotiate with someone you don't know, that you just met, or someone that you KNOW wants your money.

Negotiation can help you to close more deals, generate more revenue, and build stronger relationships with customers. Simply put, it's the process of finding a mutually beneficial solution(s) to a problem or issue, which includes listening, understanding, and communicating effectively with the other party. Basically both talk, listen, and understand each other's wants and needs, respecting both sides and making all elements worthwhile for both the prospect and the salesperson.

When you're in sales, there are a few things that negotiation is imperative for:

1. CLOSING MORE DEALS: Duh! When you master negotiation it helps to persuade customers to buy your products or service by demonstrating the value they will receive in exchange for their money.

There are certain things that you need when negotiating to close more deals.

> **a. Be a Good Listener:** Listen so hard it hurts! The prospect's needs, concerns, and what they feel is most important. When you listen, it can help guide the prospect, serving them properly, without wasting time on things that don't add value to them. Prioritizing your pitch helps negotiate better terms and proves how much you care.

For Example:

Prospect: "I'm interested in your product, but I'm not sure if it's the right fit for my business. Can you tell me more about how it works?"

Salesperson: "Absolutely. Our product is designed to make things easier for you, to minimize your effort and increase efficiency. Less time, more value. That being said, I want to make sure I understand your needs fully before we move forward. Can you tell me more about what you're doing currently and where you think our service could fit in?"

Prospect: "Well, we have a lot of manual processes right now and I'm hoping your service could eliminate some of that. But I'm also worried it's going to be out of my price range."

Salesperson: "I completely understand. That's why I like knowing as much as I can about what you do. Our service has helped many individuals like yourself, while being extremely cost effective. But if it's not a good fit, I'm just going to tell you that. Tell me what specific needs are you looking for and let's see if we can build something that not only makes sense financially, but gives you the tools you need to make this a no brainer. In the end if it's not something that makes sense, I'd rather you tell someone how well we treated you, so we can be the obvious choice in the future."

The salesperson listened. Proved that the prospect's points mattered most, but the salesperson also made it very clear that if it didn't make sense to do business, whether it be financially or in what the service offered, they'd rather just part ways to be the obvious choice to do business with at a later date. The prospect felt heard and the concerns were addressed in a way to keep the process moving, building trust through listening. Everyone wants to be heard. It's the easiest thing to do that most salespeople miss, unfortunately.

    b. Build Better Rapport: I know, I know. You're probably thinking "We know, Todd, we know!" But the truth is, I say it so much because it matters. It builds trust on BOTH sides, which makes the sales process smoother and helps eliminate having to negotiate as much on the back end. Just two people finding a common goal, having a fun conversation, and actually caring about the value add to both parties.

    c. Show Them the Value: What does your product or service do? How will it add value to their world? Make sure they fully understand the benefits of what you're offering, FULLY. When they say they do, ask them again just to make sure. Third-party stories are great here. Any evidence of success is crucial when negotiating to close more deals.

    d. Be Ready: Do you know the customer? Their wants and needs? Do you know the competition that's out there? Do you know the problems most prospects face in your world? Are you ready to show them how you can help fix that? Are you ready to be the person they can count on and actually be there when they need you? All of this is so important when negotiating. They want the expert. They want the prepared. They want the compassionate person who cares about them. They want it all, so why you? Because you're going to go the extra mile in being the person that has the answers to it all or at least know how to get them to best serve your client.

When you're negotiating to close more deals, you need to ask good open-ended questions to better understand the main pain points of your prospect. Take all the information you've learned and be flexible. What you're offering should never be a "one price or product fits all." Even the mega car dealership that says, "We don't negotiate," still negotiates. The negotiations aren't always on the price of the car, but what about the extended warranty, the service package, gap coverage. Most of the negotiations on "no haggle" car dealerships are done when you're approved and you've already done everything except sign the documents.

Work to find a mutually beneficial solution. Be willing to make concessions or adjust your offer to meet the prospect's needs. Remember, serve. Doing this can create a sense of urgency by highlighting the benefits of acting now rather than later. Offer incentives for quick decisions. Not to talk them into doing business with you, but to really give them the best deal if they move now.

2. Get the Best Revenue Outcome: Negotiation skills can also help you to maximize your revenue by negotiating higher prices, upselling, or cross-selling additional products or services.

Negotiating can help maximize revenue in sales in several ways:

Negotiating with the customer allows you to demonstrate the value of your product or service and how it can add value in their world. When they see what it can do and the worth of what you are offering, it'll lead to higher sales revenue.

a. **Referrals and Loyal Customers:** Negotiating with customers can help build a relationship with them, which can lead to more business that they'll refer to you and increased loyalty, which usually leads to them coming to you as the obvious choice for doing business in the future. If customers feel that you are willing to work with them to find a solution that meets their needs, they are WAY more likely to return to you in the future and tell everyone that you're the person they suggest working with.

b. **Upselling:** When you know what they want and meet their needs financially and what they'd get by working with you, it increases the odds of selling them additional products or services on the back end. They trust you. You've negotiated something that suits their needs, which means they're more inclined to add things you believe will impact them positively. By offering additional products or services during the negotiation process, you can increase your revenue per sale. It's not how many sales you can get, it's how efficient and profitable you are per sale that builds a powerful salesperson and team.

c. **What Do You Have That Others Don't:** When you're the person who takes time to negotiate a deal specific to their needs, that ALONE makes you stand out from others unwilling to do so. If you can offer better terms or pricing than your competitors, you may be able to win the customer's business and increase your revenue.

d. **Lost Deals Become Opportunities:** Most untrained sales representatives these days have egos so big that they'd rather lose a deal than negotiate. Now this doesn't mean you should always drop the price, but not every deal comes with the highest revenue at first. BUT it sure can turn into a long-term client for years to come. Don't miss out on deals because they're not the larger dollar amount deals we all hope for. Negotiate, close, and retain for future business. By working with the customer to find a solution that meets their needs, you may be able to close a deal that would have otherwise been lost.

3. Build Relationships: Effective negotiation skills can help you to build stronger relationships with your customers by demonstrating your willingness to listen, understand their needs, and find mutually beneficial solutions.

Building a relationship can be very helpful in negotiation for several reasons:

> **a. Make Sure They Trust You:** When you build a relationship with someone, you establish a level of trust between you and your prospect or client. Trust makes things easier. If they believe that you're honest and have their best interest at hand, it'll mean less need for negotiation at the back end. It makes them feel confident that you will follow through on any agreements made.
>
> **b. Know What They Want & What Motivates Them:** You need to be VERY VERY VERY good at finding out what's important to your prospect. What do they want out of what you're offering? What's the motivator for them to do business with you today? No silly acronym here. Just, what do they need and what can you do to motivate them to do business with you sooner rather than later? When you do this, you can tailor your negotiation approach to meet their needs, which can result in them getting what they want out of you and you closing the sale, which is what you want too!
>
> **c. Have Solutions to Conflicts:** It's normal for the first option not to be the right option. There may be something that you're offering that might need some tweaking or slight changing. You have to be good at navigating the negotiation process, leaving options for them that'll resolve any conflicts they may have when you're trying to close the deal. When they like you and trust you it makes it way easier to resolve conflicts when they come up. A

good relationship decreases tension and creates a more collaborative environment and closing process in which both parties are more willing to work together to find a solution.

When you have a good relationship with the other party, you'll start to think of options that allow both parties to do business with one another. Basically, both of you are open to finding a solution that works. This will definitely lead to more mutually beneficial agreements and you closing more deals!

4. Eliminate Conflict: Prospects will have pricing disagreements, different options they like and don't like, dates of delivery issues, and more when you're negotiating. Never ever ever get combative. Find a solution, but do it together. You're catering to their needs to the best of your ability and when you do this and it's evident, the prospect will usually bend on what they first said was "non-negotiable" and be more lenient because they see how much you're willing to work with them to make a deal happen that satisfies their needs.

Overall, negotiation is a critical skill in sales because it allows you to build trust, demonstrate value, and close more deals while also maintaining strong relationships with your customers, which to me, is the best. Nothing trumps building a relationship. Increase efficiencies everywhere and you'll be the first person they're going to refer to other prospects when they know you're open to negotiation and finding the best overall solution for everyone.

Before you even start to negotiate in sales, understand your product or service better than anyone. The features, benefits, limitations (what it won't do), pricing strategy (negotiation options). You should be able to answer any questions that the customer may have about your product or service confidently and intentionally.

You also have to know your customer. Know who's in front of you. Don't prejudge, but understanding their wants and needs is essential in the negotiation process. Their needs, what's most important, and possible budget. This helps tailor your approach to match their needs specifically. When you know your customer, you'll know their objections or concerns and be prepared to handle them all for the best outcome of both parties.

Always be ready to compromise. It's a part of sales, period. It's a give-and-take world and you have to be willing to compromise to reach a common goal, which is to do business with one another. However, don't just give it away. Stand firm, know your limits, and realize that every deal's not for them, but every deal's also not for you.

If you negotiate a deal that's not in your best interest, word can get out and it'll diminish the value of what you're offering.

Be careful not to undervalue what you're offering. A lower price when you drop will cost you deals. If you drop too soon, it'll make people wonder whether what you're offering is even worth the value at which you originally presented it. Because in the end, negotiating can potentially cost you deals too. You have to be strategic when negotiating, so you don't ever set yourself up for failure.

One of the main ways that negotiating can cost you deals is if you come across as too aggressive or pushy. If a prospect feels like they're being pressured into a sale or that you're not willing to listen to their needs and concerns, they may decide to walk away from the deal altogether.

Another way that negotiating can cost you deals is if you don't know enough about your product or service and consequently you left value that it adds out of your sales presentations. When you're on the back end, asking for the money and they give you an objection on some value that you didn't surface, it could set you up for disaster when negotiating. If you focus too much on price and not enough on the benefits that your product or service and what you personally can provide, you may not be able to justify the price to the prospect. This can make them hesitant or reluctant to close the deal.

If you want to avoid all of the above, it's important to approach negotiations in a collaborative and strategic way "TOGETHER." Always be listening to their responses and make sure they know that what matters to them, always matters to you.

Now let's dive into the "types" of negotiation. Here are 7 things you can negotiate with during the sales process or life of a prospect:

1. MONEY:

Whenever money is involved, it can get uncomfortable, but the good news is, it doesn't have to if you know how to negotiate properly.

First you need to do your research. Before any numbers start getting thrown around, know what you're negotiating for.

- The price of the item (market value) &
- The benefits you're going to receive if a deal is made (preferably written down)

All too often, I see people and companies negotiating deals and then when a deal is about to be made, they start talking about what it includes or doesn't include. Be VERY conscious of what the offer is, everything it includes, and know the market value of what you're looking at before you make a decision that isn't the best for you or the client.

You also want to see clear expectations. Such as:

- An affordable budget
- Timeline (delivery date, expectations for results, and more)
- What you're expecting from purchasing the product or service

Knowing this gives you leverage. Whenever you're negotiating for you or during the sales presentation, it's very important to understand what the leverage is and how you can use it to best serve both parties.

For instance, your leverage might be:

- A unique skill no one else offers
- Being able to accomplish something faster than others

- Your product or service is more for their money

Look, no one wants less value for more money. Everyone wants more value for less money. Knowing what leverage you have is a game changer.

One of the biggest mistakes I see salespeople make is starting too low when negotiating money. They don't give themselves resources or room to create a good value-based opportunity that suits both parties. Starting at a high price in a negotiation has several benefits.

Here are some of the best reasons to start high:

By starting with a high price, you're setting the tone of value to your prospect. I'm offering "x" and "x" is worth "y." You're influencing the other party's perception of what's reasonable. Even if they don't agree to the first price or to instantly do business with you, it shapes their expectations and influences their willingness to compromise when it comes down to deal time!

If you start with a low price, you may not have much room to move without going below your bottom line (which you should rarely do). One of the very few reasons to go below bottom line is creating a potential long-term relationship that will yield bigger and better business in the near future. I've made deals where I've lost money at start, but flourished in revenue after we proved what our value was to our clients. By starting high, you can make smaller concessions and still end up with a favorable outcome.

Remember, when you start high, you're building the value of what they perceive your offering to be. The prospect might believe that you're asking for a higher price because your product or service is that good! If you offered a lower price out of the gate, they could, on the other hand, think it's not that valuable and you may scare them off. This is one of the strongest reasons to start high. When the price is up, the prospect usually believes the quality is up.

Another reason I like to start out higher with price is because my time is worth money and so is yours and the prospect's. When I start high, it signals the prospect that I value the product or service and my time. Most of the clients will respect a higher number and that your time is money.

Starting with a high price can also signal to the other party that you respect your time. When you start lower, it usually seems like you're desperate for a deal. A higher price screams: this is the value of myself and the product or service and they're both worth your time and money. Humbly spoken of course. If you do this arrogantly, you'll lose someone instantly.

I want you to hear me when I say this: **"Be willing to walk away!"**

If the other party isn't willing to meet your minimum requirements, be prepared to walk away from the negotiation. This shows that you value your time and skills and won't settle for less than you're worth.

We know money is important, but there are so many other things that can be negotiated. You don't always have to drop the price and it's usually one of the last things I do.

Here are a few bad outcomes when dropping the price:

- Less money/smaller margins
- Smaller commissions
- They question the original value (why are they dropping the price that much?)
- Hurt your brand
- Questions quality
- Hard to go back up when you've dropped so low
- It can attract the wrong clients/prospects

So is dropping the price the best thing to do? No. For the reasons listed above, dropping the price is not always the way to go. There are so many other ways to negotiate and give yourself the outcome you're looking for and the prospect what they want.

Here are some examples:

Time

Is your time worth money? What value are you putting on the time you spend with your clients on their projects? Most prospects look for a great product or service, but look even more to the salesperson they're working with. You as the salesperson can bring even more value to what you're offering. The elite sales professionals in the world negotiate their time with their prospects as their highest value. This saves so much time worrying about trying to negotiate with just money or services. Don't underestimate what your time is worth.

Using time as a negotiating tool in sales can be a VERY effective way to create a sense of urgency and encourage the prospect to make a decision.

Here are some ways to negotiate with time:

1. Set clear deadlines:

Set a clear deadline for the deal and communicate it to the prospect. This can create a sense of urgency and encourage the prospect to decide in a timely manner. Communication is so important before and after the sale, but when you're in the negotiation stages, make sure both parties are clear on the deadline to make the decision. This way everyone is aware of the time frame to either move forward or continue the negotiation process.

2. Create scarcity:

Whatever you're offering should be emphasized as in high demand when there's a need or a solution you're offering to your prospects. This could mean limited quantities available, or pricing could increase if the decision isn't made in a timely manner. Use of the product or service might give them an edge on the competition. All of this can be used to motivate the prospect to make a decision sooner rather than later to avoid missing out on any of the above-mentioned opportunities.

3. Limited-time offers:

Some think this is "salesy" but in many cases, when true (always be honest), a special deal, discounts that are made available for a certain time, or additional items/services that can be included in the same price point for doing business now, can all be used as negotiating and motivating tools to close deals. When you do this, it usually will help the prospect make a decision much quicker because of the value of what you're offering for a limited time.

4. Highlight the consequences of delay:

Explain to the prospect that delaying the decision could lead to missed opportunities, increased costs, or other negative consequences. This can motivate them to take action sooner rather than later. Buyers don't want to miss out on things, but the fear of loss and explanations of what could "cost them money" by not doing the deal now is such an underrated tool.

5. Provide incentives for early action:

Offering additional benefits or incentives for the prospect to make a decision quickly is always a good tool. The problem with this is that if you offer it too soon, you could come across as pushy and not leave yourself tools to negotiate on the back end. It's important to save additional incentives to negotiate when you ask for the money. You can use some throughout the sales presentation.

I recommend that if you're a leader in an organization that has incentives to offer, your sales representatives need to come to a manager to ask approval before offering. Although this is a good tool, many untrained salespeople will give it all away far too quickly, eliminating the strength in what this tool is used for. When they know what they can do, they'll take the path of least resistance in offering these incentives if not controlled. Use this negotiation tool in strength. Meaning, hold out until the very very very end and only use a minimal amount of what you have to offer to still leave room for negotiation.

For example, offering a free trial or a bonus product can encourage them to take action sooner, but "when" you offer this is equally as important as the "value" of what you're offering in the incentives.

It's important to use time as a negotiating tool carefully and not come across as pushy or manipulative. Be real, transparent, and honest with the prospect, and focus on creating value for them rather than simply trying to close the deal quickly, which unfortunately most salespeople do these days. Be strong. Build value and hold out offering anything until the time is right.

Services

Negotiating the quality, frequency, and duration of a service during a sales process can be challenging, but here are some tips that might help:

1. Determine your customer's needs:

Before negotiating anything, it's important to understand what your customer needs and wants. Ask questions and listen carefully to their answers to identify their pain points and goals when they've worked with other sales representatives in the past. Knowing what they expect from you and determining the time and assistance they're expecting from you is so important. When you do this, you can then use the service you will provide to them as a negotiating tool.

2. Highlight the benefits of your service:

Emphasize the benefits of your service and how it can address the customer's needs. If you can demonstrate that your service can solve their problems or help them achieve their goals, they may be more willing to agree to your terms. Remember, once again, this includes you and your time. They want you to stick around and not just leave them high and dry after you get their money, like many sales representatives do these days.

3. Be flexible:

Negotiation is about finding a mutually beneficial solution. There are so many "one price" companies that pitch the benefits of "no negotiation," but is it really a benefit? Look, I get that some people like the "no-haggle" aspects of doing business with the one-price-only companies. That being said, it can be a little misleading. Those companies still negotiate. They might not negotiate on the price of the product or service, but "additional services" are often used as add-ons during the closing process once the buyer has agreed to the sale.

Negotiation is always used, in my opinion, and if it's not price, it's one of the many things I've outlined in this chapter. Be prepared to compromise on certain aspects of the service, such as the frequency or duration, to meet the customer's needs. Being flexible on certain items or services that you offer will and can make a buyer more ready and able to do business with you. Most of the time it provides more value, making the prospect feel like they've received the best deal.

There are many different ways to offer services. Use the list above as a tool, but I recommend you and/or your team sit down and discuss the services you believe will best suit your client or prospect's needs best, so you are clear and confident knowing how to best negotiate those services when trying to close deals.

Resources

You can negotiate the allocation of resources, such as staff, equipment, or materials, to ensure that each party gets what they need to achieve their goals. Using resources as a negotiation tool in sales can be a good way to close deals and achieve mutually beneficial outcomes.

Before using resources as a negotiation tool, you need to understand what the other party wants to achieve from the negotiation. This will help you identify which resources would be most valuable to your prospect or client and help you position them effectively when presenting an offer.

Here are some tips on how to best use resources in the negotiation process:

1. Know the resources you have:

Knowing the resources you have to use is the first and most important thing when negotiating. If you're unsure of whether or not you can do something or have a tool they might utilize or need, you will appear as if you don't know all the details of what you have to offer. This might push your prospect away, as most look for someone who is an expert in their field. These resources could include product discounts, additional services, extended payment terms, or other incentives that could be offered to sweeten the deal for them.

2. Know what to offer and when:

When you know what you have, position those resources strategically. For example, if you are negotiating with a customer who is price-sensitive, you could offer a discount, or additional services to prove more value, in exchange for a larger purchase. Another example might be if the customer needs a specific service that you provide, you could offer an extended service contract in exchange for a bigger deal, or an additional service for the same price that you know is at your disposal without increasing the price so the value is evident to your prospect.

Become a master in the process and "the what"—what you have to use and when to use those resources to help close the deal. This is a huge part of the success of the most elite sales professionals in the world.

Terms and Conditions

You can negotiate the terms and conditions of an agreement, such as payment terms, cancellation policies, warranties, or guarantees. It's important to use terms and conditions to protect your interests and ensure that both parties are clear about their rights and obligations.

Before entering into negotiations, make sure you know exactly what you want from the deal—both you and the prospect. When you're on the same page with each other's wants and needs, this can be a huge tool. This way you can prepare terms and conditions that reflect your and the prospect's needs and goals.

When writing terms and conditions, they should be written in plain, easy-to-understand language. Avoid using hard-to-understand legal terminology that may confuse the other party. Be very specific and outline the entire scope of work that details timelines, terms of payment, schedules for deliveries, whether outcomes are guaranteed or not, and anything else that both parties see fit. When this is done properly, it makes the back end much easier in the closing process. It also gives you the ability to negotiate specific things that might help solidify the deal. When it's in writing, they feel more comfortable moving forward.

Also make sure that the terms and conditions protect both parties' interests and outline what will happen if the other party fails to fulfill their obligations. Although this may seem harsh, it's also a very good way to negotiate deals, close deals, and for both parties to feel comfortable about getting the deal done.

Overall, the key to using terms and conditions effectively during negotiations is to be clear, specific, and flexible while protecting your interests.

Non-monetary Considerations

You can negotiate non-monetary considerations such as reputation, brand value, exclusivity, intellectual property rights, publicity, warranties, volume discounts, customized programs products/services, payment terms, and more.

Another good way to negotiate is to ask for feedback on how your negotiation was presented and the final agreement. This can help you improve your approach to future negotiations and ensure that your customer is satisfied with the outcome, but it can also surface their concerns in a manner that gives you a chance to get the deal done. Maybe you offer what they need, but you forgot to mention something? Maybe you did offer it, but they didn't fully understand? Many things happen throughout a presentation, and this is just a final chance to see if we can provide value that may have been missed to get the deal.

The Psychology Of Negotiating

Psychology plays a huge role in negotiating, because it helps us understand the motivations, emotions, and behaviors of the people we are negotiating with. All of these play a key role and allow you to determine specific negotiators that can tailor your approach to better communicate and persuade the prospect, anticipate their reactions, and build trust and rapport. The psychology in negotiations literally helps you manage the emotions of the prospect by understanding things they don't like or have questions about. It keeps them focused on their goals and guides you to find the solutions that will help them achieve those goals.

The pathway to fulfilling a prospect's expectations that are directly connected to their business or life goals gives you the best and most optimum outcome. It also reduces conflicts and helps you build way stronger relationships.

The psychology of negotiating involves understanding human behavior and motivations that drive negotiations. This knowledge helps negotiators to better understand themselves, their counterparts, and the dynamics of the negotiation, which can lead to more successful outcomes.

There are a few things that I train on when teaching psychology in emotions. Let's go over them:

1. Relationship building

Remember, negotiating isn't about just coming to a mutual agreement. It's not just getting the sale or trying to close a business or a person. It's more so about building relationships, which I know we've gone over a lot, but it's very much connected to psychology. When they know you more, they trust you more. It's as simple as that. The prospect has to feel like you have their best interests at hand. You're not just trying to get paid, but you want to help them find the solution that best suits them, and if you can't, you'll be honest and tell them.

2. Know how humans work

Human behavior is a massive part of the negotiation process. People come to the table with various motivations, emotions, judgments, and more which can impact their decision making and how the sales process will play out. You have to become good at understanding the other party's perspective and build rapport to establish trust. You have to let them know you're there to cooperate with them to determine the best possible outcome for them. Not for you, but them.

People just respond to people better who seem trustworthy and likeable, and who know their stuff. People will also negotiate based on their self-interest, what's important to them, as they should, but framing the negotiation in a way that benefits both parties can lead to better outcomes.

People know you're trying to make a sale. They know you're trying to close them and this is how you make a living. So be honest and make sure they know that there are beneficial goals for both parties and what's most important is that they both are aligned.

The last thing I'll say about knowing your prospect and how they work: Be very aware of their emotions, what troubles them, their judgments, skepticisms and more so you can effectively communicate all this for the best outcome in the decision-making process. Understanding human behavior during the sales process can be a book in itself, but just be conscious of learning the how and implementing it into your daily practices.

3. Know what matters to them

Interests don't always align, but knowing and identifying their interests is extremely important. When you know what matters to them, you can tailor your presentation, building a solution-based process that fits their specific needs. This is created for them, to help them and to serve them. But most salespeople just spew things they think might matter. If you do this, it could make the prospect think that what matters to them, doesn't matter to you. Make sure you're intentional about what's important to them.

Just identify the interests and needs of the prospect throughout the negotiation. This information will help you create solutions that meet everyone's needs, leading to more solution-based sales, making your prospect happier.

4. Control your emotions and theirs

The negotiation process can be stressful and emotional, but the best negotiators in the world understand that managing your emotions and remaining calm and composed at all times helps the sales process run much smoother. Getting combative at any time during the sales process has never and will never help you get more sales. This skill helps you to stay focused on the negotiation and avoid making decisions based on emotions rather than logic for both you and the prospect.

Trust me, many prospects will test you by asking you questions to see what your response will be. They'll even go as far as saying "no" or "declining" your offer to see what your reaction will be. Stay calm and focused and understanding. When this happens the right way, their guard will come down and they will be more apt to do business with you in the short and long-term.

5. Give them value

Always maximize value for your prospects. This is whether in life or in sales. People want an optimal outcome for both parties that adds value to both their worlds. When you create high value in the negotiation process, giving them solution-based options that maximize the outcome of what you're providing them, they tend to move easier without you through the sales cycle. When you master this and can show REAL value, win-win solutions become evident for everyone involved, which of course, leads to more sales.

In conclusion, fully understanding psychology in the negotiation process is so important because it give you the ability to read and respond to these psychological factors, which can greatly impact the opportunity for a sale.

For instance, understanding the prospect's interests or emotions can help you frame their arguments and responses in a way that appeals to them. You understand their concerns well enough that you're helping guide them to a good decision that they can make logicially, not letting either party's emotions navigate the sales process. Overall, psychology plays a crucial role in the negotiation process and can significantly impact your efficiencies. I recommend role playing; have someone be emotionally attached to a decision while you and/or your team help figure out logical solutions to keep emotion at bay. Use logic and understanding of what matters to them to get you to the finish line.

Body language negotiations

Does how you move matter? How you sit? How you respond physically? It all matters and more than you know. Body language plays a big role in the negotiation and decision-making process in sales. All of the above impact how you and the prospect respond to one another.

For instance, if you shake a hand and look the other direction without eye contact, it can seem as if there's lack of confidence on your part, or lack of caring about the prospect or their time. People have different take aways from your movement and rarely is there a one-size-fits-all response to your body language. You need to find the best way to approach most, but be ready to pivot based on your read of the client.

There are several ways body language plays a role in the negotiation process, but here are a few that matter most:

1. Be trustworthy when you move

Yep, you can make some people trust you when your body language proves that you are trustworthy. Making direct eye contact, not looking away when someone is speaking to you, not buying time by sitting back or deflecting when they ask you a question. Keeping calm and not throwing your hands around when you hear an objection. Keeping your arms open and free, not crossing them to show power or make it seem as if you're upset about something. Rolling your eyes, moving condescendingly when they say something that you may not agree with.

All of these and many more play a large role in whether they will feel as if they can trust you without you even having to say a word. Be aware of how you move when building trust. Prospects need to know that your movement, your body language, portrays that you're listening to them and care about them enough to be interested in what matters most to them.

2. Confidence is conveyed through movement too

Do you move in a way that's confident, or is it portrayed as not confident or arrogant or that you could care less about their time? Confidence is key when negotiating. Do you sit straight up? Do you stand tall? Do you look them in the eye more than most? Now don't do that too much ☺, but definitely do it enough where it shows you are fully vested in providing a solution through serving them.

If you slouch, it proves that you're bored or not interested. If you don't look them in the eye, it shows that you might not have a solution that you're confident can serve them. If you're constantly looking at your phone, it shows disrespect to their attention and proves that you're less interested in them and more interested in something else.

Nodding your head in agreement with them makes them feel like you hear them and that what they say matters. Something as simple as a high five when you agree on something or a thumbs up shows them they're on the right track.

You can build a prospect's confidence in you by using your body language to show that you're confident you can serve them. Show them, without speaking, that they matter and what they say is important to you. All in all, you should always be on your "A" game and understand the art of building confidence through how you move. Move intentionally. Move methodically and make sure it represents the confidence the prospect needs in who you are.

3. Show them you understand

Understanding body language and using it to show prospects that you understand how they feel is essential to your overall growth as a sales professional. Remember to mirror gestures, as we've already gone over. And again, nodding your head in agreement, leaning in to listen or to show interest in what concerns them or they would like validation on—all this proves to them that you care, you want to listen, and you're receptive. Movement is very important in the negotiation process.

4. Power movement

Have you ever been in a presentation where you're sitting and the presenter is standing? This is power movement. Again, how you move can show strength or it can show weakness.

Another power move is if someone is using hand gestures such as pointing towards something that can potentially create value for the client, getting them to look towards the position you are pointing towards. This movement gets them engaged in what you're presenting. If one person is using gestures and the other isn't, it may seem as if they're closed off or unsure about what they're presenting.

You always want your movements to be controlling the sales process, while at the same time you are very conscious and understanding of what's important to the prospect. Power doesn't have to mean dominating the presentation, it just needs to prove confidence in what you're presenting, and the prospect will see that confidence and power as something they want to work with.

In the end, body language is an important aspect of the negotiation process in sales. By being aware of your own body language and reading that of the other party, you can better understand the dynamics at play and use this information to your advantage.

Tonality in the Negotiation Process

How you speak matters. Your tone, the voice inflection through the negotiation process, is an enormous tool to help you close more deals. It's an influential part of persuasion and it will create trust and rapport and make it fun for the prospect to work with you. On the other hand, if you aren't good at when and how to use tonality when negotiating, it can also cripple your chances of doing business with a prospect. Your tone of voice proves confidence, understanding, empathy, authority, and enthusiasm when dealing with a potential client.

For example, when you first meet someone, a friendly and relaxed tone can show them that the sales process can be fun and that you're there to serve them. The honesty in your voice can help a prospect feel more open to tell you their pain points and overall just be more open to working with you. On the other hand, if you're aggressive in how you speak, it could limit opportunity to work with a potential client.

Tonality is also very important when you're trying to put more emphasis on certain value points that you're presenting. You can control how fast or slow the conversations will go and you can move towards a common goal, to do business together, reading their pace as a guide.

When you adjust the tone in which you speak, you can better control the emotional side of the sale. This makes the interaction between you and the prospect more seamless and stable, which improves the chances of them wanting to do business with you.

There are a few ways to use tonality in the negotiation process:

1. Be nice and have an upbeat tone

When it's fun and open, you're being intentional in proving that the sales process will be an easy one where you're there to serve.

When you do this, they'll be more open and receptive to talking to you throughout the presentation.

2. Have a confident tone

Don't sound soft or as if you don't know what you're talking about. When you speak with confidence about your knowledge of a particular product or service that you're offering, that energy is passed off as them working with an expert in your field. People want to work with rockstars; make sure you present yourself as one. The other side to that is feeling and speaking confidently enough that when you don't know an answer, you tell them you don't, but confidently speak in a way they know you're going to get the right answer for them. This builds trust immediately and prospects love honest people who are strong to talk about what they know, but confident to speak when they don't know something. This will put an immense amount of confidence in you so they still feel you're the person to do business with.

3. A consultative tone is reassurance

Prospects know you're trying to get the deal. They also need to know that you're willing to navigate through your service or offering to make sure you find the benefits that will best suit them. So when you're working with a prospect, using a softer tone to ensure they know you're willing to take the time to find out how to best serve them, will 10x your conversion. Potential clients don't want to be pushed, they want to be guided and this is a great way to guide them to the best solution and sound like it!

4. Be excited on the back end

Everyone wants confirmation and most need confirmation when they're making a decision to buy something. When you're influencing people or persuading them towards the close, use an enthusiastic and fun tone. This helps the buyer assume the sale will be exciting and moves them to make a positive decision. This type of tone can create urgency and put people in the right mindset to take advantage of what you're offering sooner rather than later.

5. Objection tone

Some people think handling objections is a game that the other party is trying to win. In reality, handling objections can be difficult for most when they aren't using a calm and reassuring tone. Make sure when you're speaking that they can feel, through your tone, that their concerns are understood and that they matter, whether there's validity there or not. They just want to know you're listening to them and that their concerns are serious to you. When you do this, they will organically surface objections that other sales representatives would've had to pry out of the prospects. If they feel you care, they'll start asking your opinion on other concerns. This allows you to handle them now, rather than having to handle them on the back end when it's time to ask for the money.

As many have said before and many will say after me, "It's not just about what you say, it's also about how you say it." Mastering the art of the tones listed in this chapter and when to use them will give you a huge advantage over the rest of your competition. It'll also get you more referrals and future business, as you know what to say and how to speak in certain scenarios.

Tonality is an important part of the negotiation process in sales and life because it can significantly impact the effectiveness of your message and influence others to listen and to be more open to working with you. If you're looking to get really good at sales, get really good at this!

Conclusion in Negotiating

In the end, mastering how to negotiate is extremely important in sales, for you, your team, and your company. I tell companies all the time, training, training, training will get you to the finish line sooner and help you increase all your sales efficiencies.

Negotiation is a life tool, but when directly related to sales it literally means the difference between losing sales and gaining them on an exponential level. When you get good at this, it's easier to understand the needs of your potential client, build better rapport, create solution-based win-wins, and make sure that the interests of your prospects are met intentionally and fully.

Your reputation will increase when you master the negotiation process and so will your company's. When people hear or share how you were willing to work within their needs, if there was equal and positive synergy to work together through the benefits your product or service offers without getting upset or sacrificing things that were important to them, you'll have increased revenue and long-term relationships with your clients. They won't look elsewhere as they know who you are, who your company is, and that you'll negotiate what's best for them.

Look, the art of negotiation isn't just a sales skill, it's a life skill. It's helped me in all aspects of my life, and it'll help you too. It'll help you solve conflicts easier and build a better business and overall life. Being a skilled negotiator helps you achieve your goals and create the life you're worthy of, while others who don't master this art will have a much harder time achieving their goals.

CHAPTER 25

THE "T.O." PROCESS THAT CHANGED MY LIFE

What is a "takeover" or "turn over"? They both are the same thing in the sales process. A T.O. is usually someone very skilled in the art of sales (of course), negotiation, rapport building, and handling objections in a timely manner. This person doesn't have to be a manager or someone of authority, but usually is. This process can be used throughout a sales presentation at many different times.

The takeover can come into play when a salesperson needs approval from an authority to continue in the negotiation process, or when a prospect needs to speak directly with a more educated or talented sales professional. The T.O. may also come into play when a salesperson doesn't have the best rapport with a prospect, or it may be that an authority can better assist in handling an objection that the original salesperson might not be able to handle. The takeover is very effective and helps earn a lot of business.

Turning a sale over to a manager or high-level sales professional typically means that a salesperson is referring the sale to their superior or a higher-level manager for further handling or approval.

One of the most important processes in a takeover is information. There should be guidelines to follow and meet before a T.O. should speak with the salesperson's prospect. For instance, if I'm in car sales, the approximate payment and range in credit would be ideal information for me to know prior to speaking with the prospect. I need that information ahead of time to best serve the prospect. If I'm in real estate, approved funds, size of home, number of beds and baths might be ideal information to provide the best service to that prospect.

Most of the time when a takeover is initiated, it's because there are questions or concerns that a prospect has before moving forward that need clarification. Maybe it's negotiation on the terms or maybe it's just because there's not a great rapport with the original salesperson. In any of these cases, getting this very relevant information to the person taking over the sale is essential to the overall success of this process.

Unfortunately, this process is not utilized as much as it should be. Too many deals are lost due to ego. Where a salesperson tells a manager or another person willing to help things like:

"They're not interested."

"There's nothing there."

"The guy's a jerk."

"The lady won't listen."

"I offered them everything."

"They were time closing me."

All of the above are excuses, not usually valid reasons, where ego gets in the way of possibly making a sale. Don't let ego stunt your growth in sales, because if you do, it'll stunt your paychecks too.

Why would you not let someone else try to help you get the deal? I've asked for years and no one seems to ever give me a valid reason. You know why? Because there isn't one. It never ever hurts to get a new set of eyes and ears with a prospect even after they say no.

Harvard Business School did a study. They had two categories they were diagnosing. One was how many deals out of 1,000 presentations were closed without using the takeover process and the other one was how many deals out of 1,000 presentations were closed using the takeover process while selling a new CRM software. The numbers will blow your mind.

Non-Takeover Stats Out of 1,000 Sales Presentations

31% Same Day Close – 3% Follow Up Closes and a 41% retention rate

Sales That Were Taken Over Out of 1,000 Presentations

58% Same Day Close – 17% Follow Up Closes and an 84% retention rate

This could be for a variety of reasons, such as a few stated above, but let's get into how and when they can be used most effectively.

Here are a few of the best ways to use a "Takeover":

1. THE BUMP OR SPOT CHECK:

As a sales manager, if you're on the floor with your sales team, it's important to stop by and introduce yourself as someone there to make sure their process or time with your sales team goes well. Just let them know that if they need anything, you're there for them. This is NOT the time to sell and you should talk about anything other than sales.

The bump (just letting them see you, so they're familiar with you) is an essential part of the takeover process, so if you need to assist throughout the sales presentation, they'll know who you are. When someone takes over a sale cold, meaning never been seen or introduced before, the sales wall/resistance that the representative has worked so hard to bring down will shoot back up. They usually feel as if the T.O. (takeover) is just another salesperson trying to get their money and is not there for their best interests.

You must make sure you spot check your prospect whom the salesperson is working with. Stop by, not too often, every now and then and just offer something to drink or maybe ask if there's anything you can do to serve them. When you do this, this also gives the sales representative an opportunity to confirm value points that they've presented and spark a conversation between the T.O. and the prospect. It gives them the OK to start building rapport. Again, you should never do a bump or spot check for the sake of selling, but just for familiarity between the T.O. and the prospect.

Build a rapport: When one salesperson hands over a customer to another, it provides an opportunity to build a rapport with the customer. The new salesperson can introduce themselves, learn about the customer's needs, and start to establish a relationship.

2. GET THE INFORMATION

When a salesperson hands over a prospect to a manager or another salesperson, it gives the person taking over the sale the opportunity to ask questions and guide the prospect better using the information they've received that can make or break a sale.

The salesperson should ask questions and gather information about the customer's needs, preferences, and budget. This information can help the new salesperson make informed recommendations and close the sale, but for the takeover process, it's important to make sure the person taking over the sale is serving based on what the customer guidelines and buying motives are.

There are several things that are important when using the takeover process:

A Seamless Takeover

The handover process should be seamless, with the person taking over the sale process picking up where the previous one left off. This allows the new person to have a smooth transition engaging the sales process, making sure they're concentrating and staying on the selling points that matter most to the prospect.

Time to Add Value - Upselling

When it's time for someone to take over the sale, the previous person who was serving the prospect should inform the T.O. of the possible ways to upsell or offer new services that can add value to the potential prospect.

For example, if you're selling a car, it might be gap insurance, nicer wheels, or additional warranty options that will add value to their purchase. This is good for a number of reasons, but the main statistic is that the previous salesperson who offers a ton of different options might come off as pushy. The T.O. is a new face, possibly different energy, and the T.O. should be trained on additional offers to complement the purchase, even if the previous salesperson forgot or didn't feel confident pitching the additional options.

Confirm the Value the Previous Salesperson Presented

When you hand the sale over to the takeover or you're the person taking over the sale, it's important to reconfirm the value of what the original salesperson is offering. It's a good time to ask if there are any questions about the service or product you're offering. It's also a very good time to talk about the importance and value of working with the original salesperson, their customer service, their ability to pivot as needed to provide solutions, and their honesty in only offering something that adds value to the prospect's needs.

Customer Service as a Whole

When someone takes over the sale, it's a great time to talk about the company as a whole as well. Let the buyer know how the company treats their customers. It's always good to share third-party stories here to confirm that the company will be by their side for any and all of their needs.

Negotiating

This is a great process to use when the original salesperson has offered a price, monthly payments or options they believe best suits the prospect, but the prospect just isn't convinced it's the right fit yet. At this point the T.O. can assist by negotiating money, financing terms, and/or additional services to create enough value to close the deal. Most of the time, it's good to add a new face on the back end when the original sales representative is getting pushback from the potential buyer.

The Survey Transition

This is a tool that's not used as much as it should be in today's sales world. This is when the prospect has said no and they mean no. They're done with the sales presentation and ready for it to be over. A lot of deals are missed here.

A good T.O. should be trained to ask, "How did we do?" Remember, the prospect has already said no to what you've offered. Sometimes a good T.O. can get the prospect back in by just simply asking, "How'd we do?" which transitions into, "What'd we miss?" or "What could we have done to possibly earn your business today?"

This has to be done right! If you're not trained in how to do this properly, it could upset a potential future deal with the prospect. But when done right, it could get you a sale, and if not, still keep the peace.

Let's give an example of the customer saying no on the back end and the salesperson turning it over one last time to a T.O. (the person taking over):

SCENARIO:

Takeover (T.O.): *"Hey, first off, we'd like to thank you for your time today. Your time is important to us and we'll get you outta here right away. Now I know you've decided not to buy today and we totally respect that, but your opinion matters to us very much* and I was wondering if I could ask for your help as we're always looking to get better.

How'd we do?" (shut up and let them speak)

Prospect: "You guys did great. It just wasn't a good fit for us at the moment."

Takeover (T.O.): "Totally get it and we're not always a good fit for everyone, but knowing we aren't doing business today, do you mind me asking what we missed? Like, what did we not have or what could we have added to our service that might've made you choose differently so we know for the next person we work with?"

Now, notice I keep confirming:
- That they're not doing business with us today.
- It's OK and we respect that we weren't a fit for them.

This brings down the tension a ton and the prospect truly is giving us advice on how to better serve the next person we have the luxury of serving. Let's continue the scenario:

Prospect: "To be honest, you didn't have _____ (x,y,z) and it's something we're looking for."

Or

Prospect: "The timeline to receive the service doesn't really make sense for us. We need it sooner."

Or

Prospect: "It's just out of our price range, to be honest."

There are a ton of different replies, but the objective is to get the information we need to find the reason they didn't do business with us today. Let's keep going with the scenario using the price information they gave us:

Takeover (T.O.): *"Well, that's super helpful and I can't thank you enough for your advice. Let me ask you, though, had it been something that made more sense to you financially and the value was what you needed it to be, which I'm almost sure we don't have, but would you have done business with us today?"*

So a couple of things here. I first thanked them for their advice. It's amazing to see the wall completely drop when they're trying to train, help, or give a suggestion on what we could've done differently to earn their business. I then asked them, had we had something within their terms, would they have done business with us? But in the middle of that, I also said, "which I'm almost sure we don't," which keeps the wall down, but it also will verify: was it the real objection? If they say yes, then we can possibly see if we can get where they need to be, or if they say no, we can ask them the main reason they didn't buy. Either way, conversation is sparked and we have the opportunity to either close the deal or learn from our prospect. Both are valuable for the sales team and the company.

Let's keep going if they say yes:

Prospect: *"I mean, yeah. If the price was where we needed it to be, we probably would've done business with you."*

Takeover (T.O.): *"Well, once again, we appreciate your honesty and Todd told me where you needed to be and like I said earlier, it's most likely not going to be possible, but I think it'd be a disservice to you if I didn't check on one last thing to see if we can help. Give me one second, I'll be right back."*

We've now created an opportunity to see if we can come up with something that makes financial sense and get them onboard with us. You should always be ready as a T.O. to have options and be able to create something the prospect sees enough value in to bring them on board with us. Worst case is they can say "no" and we gave it our last shot. It never hurts to try!

Now let's see how the scenario would've gone if they had said "no" on the offering something more suitable in their price range.

Prospect: *"No, it really wouldn't have mattered."*

Takeover (T.O.): *"I appreciate that. But just so I can better serve the next person, then what was the main reason you didn't do business with us today, if price wasn't the main reason?"*

Again, be quiet and let them speak. We're trying to find out the real reason the prospect decided not to do business with you. Sometimes they'll give you the reason and sometimes they won't. Using a T.O. can help by asking, "How'd we do?" as a survey-type close to the presentation. The truth is, whether they buy or not, we learn! Learning will help you in future deals, never forget that.

APPROVAL OUTSIDE MY AUTHORITY

The takeover is a great way to get approval on something the prospect is asking for that may be outside of your realm to approve. People like value. They also like to win the negotiation process or at least feel as if they did. Our job as sales professionals is to serve. Give them the best value for the money they're spending intentionally and honestly.

When a T.O. is asked to approve special financing, a price reduction, additional services that may not be normal and must be authorized approved options, the prospect feels special. The person taking over the sale should reiterate that this is not a normal process and that they're going above and beyond to satisfy the prospect's needs.

This is a very effective way to transition to the close in the sales process and probably the most used process in the take-over scope of work.

Bringing someone in to take over the sales process is a vital tool most companies aren't utilizing and it should be a regular practice even if the sales representative doesn't think it's necessary.

Many high-end salespeople like to say they don't need a T.O. and they are a "front-to-back" salesperson. This means they do it all on their own. But more times than not, their ego will cost them deals. As long as the person taking over the sale is properly trained, even if the sale is done, the T.O. can solidify how they've made the right decision, which reduces cancellation rates and increases retention of their deals.

This process is good for a fresh perspective, to better read the prospect's interest, to build a rapport as someone representing the company, but it also assists a struggling salesperson who's having a hard time connecting with their prospect. Let's be honest, there are plenty of people who don't want to do business with an energetic, loud-mouth, tattooed guy like me, so when those people arise, I turn the sale over to someone who might be a better fit. Why lose an opportunity even if you have to split the profit on the deal?

Using a takeover also shows the prospect that we care about them and are committed to offering them the best experience whether they do business with us or not. It proves we care, will try to meet their needs, even if it takes a team of people to do so.

In the end, the take-over process is primarily a strategic way to make a prospect feel comfortable in all aspects of the sales process. This ensures the best possible outcome for them and for you as a salesperson.

Use this process. Role play different scenarios where it'd be a good idea to bring someone else in. Master the art of the bump, so they see a familiar face there to serve them if need be, and learn the best way to build your dance together, if you're constantly working with the same person who might take over your sale.

Don't miss this tool like many people and companies do. Relinquish ego and you'll all close more deals, which means MAKE MORE MONEY!

SCENARIO 1: HEALTH INSURANCE (PROSPECT SAYS NO)

Setting: A modern office space. Sales representative named Hannah is discussing a health insurance policy with a middle-aged man, Robert.

Scene: Hannah: "Our comprehensive health plan offers both inpatient and outpatient coverage at an affordable rate."

Robert: "I'm not sure. I had a different policy in mind and this doesn't seem to match my needs."

Takeover Moment: Hannah: "I appreciate your honesty, Robert. Let me introduce you to our Senior Health Insurance Advisor, Grace. She has extensive experience and might be able to offer a policy that's more aligned with what you're looking for."

Grace steps in, listens to Robert's concerns, and tailors the discussion to his specific needs, eventually finding a policy that fits.

SCENARIO 2: CAR SALES (PROSPECT SAYS NO)

Setting: A car dealership. Sales representative, Leo, is showing a sedan to a young professional woman, Isabelle.

Scene: Leo: "This sedan is both fuel efficient and known for its safety features."

Isabelle: "It's nice, but it's a bit over my budget."

Takeover Moment: Leo: "I understand, Isabelle. Let me introduce you to our Sales Manager, Max. He might have some special promotions or financing options that could make this more feasible for you."

Max enters, discussing possible discounts and tailored financing options, making the car more affordable for Isabelle.

SCENARIO 3: HEALTH INSURANCE (PROSPECT SAYS YES)

Setting: The same modern office. Sales representative Hannah is discussing a premium policy with a couple.

Scene: Hannah: "Our premium plan offers extensive coverage including overseas medical emergencies."

Couple: "Sounds perfect for our frequent travels. We'll take it!"

Takeover Moment: Hannah: "That's great to hear! Let me introduce you to Alan, our Finalization Specialist. He'll walk you through the paperwork and ensure everything is clear."

Alan steps in, confirming the policy details, and solidifies the couple's decision.

SCENARIO 4: CAR SALES (PROSPECT SAYS YES)

Setting: The same car dealership. Leo is showcasing a convertible to a retiree, Mr. Jones.

Scene: Leo: "This convertible is perfect for those leisurely drives and is equipped with all the latest features."

Mr. Jones: "I've always wanted one. Let's do it!"

Takeover Moment: Leo: "Fantastic choice, Mr. Jones! Let me introduce you to Mia, our Documentation Manager. She'll ensure the paperwork is hassle free."

Mia assists with the necessary documentation, confirms Mr. Jones' choices, and emphasizes post-sale services, ensuring he leaves contented and confident.

WHY THE TAKEOVER IS IMPORTANT:

1. **Expertise**: Different team members have areas of expertise. By handing the sale over to a manager or specialist, the customer feels they are getting the best and most knowledgeable service.
2. **Building Trust:** It shows that the company is willing to involve senior members to ensure the customer's needs are met. This can enhance the trust factor.
3. **Flexibility**: Managers often have the authority to offer special deals, discounts, or terms that regular sales representatives may not be able to.
4. **Reassurance**: For clients who've already said yes, a takeover can provide an added layer of assurance and emphasize the importance the company places on individual sales, ensuring the buyer feels valued and taken care of.
5. **Mitigating Concerns**: In situations where a prospect has reservations, a manager stepping in can address concerns directly, potentially turning a no into a yes.

Now look, is there a perfect way to turn the sale over every time? That answer is no. In order to maximize this process, get with your entire team, the salespeople and the leaders, and really dive into the best possible solution to turn the sale over in almost every possible scenario.

When you train on this, get people involved in building it, you will see tremendous increases in sales, retention, cross-selling, upselling, and referrals. It's a skill no sales team should go without mastering!

CHAPTER 26

URGENCY: THE SALES' UNICORN

Hurry and get the deal already! That's what everyone wants. Less work, more money. Creating urgency doesn't mean pushing them into a deal. Creating urgency is done in several ways that we will talk about throughout this chapter, but ask yourself these questions before we dive in: What motivates me to buy? What was a time I bought something because I felt like I couldn't wait? And finally… What are my personal urgency triggers?

What's an urgency trigger, you ask? Oh, well, let me tell you about something that makes people buy more than just about any other tool in your arsenal and the good news is, there are several ways to trigger a prospect to move!

An urgency trigger is psychological ammo used to motivate a potential buyer to move towards a buying decision quicker. You need to be able to identify the best triggers in your fields.

Have you ever bought at a store online or walked by a jewelry store in the mall and you see a sign saying, "80% OFF FOR A LIMITED TIME"? The funny thing is, most never come down and most don't even have a time or date that the offer won't be valid for anymore. Why is that? To create buyer urgency. It's an urgency trigger when you see a sign that says, "Going out of business" or "TODAY ONLY 50% OFF," but is it really for "today only" or do they use that over and over and over again? The Federal Trade Commission stated that as long as you sell something for the retail price once, you can post a retail sticker on it for that original amount and show a discount thereafter. Isn't that nuts? So are the prices you see even real? A gold chain might show a retail price of $2,000 and today it's 80% off for $400, so you think you're getting the best deal ever. Is it really worth $2,000? No, it's not. I was in the jewelry business for a while and saw how they moved and offered sale prices and guess what? It was every day, a different sign showing similar discounts!

For instance, some of the most common motivating triggers for urgency are:

- **A concert with limited seating left**

How many times do you think people buy event tickets for a favorite artist or team because the verbiage on the ad says, "Tickets won't last long" or "The last event sold out in 15 hours – get your ticket now." These are mental urgency triggers.

- **Special offer that ends at a certain time**

You might go to a website and see, "Offer good for 90% until you close this link" or "90% off until close of day tomorrow." Don't believe me? Go look at some influencers, other sales-trainers pages and see if you don't see "Normal price $15,000" with a line or X through it saying, "BUT TODAY ONLY $1,499!"

You'll even see it on a lot of the stuff my company sells as a "special offer," because we are truthful and it actually is a special offer. Don't mislead people with urgency triggers because you want business, but the special offer tool works tremendously.

- **Lack of inventory**

You might be selling a product where there is only a certain amount for sale. Use that as a tool! That's a massive urgency trigger for someone looking to buy what you're offering. If there truly is a limited number of products left or that you're selling, make sure your prospects know that. It ignites an urgency trigger to get them to buy now, rather than think there will always be inventory available.

- **Buy one get one deal**

You see this in stores like PayLess ShoeSource all the time. The "BOGO" method has worked, does work, and will continue to work. The companies that offer this know exactly where their margins are and will run this as an urgency trigger once a month or quarter to boost revenue and sales.

- **VIP discount for a particular month**

If you've been working long term with someone or maybe they bought into a high-level service or product base you offered them, they become VIP in my book. You don't have to use the VIP title, but be sure to cater to a person who enjoys doing business with you. Let them know you appreciate them. Based on who they are and how you'd like to serve them, you can offer them added gifts, additional value items, or yes, maybe even a discount because they're loyal in doing business with you. This is an urgency trigger.

It also gives you a really good way to market and follow up with your VIP clients to offer them something new before anyone else gets the chance to see it. This is a very good urgency trigger and it's non-pressure, which is what I like and believe me, so does your client.

- **If you buy more, you pay less**

Buy more, pay less. This is a very common urgency trigger used in today's sales world, and to be honest, it should be. If I'm a prospect and I'm going to buy something in bulk anyway, why not give me a discount, right? Or additional products at a discounted rate, or even FREE, based on the quantity and your margins needed.

You should always prove that your prospect matters when buying in bulk. This will always work, and customers actually expect it these days. Just make sure your prices are competitive and value based. If you offer them more and don't give them a bulk price, you could lose the deal altogether. This doesn't mean always discount everything; this is just a common practice when you buy more, upgrade more, or add additional services with most companies.

- **Since you bought this, you can get this add-on item cheaper only if you do it now.**

This is common using sales funnels, but it is prevalent in all sales. These are usually add-on items. You bought this and because you bought this, you get this other item cheaper than we'd normally offer it for. It's that simple and gets people upsold all the time. Learn how to bundle your packages, have discounted upsells that are no-brainers to add. You can do this after they've said yes, or use it as an urgency tool to get the deal now.

- **Seasonal product or service**

This is as simple as it reads. An example would be the "Pumpkin Spice Latte" at Starbucks. Not sure why, but I love that drink and I hate that it's seasonal, but when it's in season, they post it all over the place, which creates an urgency trigger to get to Starbucks while they have it available. For Starbucks, that means they're getting prospects to go there when they normally wouldn't and they're probably not just buying the Pumpkin Latte, are they? The answer is NO. They buy more and it's a genius urgency trigger.

- **Signage or banners showing discounts**

Banners on websites. Banners in the mall. Signs on social media, your stories, your pages, anything like this where you can show that there's a discount to buy something with the product or service you're offering is an "in your face" approach that has worked for 100's of years.

If they don't know you have a sale, why would they assume? This is an urgency trigger.

- **Deadline Trigger**

Maybe you're the person who can get something done sooner than others. Maybe you're going to prove to them how you're going to go the extra mile and make sure you meet their timing needs. This is a great way to urge people or nudge them in the right direction and the best part is it doesn't involve a discount!

When a prospect has a deadline to reach, it's a great way to earn business. Just be truthful when you say you can get it done, because if you don't, that's the last time they'll buy with you. If you do, they'll be a repeat customer for a very long time!

Showing proof and testimonials of others whom you've done business with, their reviews and more, definitely creates a high level of urgency, because they see how well you take care of your clients and it demonstrates that your product or services work well. Many sales representatives don't do this and leave the prospect wondering if they should trust your word. By showing them all of this, it will increase your chances of getting your prospect to move sooner rather than later by four times. I'll take those odds all day long.

Have a testimonial book, videos of clients, pictures of happy customers, reviews on hand, BBB (Better Business Bureau) links ready to click if you're in the U.S. Just be prepared to show them how it has been for others who've made a similar decision that they're about to make.

The thing is, when you're out shopping for something, you have a mission to find what you want and that's enough to buy it. You're creating your own urgency. But why should they choose you to work with?

Well, much like the "limited time offer" approach, another way to create urgency is a common term called "FOMO" or Fear Of Missing

Out." People may say they don't want to be first to have something or create a trend or show off the new shiny item that they own or that's making them a ton of money, but THEY ALL do!

Look, we understand that we're in sales because we want to make a ton of money serving others, by offering something that will impact them in a positive way. Creating a sense of urgency will put them in the picture and get them to move faster. No delays. No waiting. No thinking about it. If you can find out what triggers them by asking good questions, you can fine tune what will create the most urgency for your prospect.

My personal favorite way to create urgency isn't any fancy words, signs, or sale offers, its VALUE! Value in YOU and what you're offering. When a prospect sees and believes that you're the best person to work with, that alone creates massive urgency. Now couple that with an amazing product or service and the prospect hit the jackpot by getting both!

Ask what they expect out of you. Give them examples of how you've served others in the past who are still working with you. Explain what the product or service you're offering will do for them and how you're going to prove that and then ACTUALLY do it.

Another good way to create urgency is, what are they losing by not doing business with you?

For instance, you're selling pest control and the homeowner doesn't want to do business with you right now. There's no urgency. You might talk about how previous owners who waited, due to the weather and more critters and bugs surfacing, started seeing roaches in their kitchen, termites finding a home within the walls, and an attic full of spiders and squirrels.

Giving more details on how they might be negatively affected by not doing business with you can potentially create urgency. You are putting them in the picture and showing them that the only way to make sure that bad stuff doesn't happen is to do business with you now.

My partner Brandon and I use the negative approach naturally. Don't get me wrong, we love talking about the good we can do for a client, but what if they have a sales and leadership team, they've inquired about the cost of our services, and they tell us, "It's just too much money"?

Our response would go something like this:

"First off, I completely understand and hear you, but I will tell you we have a very similar client who wasn't running as efficient as they'd like to be. They also thought that the $25,000 for a 3-day deep dive of their company was way out of their price range, so we asked them their Cost Per Lead (CPL) and what their Cost Per Acquisition (CPA) was. The client didn't know. They guessed, but they really didn't know. So Brandon and I gave them an hour of free consultation and we found over $50,000 in quarterly revenue they were lighting on fire the way they were doing business. So we just asked them: Is it worth $25,000 to save $200,000 a year?"

And noooooooooooooooooo, we didn't use the corny, outdated, horrible phrase, "The real question here isn't whether you can afford it, but more like can you afford not to?" Damn, I just threw up in my mouth typing that. If you're using that, STOP IT NOW! It's my top 3 worst sales closes of all time.

Anyway, we basically told the client,

"Look, there's a list of things we've just mentioned that are running bad. We can help and we can definitely show you the value like we've done many times for other prospects. In fact, I'm so sure of it, if we don't save you or make you at least $25,000, then don't pay us a dime. Deal?"

Don't underestimate your product or service and the value it provides. That VALUE URGENCY has closed MILLIONS AND MILLIONS of dollars in deals for our company. BUT, we've always done what we said we would do. Our name, our history, our reviews, tied to the value we bring and the service we offer, is an urgency trigger in itself. To get on to our schedule, you need to move and we'd love to be the one to serve you. #closed

Urgency doesn't have to be hard. It can be as easy as making it easier to do business with you than it is to work with someone else offering something similar. How do they sign up, how easy is it to use, and how fast can I see the results? All urgency triggers.

Just be smart when creating urgency. Don't get pushy. Don't force the idea of "buy now" or drop seeds of limited products too early or too often, because it can also turn a prospect off. It's super important not to sound salesy, always be ethical, without pressuring. Yes I know I've said it twice, but I just get so frustrated watching strong salespeople lose deals because they're not trained properly in how to use urgency the right way.

In conclusion, urgency is a powerful tool to have in an arsenal of techniques when serving a prospect. When genuine, and all of us should be, you're truly helping them make a decision they might not have. A lot of people miss out on deals because they talk themselves out of buying now. Then disappointment sets in later.

Yes, it might put a little pressure on them to make a decision, but it's better than regretting that they didn't. Our job is to have enough value, present it as so, and prove to the client how that value will impact their lives. Urgency helps them take action, it increases perceived value, not only in the product or service, but IN YOU!

My recommendation is to get together with your team—or just by yourself, if you don't have a team—and write down the top 5 things that you believe create the most urgency for your prospects when you're working with them. Know those top 5. Master them and implement them. When you do this, you'll make more sales and serve more people. When you add value to their lives with a decision you helped them make, the real reward is them telling you how grateful they are that you did! That, my friends, is what urgency is all about!

Now in order to help you and your team get better at it, I've added a few different scenarios for you to learn from. ENJOY!

SCENARIO 1: ROOFING BUSINESS - IMMINENT WEATHER ALERT

Setting: A homeowner's living room. There's a weather bulletin on TV warning of a severe storm approaching in the next 48 hours.

Role Play:

- *Salesperson*: "I noticed some potential weak points in your roof during our inspection. With the storm approaching, it's crucial to get those addressed immediately. Waiting might result in leaks or more extensive damage which could be far more expensive to repair."

- *Homeowner*: "I was thinking of getting it fixed next month."

- *Salesperson*: "I understand. However, with the impending storm, waiting could be a costly decision. We can prioritize your roof and ensure it's secure before the storm hits. It's not just about saving on future repairs, but also ensuring your family's safety."

SCENARIO 2: TIMESHARE BUSINESS - LIMITED AVAILABILITY PROMOTION

Setting: A vacation resort presentation room. A screen displays images of a luxurious property.

Role Play:

- *Salesperson*: "This particular property you're interested in has a unique promotion for the next 48 hours. If you decide to invest now, you'll get an additional week every year at no extra cost."

- *Prospect*: "It sounds tempting, but I need more time to think."

- *Salesperson*: "I totally respect that. However, given the high demand and limited availability, I can't guarantee this promotion will be available after the next 48 hours. If this property truly resonates with your vacation desires, it might be worth seizing the opportunity now."

SCENARIO 3: REAL ESTATE BUSINESS - COMPETITIVE MARKET INSIGHT

Setting: A modern condo with a city skyline view.

Role Play:

- *Realtor*: "This condo has all the features you've been looking for, and in this fast-paced market, properties like this are getting multiple offers within the first week."

- *Buyer*: "I do like it, but I want to explore a few more options before making a decision."

- *Realtor*: "Absolutely, it's important to be sure. Just to give you insight, three similar condos in this building were sold last month within days of being listed. Given the demand, it might be wise to make an offer if you're genuinely interested, so you don't miss out."

Key Takeaways from the trainings above:

1. **Use Real and Immediate Factors:** The impending storm in the roofing scenario is a genuine concern that can create urgency. Real threats or challenges can motivate quicker decision-making.

2. **Offer Time-Limited Promotions:** The timeshare scenario uses a promotion with clear benefits but available only for a short period. This "limited time offer" approach pushes the prospect to decide quickly to benefit from the promotion.

3. **Provide Market Intelligence:** Knowledge is power. In the real estate scenario, the Realtor educates the buyer about the competitive market, prompting faster action. Sharing relevant market data or comparisons can influence urgency.

4. **Build Trust and Offer Solutions:** In all scenarios, the professional is not merely pushing for a sale but offering a solution to a potential problem or providing value. Establishing trust and showing genuine concern for the client's needs is crucial to effective urgency-driven sales tactics.

In the end, there are so many different ways to create urgency. Build that list for your industry and with your team. Then create role-playing activities for the urgency training on your team. Get them to create it at least 3 different ways, so they can have an arsenal ready when they need it. Without practice, you can't get better.

CHAPTER 27

SUGGESTIVE NUMBERS

This is one of my favorite tools to use when negotiating or dropping seeds on cost. I use this personally so often, just to pull out what a cost of something might be that someone isn't wanting to tell me, or to negotiate a deal on a service or product I want to buy.

Suggestive numbers can be used to persuade someone to make a buying decision. They're usually numbers dropped within or throughout the sales presentation for a customer to hear, to assist with price objections, or to just give the prospect an idea on cost. They're also used to influence a prospect to make a decision when they feel the number suggested makes sense for them to buy your product or service.

Another way to use suggestive numbers is to ask a prospect what they think the cost is. For instance, if I'm selling a vacation package to the Maldives for a family, I might say something like this:

Salesperson: "So if you were to guess, how much do you think this package costs?"

Prospect: *(is thinking)*

You notice they're thinking and before they say anything you "suggest numbers" like so…

Salesperson: *"What do you think like $15-$20-$25,000?"*

Now there's a couple of main factors to know here. You should always suggest a number that's higher than the price of the product or service you're offering. This isn't to mislead in any way, but it's a good way to see what they think the value is on what you're offering.

In this case, we're selling a vacation package to the Maldives and the actual cost is $5,997. They don't know that yet, but by suggesting a higher number, psychologically, the prospect normally will choose the one in the middle. They think, *"Well, it can't be that cheap and I doubt it's that expensive, so I'll say the middle one."* This is the same psychology when offering three offers.

They might think about it more and say, "No way it's that much," and guess what, it's OK that they do. You just know you have some work to do to build more value in what they believe this vacation package is worth.

What if they say $2,000, before you have a chance to suggest numbers? What do you do then? You just ask good questions to find out why they think it's that price. By the way, never put down someone by saying something like, "Why do you think it's so cheap?" Because $2,000 could be a ton of money for them and that would be an insult, rather than a good question to ask. All you need to know is they feel like it's worth less than the actual cost is and it's time to get your grind-in boots on and start building some more value up and find out why they feel it's worth $2,000. Their opinion matters to them, of course, but try asking them properly why they think it's (don't use the word "only") valued at $2,000, and you'll get a ton of good information that will help you navigate through the sales process better.

Now I can build the value even more, where they might say the higher number, like so:

Salesperson: *"So if you were to guess, how much do you think this package costs... with a cabana in the middle of the ocean, your own butler, all-inclusive, a private pool, a private jacuzzi and a shuttle included to and from the airport.... What do you think something like that would cost?"*

Prospect: *(is thinking)*

You notice they're thinking and before they say anything you "suggest numbers" like so...

Salesperson: *"What do you think like $15-$20-$25,000?"*

See, in this version, I beefed up the value chat! Started listing the features and benefits about the vacation instead of just asking, "How much do you think this package would cost?" Personally, I like this way better, although both work well.

Remember not to pitch too many of the benefits, because then it might become "too good to be true" in the prospect's mind, even when you're being completely truthful.

At this point, the prospect might say, "Well, obviously $25,000 or more with all that included." So did I guide them through suggesting numbers? Yes, I did. This is one way to use this tool and it's very, very effective.

Another scenario might be:

Salesperson: *"So if you were to guess, how much do you think this package costs... with a cabana in the middle of the ocean, your own butler, all-inclusive, a private pool, a private jacuzzi and a shuttle included to and from the airport.... What do you think something like that would cost?"*

Prospect: *"I don't know. Like $20,000."*

At this point, ask them the same way you would if they thought it was worth $2,000. Ask them why they believe the value is worth $20,000.

Salesperson: *"Why do you think it's a $20,000 trip?"*

Yes, we know the price is only $5,997, but letting them speak the value. Their saying it, not you, means they own those words. You can use this information to help close them on the back end if they give you a price objection.

Salesperson: *"So the price doesn't make sense for you?"*

Prospect: *"Yeah, it doesn't make sense."*

Salesperson: *"So earlier when you said it was worth $20,000, what were the features you felt brought you to say that number?"*

See, I'm reconfirming in a nice way that earlier they told me they believed the vacation package total cost was $20,000 and if they truly believed it was worth that, then tell me why you said it was. Remember, they said it, not you. When they speak it, THEY OWN IT. It's very hard for someone to use price as an objection when you use suggestive numbers, building the value to where they agree that the number/value is much higher than the actual cost of the offer. You basically blocked that objection by using this method.

There are many ways to use suggestive numbers. In car sales, they might start the price of the car the prospect is looking at for a larger number, but instead of them saying the number, they might ask the prospect something like this:

Salesperson: *"I see you like the Cadillac Escalade. This is our newest model and one of our top sellers, so if you had to guess what something like this goes for, what would you say ... $80-$90, $100,000?"*

The real price might be $75,000, but you're building perceived value, which is also called anchoring when suggesting a higher number.

Prospect: *"I don't know. I'd say $90-$100,000 for sure."*

If the Escalade is $75,000, you have a perceived value, anchored at $90-$100,000. This means that when you offer the price, there should be sticker shock in a good way. Again, if they speak it, they own it. Just remember, if they had said $60,000, it's not the end of the world; you just have to build value on why it's much more than that.

Others will use suggestive numbers from a psychological aspect. If you see something for sale at $99 instead of $100, it's a scientific fact that the brain reacts to it differently. So you're not even speaking and using "suggestive numbers."

How about something that's priced at $999 but it's got a huge sign on it saying that it's 25% off? Is that another form of suggestive numbers? Yes, it is. The prospect automatically perceives the value to be higher and they feel like they're getting a deal. Many retail companies use discounts like this and again, don't even have to say a word; it's evident through the percentage off.

The main focus on suggestive numbers is getting the customer to speak it so they own it and building a perceived value in their mind, so when you give them the value matched with a price lower than what they perceived it to be, it becomes a deal they can't pass up in their mind.

This is probably one of the most powerful, underutilized sales skills in today's world. If you spend time mastering how to use this in your presentations and get the prospect to believe in the value of a higher price that they speak, not you, you're on your way to solidifying a sale WAY FASTER than the average salesperson. Oh, and guess what? Your retention will be higher too, because the prospect not only feels good about their purchase, but they know they got a great deal because you did your job, they spoke the higher price and you transitioned them into a buyer by offering a lower price than what they thought it was.

This skillset you should practice daily!

CHAPTER 28

MASTERING THE CLOSE

You're reading this book to learn about sales. Mastering how to close/serve a prospect when it's time to get down to the money is one of the most important parts of the sales process, but one in which most salespeople are untrained.

A prospect should transition to the close seamlessly, but that's not always the case. People buy differently and you have to understand how your buyer buys. If you randomly use corny closes, the potential of you getting the deal goes WAY down.

It didn't matter what I was selling and it still doesn't, because people don't feel forced or pushed into the sale. Most don't even know how to ask for the money and because of that, they lose sales consistently.

Here the top 7 no-no's when closing the sale on the back end:

1. DON'T FORCE THE SALE OR BE PUSHY.

I know, personally, if I feel pressured into making a decision, I'll shut down immediately. This is the case for most buyers. You make the customer feel so uncomfortable after you just spent an ample amount of time getting them to trust you or at least broke the resistance wall down and when you're pushy it just builds that wall right back up. The pain doesn't stop at losing the sale either, they'll tell others how pushy you were, how they felt pressured and could hurt the company's name as well, which inevitably could cost you your job.

Another reason being pushy is horrible, is that the prospect is open to hearing what you have to say, but the minute they seem uninterested and you begin to be pushy, it can send a signal that you're trying to take advantage of them. That you care more about the money than you do about them.

Overall, you'll have a tiny percentage of repeat business, getting referrals from them, and they could leave a bad review on you and the company which will reach other potential clients. In the end, DON'T BE PUSHY! It's the worst sales "tactic" ever and a weak way to sell.

2. DID YOU EVEN HEAR THEM?

A lot of salespeople will go into the close offering a price or service/product with features and benefits that don't even suit their needs just to try and get a deal.

Don't try to close the deal using things that the prospect hasn't told you is important to them. They will feel unheard. They will think you don't care about what matters to them, resulting in no sale.

Many will try to offer something just to see if they "might" like it. Listen to your prospect and close them by serving them for what's important to them. You seem desperate and desperation is super unprofessional and it really diminishes the value of what you've been offering the entire time.

Why offer something that isn't important to them anyway? It just wastes your time and the prospect's time. If it doesn't add value tell them. I've made more money through honesty and telling the customer the absolute truth always, because the customer is surprised in today's sales world that honesty still exists. They bought even though they didn't necessarily need what I was offering. Still, they found a way it could add value to them, BUT I WAS TRUTHFUL and listened to their needs.

In the end, if you don't listen to what's important to them and just try to guess what their hot button might be, you look unprofessional and desperate. Tailor your close around them and you'll start selling more deals.

3. DO THEY EVEN KNOW WHAT THEY'RE BUYING?

If you're too vague when offering something to a prospect, it'll confuse them on what they're even buying. I mean, if I feel like I don't really know everything I'm getting when buying something, I won't buy. That's not just me. A study from Harvard Business School stated that salespeople who were too vague in what they offered had a 61% overall less closing rate than the ones who were clear and concise on what they were offering. It just makes people skeptical and unsure, and pushes them more times than not to the answer you don't want, the word NO!

The other truth is that when you're too vague about what you're offering to the prospect, it can seem as if you don't know what you're offering. They feel as if you're not the expert in your field or maybe you're just incapable of answering questions they might have, so you try and keep it vague enough to just get their money.

If you don't seem confident in what you're offering, they will question other things about the sale as well. Maybe return policy, warranty, extended warranty, price, approximate date of completion or delivery.

Be specific and trained enough to close with confidence. Being vague isn't that.

4. MY FAVORITE NO-NO: DON'T LIE TO GET THE DEAL. EVER!

First and foremost, the liar is the weakest salesperson in the world. You're stealing from people, you aren't "closing" anyone, you're lying to get them to buy something that doesn't and will never do what you say it will.

This might hurt some of you reading this, but if you're lying or misleading people to get a deal, you're a good thief, not a good sales professional. A lot of less than ethical individuals do this when they feel like there's no other way to get a deal. All they care about is the money, not the prospect. I'm not sure how they sleep at night, to be honest.

First, you'll never ever get repeat business. Second, you could be ruining someone's life if they're financing something and can barely afford the payments based on a lie you told them. Third, you could be forcing them to spend money on something that they would've never bought had you been honest.

This is the all-around holy grail of shitty people in my book. If you want to be a closer, tell the truth. We can measure your performance there. You can't measure performance on lies. The sad part about this, too, is that there are several companies who let their representatives lie, just to hit their quota. Makes me want to throw up.

Don't lie. Sell to serve. Always be honest on the back end about what you're offering.

5. DON'T BE UNPROFESSIONAL.

There are several people who fit the "salesperson" persona today and that's not a compliment. They're joking around too much on the back end, cuss, smirk condescendingly. They might even allude to the price being "cheap" (which, by the way, NEVER use that word) when the price might not be "cheap" to the prospect. It's the biggest turn off ever.

Just treat the very crucial and emotional back-end process professionally always. It's the time for them to make a decision. They want to do business with people who care and are professional. Period.

Acting unprofessionally, using inappropriate language or behavior, can turn off customers.

6. ARE YOU SURE THEY UNDERSTAND WHAT YOU'RE SAYING?

There are a ton of people who love to use acronyms or big words during the back end of a close to seem more intelligent about what they're offering you. But have you ever wondered if the prospect even knows what you're talking about!?

I know I'm not the smartest guy in the world and every time someone is speaking using big words or terms or acronyms that I have no clue what they're saying or even mean, I feel stupid.

Let me give you a tip you should never forget. You will never close more deals by making someone feel like they have no clue what you're talking about. For me, I'll tell you I don't understand and make you explain it. For others, they won't make you explain it and, guess what, they WON'T be buying either, because they'd rather just say no than make you explain something to them because it might risk you thinking they're dumb. They might feel intimidated, too. Long story short, don't do that. Keep it simple always. Explain thoroughly always.

7. COMMUNICATION IS KEY.

When you're offering something that might need a follow up, FOLLOW UP! When you forget, you lose the deal. If you say you're going to call, text, email, contact them by a certain time or day, DO IT that certain time or day. You will never close a deal that requires a follow up if you contact them saying you forgot.

Make them feel like a priority, not out of mind.

There's plenty of things that can hurt you on the back end, such as your body language, facial expressions, terms you use. Just be conscious of the buyer in front of you.

There is a closing tool that goes both ways, though. If you use it properly, it can help you get the sale; if you don't, it will most likely stop you from closing the deal and that, my friends, is: Assuming the sale. Let's dive into this a little deeper.

Assuming the sale can be really salesy. It can sound super corny and it can also be the easiest way to transition into the close and get the deal. Like I said, there are good and bad things about assuming the sale.

The good outweighs the bad when you're trained properly.

1. SAVES TIME ON THE BACK END

Assuming the sale can save you time. Instead of pitching all over again before they offer a price, like most salespeople do, they assume the close and it eliminates an opportunity to talk past the yes. By assuming the sale, you also limit any unneeded tiring negotiations going back and forth with your prospect.

2. PROVES CONFIDENCE

A lot of salespeople that assume the sale the right way are confident when they do it. It shows the prospect that they're making the right decision and when they feel that confidence from you, its transferable energy that makes them feel more comfortable.

3. YOUR CHANCES GO WAY UP

When you care about their time and confidently assume the sale, you'll get more deals, period. Too many salespeople try to tread too lightly when trying to close the deal because they're afraid of hearing the word "no." You'll be surprised how many people will say yes if you just ask for the sale. Yep, it's that easy.

There are several different ways to assume the sale, some as easy as: handing your prospect the pen to start filling out the paperwork in front of them.

Others assume the sale by asking questions like:

- How many would you like?
- What's the best day to deliver?
- What's the best time for us to install?
- Whose name should I put this under?
- What's an email address to send you your confirmation?
- I'll get the order set up; who's name do you want it under?
- Who's going to be the primary on the account?
- Which payment method would you like to use?

You get the picture, right? Just make sure when you're asking, you don't sound pushy and you're not being arrogant or cocky. Confidence is key, arrogance is different.

You can also get the deal by providing the next move they're going to make as if they've already said yes, like:

- When you get the email with the purchase confirmation, you can download it as a pdf for your record keeping.
- Once we get you approved, you'll click this link to access your service.
- We ship everything right to your home. Can you verify that address please?
- We'll get you ready to go, but you'll have my information if you ever have any questions. Write this down: (then give them your email when you hand them a pen).

- We're going to start building Tuesday. Is that the best day to get started?

See, these statements and questions assume the sale in a very non-pushy way. This doesn't mean they're always going to say yes. If they don't, worst case is that the objection will surface for you to handle, which ALSO saves you time.

Affirming verbiage is always a great way to assume the sale as well, such as:

- Once you start using this, you're going to be so glad you chose to have it.
- It looks like this is going to definitely add value to your world.
- You're going to be able to save so much time by having this.
- Think about how much safer you're going to feel when you have this.
- Honestly, I'm so glad we had a solution that is going to exceed your expectations.
- I can't wait for you to call me after you've seen how this will impact your life.
- This really is the best solution for you. I'm glad we are able to help.

Now remember, how I say it might not be how you say it. So some of the above list might seem corny to you, but you get the drift. Say positive things, receive positive responses. Keep the energy positive and the decision from the buyer will be positive. By inserting some excitement, you're just giving them affirmation that they're making the right decision, which will absolutely make it easier to close more deals.

Here are some scenarios on assuming the sale:

Salesperson: *"I can't wait to see you use this. I'm so glad we were able to find a solution for you. Whose name would be the primary on the account?"*

At this point, you do not look at the prospect. You put your head down and have the pen ready to write. The prospect might think for a second, but if they're interested in what you're offering they'll say something like this.

Prospect: *"Put my wife's name down first, please."*

Easy right? Because it IS THAT EASY! But most untrained salespeople will sell so hard on the back end when they don't have to!

See, there's two things in a scenario like that. Either they're going to give you a name or say something like this:

Prospect: *"Well, before we do that I have one more question"* or *"We're not sure this is the right fit for us."*

And many other things they could say at that point, but at least you're maximizing your time and getting the objection quicker too, right? This is how powerful assuming the sale can be.

Here's another scenario:

Car Salesman: *The prospect just test drove the car they're looking at.*

Salesperson: *"We have several different financing options I'm sure will suit you. Where do you need to be to be comfortable?"*

Prospect: *"Around $300 a month."*

Salesperson: *"Great, I'll tell you what, when we get back I'm going to see if I can get that done for you. Is this the color you want?"*

Prospect: *"I prefer red, actually."*

Salesperson: *"I think red's a great choice. So let me see if I can get everything you want inside that monthly payment, so we can get you driving out of here with the car you want today."*

See, once again, not pushy, just gradually leading them to the close. This is the right way to assume the sale.

Let's do one more. A real estate agent is showing a home and they want to assume the sale.

Real Estate Agent: *"I can see you guys like this home and I can see you in it. When are you looking to close by?"*

Prospect: *"We're really not sure."*

Real Estate Agent: *"I totally get it, making a decision like this is a big one. But I can see how excited you guys are about this property. Why don't we look at some financing options to make sure you're happy with the payment. I don't want you losing your dream home."*

Prospect: *"OK, we can do that."*

Once again, does it always go this smoothly? No. But it CAN! All you have to do is try. Most of the time a real estate agent shouldn't be wasting time with a prospect without a pre-approval anyway, so this is always a great way to assume the sale.

Now let's get into the best way to close a sale with multiple options. Transitioning to the close on the back of a sale doesn't have to be awkward or hard, but you do have to know the best way to do it, and you also have to role play and practice doing it.

Here's a guideline to follow that'll get you trained to be conscious about how you do it and teach you to execute it the right way every time.

1. SUMMARIZE THE BENEFITS THAT MATTER MOST TO THE PROSPECT.

Stop wasting time on things they don't care about. All the perks, bells and whistles that they haven't shown interest in, are a waste of time on the back end. When you summarize what matters most to them before asking for the money, it shows you've heard them and you care, but it also reconfirms the things that matter most to them to get them in the buying mindset from the value of that confirmation.

2. BRING UP THE OBJECTIONS AND ASK THEM IF THERE'S ANY OTHER BEFORE YOU MOVE FORWARD.

Confirm that you understand what their concerns were and you want to make sure you've handled those concerns to their satisfaction, such as:

- "I know that you said this has to be affordable."
- "I understand you're worried about the life of the product."

"I've addressed both of those concerns and I know you'll be pleased with the solution for both. Are there any other concerns or reasons this might not be a good fit for you before we move forward?"

If they say no, you gave them a chance and proved that you heard what their concerns were throughout the presentation and wanted to make sure there were no other concerns before you moved forward. This is important and always shows you care.

3. PICK YOUR CLOSE.

There are many ways to close when working with someone.

- **The Choice Close**

It's always best to offer three options. Most will land in the middle. With this type of closing technique you are offering two or more options, the optimal number being 3, please, if you want the best results, of course. This close is powerful because the prospect feels like they're in control. They get to choose between option A, B, or C. You're listing the differences (features and benefits) of all three options based on the customer's needs and waiting for their feedback on which option they believe best suits them. With this type of process, it's much easier to upsell and negotiate without having to negotiate your process. Choose the one that you believe best suits their needs, genuinely of course, and explain why.

The good news about a choice close is if you offer three options and they even take time to review them, you're on your way to a sale most of the time. It's one of my favorites!

- **Urgency Close**

You can use this type of close many ways, but it's usually tied to lack of inventory, limited time offers, buy one get one, adding additional benefits without increasing the price.

This is used to get your prospect to make a decision now rather than later. You're trying to persuade the prospect with an offer that they can't refuse. It's really well used when you have an indecisive prospect who's about to make a decision but they just can't be pushed over the edge. In that case you might say something like this:

> **Salesperson**: *"I know you're having a hard time making this decision, so here's what I'm going to try and get done. I'm going to extend this service from 12 months to 18 months, which basically gives you way more value. Now I'm not sure if I can get that approved, but I know how important it is for you to get the most value. If I can get that done, I'm sure you'd see the value in getting this done today, right?"*

See, urgency. Offering an additional benefit for the same money, I'll go ask for approval to prove that it's not something we just give away, which increases perceived value, to get the deal done now.

An urgency close can also be as easy as:

Salesperson: *"If we knock this out today, I'm going to get you 20% off. That saves you $XXXX. But if I go ask for this, my manager is going to want to know you're serious. This isn't a normal thing, but it's the end of the month and we need to hit our sales quota, so it'll be for today only. If they say yes, are we good?"*

The urgency close is about doing business now. Not tomorrow or the day after, but as soon as we possibly can with a limited time offer on a benefit and delivering that to the customer so it doesn't sound corny or salesly. You're simply motivating your prospect to make a faster decision. But do me a favor, once again, make sure you're using this ETHICALLY and not to manipulate the sale. For those of you reading this or listening to this who aren't using it the right way, you're the reason why the sales world has a bad name. Change now. It's not too late to have some integrity.

- **Assumptive Close**

We went over this in detail above.

- **Summarization Close**

This is simple. You're basically offering everything of value that matters most to the client and are simply asking for the sale like this:

Salesperson: *"I know you said in order for this to be the right fit for you it has to have x, y, and z. Assuming we have everything that you're asking for and it's within an acceptable price range, is it fair to say I can earn your business today?"*

Yep. Just that easy. Summarizing what they like most about your product or service, making sure the money makes sense to them, not you, but to them, and then just asking: can we do business?

- **Direct Close**

Another simple close, used in retail a lot. Someone's walking around with 4 pairs of jeans and you just ask: *"Are those the ones you're getting?"*

Or maybe a golfer is looking to buy a new set of clubs and the salesperson simply walks up to them and says: *"Looking to buy a new set of clubs?"*

A yes or no response, sometimes a maybe, but either way, you'll know how to move once they respond. Very direct.

- **The Conditional Close**

This is very similar to the "if I could… would you…" old way of doing things, but just delivered differently. A salesperson might say something like this:

Salesperson: *"I'm not sure if I can, Todd, but if I can get x, y, and z together for you and it doesn't cost any more money, can we lock this deal down?"*

Another way to use the conditional close is:

Salesperson: *"OK, in order to get this deal going, we need x, y, and z from you to make sure you qualify for this."*

People love to qualify! All of 'em. No one wants to be declined and sometimes it's not attached to credit rating or income; there are plenty of other ways people can qualify for something. The conditional close is used in multiple scenarios and is good to keep as ammo in your back pocket.

- **The Question Close**

This is a pretty common way to see how serious someone is about buying something from you on the back end of the sales process.

When you ask a question in a way that not only assumes the sale, but makes it so the deal is done with their answer, the salesperson just leans over and starts filling out the paperwork. Like "assuming the sale," it's a quick way to a yes or no, but only if you ask the questions the right way.

For instance, here are a couple questions to close the deal:

"I want to make sure you understand everything fully and I'm serving you properly. Are there any questions about how this works before we start filling out the paperwork?"

"I know we have the car in yellow, but you really wanted red. If I can run down to the other dealership and get you the red one, can we lock this deal in?"

Yes, this is similar to many of the other closes. You'll see a lot of each in the question close, but it's a really good way to get the deal or find out why you haven't. You're literally directing the sales process right to a yes or no. Both answers give you the information you need to move properly.

THE TRIAL CLOSE

The last and final option is the TRIAL CLOSE: a MUST to master if you want to be part of the elite in the sales world. You can use the trial close at any point in the sales presentation, if used properly.

The goal of a trial close is to predict the level of interest your prospect has in what you're offering. How do you know unless you ask? Another goal is to use the trial close to surface objections to handle NOW, so the prospect can't use them against you on the back end when you're asking for the money.

A trail close is also similar to many that we've already talked about, but its use is not just for the back end of the sales process. It can be used in every part of the process to make sure the prospect is engaged and interested in what you're saying. As many of the most elite sales professionals in the world will tell you, it's very important to use the trial close in multiple areas of your presentation.

By asking trial closes, you're building rapport and trust, and you're showing the prospect that you care about what matters to them and that what you're offering actually adds value to them. Using the right amount of trial closes is important too. You don't want to overuse them, but you need to use them. If you're asking for the sale multiple times throughout the presentation, it will get annoying and can cause you to lose the sale, but when used right and by asking the right questions that aren't always a "are you ready to buy" question, but more for verification purposes, then you will get the best out of using them.

Here's some trial close questions I like:

- How does everything we've talked about so far sound to you?
- What do you like best about what we've gone over so far?
- If you could pick the best thing that sticks out to you most, what would it be?
- How do the terms look to you?
- Is there anything you'd want to change about the offer before we move forward?
- What's missing that you think we might need to do business together?

Those are all used often and in multiple different industries. Sit with your team and figure out the best trial closes to ask your prospect and then master when and where to use them.

So when is the best time to use a trial close?

1. At the introduction:

A lot of industries aren't breaking the ice well enough when you meet a prospect. For instance, I was working in the timeshare industry many years ago and now we consult for many of the high-end brand-name companies. One of their biggest problems was getting their sales team to get the prospects to smile when they've been bribed by a gift to go to a presentation they never wanted to be at in the first place.

So we taught them to trial close the minute they shook the prospects' hands. They knew that most of them didn't want to be there, just as when I was selling timeshare we knew the prospects probably weren't interested and this was most likely the last place they wanted to be. This particular trial close was created to be more humorous to break the ice, but also let them know that we know they don't want to be there, so let's get through it quickly and have some fun.

Here's how it went. Prospect waiting in lobby to meet the sales representative, the sale rep walks up, introduces themselves, and here's where the trial close broke the ice with humor, but also made it possible to gauge how interested in timeshare the prospect was:

Salesperson: *"Are you the Speciale Family?"*

Prospect: *"Yes, we are."*

90% of the time they're annoyed that they're even there. Salesperson shakes their hands and says:

Salesperson: *"Look, I'm guessing they gave you guys a gift to be here today and I'm also going to guess that you'd rather be outside by the pool than stuck with me for the next hour, right?"*

Prospect *(most likely shocked but laughs)*: *"Well, yes, we'd rather be in the pool with our kids for sure, no offense."*

Salesperson: *"No offense taken at all. I appreciate the honesty, and I'll also be honest with you. So here's the deal, you know I'm going to try to sell you something, right?"*

Prospect: *"Yes."*

Salesperson: *"Great. And I know that when I ask you to buy this timeshare you're going to say what?"*

Prospect: *"No."*

Salesperson: *"Great. So here's the honesty. You know that I'm gonna try to sell you something and I'm in sales, not just a tour guide of the property like someone else might've told you. I know that when I ask you to buy, you're going to say… (let them answer again)"*

Prospect: *"No."*

Salesperson: *"Exactly. So let's do this, since we've got that out of the way, we're both being brutally honest with one another and you have to be here for an hour anyway, all I ask is this. You be honest with me, I'll be honest with you. Since I know you're going to say no anyway, just keep an open mind and in 30 minutes, half the time of your presentation if nothing I say adds value to your vacation lifestyle, I'll get you out of here sooner than later, cool? But you have to truly keep an open mind, deal?"*

The trial close here was getting the family to just keep an open mind and confirm that they would by offering value of half the normal tour time if they weren't interested in anything I had to say. Brutal truth from the jump and a trial close on getting them to keep an open mind. In that 4-minute intro or less, I build the amount of trust it would take an untrained timeshare sales representative to make in hour or if ever. People want honesty, so give it to them, then trial close them on giving you a chance, even if it's a small one.

2. During the opening of your pitch:

A lot of untrained sales representatives miss this crucial place to ask a trial close. It should never be to assume the sale or go for the jugular, but it's a good time to gauge the level of interest in what you're offering so far. You might've given an opening statement to what your product or service is about and it's always helpful to see what their honest feelings about it is to help you navigate through the sales process, catering your presentation to best suit this particular prospect.

For instance, you might ask:

"Based on what we've gone over so far, does this sound like something that might add value to you?"

"I know we've just started, but I really want to cater to what's most important to you. What about what we've discussed so far would add the most value to you?"

Very non-threatening questions to see where their minds are at. It's good for many reasons; sometimes at this point they might say different things like this:

"I actually had no idea your product did all that. I'm intrigued."

This type of response is obviously great. But now you have one little trial close that's proven to you there's real interest in what you're offering. Proceed.

"From what I've heard so far, I don't think it's really what we're looking for."

In this case, your response should be confirming you've heard them and then asking something like this: "I totally respect that and I don't want anyone I serve to ever get anything that won't add value to them, so let me ask you, what are the most important things to you so I can see if this is even a good fit for you?"

Either response is fine as long as you know how to respond. Right after the opening is a great spot to ask a nice, soft trial close to see where their level of interest is.

3. Throughout the presentation at identifying moments:

Look, there's times throughout the sales presentation that you're going to gain interest. You're going to say something and they're going to say something positive back. This is a great time to ask a trial close, again, as long as it's not an aggressive one. It's always good to get them to confirm their level of interest when they respond verbally or by body language that they've seen or heard something they like. For example:

> **Salesperson**: *"One the best parts of how our sales training company works is that we bring an outside perspective, which saves you time and cost for in-house sales trainers and the best part about it, we guarantee results. If the results don't increase, you don't pay. How's that for customer satisfaction?"*
>
> **Prospect**: *"Wow. So if we don't increase sales and efficiency, we don't pay?"*
>
> **Salesperson**: *"That's right. Knowing that, I bet it's worth having our team show you what we can do, right?"*
>
> **Prospect**: *"What do I have to lose, right?"*
>
> **Salesperson**: *"More than you think, sir. There's a reason why we guarantee our work. We're not in the business to work for free either. We know what we're capable of when we go into an organization like yours. But what you'll lose is a massive jolt of energy, increased efficiency, and more sales with higher retention. That's what you have to risk by not having us."*

Damn, I'm not gonna lie. Typing that got me pumped up. That person just got closed. See how it's good to use trial closes at positive identifying points throughout the presentation? It wasn't "if I could… would you… " corny stuff; it was confirming they just heard or saw value in something and we planted a seed, with their confirmation, that they're more apt to do business with us now.

4. When you've finished presenting what your offer is:

This is a crucial part of the sales presentation. You've presented your offer and a lot of salespeople fall apart right here. They're so afraid of getting negative feedback that they tiptoe around getting a real answer to the level of interest the prospect has in their offer. Don't be afraid to hear constructive, negative stuff or even "I'm not interested at all." It's all discovery information to keep the sales process going. It doesn't mean you've lost the sale. But if you ask a good trial close here, you can get valuable intel almost instantly.

Try asking something like this:

Salesperson: *"Based on what we've gone over so far, do you think this would be a good fit for you?"*

They might respond yes or no. To be honest, it doesn't matter. What matters is that your trial close has given you the information to ask questions to further the presentation or just to assume the sale if the response was positive. Without asking, you'd only find out after you've asked for the money and it's much better to know well before that.

5. The Objection Trial Close

Some of the best ways to handle an objection—and, as you know since we've already gone over that chapter, there are many of them—is using a trial close.

For instance, the prospect may surface an objection and say:

Prospect: *"Those terms don't work for me."*

Salesperson: *"Totally get it. So what you're saying is if the terms made sense to you, then we could move forward?"*

Like in the handling objections chapter, in this chapter I'm asking a trial close with a question to find out if that objection is the "real" objection. If they say yes, we got a deal. If they say no, then that's not the real objection anyway. But using a trial close, responding to their objection with a question to get to the close, is a winning scenario either way. Once again, you're getting information you need to continue the sales process in the right direction.

6. The Price Trial Close

Another good spot to do a trial close is when you've presented the prospect with your pricing options. Many untrained salespeople don't like talking about the money, but you have to get very, very comfortable with it. It's exciting for the elite. It's what they look forward to, because if you follow the steps in this book, the money portion of the sales presentation is when you get paid too!

There are several different trial closes on price. Here are some examples:

"So which option works best for you: A, B, or C?"

"So based on what we agreed upon earlier, we can agree the price makes sense, right?"

"Knowing that many of the benefits add value to you, do you agree the price is fair?"

"Would we agree the price is worth the investment?"

"This price is catered to your needs and the 10% off you've requested is approved. Are we ready to move forward?"

When talking about price and the prospect is trying to negotiate, make them work for it. Before getting approval on what they've requested, confirm with the prospect that they will do business with you if the approval is granted.

For example, say you're a door-to-door salesperson offering any product with a price attached to it and the prospect is just that hardcore negotiator who needs a deal. They're the type of client who wants a deal better than everyone else.

Whether you're in person, over the phone, or in virtual sales, it all works the same. Say something like this:

Salesperson: "OK, Mr. Speciale, what you're asking for is a lot and it's EXTREMELY doubtful I'll be able to get this approved. BUT, and that's a big BUT, I don't want to go to my manager, beg for what you're asking for, come back out here, and you still say no."

- (if you're in person, continue with this) ... "so I'm going to write the price down on this piece of paper, I'm drawing a line right here, you sign it saying you'll do the deal if he approves it. If he sees that he'll know you're serious and you and I can shake hands before I go ask hoping for the best, deal?"
- (if you're in phone sales or virtual sales, continue with this)... "so do me a favor and text me real quick saying that if I get this approved, you'll do the deal at that price. That way he will know I'm serious when I ask him, deal?"

All we're doing is triple confirming that their level of interest is as they say it is when it comes to the price they want or the discount they're asking for. Then go ask for approval if you need to, wait some time, and then come back with the paperwork, shake their hand if in person, or if it's virtual give them a big smile, if it's phone use increased tonality proving excitement like they won, and say:

"Not sure how we made it happen, but welcome to the family. Start filling this out."

See, too many untrained sales representatives miss deals because they think they can lower the price without confirming that the prospect will buy, and then they come back with a lower price and the prospect still says no. So was it really the reason they weren't buying? Maybe they're going to ask for more of a discount because you got that one? You MUST confirm when someone's asking for a discount, that if you get it done, they're going to do the deal. It eliminates a lot of other unnecessary negotiation time.

Trial closes on price is a mastered skill you have to have in your arsenal.

7. Back-end Trial Close

You've talked benefits, you've talked price, and now it time to make a decision, so just ask! You gotta ASK! Don't be afraid. A trial close here is a softer way, but it's also a good way to see where they stand.

Something like this is always a good trial close:

"Based on everything we've gone through today, are you ready to move forward?"

Now remember, it doesn't matter what sales book you read, who's training you, what you listen to, you don't have to use our words. Make these questions and responses conform to your personality, how you'd say it. Your presentation needs to be natural and meaningful and you can't do that reading a script or trying to say things like someone else would. Be you; it's the best version anyway!

The trial close, at any stage, with any form, is supposed to test the level of interest a prospect has. How committed to purchase are they? Do they really want what you're offering? By intentionally using trial closes at multiple points throughout the presentation, you can literally guide your prospect to the close like a navigation system with the most optimal route! Also, don't forget to tie in social proof, good reviews, testimonials, and third-party stories when closing deals. They're very effective and if told properly can put the prospect in the shoes of someone who has yielded value by purchasing what you're offering.

THE MONEY

You know the closing techniques; now let's get into asking them for money! It's hard for some, but it can be simple if you have the confidence and understand that no is a real thing you're going to hear a lot and you should get excited when you do. You might be asking yourself, is Todd crazy? LOL. Maybe a little, but the truth is, the "no" is a great thing. I know there are plenty of theories on how many "no's" it takes to get to the "yes" and, to be honest, I'm not sure anyone knows the real answer, but I can tell you that hearing no is a good thing!

Let's make the uncomfortable, comfortable. There are many different ways you can ask for the money. Below are some common options to choose from.

> "This is a great investment for you. When would you like the monthly payment to start and how would you like to handle the down payment?"

> "We have several different payment options. Do you plan to pay it all in one lump sum, or just use a down payment and get your monthly payment comfortable for you?"

> "How would you like to pay for it, credit card, cash, or finance it?"

> "Would you like me to run your card now, so we can get those added benefits we got approved for you?"

> "Sounds like you're ready to get the ball rollin'. How would you like me to process the payment?"

> "A lot of our clients use our 12-months same-as-cash option. Would you like to just pay for it or take advantage of that option?"

You have to be ready for the yes, best outcome, or the no, not as cool as a yes, but we can still get the deal.

One of the biggest mistakes salespeople make is asking for the sale, getting it, and then talking past the close. You got the deal! That was the goal! They've said yes! Shut up and fill out the paperwork. Time is money. But you'd be surprised how many deals are lost because salespeople just can't be quiet but continue to pitch after the prospect has already agreed to the deal.

- Hubspot conducted a survey and found that 69% of buyers said that the most influential factor in their purchasing decision was a salesperson who listened to their needs. Who spoke less and made the closing process short and sweet.

- Another study by Gong.io researched over 100,000 sales calls and found that the most successful salespeople spoke for only 46% of the call, while unsuccessful salespeople spoke for 65% of the call.

So what does this mean? Be quiet. Listen more and get the paperwork done. You waste so much time by continuing to pitch or discuss the product when a customer has already made their decision. This is wasting your time and more importantly theirs. You also create doubt. They're thinking, "Why is Todd still pitching me after I already said yes?" It can literally make them rethink doing business with you. It's also super annoying to someone who's probably been with you for an ample amount of time already and all they want to do is buy what you offered and get out of there as quickly as possible. Trust me, you don't want their first experience with you to be a bad one after they've said yes and you keep going. You might get lucky to get that deal, but it'll reduce the chances of them coming back to buy from you again tremendously. Let's not forget, if you do talk past the close, it'll most likely eliminate any opportunity for referral business as well.

Moral of the story: they say yes, you stop pitching, accept the yes, keep it movin', and get the sale completed promptly.

So what if they say no? Well, by this time you know how to ask good questions, you know how to do a discovery, you know how to handle objections, BUT what if there were a way to close a few of those super hard-headed people who just love to say no? What if I told you some secret sauce right here that's made me millions in sales?

Well, get ready, this one is GOLD!

Years ago, I racked my brain for months trying to figure out how to convert even 10% of my "hell nos" into a yes. Like, literally turn them around before they leave my office even after they've been adamant about not doing business that day. Well, guess what? I figured it out and I've implemented this process in multiple different industries and it's GUARANTEED to increase your numbers if you just USE IT!

So here it is: I call it **The How Did I Do Revival Close**

You've worked with this prospect for quite some time, you feel like you've handled their objections well, and they still have said no. You've given up and can't put a finger on why they're not doing business with you. Welp, there's one thing people love to talk about: themselves. They also love to give advice. So let them do both.

Prospect: *"Nope, sorry, I'm just not going to buy today. Thank you anyway."*

Salesperson: *"That's OK, ma'am. One job won't change the financials of this company, but your happiness will. We just want to make sure you leave feeling served, whether you do business with us or not..."*

(BTW, if you have any type of pitchbook or paperwork here, fold it up/close it and put it to the side. That's a psychological signal that the presentation is really over.)

(continue with)... *"But since we know we can't earn your business today, I was wondering if you wouldn't mind helping me with a small favor before you leave? I really value your opinion and I know you could help me."*

Prospect: *"Sure, how can I help?"*

Salesperson: *"We are always looking for better ways to improve our product and I'm personally always looking for ways to get better at serving our potential clients, so my question is: what did* *we miss? What could I have done better to earn your business, but equally as important, what did the product not have that if it did, we could've possibly earned your business?"*

HA! Watch them give you their advice, hopefully sound, but some will just speak to hear themselves speak. But in the meantime, they're telling you the things about your product or service that it supposedly didn't have. Rarely, if you're good at your job, will they say anything about you. It's not in most people's nature. But they will surface the things your offer didn't have.

Here's what I found out about that. Most people miss a lot of the sales presentation. When you use this tool, you'll find that a lot of what they say your offer didn't have, it actually has. So your transition back in is always an apology, it's always your fault, but you just wouldn't feel right letting them leave unless they had all the information they need to make an informed decision so they don't lose a great opportunity for something that will add value to their lives.

Say something like this:

Salesperson: *"Oh, I'm sorry, Mr. Speciale. I really need to apologize, because our offer actually has what you say it didn't and more. I wouldn't feel right if I let you leave without showing you this before you go, look here..."*

BOOM! You're back in. It doesn't work all the time, but remember, when people are speaking, most of the time the person listening is only retaining 30% of what the speaker is saying. Give it that one last shot to see if you can potentially get a deal. They are the most fun deals to close by far because most believe the deal is dead, when it's far from that!

Another way is called: **The Survey Revival Close**

Same concept, except the sales manager, a co-working salesperson, or a T.O. (take over) speaks to your prospect and asks how you did, what did we miss, what value is the product or service missing? Then this person transitions back into the sale in the same way as above.

Mastering the closing process is very detailed and intricate, and it's something that should be worked on daily and role played daily. I can teach a person who has never been in sales before how to master this section only and they can compete with some of the higher end reps in the world today. This is crucial to your career in sales. Learn it. Live it. Use it! TRAIN IT!

Here are 3 different scenarios using specific closes to train on. Go back through this chapter and get with your leaders and your team. Figure out the top 3 closes that'll be the most beneficial for your world and start training on them immediately. The faster you can close your own deals and be trained on different ways to do that, the faster your personal brand and business begins to grow!

SCENARIO 1: SOLAR BUSINESS (ASSUMPTIVE CLOSE)

Situation: The client has just listened to a detailed presentation on the benefits of solar energy, the long-term savings they will enjoy, and the environmental benefits of making the switch.

Close: "So, Mrs. Smith, based on your home's location and energy needs, we'd recommend the mid-sized panel system. Should we schedule the installation for next Tuesday or would Thursday be better for you?"

Benefits:
1. Projects confidence: It presumes that the customer has already made the decision to buy.
2. Smooth transition: It transitions seamlessly from presenting to closing without an abrupt change in tone.
3. Reduces decision-making stress: Instead of deciding "if" to buy, the customer is simply deciding "when."

Key Takeaway: Use the assumptive close when the customer seems very interested and is showing few objections. It's a gentle push that can expedite the decision-making process.

SCENARIO 2: LIFE INSURANCE BUSINESS (DIRECT CLOSE)

Situation: After discussing the importance of providing for loved ones, highlighting potential risks, and walking the client through various policy options, you sense that the client understands the value but is hesitant.

Close: "Mr. Johnson, based on our discussion, I believe that the Gold package would be the best fit for your family's needs. Would you like to proceed with that policy today?"

Benefits:
1. Clarity: A direct approach leaves no ambiguity; it's clear what's being asked.
2. Efficiency: It brings the customer to the point of decision without further delay.
3. Honest and Transparent: Some customers appreciate and respect the straightforwardness.

Key Takeaway: When the customer understands the value proposition and simply needs a nudge to commit, a direct close can be the most effective approach. It's candid, concise, and cuts to the chase.

SCENARIO 3: FURNITURE SALES BUSINESS (CONDITIONAL CLOSE)

Situation: A couple is looking at a luxurious sofa set but are concerned about the price.

Close: "If I could get you a 15% discount on this sofa set, would you be willing to make the purchase today?"

Benefits:
1. Overcoming objections: This close directly addresses and potentially removes a primary barrier to the sale.
2. Creates a sense of partnership: It shows the customer that you're working with them to find solutions.
3. Provides valuable feedback: If they still hesitate, there might be other objections you haven't uncovered.

Key Takeaway: When faced with specific objections, the conditional close offers a solution on the condition that the client will buy. It can lead to a win-win scenario, resolving the customer's concerns and securing the sale.

Each closing technique has its place, depending on the customer's needs, objections, and the sales context. Salespeople must be adept at reading the situation and applying the most effective close. The goal is always to create a positive outcome for both the seller and the buyer. Practice these techniques by training daily in scenarios specific to your industry, refine them based on feedback and experience, and you'll be well on your way to becoming a master closer.

CHAPTER 29

THE GREATEST LEAD IN ALL OF SALES

Talk about working smarter, not harder. Most companies and sales individuals don't spend enough time training on this and it's costing you and your company tons of money! The time spent on training in how to get referrals is at minimum a 100% return on your efforts. Most don't even ask! It's crazy to think, but it's very, very true.

Asking for referrals is crucial for many reasons. You make more money. You're getting opportunities most won't even ask for and it'll grow your customer database to extreme levels for future business, whether they buy from you now or not.

Let's dive into why it's important to be a master at pulling referrals:

1. YOUR ODDS OF CONVERTING GO WAY UP WITH A REFERRAL.

If your closing ratio is 40% for example on a non-referral opportunity, it's double with someone that your clients have referred to you.

I don't know about you, but I personally would love an opportunity that converts at double what a normal one does.

They're easier to close because someone they know and trust referred them to you. This shows the referral that they believe you're a good person to do business with, so the wall you have to fight to break down with a non-referral is already broken down for the most part. I'm not saying you don't still have to build a great rapport, but it's way easier when someone they know has already done business with you.

2. COST PER LEAD/ACQUISITION COST WAY DOWN.

Most sales representatives and companies track what a lead actually costs them. For instance, if you're advertising/marketing your product or service and the cost to generate one lead is $100, then your cost per lead/opportunity is $100. If you close 33% of those, then your cost per acquisition is $300 per sale. That's one deal for every 3 opportunities.

Now here's the gold with referrals: if you get 5 referrals from your client and the closing ratio is double at 66% close because they were referred to you by someone they know and trust. That means for every 5 referrals you get that you have the potential to close, you'll make 3.3 deals.

So let's put that into perspective on a cost per lead and acquisition base. If you and your team are trained in how to ask for referrals, that means for every one deal you pay $300 for, you can close 4.3 deals when asking and getting 5 referrals for an averaged out closing rate of 53%. That's increasing your closing ratio by 20% and reducing your cost per lead to $37.50 (getting 8 leads instead of just 3). Take the $300 and divide it by 8 leads generated. Three from marketing and 5 referrals. Now you have 8 leads with a closing percentage of 53% netting you 4.3 deals. This also brings your cost per acquisition to only $69.76 rather than $300 per acquisition.

The closing percentage goes up and the cost per deal goes down. Why would anyone not want to get referrals. More sales for the representatives and less cost to the company. WIN-WIN!

3. SAVES YOU A TON OF TIME!

When you get good at getting referrals, it'll save you time. You won't have to cold call as much; you won't have to do as many presentations that aren't referral based. Don't have to prospect near as much. As a matter of fact, most sales representatives who are beasts at getting referrals work off of only referrals.

I mean, why wouldn't you? Less work. Higher closing percentages and saves you time prospecting, closing percentage is way lower, and cost per lead and acquisition is way up. Sounds like a no-brainer to me. So why don't people do it? They're afraid to ask and aren't trained in the best way to pull referrals, which lucky for you, you bought this book or audio version and I'm going to teach you how!

4. REFERRALS LEAD TO REPEAT BUSINESS.

Truth. Salespeople have a bad name most of the time in today's sales world. When a customer is referring you to a friend or family member, they usually have all good things to say about you, they trust you and believe you'll guide whoever they referred to you properly and create a relationship based on integrity.

When you take care of them and treat the people they refer to you too with equal care, you're building a client base that will become super loyal to you and give you opportunities to work with them in the future. Once again, your good work ethic and always being honest about your product or service creates a positive long-term relationship profitable for you and gives people peace of mind that when they do business with you, they'll be led down the right road always. This is good for your clients and gets you good referrals.

5. REACH AN AUDIENCE YOU MAY NEVER OTHERWISE HAVE.

Referrals give you a huge range of opportunities. For instance, we've done some consulting for insurance companies in the past where the sales representatives were licensed to do business in multiple states. If you're in Florida like I am and you get a referral to work with someone in Idaho, would you have ever really prospected in that area without your client giving you that referral? We'd like to say yes, but most won't.

When you get that referral in Idaho, you can start to pull local and out-of-state referrals from that client as well. I used to use red pins to mark on a huge map where I've done business. I used to love putting the first pin in a state and then flooding the state with red pins for all future business I pulled from referrals in that area. It was a blast and also a competition for my team and me. How quickly can we expand in that state? When you're concentrating on getting referrals, it makes it fun, everyone makes more money, and you reach people you may have never reached had you not asked for a referral to begin with!

6. YOUR REPUTATION AND HOW YOU DO BUSINESS IS BUILT FASTER AND STRONGER WITH REFERRALS.

With referrals, you're constantly expanding your network and people are reaching out to you as the "go-to" person in your industry. If you are the person who finds solutions, is honest, fair priced, and provides the best value, then your reputation will be as such. If you treat people badly, lie to them to get the deal, treat their referrals badly, and fail to communicate, your reputation will be as such.

When you do the right thing, business will flow naturally your way and your referrals will be abundant enough for you to build a huge client base, by just being a good, ethical, and hard-working sales representative for your clients.

Now that we know why getting referrals is key to your overall success, let's teach you the best ways to get them! This part is fun, so if you're listening to this, get a pen and paper out and start to take notes. If you're reading this, get a highlighter out and let's start highlighting the ways you think best fit you and your business.

Just remember, there isn't a one-size-fits-all way to get referrals. Some methods will work better for you than they will for others and vice versa, but mastering each and trying them all should be done to find out what works best for you and your team.

So let's go over some great ways to get a ton of referrals.

1. JUST ASK! MOST DON'T.

There's a fear of asking for referrals in the sales world that seems to be spreading like a cancer. What many people and companies miss is that the training to teach people how to ask for referrals is at an all-time low. If you aren't trained, you will be scared or unsure if you're doing it properly and because of that, most won't ask at all.

You have to learn and role play daily to get really good at asking for referrals. When the value you provide is backed up by communication and exemplary service, asking the client to recommend others who might benefit from your offer will be seamless.

2. GIVE THEM SOMETHING!

Everyone likes perks. Everyone likes value. Less money, more value. If they're already a client of yours, offer an incentive to get them to feel the urgency of giving you referrals. This is a great and proven way to gain plenty of referrals for your pipeline.

The more you give, the more referrals you'll get. Don't give them everything at once; save some cool stuff to negotiate even more referrals.

This might be free services, a free month of what you're offering, or any other additional perks that they see value in. Giving these freebies will give you some new opportunities.

3. SERVE YOUR PROSPECTS!

There's a very common balance that needs to be created in a sales process between selling and serving. Yes, we are selling. Yes, we are closing. But you equally need to serve your clients to the highest. When you do this, referrals will come more easily and more organically.

So many sales representatives are literally NONEXISTENT after they make a sale. They don't answer phone calls, emails, or text messages. The communication goes away, which makes the client feel like they don't matter. This happens more often as your client base gets bigger and bigger. When your prospect knows they matter, that you're there when they need you, they will give you referrals because they know that you're the person who will serve their friends and family members equally as well. Don't do this and you'll have a hard time getting referrals.

4. STAY IN TOUCH!

As in the previous step, sales representatives who are all about the money and not about the client lose tons of business when they don't follow up or just keep an ongoing relationship with their sales pipeline.

There is SO MUCH business earned from keeping in touch with your clients that's missed when you don't. You can set reminders, or have some new AI software that will continually send out texts or emails, or drop a call personally to your client base to let them know you're still here and available to serve them as they need you.

Simple things like ending the conversation, in any instance, with a question eliciting a response like this is a very good and efficient way to stay in contact with your prospects:

Email, Text, or Call:

"Hey, Todd, hope all is going well. I just wanted to make sure everything is going well and to let you know I'm here to serve you. Do you have any questions about your purchase that I can answer for you or is everything good?

Let me know and have the best day."

The problem with most salespeople following up with clients is that they're always trying to sell something at every turn. The client then feels like the only time you want to connect with them is when you're trying to get their money. What if you genuinely cared? What if you were really proving you're following up with them to just make sure they're good?

When you do this, the follow-ups can lead to additional sales from the client. An easy way to reply to their reponse like this:

"I'm so glad everything's going well. I just really want to be your point of contact and for you to know I'm available to serve you as needed. Also, if you know of anyone else you think might benefit from our service, we're running some great deals this month and of course I'd serve them as I am you. Got anyone in mind?

Thanks again and I'm really glad things are going well!"

See, that right there alone will get you a ton of business and even if it doesn't, it'll show your client you care, which at worst case will create repeat business for you.

5. MAKE IT EASY TO GIVE YOU REFERRALS

They should have an easy way to share your information. Give them an e-business card to share. I'm not a huge business card fan, because most people just toss them anyway. If it's digital, it's way easier to send through a text or email. If business cards is all you have, then leave a stack with them. Also, make sure your client has your information at least stored in their phone to share with potential referrals.

You might create marketing material to leave with them for referrals as well. QR codes are easy to get these days and they are cheap options to scan with their camera on their phones to provide your personal information or some material on what you do and your offer.

6. PAY THEM!

As funny as that may sound, clients love cash or some sort of gift that has monetary value. Cash referral fees are a sound and very effective way to get referrals. It promotes greed, and usually the best time to offer referral fees is when they're finalizing a deal with you. Offering referral fees can offset their cost to you for your product or service they're buying.

For instance, if you're selling something that's $1,000 and they've agreed to purchase it, you might offer a referral fee of $100 for every person they refer to you. This creates greed as most prospects would think, *"If I refer 10 people to this person, it just paid for my purchase!"* This is a very good way to get referrals, and cash, as they say, is king!

7. OFFER THEM A REFERRAL

I know what you're thinking. Why? At this point in the presentation, you should have built a good enough rapport that you know what they do for a living regardless of what you're selling. Sometimes offering them a referral—but only when being honest about it—will get them to do the same for you.

It's a great way to break the "asking for referrals" ice. You give them something, they give you something. Many clients appreciate you recommending people to them as well. They have a business, they have to earn a living like you, so why not support them and the support usually comes back equally, if not more. Especially when you offer a referral first. If you haven't tried this yet, you absolutely should.

In the end, referrals convert higher, the retention is higher, the customers trust you more, and most turn into long-term clients when treated right. This is one of the easiest ways to build your book of business and use it as tool to create extraordinary wealth.

The Wharton School of Business conducted a study on the difference between a referred customer and a non-referred customer. They found that a referred customer has a 16% higher lifetime value than a non-referred customer. That basically says that they're more likely to do business with you again in the future.

Another study by Nielsen said that people are four times more likely to buy a product or service when it is referred to them by a friend or family member. Why? Because if a family member or friend refers you, it's telling the person they're referring that they trust you. This makes every sale much easier to close.

The *New York Times* also said that 65% of new business comes from referrals. This statistic alone proves that referrals are a huge source of additional business. Isn't it crazy that this isn't even role played or taught very often? If this doesn't get you to want to ask for referrals, nothing will.

It's important to practice asking for referrals even if you fail miserably. Eventually you'll get better and better. This is one of the most underrated skills that is trained the least, but has tremendous value. Get good at it! You'll thank me later. I've added a few ways to get referrals below. Train on them and enjoy!

SCENARIO 1: HEALTH INSURANCE

1. Customer Didn't Buy:
- *Scenario*: A salesperson named Jane is presenting a health insurance package to a prospect named Lisa. After the presentation, Lisa decides the package isn't the right fit for her.

- *Jane*: "Lisa, I appreciate your time today and respect your decision. Even if this plan isn't the right fit for you, perhaps you know someone who might benefit from our offerings? Do you have any friends or family looking for health insurance currently?"
- *Lisa*: "Actually, my sister mentioned she's looking. Maybe she'd be interested."
- *Jane*: "Great, would you mind sharing her contact details with me or would you prefer to pass along my details to her?"

2. Customer Bought:

- *Scenario*: David purchases a family health insurance plan from a salesperson named Robert.
- *Robert*: "David, thank you for trusting us with your family's health needs. Many of our clients come through word of mouth. Do you have friends or family who might be interested in exploring our health insurance options?"
- *David*: "My friend Paul was just talking about this. Let me give you his number."
- *Robert*: "Thank you, David. I'll reach out and see how we can assist him."

SCENARIO 2: DOOR-TO-DOOR SALES

3. Customer Didn't Buy:

- *Scenario*: Mark, a door-to-door vacuum cleaner salesperson, gives a demo to Sarah. She decides not to purchase.
- *Mark*: "Sarah, thank you for letting me demonstrate the product. If you ever change your mind, you know where to find us. By the way, do you have any neighbors or friends who might be interested in a demo?"
- *Sarah*: "The Smiths next door were looking for a new vacuum. You could try them."
- *Mark*: "Would you mind giving them a heads up, or should I mention you referred me?"

4. Customer Bought:

- *Scenario*: Ellen purchases a vacuum cleaner from a door-to-door salesperson named Amy.
- *Amy*: "Ellen, thank you for your purchase. It means a lot to us. I'm sure you have friends or neighbors who might benefit from this too. If you could refer me to them, it'd be much appreciated."
- *Ellen*: "Of course! My friend Nina was just complaining about her old vacuum. Here's her number."
- *Amy*: "Thank you, Ellen. I'll be sure to give her a call."

Importance of Getting Referral Information:

- *Builds Trust:* Referrals come from a place of trust. When prospects are introduced through referrals, they are more likely to trust the salesperson because someone they trust has vouched for them.
- *Efficiency and Cost-Effectiveness:* Acquiring a customer through referrals is less costly than traditional marketing and advertising. It's also more efficient as the sales cycle is often shorter with referred leads.
- *Higher Conversion Rates:* Referral leads tend to convert better than cold leads. They already have some level of interest or need, as suggested by the referring party.
- *Strengthening Relationships:* Asking for referrals can help in solidifying the relationship with the current customer. It shows that the salesperson values their opinion and network.

Importance of Each Scenario:

1. *Customer Didn't Buy (Health Insurance):* This showcases the ability to see value in every interaction. Just because a sale wasn't made doesn't mean the relationship isn't valuable. A non-buying customer can still be a source of future prospects.

2. *Customer Bought (Health Insurance):* Happy customers are the best promoters. Their satisfaction can lead to more sales through referrals.
3. *Customer Didn't Buy (Door to Door):* This highlights persistence and optimism in sales. Every door knocked on or demo given has potential, even if it doesn't result in an immediate sale.
4. *Customer Bought (Door to Door):* A direct transaction in door-to-door sales can create a ripple effect. When neighbors see a purchase, they become curious, and a referral amplifies the salesperson's credibility.

I'm sure a lot of sales trainers will try to convince you that there's a one-size-fits-all training on how to get referrals and their information. Truth is… There's not. Personalities are different. There's always going to be different situations where they don't want to give you someone's information and that's OK!!!

Just remember the MOST IMPORTANT RULE in referrals, "You gotta ask."

CHAPTER 30

FOLLOW-UP: HOW TO ACTUALLY DO IT

How you follow up matters. I see so many mistakes with how sales representatives follow up these days. Many companies are using a new role created specifically for following up with customers just to make sure they're happy and everything is going well. That position is called a: Customer Happy Agent.

Their only job is to follow up with clients within their organization to make sure they're getting communications, not offering anything for sale, but to make sure they have what they need from the product or service they purchased and if they don't, the Customer Happy Agent makes sure they do!

What a genius idea. Hiring someone to just keep your clients happy. So the real question is, can you do this if you're a sales representative and it's your book of business? The answer is yes. There are so many virtual agents you can pay to just stay in contact with your book of business, asking them if they can be of service or if your clients need anything that they can help them with. VAs are cheap and worth every single dollar and way more!

So how important is the follow up? Very. The amount of trust and loyalty to your clients after you've made the sale just proves to them they matter beyond the money you made from them. The complete satisfaction they get by knowing that you care about them enough to make sure they're getting the maximum value out of what you've sold them, goes way further than you think.

When following up with a client, you can address concerns, which shows you're the person who's going to take care of those concerns when they arise. This can get you good reviews. If you don't follow up and take care of your client's concerns—especially when the client reaches out and you don't respond—this can turn into negative reviews. Not good for either of you.

The follow up isn't just about what happens after the sale. What about prospects you're trying to convert into sales? It's just as important. I won't sit here and say one is more important than the next, because they both generate tons of business.

One thing you should never say is: "Hey, Todd, I'm just following up…"

- On that email

- On the information I dropped off

- On the text I sent

I hate the words "I'm just following up." Is that as creative as you can get? You might as well just say, "*Hi, Todd. I want your money.*" Don't be that person. Start every follow up with a creative way to engage in a conversation.

Harvard Business Review did a study that stated companies that follow up with leads within an hour are 7 times more likely to qualify the lead than those who wait even just one hour longer. This is proving that "time" matters in the follow up. Another study by Insidesales.com found that 35-50% of sales go to the vendor who responds first.

So if a lead is generated in your pipeline, you or your team needs to respond and fast.

As a matter of fact, HubSpot said that 82% of customers feel that a quick response to their inquiries is important when the prospect is trying to make a buying decision. Having a good product or service is important, but if someone is offering something similar to what you are and you don't respond in a timely manner, like the fastest, you could be costing yourself tons of business.

A few of the top reasons to follow up also include:

1. BEING PRESENT

Have you heard the saying "Out of sight, out of mind"? It's very true, especially in sales. If you're constantly checking up on your clients and prospects, your name, your presence will be known and if they see it often, you'll most likely be the go-to person to do business with. People will literally work with you based on a high level of respectable persistence. Just stay in touch. You can do this through automated messages, but nothing beats an old-fashioned phone call or in-person surprise visit to just say hi and make sure they're good.

2. WHAT THEY THINK MATTERS

Another good way to follow up with your clients or prospects is to ask them how YOU are doing. For example:

> "Hey, Todd, hope all is well. If you don't mind, I've been trying to fine tune how I serve my clients and would love some advice of what you think I could do better to take care of my clients or what I can add to my service that it may not have. I'd appreciate all feedback. Any suggestions?"

Simple, yet very effective. When they give you feedback, by the way, take it. No one will teach you how to grow your business better than the people you've done business with. Also see how I ended that statement in a question? Get that literally ingrained in your brain. Asking a question elicits a response and just sparks a conversation. Clients love to give you feedback.

3. UPSELL THROUGH THE FOLLOW UP

Following up shouldn't always be about selling, but it's OK if it is every now and then. When you stay in contact with your clients, it does give you plenty of opportunities to upsell or cross sell. You may have a special promotion or a new product or service you can bring up in the conversation casually that can increase your revenue and give you an opportunity for a sale.

4. BUILDS A BOND

Your clients should know you and you should know them. Building rapport and understanding who they are as people, getting to know them or their family by sending birthday cards or holiday cards just so they know that you care, is a great way to get closer to your clients and make sure they know they matter more than their money matters to you. Do this consistently and you'll always be the one they come to for advice or potential opportunities in the future.

5. GIVE THEM SOMETHING

A simple gift goes a long way. When you follow up with someone and you're not selling them, but you're giving them something, it's just nice! Most people are constantly selling when they're reaching out to their clients. Be creative. Giving thank you gifts for simply staying loyal and being a part of your network is a great way to be the obvious choice to do business with in the future. Many times, they'll respond with questions that open a dialogue up to maybe serve them again. The gift of giving is never ending.

The truth. Customers just want to feel very appreciated. They're spending their hard-earned money with you and we both know they have plenty of choices on who they could do business with. When you stay in touch and prove that you're loyal to them, they'll become loyal to you.

Here are 5 statistics on follow ups you should know:

1. A study by the Marketing Donut found that 80% of sales require five follow-ups after the initial contact, while the average salesperson only makes two attempts to reach the prospect.

2. The *Harvard Business Review* states that clients appreciate follow-up emails that come one week after the initial contact.

3. According to a study by InsideSales.com, it takes an average of 18 calls to reach a prospect, but only 10% of salespeople make more than three attempts to contact their leads.

4. A study by MarketingSherpa found that sending follow-up emails between one and two weeks after the initial contact resulted in a 50% increase in sales.

5. A report by Salesforce found that companies that follow up with their leads within five minutes are nine times more likely to convert them into customers than those that wait 30 minutes or longer.

So timing does matter. You have 5 different reviews from very prestigious companies proving that you need to follow up be persistent. There is a direct correlation to the fact that sales representatives waste leads, just because they don't take the time to follow up as much as they need to. Be different, keep going!

The best of the best know the statistics. They have a regimented schedule they follow based on the moves and the amount of times that are necessary when following up with clients and prospects they're trying to turn into clients. Create a really organized plan of action to STAY IN TOUCH! Most people just want to know they matter more than the money. When you make them feel that they matter, the follow up will get you rich and quick, but most importantly build one of the most loyal client bases ever.

Here are a few different examples of following up and why honesty is ALWAYS the best way to reconnect.

SCENARIO 1: REAL ESTATE

Scenario: You recently gave a tour of a beautiful property to a potential buyer. A week has passed, and you haven't heard back from them.

Reengagement Approach: "Hello [Client's Name], I hope you're well. I was just thinking about our visit to [Property Address]. I'm always looking for feedback on the property itself and how I served you. I'd love to hear your thoughts on both and if there's any other information or assistance you might need. So what'd you think?"

Importance of Reengagement through Honesty: In real estate, a home is a significant investment, both emotionally and financially. By reconnecting without pressure and genuinely asking for feedback, you're showing that you value their opinion and are not just after a sale. It fosters trust and can make the potential buyer feel more comfortable sharing their concerns or wishes, leading to a more tailored service.

SCENARIO 2: CAR SALES

Scenario: A couple visited the showroom last weekend and showed interest in a specific car model. They seemed excited but needed time to think it over.

Reengagement Approach: "What's up [Client's Name], I trust you had a good week. I've been thinking about your interest in the [Car Model]. If there are any more specifics or clarifications you'd like regarding its features or financing options, I'm here to help. The only way I want to earn your business is if this car is everything you want. I'd also like to ask for your opinion on the car itself and how I treated you.

Whether we do business or not, it's the only way we get better. Do you mind helping?"

Importance of Reengagement through Honesty: Cars, like homes, are significant purchases. By expressing genuine concern for the customer's comfort and understanding, you're reinforcing that their best interests are at heart. A transparent approach can alleviate their apprehensions and can lead to a more informed and confident decision on their part.

SCENARIO 3: HEALTH INSURANCE

Scenario: An individual requested information on different health insurance plans two weeks ago. They received the data, but there has been no communication since.

Reengagement Approach: "Hey [Client's Name], I hope all is good. Honestly, I just wanted to touch base regarding the health insurance plans we discussed and the customer service we provided you. Obviously, we'd love to earn your business, but if we're not the right fit, I'd also love to know why, so we can better serve the next person. If you don't mind me asking, how'd I treat you and what are your true thoughts on the coverage?"

Importance of Reengagement through Honesty: Health is a sensitive topic. By focusing on the well-being of the individual, you're emphasizing the human aspect over the commercial. A sincere approach in this industry can assure the prospect that they're not just another sale but that their health and peace of mind truly matter to you.

Notice how I ended each reengagement opportunity in a question to elicit a response. In each of these scenarios, the focus is not merely on making a sale but ensuring the prospect feels valued, understood, and genuinely cared for. This approach can often lead to stronger relationships, higher trust, and a more positive reputation in the industry. Use these as examples and keep practicing.

CHAPTER 31

SALES SCRIPTING

How you speak, pause, listen, and what you say matters. The most crucial thing you have to understand when building a sales script, whether its phone, face-to-face, or virtual sales, is that the script is only a guide with crucial points you have to learn in order to get the highest efficiencies when closing sales.

A good sales script helps ensure consistency so you and/or your team are presenting a common and consistent message when speaking to your prospects. Some will say to use the same language on the script, but I disagree totally. You have to read the script and then speak it—role play it in your own words. You're saying the same thing, but you might use different words than a high-level intellect might use or if you're the high-level intellect, you will use different words than someone who may not use the same language. Build it, practice it, and rewrite it as if you were speaking it.

When you're building the sales script, remember that another reason for having one is to make sure the value proposition is clear and concise. Outlining specific features and benefits so you don't forget or miss key components of your offer is highly recommended. The truth is that salespeople miss plenty of sales because they forget to do the things that made them successful to begin with. Having a script that's clear on the important points of your offer is imperative to your success.

You also save a ton of time when you use a script. Again, a great sales script should be used as a guide, not read word for word. You can save a ton of time, identify the specific needs of your potential clients, and cater your script to extract the information you need to save you and the client time. No one wants to waste time and a good script saves you time!

Also one of the best things about having a sales script is that it gives you confidence in what you're pitching. If you use that guide every presentation and re-word it so it sounds just like you, the words will flow and you will begin to sound like it's not a script at all. Your confidence will go through the roof and you need confidence in sales to be one of the elite. Constantly training yourself to use the script and practicing it with people who KNOW YOU and the way you speak is so crucial to your overall success. TRAIN, TRAIN, TRAIN until you can recite it like the back of your hand.

When writing a script you should avoid using proper terms. Write the script as if you're speaking it. You can always build an outline and let someone read it to make sure it sounds like you, your personality. For instance, when I'm writing a sales script I remove the proper "I am" and insert "I'm." Here's an example of what I mean:

- "My name is Todd Speciale; I am your point of contact. If there is anything you need, do not hesitate to contact me."
    o To me, that sounds super scripty. For me, I'd re-word it to this:
        - "My name's Todd Speciale; I'm your point of contact. If there's anything you need, don't hesitate to ask."

Taking the "name is" and making it "name's," the words "I am" and making it "I'm," the words "there is" and making it "there's," the words "do not" and making them "don't" sounds softer and more genuine. You sound like a real person, rather than someone reading from a script.

Like I said, make the script your own. Even if you work for a company that has a prepared script and it seems very formal, rewrite it and get with your manager to make sure they're OK with how you've re-worded it. The problem that may occur with that is that if you're working with a manager who is ego based or doesn't understand the importance of rewording a script based on personality, they might tell you not to do it. My advice, do it anyway. Your results will thrive and you'll see a major upswing in your sales efficiencies. When you start outselling everyone, your manager won't complain. I promise.

When creating a proper script, you have to know several things in order to create a great script:

1. WHO ARE YOU TARGETING?

Knowing the who and the where of your audience can change a script drastically. The audience in Texas may require different triggers than those in New York City. Know the demographics, how your buyers buy, and tailor your script to the needs, tastes, and desires of your listeners.

2. BE AN EXPERT ON WHAT YOU'RE SELLING.

Know your product and every service it offers. Know all the features and benefits fully before you build a script. Missing key components of your offer will cost you millions. If you don't highlight the appropriate value proposition, your efficiencies will go way down.

3. WHAT MAKES YOU AND YOUR OFFER DIFFERENT OR UNIQUE?

Knowing your Unique Selling Proposition (USP) is what will set you apart from your competition. Knowing the exact reasons why your offer is different, unique, and how it will impact your prospect in a positive way will help you and your team sell more and immediately find out how you can best serve your potential clients.

4. BUILD A STRUCTURE THAT'S EASY TO FOLLOW AND GUIDES YOUR PROSPECTS TO THE CLOSE.

You want to build a guided, intentional sales script that's easy to follow for you or anyone who gets the luxury of using it. Clear process-driven, impactful scripts with tie downs and key points give you ways to create buying opportunities when they reply to the script you've built.

5. HOW YOU START MATTERS EQUALLY TO HOW YOU FINISH!

Your opening statements in your sales script should be intentionally strong, while grabbing the attention of your prospect. Every hook should be placed properly, not just at the beginning, but also later to regain their attention through more of the not-so-fun but necessary parts of the presentation. The object of this is to gain interest. This step will get them to engage and ask questions because your hook has made them curious.

6. HOW WILL YOUR OFFER BENEFIT THEM?

This isn't the feature section, nor is it the benefits that your offer provides. This step is to list the benefits and rewards your prospect will see by having the features and benefits that your product or service offers. What Return On Investment (ROI) will they have by using your product or service the right way? What are the key positives they will see from doing business with you? Most scripts concentrate so much on what the offer does that they don't really dive into the results your prospect will have from the features and benefits of your product.

7. DON'T LEAVE OUT WHAT YOUR PRODUCT WON'T DO: THE NEGATIVES.

Very, very few sales scripts talk about or surface the negatives about your offer. The truth is that most people are afraid to talk about what it won't do, as they think it'll put them in a position not to earn a sale. BUT if you're different, if you're honest, if you really dive into the downside, proving that there's no PERFECT solution for everyone, it builds immediate trust and the rapport skyrockets almost instantly. Why? Because most sales representatives aren't trained on the benefits of the negatives in a sales presentation. Know what it will do and know what it won't and share that information with your potential clients. It will surface objections sooner and give you a chance to handle them, so they can't use them against you on the back end.

As in my earlier chapters, if you know everything about what you're selling, you know the top 5 objections you receive from your prospects and you should also know the most common negatives about your offer. It's OK and it's very valuable to bring them up to prove your offer is real and you're going to explain the limitations it has so they are clear on what your offer will do and what it won't.

8. KNOW THE OBJECTIONS AND BLOCK THEM IN YOUR SCRIPT.

Again, you should know the most common objections and a great sales script guides you to surface them, talk about them, and offer a solution to those objections before the prospect ever has a chance to bring them up. What does this mean for you? When blocking and handling objections intentionally in your sales script, you eliminate ways out for your prospect on the back end. It also shows them you know what you're talking about. The strongest script brings them up and handles them to the point where your prospects are more than satisfied by the solutions you offer.

9. ASK FOR THE BUSINESS!

I know this might be crazy to hear, but most sales scripts are built to get people to the ALMOST finish line. Basically, it gets the prospect right to the point of asking for the money, but it is not created to actually get you to ask for the sale. Your job as a sales professional is to offer a product or service that has enough value that it's easy to transition to the close. The scary part is, a lot of representatives will end the sales script with something like: "So whatcha think?" Crazy, right?

You need a very clear call to action. It's got to empower, motivate, and get your prospect to take action by the end of your sales script. When you build this, go back to the "closing the sale" chapter as a guide with the multiple ways I've outlined in that chapter and create something that's yours! But most importantly, YOU GOTTA ASK!

10. COULD YOU HAVE DONE SOMETHING DIFFERENT?

Many companies and sales individuals miss opportunities to close deals because they don't ask the prospect, when they've said no, questions like:

> "Although this wasn't the best fit for you today, I'm always looking for ways to better myself and our product/service. So before I go, I'd really love some tips on what I could've done better and/or the reason(s) why you didn't think this was a good fit for you."

"I truly thank you for your time today most importantly, but I love prospect feedback. If you don't mind helping me, what could I have done differently?"

Prospects LOVE when you ask for their opinion and a lot of times, when speaking about your product or service, they might say something that you actually do offer but that either they didn't hear you say or you forgot to say. This helps bring them back into a potential buying state of mind. This is one of the strongest and missed sales skills every professional must have!

Now that we have a process of what and how to build, let's get into some of the most common missteps sales representatives have when starting a conversation with generic greetings like this:

- "Hi, how are you?"
    - o Do you really care? Let's be honest here. If you care, I love that, but you're calling someone to possibly turn them into a potential client of yours.
- Don't talk about you so much. The call is about them.
    - o The statistics about you matter, but there's a certain time for that. Get to what the conversation is about and do it in an enticing way. Have a hook.
- Being direct is good, but don't be pushy.
    - o There's a fine line between getting to the point and being direct about your intentions and trying to force a sale.
- Be the expert, but not the arrogant.
    - o People want to work with winners. Any way you look at. But when you're building a script, be the servant expert, not the arrogant one.
- Simple and understandable
    - o Don't use acronyms and hard-to-understand verbiage to make yourself sound smart. You could have an entire conversation and if you're using industry words they don't

know, it's a waste of everyone's time. Most won't even tell you they didn't understand what you've said, because they might be embarrassed to say they don't understand. Keep the verbiage simple.

Utilizing a script, regardless of its verbiage, is supposed to give you an outline to follow and then present AS YOUR OWN! No one person sells the same or sounds the same when they speak. If they feel like it's scripted, you'll lose the attention of the prospect immediately. For instance, how many times have you received a call and the sales representative started out with things like this:

- "Hey, is this the person in charge?" or "Hi, my name is Todd from _____. Am I speaking to the person who can make buying decisions?"
    - o Here's the thing. You're already questioning the authority of the person you're talking to. This is aggressive and doesn't make people feel like they're valuable to speak to. Not a good option for a script.
- "Hello and thank you for taking my call. My name is Todd and I'm with _____ and the purpose of the call today is _____"
    - o This is too lengthy and literally sounds scripted. It's not the best way to gain a prospect's attention and usually results in someone hanging up the phone or an inner eye roll as you sound just like every other salesperson they've spoken to.
- "Hello, I'm not sure if you're the person I'm looking for, but would you be interested in _____?"
    - o What if they are?! And if they aren't, you're leading into something without allowing them to answer the first question. Never lead with this. Once again, it makes the person feel like you don't know who they are, or if they aren't the person you're looking for, do they even matter?

- "Hey Mr. _____, quick question... are you interested in saving money?"
    - o Way too vague and it's an obvious question, isn't it? I mean, who doesn't like to save money? Duh! Rhetorical questions are OK in some cases, but not when you're first speaking to someone and trying to build a rapport so they feel comfortable talking to you. This is VERY salesy and most get turned off immediately.
- "Hi, ma'am. My name is Todd and I'm calling from _____. Would you be interested in _____?"
    - o Jumping right into selling is one of the easiest ways to get someone off the phone or turned off if you're selling face to face.
- "Hey Mrs. _____, this is Todd from _____. Do you have a second to chat?"
    - o Some might think this is OK, but the prospect doesn't even know who you are yet. Why should they speak to you? What questions do you have for them? Why are you even contacting them? The immediate reply would be, "Who are you and what's this about?" The minute you tell them, if it's a sales call from a representative without proper training, they're hanging up instantly or they'll say they don't have the time if in person.
- "Hi Todd. First off, I'm not trying to sell anything, but I wanted you to know who I am in case you needed anything in the future."
    - o One of the worst things to say ever is "I'm not trying to sell anything." Because YES YOU ARE! If you want to lose most of your potential sales, start off with this one. It'll fast track you to minimal income and it's the easiest way to break trust instantly!

- *"Hey Todd, we have some new specials I wanted to go over with you. It'll only take a few minutes."*
    - o Again, selling from the start. Not a good idea. No one has time for specials unless something has been requested or someone has asked to be contacted. A few minutes in the business world is a long time. Try some of the best opening sequences in the script building in this chapter.
- *"Hey Todd, can you tell me a little bit about your business?"*
    - o For what? Again, who are you and why do you need to know about my business? What are you calling for? These are responses you're going to get and you'd have to start all over anyway, but unfortunately people use this and you shouldn't.
- *"Hey Todd, I'm calling to follow up on an email I sent last week that I'm sure you were too busy to view."*
    - o Were they too busy? I know some might think that's respectful, but it can be taken in many different ways. If they didn't reply to your email, it's OK to say you've been trying to contact them, but not from the start of a conversation.
- *"Hello. My name is Todd and I'm calling from _____. We are the leading company in our industry..."*
    - o Great, so what's this about and why are you calling me? People want real people. Get to the point and hook the person with tangible steps we will go over in this chapter.

It's important that you know what not to say, so you can build on what you should say. Remember though, you can take every "not-so-good" way to speak to a prospect through your script and switch a few things around that you like and immediately turn it into the best script you've ever written.

A lot of sales trainers will say "live by their way only." I'm not that guy and I never will be. You have to put yourself in a position to understand your product or service and what works best for you. I've seen some of the best sales professionals in the world use many of the most common mistakes listed above, add a few key words and it works great. Remember, this is YOU, this is YOUR TEAM, just stick to what works for you, but get multiple opinions and reviews on what works best. Other people will see and hear things you may miss. LET THEM!

So let's get into some of the great ways to speak to a prospect using a sales script. First, you have to define what type of script you need and for whom. I'm going to give you a couple of cold scripts to, again, customize and make your own, but at least you'll have a base to grow from.

- General cold script: you've never spoken to anyone about your offer before.

Hey or Hi (potential client's name)

Thanks for giving me some of your time; I appreciate that. I know we're all busy, so let me get to the point. I work with a company that specializes in _____ (insert hook. What you do. Short and sweet like....) *helping get you more leads at no upfront cost and you only pay when we help you make more sales.*

Insert the real – *"I'm sure you've probably spoken to tons of people who say they do what we do, but if you give me a small portion of your time, I'll prove it."*

Insert questions that are intentional and transition smoothly. *"What I don't want to do is waste your time or mine. So let me ask you a couple of questions to see if there's a fit here. If there is, it'll be good for both of us. If there isn't, we can get off this call right away so I can respect your time. Sound good?"*

If the prospect agrees, you need to have your script ready with very good questions to pique interest and also get the information you need to best present your offer to them. Something like:

"We know lead cost can get pricey. We also know most sales organizations want to reduce cost and generate more sales. As great as that sounds, it's hard to do for most. Which is what we're experts in. What do you think the top 3 challenges are that you face when generating more leads?"

"Most sales companies are great at sales, not marketing. Which is why partnering experts in marketing like us with companies like yours who are experts in sales usually solves those problems that may be hindering your growth. What about your current process do think needs help the most? How do those issues affect your business the most?"

Again, there's no one-size-fits-all question. Some work in any field, some are very specific. But if you sit down and really think of questions that can hook someone you've never spoken to before, while dropping seeds of the value you can provide, you grab their attention and get them thinking, "They might be able to help me."

At the end of the day, you're getting information you need to see if there's potential synergy. Without this information, you're just guessing. A lot of scripts are built to just throw all their features and benefits at someone just to see if one interests them. It's not the way to sell. It takes more time, the very limited time you have with a new prospect, but if you get crucial information and truly dial in to what matters most to them, then you have great time management and a more intentional sales process. This isn't a call to hard close, this is more of an initial discovery call to build rapport and follow back up with them with a solution or possible offer that adds value to their lives.

- **Building your brand and who you know script**

"Hey Todd, my name's Brandon from (insert your company name). I've been working in (insert the industry you're in) for over a decade. I've worked with some people you may or may not know, like (drop names. Remember, they might be competition to

the person you're speaking to as well). We've just found a way to support one another on challenges we have. To save time, I'd love to set up a time to talk more about this with you. If you're open to it, I will make time when you're free. Do you use Zoom or Google Meet, and when's the best time to set this up?"

Again, a lot of cold calls or warm leads are pushed too hard on that first call. Here are some statistics from huge sales organizations that are very similar.

A study by The Marketing Donut found that it takes an average of 8 cold call attempts to reach a prospect. Another study by HubSpot found that it takes an average of 18 calls to actually connect with a buyer. That same study from HubSpot found that it takes an average of 6 to 8 touches (which was calculated by phone calls, emails, face-to-face meetings, and other interactions) to generate a viable sales lead.

A similar study by InsideSales.com proved that the best number of call attempts to make before giving up on a lead is between 6 and 9. I personally believe that number is real, based on when the call is made. You have to change the times you call or try to contact your prospect.

Too many companies lose conversion on leads because they call them at the same time every day and expect them to answer. Take the same leads and run them at different times throughout the day and track them by time. If you do that well, you can understand the value of that lead by your eighth call or so. Another study by the Sales Management Association found that it takes an average of 8.42 cold call attempts to reach a prospect when you're intentionally calling at different times throughout the day.

What do these stats mean? KEEP CALLING! KEEP REACHING OUT! Don't give up after your third or fourth attempt. If all of these powerful companies who've had massive success tell you that it takes approximately 8 times to reach a cold lead, listen to them. The sad truth is that Harvard Business School found that most sales representatives don't try contacting their leads at different times and that they give up after the third attempt. Not good. Don't be like the norm; put yourself in a position to win! Follow the process of the best.

Here are some additional things that will help you build the best scripts.

1. Break the ice the right way!
- o Make sure your introduction is swift and effective and you're introducing yourself the right way. Your job here is to reduce prospect resistance and get them to be OK just having a conversation with you. Because here's the deal, if you don't master a real and honest introduction, sales resistance stays high and you increase lead cost and lower conversion. The intro is the most important lead into your potential opportunities.
    - They need to know your name.
    - Be polite about asking for their time.
    - Brief and intentional hook on why you're contacting them.

The most important thing here is NOT TO SOUND scripted. Do not read off a script. It needs to be natural with a tonality that matches the reason why you're calling.

2. Make a great first impression.

Be grateful they've taken the time to speak with you and make it clear you're going to respect their time by getting to the point. It's always good, if possible, to have done some research on who the prospect is to drop seeds to show them you've done your research. People love that other people know about them and that you've taken time to find out more about who they are and what they do.

Identify and know the most common issues your prospects face when presenting your offer. If they know that you know the most common problems people have in their industry, it'll prove to them that you understand and have felt their pain. This usually piques the interest of the prospect because you're showing you know your stuff!

You also have to know the common interests that your prospects have among each other. Again, finding them or their company on social media is a great way to find out things they like, how they live their lives, and the industry specifics you can help them with.

Always mirror or match how your prospects speak to the best of your ability. People love to work with people and feel more comfortable working with people who are easy to talk to.

3. Ask questions that get them to speak!

Most salespeople talk so much that they don't give the prospect a chance to speak, nor do they get a chance to listen, because you as the salesperson don't know how to ask questions to get them to tell you how to sell them and build the best rapport.

Questions, especially good questions, force you to listen and listening drives sales. Why? Because your prospect is thinking how to answer the questions you have prepared.

Suggestions to find out about the prospect:

- Find out their problems and have solutions ready. You should already know what those problems are, but when they speak it, they own it, and you have what they need to solve it.
- Uncover their goals.
- Ask what they like and don't like about how they currently do business.

In asking the right questions, go review the open-ended questions section and dial in the questions that get you this information. Ask the questions, shut up, and let them speak. The first person who speaks loses. Let them guide you to the close. Be direct in order to save time and to show that what matters to them, matters to you.

4. Strong value statements gain curiosity.

You have to be prepared to present and know the value that your product or service offers. Knowing how you can help them is key to moving the sales process along. You have to have very intentional value statements that drive engagement.

> o We know the problems you face and here's how we've helped other people/businesses like you.

You can't just tell them what your product does without driving the emotion of how it can serve them.

5. The prospect needs to know who you and your company are.

They need to know you not only know what you're talking about, but you have the credentials to back it up. It's always good to give examples of how you've helped others in the past and possibly send some testimonials or reviews their way after the initial call. Building this type of credibility goes a long way when trying to earn the respect and business of a potential client.

The sad part is that most salespeople don't even ask for video testimonials or reviews. It's something you need to do. Having real, powerful client statements about you, your work ethic, and how your product or service has helped them is the easiest way to build credibility. But if you don't have them, it's your word they have to trust.

Key points to hit:

- Talk about results that were driven by you and your offer.

- Milestones you've helped other prospects achieve.

- As I stated earlier, name-drop other companies or people they might know whom you have served.

- Make sure they know you have the knowledge and that you stay up to date with new industry standards.

When you do this, you prove to them that you're the person they need and should want to work with. Most people forget that being credible can turn a prospect into a client, and without it, you can turn a prospect into a dead lead easily.

Remember to have a closing statement in every script. There are several ways to wrap up a script and have a power statement that leads to future meetings. You can have product-based closing conversation statements, service-based ones, and consultative wrap-up statements. The verbiage used during this process doesn't always have to be closing the prospect either. It could also be to set up future appointments and potential meetings to further discuss their options. Let's go over each of them.

Product-based Scripts:

- Do you have any questions before we move forward?

- If you're ready, I'd love to help you get the best out of this product.

- I appreciate you giving me your time. What were the best parts of the product you liked most?

- Summarize the product's features that they like the most.

- When (assuming) we move forward today, the shipping dates will be…

- The product will be ready for use by …

- The service will be active and start by …

Finally, the MOST IMPORTANT THING YOU CAN DO IN LIFE AND IN SALES is end the conversation with gratitude!

- o All you really ever need to do when you're speaking with a client is
    - Let them know you care
    - Their time matters
    - That you're grateful for them considering your offer
    - And just be grateful for the connection whether they buy or not
- o Show that you're a professional

- The money matters, but they matter more! Always!
- Shows how much you respect them.
- Proves that you are attentive and that you're a serious professional.

o Does it matter if they buy now?
- You want the sale, but some sales processes take multiple touches. Too many salespeople push so hard for the sale at first touch that they lose any chance of a sale moving forward if the prospect believes that now isn't the right time for them. Don't lose future business like most.
- When you end a conversation with gratitude, it proves how you care more about the relationship long-term rather than just the money now. Prospects need to know you're the person who will be there to serve them always. Regardless of whether it equals dollars in your pocket or not.

Service/Consultative-based Scripts:

- Revisit the pain points and how your service can and will solve problems you know it will.

- You want to handle any and all objections or concerns before you end the presentation.

- Make sure you give them referrals or testimonials to prove you've given plenty of people just like them great service and helped them greatly.

- Most will doubt what the service can actually do. Surface that doubt and be there to explain how, by giving you a chance, you will prove to them the value that your service has.

- End your conversation with excitement and how you can't wait to serve them because you know how much value you can add to their lives.

- And again, like above, thank them for their time and consideration, and be extremely grateful they even gave you a chance to speak to them.

I do want to say, a lot of sales trainers will tell you that your time is just as valuable as the prospect's, and I too believe this to be true. That doesn't mean that you don't end your conversation, either over the phone or in person, with massive amounts of gratitude.

The last thing I'll tell you about building scripts is that it is forever changing. You have to be open to making pivots in the verbiage and economical shifts. Don't get worried, frustrated, or misunderstand when making changes that it is an absolute must to stay current and give you and/or your team the best opportunity to scale accordingly with the best written script possible.

Get team buy-in! It's also extremely important to make sure that if you're working with a team, whether new or not, you ask for everyone's opinion. It doesn't matter if they're brand new or not. Their opinions can make you millions, but the problem is most let ego or title get in the way and never understand the importance of every single person's opinion. Also, don't limit it to just the people you work with. Practice your scripts with those that have nothing to do with you or your company as well. Outside opinions, true opinions on how your script is built, are beyond crucial. Real clients, real opinions, real feedback can help you build the best script to guide you and your team ever!

Finally, PRACTICE PRACTICE PRACTICE! You and your team should spend a minimum of 20-30 minutes daily on role playing your script to get it mastered and sounding genuine, pitching from personality, not just reading a script. You should be able to recite it, but as your own. There will be things you'll do or say that may be great tools for your team to hear, and then there will be things you may or may not do that are hindering your success.

The hard fact that salespeople misunderstand the most is that you should be talking a maximum of 30% of the time. I personally like 20%, but let your prospects speak 70-80% of the time. Your script should be built around listening more than you speak. Ask the right questions, insert the right tie downs, serve, offer solutions, transition to the close.

Remember, build your script to guide, not to read word for word. Make sure that if you or your sales team have to read it word for word in the beginning that it's written like you'd speak it. A robotic-sounding script or making people hear it as if someone is reading it will reduce prospect conversation rates by more than 80%. Build it like you'd say it! Now get to work. Take your script, dissect it, get everyone's opinion, and put yourself and your team in a winning position!

CHAPTER 32

REVIEWS AND TESTIMONIALS: USING THE PSYCHOLOGY OF SOCIAL PROOF

Is it enough to just tell someone how great you are? Is it enough to show your awards and present your accolades to gain client trust in your credibility? It can be, but most of the time it's not. Customers want to hear from other people whom you've served. Speaking to someone you've worked with privately, seeing a video testimonial, or being able to look you up online gives them an opportunity to do their own research where they won't feel any type of salesy conversations between themselves and the salesperson.

When you're speaking to a potential client as well, you eliminate any aspect of ego-based conversations. A testimonial from someone else about you or your company gets rid of any chance of the prospect feeling you're arrogant or conceited, which are two of the worst sales attributes. You DO NOT want anyone ever thinking you have them.

Reviews and testimonials are crucial to your success and your reputation. Reviews provide an extraordinary way to offer social proof of who you are and how you've served someone. People just love to know what other people's experiences have been with you or your company based on customer service and product/service positives and negatives. Reviews help with that in a way that doesn't seem forced. It's an instant trust builder when they see positive experiences. Testimonials and reviews also can assist in any objections that may not get surfaced throughout the sales presentation.

For instance: It might target specific questions the prospect may have, such as:

"One of the best things about Todd is that he communicates faster than anyone we've ever dealt with in the past. If there was a question, one text, email or call and he handled it instantly."

This type of review helps eliminate any fears about lack of communication or questions about whether you will be there after the sale is made.

"The product shipped immediately, on time just like they said it would be. No delays at all!"

This type of review proves, when we say you'll receive it, you will.

"We had trouble using the software even after the training, BUT I will tell you it wasn't from lack of training, it was more our understanding of how to navigate through the software properly. We made ONE CALL and they hopped on a Zoom and walked us through it right away. We didn't have to schedule a time to speak weeks later. This company cares and wants you to get the best out of what they're offering! Highly recommend."

This type of review shows we care, that we won't make you wait when there's a problem, and that we offer training, but if you don't fully understand how to use this software, we will make sure you do!

So testimonials and reviews can help with questions, doubts, and objections they might have when implemented properly.

Let's dive into some great ways to get reviews.

1. ASK YOUR CUSTOMERS WHEN THEY CHOOSE TO DO BUSINESS WITH YOU.

When a prospect is in a buying state of mind and they are ready to move forward with you, it's a great time to ask for a review on how they were treated throughout the sales process and how you served them.

When a prospect says yes, it's confirming they see value in you, the product/service, and/or all of the above. A positive review here is almost a lay down.

2. ASK YOUR CUSTOMERS WHEN THEY CHOOSE NOT TO DO BUSINESS WITH YOU AT THIS TIME.

Even when a prospect decides not to do business with you and you handle it professionally, hopefully securing a future opportunity as someone they'd like to do business with, ask them to write a review on how you weren't trying to force them into a deal and that what matters to them, matters to you most.

That you weren't trying to convince them to buy, but rather you wanted them to do business with you when they're ready and ONLY when they saw value in what you had to offer.

That even though they said no, you understood and you respected their decision. When you do this the right way, you can get some great reviews that will open up opportunity to earn business you wouldn't have, just by how you handled their choice not to do business with you now. They might not say yes now, but how you handled this, when done properly, doesn't mean they'll "never" do business with you.

Remember, there's many opportunities in the "no", if you handle them with professionalism, when most salespeople will just move on and miss out on a lot of business.

3. OFFER INCENTIVES FOR REVIEWS.

As long as this is prefaced the proper way, you can gain some really great referrals. Everyone loves incentives. Sometimes, you can entice people to leave some great reviews or get them to reach out to others whom they may know have done business with you or your company in the past and get them to leave even more reviews! Free stuff, discounts, future services you might be able to offer at a discount or at no cost are all good ways to get some great testimonials.

4. MAKE IT EASY TO LEAVE A REVIEW.

You'd be shocked at how many companies I've worked with whose teams don't even know where or how to guide a prospect or client to leave a review. It's absolutely nuts to me. Have the link to your Google business, make a QR code they can scan, have links to Yelp, Bing, Better Business Bureau, Facebook, Angi, Consumer Affairs, HomeAdvisor, Glassdoor, Merchant Circle, OpenTable, TripAdvisor, and so many more. Wouldn't we all love to have them copy and paste a great review for us or our business on all of the platforms that are relevant? The answer is YES! The only thing that keeps them from doing so, more than not, is not having quick access to each. If you know how to get them there with ease, they will leave a review there with ease!

5. RUN A CONTEST.

This is another really great way to get reviews. Get with your client base and tell them you're trying to ramp up your reviews by running a contest. Whoever leaves the best review(s) on multiple platforms will get an incentive.

6. JUST A FRIEND.

Even if you haven't done business with someone you know, it's okay to ask them to leave a character review on you and your work ethic. Tell them to be real and honest and talk about how they feel about you and what you do. Character reviews are just as important, if not more important, than a product or service review.

7. SOCIAL MEDIA REVIEWS ARE GETTING BIGGER AND BETTER.

Have your clients go post something on your social media pages. Give them easy instructions on how to find them. It's even better if you have a business page on social media where you can share those reviews on your feed. You'd be shocked at how much business I've gained by sharing reviews on my personal page and earned business from friends that didn't know the extent of what I did for work. This is a great way to build your presence. Hate it or love it, social media can be the gatekeeper to huge success.

Now let's dive into which reviews are better, video or written testimonials? Both are powerful, but in today's world, people love to see the emotion and raw expressions of someone's face. You see them, you hear them, you watch their movement, body language, and facial expressions, which all bring you closer to the emotion behind their purchase with you or your company.

"According to Google, video testimonials can improve your search engine rankings through Google's algorithm which will prioritize your page based on having engaging video testimonials."

Written testimonials are very good too. They used to be easier to share, but once again, with today's technology, sharing a link is usually shorter and it's equally as easy to say "click here" than it would be to send a screen shot. Do I still recommend written testimonials? Absolutely yes. Not every prospect or client will make a video for you. Take what you can get. Any testimonial that's positive is good for you and your business. Written testimonials are also great to put on your website, along with the videos.

"According to *Harvard Business Review*, positive and consistent customer reviews increase sales by over 18% by just having them."

Who doesn't want to increase their business by 18%? I do. You should too!

Truth? Which one is more powerful depends on the person viewing them. Some will watch the video. Some prefer just reading the quick good ones. Don't limit your audience based on your opinion on which one you prefer. Always have a combination of them all.

There are many types of reviews; here are the most common:

- Comparative Reviews
    - Where the review weighs you or your company against similar products or services offered.

- Expert Reviews
    - These are very powerful, because the prospect is getting the thoughts of a professional who's an expert in what you offer.

- Product/Service Reviews
    - Obviously these are tied to the product or service you're offering.

- Service Reviews
    - How did you serve the client? Were you easy to work with? Did you make the buying process easy? Did you explain everything thoroughly?

Again, these aren't all the types of reviews available but some to think about asking for, so your review game covers the most important ones. Having different types like those above really gives you the best opportunity to gain a new prospect's interest.

What I would think about at the end of this chapter is:

- Do I know how many reviews I have?

- Do I have a mix of written and video testimonials?

- Do I have easy access to share the review platforms with my prospects?

- Do my reviews cover the most important categories listed in this chapter?

- Do I, or my team, know how to ask for reviews the best way?

- Do I have accounts or all the platforms that are the most popular where someone can leave a review?

- Am I, or my team, even asking for them?

- Do I fully understand the importance of reviews and testimonials?

I'm sure you'll be able to think of plenty of other questions to elevate that review and testimonial game as the badass sales professional that you are now. Just do me a favor. Don't forget about this chapter. Getting reviews helps build trust, credibility, social proof, and so much more.

Here are some statistics on the importance of reviews to end this chapter with a bang!

"According to the Online Review Statistics, potential clients read an average of 10 reviews before committing to someone to do business with."

"Video testimonials are the most effective type of video content for driving sales, with 64% of consumers saying they are more likely to make a purchase after watching a video testimonial, according to a survey by Brightcove."

That's the good, but let's review a statistics you need to know.

"Negative reviews can also have an impact, as 94% of consumers say an online review has convinced them to avoid a business, according to a survey by ReviewTrackers."

Be on top of all of your reviews, because if you aren't keeping track of the negative reviews, it can cost you millions. If you receive a negative review, you or your company would be wise to reach out to the prospect or client and plead with them on how you can make this better. Not just to get rid of the review, but that's always a bonus.

Any time I've gone above and beyond for someone who's left a negative review, they end up being some of the best reviews I've ever received. Don't leave them there without follow up. Do the right thing, serve them, and the payback will be ten-fold, I promise.

In the end, master how to get reviews, maintain them, and get a plethora of different ones to expand your reach. Reviews are money, period.

SCENARIO 1: NO SALE ACHIEVED – PRODUCT MISMATCH

Background: The customer had a specific need but the product offered did not match.

Salesperson: "I truly appreciate the opportunity to show you our product, even though it wasn't the right fit for your needs this time. We're always looking to improve and understand our customers better. Would you be open to leaving a review or a testimonial about your experience interacting with us? Your insights could be invaluable."

Takeaway: Even if there wasn't a sale, the salesperson showed they valued the customer's time and opinion. They created an opportunity for potential feedback to improve product offerings and understand gaps in the market.

SCENARIO 2: NO SALE ACHIEVED – BUDGET CONSTRAINTS

Background: The customer liked the product but couldn't make a purchase due to budgetary limitations.

Salesperson: "I understand that budgeting is a crucial part of every decision. While we couldn't find a solution this time, I'd be grateful if you could share your experience with us in a review or testimonial. It's a way for us to understand how we can better serve customers like you in the future."

Takeaway: The salesperson empathized with the customer's situation. Asking for a review in such instances can lead to insights on pricing, potential discounts, or other financial incentives.

SCENARIO 3: SALE ACHIEVED – PRODUCT MEETS NEED

Background: The customer found the product to be a perfect match for their needs.

Salesperson: "I'm thrilled that our product met your needs! As we aim to help more individuals and businesses, would you consider leaving us a review or a testimonial? It helps others understand the value we provide and can really make a difference for us."

Takeaway: The success of the sale is leveraged to garner a positive review. The salesperson underscores the significance of reviews in helping other customers in their decision-making process.

SCENARIO 4: SALE ACHIEVED – EXCEPTIONAL CUSTOMER SERVICE

Background: The product was good, but what sealed the deal was the outstanding customer service.

Salesperson: "I'm glad you appreciated our service. We strive to give our customers the best experience possible. If you could share your positive experience in a review or testimonial, it would mean a lot to us. It not only helps us grow, but it also sets a benchmark for the quality of service we aim to provide consistently."

Takeaway: The salesperson understands that a sale isn't just about the product—it's also about the experience. By asking for a review, they highlight their commitment to service quality and also reinforce the importance of exceptional customer interactions.

IMPORTANCE OF GOOD REVIEWS AND TESTIMONIALS:

1. **Building Trust**: Good reviews and testimonials help establish trust and credibility in the market. They act as a form of social proof that a company delivers on its promises.

2. **Improves Online Visibility**: Positive reviews can improve a business's online presence, making it more visible in search results and thereby driving more organic traffic.

3. **Informs Business Strategy**: Reviews provide businesses with direct feedback on what they are doing right and where they can improve. This can influence product development, marketing strategies, and customer service initiatives.

4. **Increase in Sales**: A positive reputation can lead to an increase in sales as potential customers often look for reviews before making purchasing decisions.

In each of the scenarios, the salesperson showed they understand that every interaction, whether it results in a sale or not, is an opportunity to gather feedback, improve, and solidify the brand's reputation in the market.

As a salesperson, you MUST understand the importance of this. It builds you and your product or service whether you got the deal or not. Most salespeople miss this. YOU BETTER NOT! Get to training.

CHAPTER 33

DON'T LET THE SPONGE DRY

KEEP OUT-TRAINING EVERYONE!

Kobe Bryant said: "Why would I pass the ball to you if you haven't even trained properly?"

It's something to think about, right? His mamba mentality has changed the lives of so many elite athletes in the world. It came through preparation and training. That's what made him. Out-train everyone!

People who have been in sales usually think they know everything. Have you ever heard, "I've forgotten more than you'll ever learn," or "It's hard to teach an old dog new tricks"? The most successful salespeople in the world are CONSTANTLY open to learning, removing ego, role playing daily and interested in new ways to grow.

If you think you're the best, you need to get around people who are better than you. Have you ever heard, "If you're the smartest or best person in the room, you're in the wrong room"? It's extremely true!

I was in the timeshare business for a while. When I was about 4 months in, I didn't know much, but I was closing over 60% in a burn-and-turn track, which is an insane ratio considering the tour quality and actually pitching the product properly. I was just a sales representative at the time and naturally I was being asked what I was doing and how I was closing so many deals, since I had less knowledge than others who had been in the business much longer.

We can probably identify several practices that allowed me to reach the levels I did in that industry, but what shocked me the most was how unprepared people were. How limited the training was outside the generic corporate structured training. Personally, I go all-in when I work in a new industry. I want to know the most. I want to be the most committed, but most importantly, I want to help others. That being said, why are so many of the so-called top producers in sales in any field so scared to share their knowledge or the golden sales tips that make them so successful?

One of the main reasons is they like being on top. Most high-producing sales individuals that get a taste of victory lane or of constant praise get addicted to it. They're truly afraid if they share their secrets with you, you might be a threat to their throne. Another reason a top producer might not share their tips is because they're pitching heat (for those of you new to sales, heat means: they're lying their ass off). The "top producers" who are lying or stealing or cheating people by embellishing, stretching, or creating a new so-called truth are scared to share what they're doing because they might get caught! They won't risk that and if they even say they will, be careful as some will tell you something different from what they're doing, just to act as if they're helping you, but really aren't.

It's crazy to me how defective the cultures in sales organizations are these days. We'll get into culture later in this book, but it directly impacts preparation and I'll tell you a story now of why it does.

When asked to help or train others, I instantly agreed. If I could add value to assist in the growth or well-being of another, I was in.

One of the managers, a T.O. (takeover or manager who helps close deals) who I wasn't associated with, had all of his reps sitting at three tables. He came to me and said, "Hey Todd, thank you so much for doing this. The crew is super excited to learn." I obviously was humbled and ready to impact some lives. I walked over to the tables, sat down, and started sharing literally everything I knew. I didn't leave out one ounce of what I've learned. Not one ounce of how I handled objections. I told them everything I knew that helped my sales career elevate over the years.

Then as I'm in the zone, training hard and with several people listening equally as hard, my manager at the time walks up to the tables. He has been paying close attention to how I'm helping a team that we don't earn anything off of. Loudly, so everyone can hear, he says, "Yo, Todd, you have a phone call downstairs." I said OK, stopped training for a moment, told them I'd be right back, and headed downstairs to get the call. As I'm walking down the stairs, I notice my manager was following me and when I asked him where the phone call was at the bottom of the steps, he said this: "Bro, there isn't a phone call. I had to pull you off that training because you're giving them all you got and I wanted you to know they aren't gonna do shit for you. There's no reason to help them."

If you know me or not, by now I'm sure you can imagine my response that I won't write in this book, but I was pissed. My partial reply was, "So you only help people for your own personal monetary gain?" He stuttered a bit. I stopped him and said "Look, brother, I know you're my manager and I mean no disrespect, but you and I aren't the same. I help others. Not for monetary gain. Not for my personal advancement, but to impact lives. Now I know that's not your thing, but it's mine. So if you'll excuse me I'm gonna get back to giving others some knowledge."

I was literally shocked that he actually didn't want me to help another team because it didn't directly benefit us. But he WAS SO WRONG! Now don't help people for this, but because I trained them just to help others thrive, when I became a manager, who do you think they wanted to work with? Personal gain? Maybe or maybe not. There's no guarantee that they'd want to work with me, but the odds are in my favor if I'm a genuine person who actually cares about their success.

Let's revisit what my manager thought was no personal gain. Now I'm going to reiterate, DO NOT HELP OTHERS because you're seeking something in return, but the real question is do you benefit from it? The answer is yes in many ways. Helping others prepare, role playing, constant training of any kind has helped me get back on track so many times. Yes, you heard what I said. We all go through rough patches in sales. Some great moments. Some not so great. It's all about creating a level of consistency. Some non-educated trainers will tell you that sales is a roller coaster. Well, it doesn't have to be and one clear way to stay on track is to help others!

When I wasn't performing at my peak and others would ask me to help train them, I thought "Would I benefit them at all since I'm in a slump myself?" Because I always want to add value, always. But what I realized very quickly is that when I trained others, I would remember things I used to do that led me to success. Funny, huh? You get yourself back on track by serving others with no intention of receiving anything, but just because you truly want to help. I also enjoyed the trust they had in me to be the person to elevate them. I listened and learned just as much as they did.

I started holding trainings regularly. They were really going well. We started training at a restaurant after work. We'd stay for hours handling objections back and forth and trying different sales methods, sharing all of our best practices. There were always about 7-10 of us, then it grew to 10-15 and we couldn't have trainings at that restaurant anymore. So we moved them to one of the large banquet rooms full of about 200 tables and started doing them there. The trainings were growing so fast. More and more people from all over the place, other resorts, other companies would just show up. They went from

15 to 40 people. Then from 40 to 60 people. Then over 100+ people were coming regularly. I had 30-year sales veterans, directors, senior managers, all sorts of high-level executives, including that particular company's training staff there just to make sure that I wasn't teaching anything I wasn't supposed to.

What was mind blowing to me was how hungry the sales and leadership team was to learn and more importantly how excited they were to show up to these trainings. I'd say I'm holding one, everyone would come. The corporate training team would try to hold a "mandatory" one and no one would show up. People looking to grow and accelerate their success are always looking for new and innovative ways to expand their talent. I realized after several of those trainings, how ABSOLUTELY important training, giving back, and helping others rise higher or bounce back was. THAT, to me, is the biggest reward in doing what I do.

I remember one day I told just my team of 10 that I was going to do a training and to meet me in that banquet room at 2pm. I was running a little behind turning in a deal and called Jake Cohen, one of my life-long friends whom I consider family who was upstairs with the team in that large banquet room waiting for me. I said "Hey, bro, do me a favor so we're not here all day. Put 3 tables together and grab some paper and pens so we can start right when I get up there, please." His response was, "Umm, yeah that's not possible." I said, "Which part? The paper and pen or pushing the tables together?" He said "the tables," laughed, and said I'd understand when I came upstairs.

Of course I was curious, so I hurried upstairs and opened the banquet rooms doors and there were well over 130 people in the room waiting on me to train them. They had come from all over to learn. To listen. To grow. I was humbled and grateful. That day changed me. It proved to me that if you're a fun, talented, and caring expert in your field, the people will come.

I did those trainings for about a year, before the company training department actually forced me to stop since no one was showing up to their training, rather than being grateful that I was helping the entire company grow without any pay to me. I did it because I cared and I loved how determined and really good people were ready to learn. I was shocked the day I got called into the office and they demanded I stop. Crazy, right? Some companies and people would rather stay stagnant than allow someone other them themselves to get credit for providing real value that led to real change!

MORAL OF THE STORY. DO NOT EVER STOP TRAINING! It stimulates you whether you're the one learning or teaching. It keeps you current. Relevant and on top of your game. But remember it can also help you bounce back when you're not performing at your best.

As chapter 1 states, don't be a liar. As chapter 5 says, serve vs sell. Proper preparation is so crucial to you and a company's efficiency and scalability. Teach the right way daily. No bullshit tactics or pitches, just truth and honesty in serving the people you work with and the ones you're trying to gain as clients.

Remember to always record your trainings as well. You will forget certain things you do. The best sales professionals in the world always record their pitches and the trainings they give or trainings they attend so they can refer to them as needed.

Switch up the people training too. It's boring as hell to have the same person training every day. Yep, even if it's me. People have different ways of doing things which may resonate better with others than I do. They also have knowledge that I might not have. Changing the face of who's getting your team prepared and trained often is a good way to keep training fun and relevant. Also, it doesn't always have to be the training staff that teaches. Get a brand-new representative involved. Get a seasoned one. Get anyone other than always you, if you're a leader that usually does the training. This helps individuals at all times in their career. It gives them the sense that you care and what they know is important to you. It's powerful to say the least, when you watch someone who may not think they matter, realize they mean so much, that you're asking them to train others. Empowering, for sure.

Make it fun also. You can google sales training fun and a million things will pop up. It gets people moving and laughing, instead of being stuck at a desk with a pen and piece of paper. Sales training daily gives you a huge edge on others not doing it. Spend money on your training too. When you pay for something, you'll use it more. Constantly look for new outlets, spending your time learning from platforms and people that fit you. This will help your brand, drive revenue, retain your salespeople or elevate you, so you can retain a stronger and longer salesperson-to-client relationship.

Remember, it's not just sales you need to learn about daily. Here are some examples of what high-level sales individuals and teams do daily that include personal training and sales:

- **Live a life of gratitude.**

You have to create a habit of training yourself to be grateful for the good things in your life, but not limited to. The "hard" also are life lessons that allow you to be more grateful when things are going good. Remember it could always be worse. When you're grateful, you perform better.

- **Listen to something motivational daily. (YouTube motivation or do the right thing and listen to more of me. LOL).**

Whether it's scrolling through your feed on Instagram or Facebook, just force yourself to hear something positive daily. It's so important to keep a positive, motivating mindset. I personally like to listen to perseverance stories online. It just pushes me past what I even thought I can accomplish.

I'll tell you that for years, I thought that motivation wasn't real, but it is. Les Brown changed and saved my life in the hardest moments. Listening to people like Les who had similar struggles and made it to the top proved to me what was possible. Make it a daily practice.

- **Read or listen to an audio book for at least 30-45 mins daily.**

Your car is a mobile university. If you drive at all, you have time to learn. Search the top books in your industry and listen to them while you're driving. If you like to read, set your alarm for 18 minutes early each day and read for just that long. Why 18 minutes, you ask? Well, statistically if you read about a particular thing for 18 minutes a day, which is 100 hours a year, you'll know more than 95% of the world in that specific field. Genius, I know.

- **Recognize your or your team's successes daily, monthly, quarterly, and yearly.**

Recognition is key. We all need it. Some say they don't; welp, they're lying. There's not a person in the world who doesn't feel good when someone is lifting them up, speaking good about them, or recognizing their accomplishments. Brag on others. That feeling is irreplaceable.

- **Goal planning – write it down!**

Set goals. Set daily goals. Set goals that have intention. Not just "I wanna make a million." Create an intentional path to that million. Also remember to set goals that are attainable in some cases. For instance, a daily goal should be to go to the gym for 45 minutes. Mark it as complete. It's a neurological fact that you'll feel more accomplished when you actually accomplish something you set out to do, which in turn, helps you produce even more!

- **Product knowledge training**

If you're not the expert in your field, then they will find someone who is. Now look, I'm not saying you have to know everything, but you should strive to. Being new and not knowing is OK, just be honest with the customer and say you don't know, but that you'll get the right answer. They respect that way more than trying to make up an answer.

Just constantly learn about your product or service, your competitors, what makes someone successful in your industry. New ways to gain more referral business and maybe come up with something personally that sets you apart from the competition. In the end KNOW YOUR BUSINESS and what you're offering. People may not say it, but they want to work with the best.

- **Role Playing Is a Must**

The question I get asked all the time is, "How often should we role play?" The answer is: EVERY. SINGLE. DAY. If it's not in a group setting, get with another salesperson and make it a habit of doing it as often as you can. You have to master your sales process to give you the highest level of conversion by serving your prospect properly, and the only way to do that is to put yourself in situations that are common so you can be prepared.

There are several ways role playing helps in the sales process; here are my top 10:

o *Helps Your Communication Skills*

When you role play, you help yourself and the people you're role playing with figure out how to best communicate with a potential buyer. You can practice several different scenarios in your industry that will teach you how to respond in the best way to get your point across most effectively.

o *Improves Product Knowledge*

You may know what you're selling, but you'd be surprised at what you may not know. When you role play with your fellow sales representatives, you start surfacing services and values you may not have known were crucial to the product or service that you're offering.

When you constantly role play on the different benefits your product or services offers, it gives you a deeper and better understanding so your customer can feel and see the benefits more clearly. It also gives you the ability to answer questions about the features and benefits of what you're offering.

o *Confidence Is Key*

When you dig deep and force yourself to role play more, you'll start feeling way more confident about what you're offering. Confidence is key in sales and the more you know, not just about the product, but about how the customers may respond, you'll feel fully prepared to serve them in anything that you have not felt as comfortable dealing with previously.

o *Listen With Intention*

When I role play, I've learned to listen more than I speak. This is a real and tangible skill that most salespeople don't work on. We as salespeople LOVE TO TALK, but it's more important to listen than it is to just throw a ton of stuff at them that may not even matter. When you listen, the prospect can tell you how to serve them. Practice listening when you role play and try to find the buying signals, target what's important to the prospect, and make it fun.

The person you're role playing with should already know what their dominant buying motives are that they're going to talk about. Practice finding out what they are. This teaches you to listen with intention.

o *Real Scenario Training*

If you're not using real scenarios that are common and also uncommon ones that might pop up every now and then, then what are we training for? You should have a list of the most common scenarios to practice from and master each. You should also have a list of uncommon scenarios that you know have stumped other salespeople before, and be prepared for those as well. Don't make up stuff that doesn't happen in your industry. Be very real when you're role playing so you're ready for it all!

o *You don't know what you don't know.*

Many of us never give ourselves the opportunity to see where we need to grow. Other people can see or hear things we do that may not be favorable to the outcome we're looking for. Also, what if there are good opinions from others on what we can add to our sales presentations that we don't currently have?

When we find our areas of growth and the main issues the team needs to work on as a whole, we can create training programs specifically designed to help in those areas. It's the best way to identify the stronger and weaker points of our presentation(s). When you're consistent at this, your efficiencies will increase across the board.

o *Helps with your empathy game*

Understanding empathy is very important during the sales presentation. Many salespeople miss this and the only true way to see how they react and where their level of empathy is, is to role play a real scenario. This helps you master the art of understanding a prospect's feelings about working with various other companies and people.

When you're the prospect and you're showing your emotions role playing, it gives you a better understanding how your prospects feel in a sales presentation. You have to put yourself in their shoes. Understand their emotions connected to concerns they might have about your product or service. Then swap roles and practice what you've learned.

If you really practice this, it'll help you build better relationships with higher emotional intelligence, which will mean more deals for you!

o *Keep It Movin'!*

A lot of salespeople lose deals because they spend too much time in certain areas of their pitch that may not matter as much to a prospect, and less time in the areas that matter most.

Role playing gives you a better understanding of how to keep your presentation moving and moving in the right direction. When you do this, you're respecting the prospect's time and that matters way more than you think.

o *Helps you get more sales! Duh!*

Look, if you're not role playing, you need to. Every single day! You start learning things that other successful representatives do and begin to fine tune your pitch. After that, it's just learn more and repeat best practices.

o *Builds a Stronger Team connection and culture*

Role playing is one of the easiest ways to get to know your team better. It's fun. You laugh with people, not at them. When they fumble you support them by giving good feedback. When they crush it, you empower them by telling them how awesome they were. All this may seem small, but it's HUGE and one of the MAIN cornerstones to our success at MSGA, helping companies build the strongest, converting teams with the highest and best retention rates.

Role playing is a HUGE part of your culture. If you don't do it, it's just people working with people. Not a team serving one another.

If you're just one person, working by yourself, call someone, Zoom them, and pitch them. There are so many ways to learn. Get a sales coach. It doesn't have to be me, I mean it should be, but it doesn't have to be. LOL. It's important to keep growing and constantly learning.

Now, if you're an organization and you adhere to the highest standards of consistent training, you'll attract way more talent than your competitors. You will be known as a company that is innovative and completely dedicated to giving the ones who work "with" (not "for") them the highest and best chance of being successful. Attracting talent like this will also lead to higher retention rates and keeping your cost per hire down.

The U.S. Bureau of Labor Statistics states that 54% of companies that provide additional training from outside sources, combined with daily training and preparation that they do themselves, overcome talent shortages. It stated that if you are consistent in providing captivating and authentic integrity-based sales practices, you're 38% more likely to attract top-tier talent, which also greatly impacts personal recruiting as well.

Constant training allows you or your company to redirect funds you're spending on less targeted quality training. You get way more bang for your buck when you vet trainers and get quality knowledge. I personally still look for speakers and coaching events daily and pick several throughout the year to attend. I spend a lot of money annually on personal development, but most of you would rather choose $500 dinners than spend $500 on giving yourself a chance to grow. It's so crazy to me that you'll spend $2,000 on a pair of red bottoms, but won't spend $500 for a growth conference or on hiring a trainer to help you rise!

Be a part of something bigger than you are. Learn from someone you believe to be more talented than you are. Challenging yourself comes from working with or getting coaching from someone who's grown to levels you're trying to reach. Providing opportunities to train and learn new skills is a smart way to motivate, engage, and empower you as an individual or your team. It shows you're invested in their success and unfortunately, that's more than most do these days.

Harvard did a study on over one million salespeople in a two-year period. The study proved that those who train daily or are being given training daily:

1. Have a much higher level of job satisfaction

2. Were more organized

3. Improved their overall performance

4. Were much more motivated

5. Had way lower turnover

6. Will improve the customer experience dramatically

Harvard's second study proved that higher-level sales individuals gave a client or prospect a 68% better customer experience. They focused on educating and challenging their customers, which was a direct result of staying current on trends.

You know what's crazy to me? Sales is the most lucrative and rewarding profession to have in life for individuals and is the driving factor in all companies. Without sales revenue you have nothing. Which is why I'm shocked at how lenient so many people are and don't give one shit about bettering themselves. I'm equally shocked at organizations that don't understand this or won't spend the money to bring outside talent in to help them scale. It's absolutely insane. The ROI (return on investment) you get from choosing the right sales/businesses coach is proven to be the most profitable move you can make in your career.

Give yourself that edge! Give your team an edge. Stimulate your mind and theirs. I really, really hope you start to implement this in your lives or your company's now and finally see why preparation and constant training is non-negotiable!

Here are some really fun interactive trainings to do with your team! Keep training and make it fun! Use this list below to get your team involved. Their opinions and engagement matters more than you'll ever know!

Role-Playing Games: Divide participants into groups and assign them roles such as the salesperson, customer, and observer. Create scenarios for different sales situations and have groups perform role-play interactions. After each role play, provide feedback and encourage discussions about what worked well and what could be improved.

Sales Obstacle Course: Set up a physical obstacle course that represents different stages of the sales process. Each station can focus on a specific aspect of selling, like approaching customers, handling objections, and closing deals. Participants move through the course while performing tasks related to each stage.

Sales Scavenger Hunt: Create a scavenger hunt with clues related to sales techniques, product knowledge, or customer scenarios. Participants must solve the clues and find hidden items or information throughout the training space. This encourages active participation and collaboration.

Speed Selling: Organize a "speed dating" style event where participants switch partners every few minutes. Each round, they have a limited time to pitch their product or service to their partner. This activity helps them practice succinctly presenting their offerings.

Interactive Quizzes: Use technology to conduct interactive quizzes in which participants answer sales-related questions using their smartphones or tablets. Display the real-time results on a screen to create a competitive and engaging atmosphere.

Elevator Pitch Olympics: Have participants create and deliver elevator pitches for different products or services. Set up a friendly competition with judges who evaluate the pitches based on effectiveness, clarity, and creativity.

Product Showcase Booths: Divide participants into teams and assign each team a product or service to showcase. Provide them with materials to create a mini-exhibit, complete with visuals and demonstrations. Then, have the groups rotate to each booth for interactive presentations.

Sales Improv: Incorporate improvisational theater techniques into sales training. Give participants scenarios, objections, or customer personas, and have them come up with spontaneous responses. This helps improve adaptability and quick thinking.

Sales Charades: Similar to traditional charades, participants act out sales-related words, phrases, or concepts without speaking. This activity encourages creative thinking and communication skills.

Interactive Case Studies: Provide participants with real or fictional case studies. Break them into groups to analyze the situations and come up with sales strategies. Encourage them to present their solutions to the larger group for discussion and feedback.

The Objection Ball: Get a white soccer ball or volleyball, put the top objections you get within your organization on all sides of the ball. Toss it around to your representatives and wherever their right thumb is on the ball, that's the objection they answer.

The Ball Toss: Get a small ball, could be anything. You list 5 objections or areas of growth in a pitch that need to be trained on. You pick one person to toss the ball to handle the objection or give them your pitch, and they get to choose who they throw the ball to next. You want everyone in the room to give their take on the SAME objection or pitch at least 5 times. Then move on to another objection or pitch. This gets you and your team engaged and you hear all sorts of different ways to train in areas of inefficiency.

Sales Olympics: Create a series of competitive challenges that mimic different stages of the sales process, such as prospecting, qualifying, pitching, and closing. Teams compete in these challenges, earning points for successful execution. The team with the most points at the end wins.

Escape Room Sales Challenge: Design an escape room experience with sales-related puzzles and challenges. Teams must work together to solve these puzzles, which require effective communication and problem-solving skills, to "escape" within a set time limit.

Sales Role-Play Showcase: Divide the team into groups and assign them different sales scenarios. Each group prepares a role-play performance that demonstrates effective sales techniques. After the performances, have a feedback session and vote for the most creative and effective role-play.

Pitch Battle Royale: Teams compete in a pitch competition where they present their product or service to a panel of judges (or their colleagues) within a limited time frame. The emphasis is on delivering a compelling pitch that stands out.

Sales Scavenger Hunt: Organize a scavenger hunt within your company's premises or a specific area. Participants follow clues that lead them to different "sales challenges" related to product knowledge, objection handling, and customer interactions.

Interactive Sales Charades: Create a game of sales-related charades in which participants act out sales concepts, objections, and scenarios without using words. This encourages creativity and quick thinking.

Negotiation Poker: Use a poker-themed game to teach negotiation skills. Each participant receives a set of "cards" representing negotiation tactics and techniques. They must strategically play their cards during negotiation scenarios to achieve their goals.

Sales Bootcamp Challenge: Set up a series of physical and mental challenges that mirror the skills required in sales, such as quick thinking, adaptability, and teamwork. The challenges could range from solving puzzles to physical activities that require coordination.

Product Launch Showdown: Divide participants into teams and assign them a hypothetical product to launch. Each team plans a complete product launch strategy, including market research, marketing tactics, and sales pitches. Teams then present their strategies to a panel of judges.

Customer Persona Swap: Teams create fictional customer personas with unique characteristics. They then "swap" personas with another team and create a sales pitch tailored to the new persona. This exercise helps salespeople adapt their pitches to different customer types.

Remember, when you do these things customize them to how you believe you and your team can add the best value in helping people grow. This is about IMPACT! This isn't just knowledge. How these trainings go, encouraging people, pushing them, believing in them, giving them hope… it ALL MATTERS! NEVER EVER STOP TRAINING. It's the backbone to growth.

CHAPTER 34

BE COACHABLE: THE MOST UNDERRATED SKILLSET

Are you coachable? Really think before you answer that. No one is going to hear your thoughts, but be extremely honest about answering that question. See, many tenured salespeople have a hard time accepting any type of coaching or training from someone who hasn't been in the sales game as long as they have. It could be pride. It could be ego. It could be that they're just super stubborn. So the question is, what does it cost you when you're not coachable?

> *"In a study conducted by the American Management Association, participants who underwent coaching saw an average return on investment of 5.7 times the initial investment."*

That's 5.7 times your initial investment! That could be in dollars, time, education… But who doesn't want that type of return? We all do, period. So why aren't people coachable? Let's talk about it.

Here's a great list I've created to get you to think about which one of these is you. If you're being real, we've all been one of these at one point in our lives and it's costing us REAL MONEY! Here are my top 10!

1. TOO PRIDEFUL

If you're too prideful, you won't be open to learning something new and you'll listen to others less. You don't take constructive criticism well and block out any and all advice. You're basically missing out on information that can really help you earn more and be more.

2. ARROGANCE KILLS

Remember, there's a difference between confident and arrogant. A massive difference. Confidence can turn into arrogance when sales are flowing in. When they're not, arrogance can still surface by placing blame on everyone else and not taking any accountability. There's nothing good about arrogance. This one will completely kill any chances of letting someone coach you to get the best out of who you are.

3. HAVE TOO MUCH MONEY TO CARE

People who have a pipeline of business and are usually not too receptive to coaching are often those whose net worth may or may not be larger than the person coaching them. It's imperative to understand that a knowledgeable salesperson at any level who may be able to coach you into being more successful is worth listening to.

4. NOT OPEN TO LISTENING

There are many people who just don't ever really listen to feedback from anyone. They're closed minded and think they know it all and feel like any coaching at all won't change things for them.

5. RESIST CHANGE

A lot of people hate change and resist any type of coaching at all. This is bad for multiple reasons, but the main one is: What value do you get out of NOT listening to someone offering to help? You don't have to use everything someone is teaching. You can pick the pieces that you like from what they give you. Try some suggestions and use the ones that work and don't use the ones that don't. Not trying them shouldn't be an option. You'd be surprised at how many people try things they thought would never work and that actually do work.

6. FEAR THEY MIGHT FAIL

When your income has been consistent and you're afraid or not willing to try something because it might, at first, be a failure, it'll hold you back from being open to try something new or listening to a trainer or coach. Don't be afraid to make adjustments based on compensation or the fear of failing. Without risk, there's minimal reward.

7. NOT SELF-AWARE

Most people aren't willing to be coached because they refuse to hear or see the things that they need to know about to promote real change that can impact them in a positive way. One of the hardest things for me to do in life was being self-aware. I refused to take the time to hear about things that others can see from the outside looking in that I didn't even know I was doing but that was hindering my success. Be OK with areas of opportunity in your life. It's OK, no one's perfect. When you understand these things, you can fix them. When you don't know, you can't.

8. ZERO TRUST

Most people have a hard time trusting other people. You're in sales or wanting to be in sales if you're reading or listening to this book and you have to compare your ability to trust and be coached to serving a client where you're trying to earn their business. They don't trust you. You have to build that trust and you're asking for that opportunity every time you speak with a new prospect. Give a coach or a trainer that same opportunity. You never know how much they can help unless you trust them to teach you something you may not know.

9. NOT COMMITTED TO BEING GREAT

A lot of people talk a big game. They have huge goals. They want to make all this money. They want to be at the top of their game. Most talk, but few move that way. You have to be fully committed to read a book like this and in sales, you have to be equally committed to wanting to be the master at your craft. Anything other than full commitment to being in the elite class of sales professionals is robbing you of income and a life-changing role. Be committed and do what's necessary to educate yourself to be the best.

10. LETTING PERSONAL THINGS HOLD YOU BACK FROM GROWTH.

I know, I know, this is way easier said than done, I get it. In my decades leading sales professionals and coaching companies, I find that way too many people let their personal lives interfere with coaching and training. Yes, it's difficult at times, but you have to leave your personal problem at the door when you're ready to grow in your career. Don't let personal problems get in the way of being coached into a life of new opportunities. This has crippled many people whom I know could've had extraordinary sales careers.

All of the above could be for paid coaching, in-house training, or free coaching offered to you. So let's get into why the best of the best pay for coaching outside of their work environment. Whether it be sales coaching, leadership coaching, finance coaching, or life coaching, there's massive value in getting outside non-biased training from people who are the masters at what they do.

Here's the thing, it's a statistical fact that if you pay for something, you're going to use it more than if it were given to you for free. It's like you paying for a trainer in fitness; when you pay for it and you know someone's going to meet you at the gym, you will show up. If you don't pay for it and someone's not there for you to meet, you most likely will choose not to go. Paying for coaching is good for a number of reasons, so let's review the top reasons to get coaching.

1. CREATE ACTIONABLE PLANS PERSONALIZED SPECIFICALLY FOR YOU

When you have a coach, their sole job is to create plans based on your goals. They are experts in building plans with action steps that will give you the road map you need to success.

2. HOLD YOU ACCOUNTABLE

Some people don't like this, but when you're held accountable to hit your goals, coaches force you to win! They encourage you to keep moving forward through any and all obstacles you might face along the way to the success they know and you know you're capable of.

3. HELP YOU GET CLEAR ON YOUR GOALS

You have to understand fully what your goals are. You need to have clear and certain objectives so you can be guided properly to achieve the goals you have set for yourself, your team, or your company.

4. SOLVE PROBLEMS

A good coach that you spend money on isn't only obligated to help you reach new heights, but they're also someone to help you solve problems and get through obstacles that arise throughout your journey. Lean on them. That's what they're there for.

5. CONFIDENTIALITY

You may share things with a coach that you don't want to share with anyone else. It could be personal. It could be about your finances and other things that you would like to keep between you and them. They're also great people to talk to about things going on in your life that may be stunting your growth. It's good to have an unbiased, professional opinion where you know you can trust them.

6. A NEW OUTLOOK

A good coach will give you insight into new and effective ways to achieve more. When you're paying someone and have vetted them well, they'll usually give you great advice, tools, and processes that may be new, but also very effective. Most of the times, the people you're currently around may have the same outdated look at things as you do. It's good to gain new perspectives always.

7. IT'S WORTH THE INVESTMENT

When you are investing money, you always need to figure out what type of ROI (Return On Investment) you are looking to achieve. With coaching it's no different. A lot of people don't see the value in paying for it, but the time it takes someone to achieve a high level of success without help, historically, is much longer than if they were to hire a coach. They'll get you reaching your goals faster. Time = money, right? So don't waste time trying to do it yourself when you can be guided there faster and more efficiently by someone who's trained to get you the results you're looking for.

"A study by Manchester Consulting found that coaching produced a 529% return on investment for the companies that participated in the study."

You have to be open and stop doubting people who are great coaches and dive in fully. Most of you will spend $2,000 at a night club for bottles without a care in the world, but you won't spend $2,000 investing in yourself and your goals in life? Seems weird, right? Well, its very common and unfortunately its costing them a chance at a life they've always dreamed of.

I'm a huge advocate of coaches. Whether it's me or not. Find someone you resonate with and be completely open to coaching! Please trust me on this. You won't regret it.

In conclusion to this chapter, I can tell you that in my decades of leadership and sales experience, I have learned something from people of all ages and tenures in the sales world. From young adults with zero experience to tenured professionals who are also more tenured in life and experience. Just because someone is new doesn't mean they don't have something powerful you can learn from.

Keep an open mind. Grow using the tools that are there for you and get a mentor or a coach who knows how to set you and your life up for success. Life's too short. Lose all the things stopping you from being great and take all the things that will help you reach the goals you have set for your life.

CHAPTER 35

KNOW YOUR NUMBERS

Can we have a real conversation here, please? This chapter better really hit home and you have to promise to use everything I'm going to teach you here. Why? you ask. Because I've heard horrific stories of how salespeople have lost commissions and how they stay stagnant because they don't truly know their personal statistics or KPIs (Key Performance Indicators).

Let's talk about tracking your success. First, you should keep track of every deal you make and every deal you don't. Without this, how can you really see how you're progressing or digressing? It'd be a guess, and guessing doesn't give you the best chance at being elite.

There are so many apps out there that can help you can track your deals, but even a simple Google sheet, Excel, or any app you'd like to use would be fine. The MOST IMPORTANT thing is to just do it. Companies have technology that is usually run by humans (notice how I said usually), all of whom have the ability to make mistakes. You want to protect your money at all costs. I'm not saying anyone would intentionally do anything to harm you or your business, but wouldn't it be much better to have access to any and all information you need to prove the monies that are owed to you if there's even a conflict? I'm glad you agree. Me too.

Tracking your activity not only protects you, but it can evaluate your entire sales performance. Again, track the deals you did and the deals you didn't to understand your closing ratio, your average price per deal, and your average cost per acquisition, which will help you set proper goals in the future.

There are several ways to track your success:

1. EXCEL (OR LIKE) SALES FORECASTING.

- You should know exactly how many deals you've written
- The value of each deal
- The commission you're owed on each deal
- How many canceled deals you have and why
- Any freebies or incentives you gave away on each deal

You need to LIVE BY THIS! You can easily build the correct strategy you need to maintain and/or set higher goals to achieve. If you're a company, this will give you an exact idea, based on REAL production, that will help you leverage how to increase your revenue by metrics like these below:

    a. Closing percentage

    b. Average sale price

    c. Cancellation percentage

    d. Cost of incentives

    e. What percentage of deals did you have to use incentives on

    f. Cost per acquisition (tied to lead cost)

    g. Cost per lead

    h. Average volume per guest

    i. Keep track of all bonuses – which deals include them and what the bonus was

These are several good ones, but create your own as well. For instance, if you're in telesales:

- How many calls does it take to set up an appointment
- How many appointments does it take to get a deal

If door-to-door sales:

- How many doors do you knock on to speak to one person
- How many people do you speak with to get a deal

You can create some cool metrics to measure your success and give you and your company the best opportunity to grow. If you know the numbers, if you want to increase revenue by 10%, it will be as easy as increasing your average sale price by 10%. Everything else can stay the same. If you want to increase your year-end sales volume by 10%, it's as easy as increasing your closing ration by 10%. The point is, when you have these metrics, you're setting yourself up for the easiest way to produce more. Without them, you don't really have a guideline to what you need to focus on the most. This is the biggest enemy for people and companies looking to grow.

Review your metrics daily, weekly, monthly, and quarterly. Know where you want to be and use these metrics to step up your game. Find areas that need help, get the help, and start making more money. People really don't get how easy it is to increase efficiency on all levels when you track your efforts. The truth is that most don't want to know, don't care to know, don't want to be embarrassed if their numbers aren't amazing, but if you don't know where you need growth, how do you grow properly?

> "According to a survey conducted by HubSpot in 2020, salespeople who tracked their sales metrics and activities were 2.3 times more likely to meet or exceed their quotas than those who did not

track their metrics. The same study found that 60% of salespeople who tracked their sales metrics also reported feeling motivated to achieve their goals."

Finally, once again, please, please, please remember to track your commissions, you guys. There's a list of reasons why it's important and I'd like to finish this chapter with that list.

1. Allows you to track how much you're earning.
2. Gives you a really good way to track any types of trends, good or bad.
3. Know your timeline on best months for the highest income opportunities.
4. Helps you budget your life financially.
5. Protects you if you know you're owed money and can easily access the deal you sold.
6. Helps you keep track of bonuses or spiffs owed to you.
7. Motivates you to set bigger goals and teaches you how to achieve them easier.
8. You have a clear and concise understanding of your overall performance.
9. If you're working for a company and your production gets better, you can show proof to be able to negotiate higher pay based on your performance.
10. Helps you understand your performance over time. Per week, month, quarter, and year.
11. Gives you a clear understanding of the money coming in and when.

And the main one:

12. It gives you proof of your performance, the monies owed to you and when, which allows you to be prepared for any and all discrepancies in pay.

Whether you're a sales professional or a business, you are ultimately responsible for keeping track of your pay and your KPIs. The deal is simple: with this, you're protected. Without this, it's your word against theirs. With this, you can scale all of your efficiencies with a target based on real numbers. Without this, you're guessing on areas you need to work on.

"Another survey conducted by Xactly in 2019 found that 80% of salespeople who tracked their commissions reported feeling more motivated to achieve their sales goals, and 70% reported feeling more engaged in their work."

Guess what? Times haven't changed. It's more important now than ever! If you want to be one of the elite sales professionals, leaders, or companies in the world, TRACK EVERYTHING! As difficult as it sounds, it's super easy. BUT even if it were difficult, it's without a doubt worth the effort.

Companies need great cultures to thrive. If they spend time coaching, teaching, and giving their teams access to the tools that have made so many others successful, they will thrive and you will achieve better results than you ever thought possible!

CHAPTER 36

CULTURE IS KING

Ed Mylett, one of today's biggest, brightest, and most extraordinary people in the coaching and motivational world said, "Leadership is everything and CULTURE is the KEY to leadership!"

Culture stems from so many different things and the truth is, they ALL matter. I know you've probably heard a ton of gurus out there talking about discipline over culture. That the world is so zoned in on culture that they don't teach their team's discipline. There's definitely truth to that, but you have to have both, in my opinion.

Discipline without culture can get you results but let's say you're working with a company that gives you potential to earn because you're disciplined, but the culture sucks. The leadership talks down to you. The environment is negative, people come and go, the morning meetings suck, the leaders care about the titles more than proving who they are as good people and leading by example. This is all CULTURE! Without it, you can keep disciplined people for a while, but eventually if they're successful because of their discipline, other companies will reach out to them, other companies will offer them opportunities, other people will explain how much fun it is to work with their organization. Believe it or not, I've seen people take pay cuts, make less money, or go places that offer less opportunity in order to work with companies that respect them and that are great fun and have uplifting cultures.

There are also companies that believe just because you have great earning potential, you'll be willing to stay. Not true. Earners, performers, people with drive and discipline will eventually find better opportunities.

So the question is, how do you create a great culture and what does that entail? Yes, you need discipline. Yes, you need opportunity (money, promotions, growth). Yes, you need culture. If you just have a great culture with no earning potential, they won't stay. If you just have earning potential with no culture, most won't stay long. You need culture and opportunity, driven by discipline.

Culture starts with leadership. If you're a leader all the way up to CEOs and you're not a good person, you're not culture oriented, it sets the tone for what's acceptable and trickles throughout the hierarchy. This will cripple you, a sales organization, a company and teams. You spend more time at work than you do with your family. It's not OK to go work with someone who makes you feel as if you work FOR them and who creates a tough environment that you don't want to show up to every day.

- Companies with highly engaged employees outperform their competitors by 147% (Gallup).
- Engaged employees (powered by culture) are 87% less likely to leave their organization than disengaged employees (Corporate Leadership Council).
- Highly engaged teams, that are given cultures they enjoy being in, show 21% greater profitability (Gallup).

What are some of the key factors for creating an extraordinary work environment? Below is a list of must-haves if you want to create the best culture.

1. CARE

You must prove that you care about the people and their success. We spend so much time in every aspect of business, weighing our "care" on production, rather than the people. Caring for the people drives production.

Too many leaders don't get to know their people. They don't get to understand what their goals are. Dream vacations, dream homes, what their why is; for example… why do they work so hard? Who for? What's the real reason they want to create a better life for themselves and their family? In order for people to care, you have to. When you're driving culture, talk about anything other than the company every now and then. Talk about them. Let them be open and honest about what matters to them.

Culture is a byproduct of success. That being said, don't show interest and concern just to get results; be genuinely interested in others. Your livelihood depends on it. People will stay by your side when you show you care about them. Unfortunately, "care" is less common than it should be in today's sales world. Be the difference.

2. NO NEGATIVITY

Look, if we're being honest here, negativity is something that is just in people. It's hard to transition them out of that mindset, but it's possible. From the top all the way down through the hierarchy, there must be a "no negativity" culture. Do everything in your power to eliminate that. A lot of it can be reduced by the first component of culture, "care."

People are going to go through stuff, personal, financial, lack of results or achieving certain goals they set out to do. When they're down, production usually falls as well, but one of the biggest cancers in a sales environment comes when leadership allows people to bring any type of negativity into a group environment.

Negative people affect you and your entire team. If you're having a bad day, which we all have, keep it to yourself. Especially if you're a leader. Your job is to inspire, motivate, teach, even when times are tough. I'll give you an example. My father had been sick for many years before he passed away and the day he passed away, I made him two promises while lying next to his death bed. He made me promise him that I'd speak to the world and tell my story on stages for people to hopefully be inspired that change is possible and the other was to finish my book *The Things I Do Know*, which I had been procrastinating on for over a year. When he passed, I was a leader at a very well-known organization. That next day, I went to work. Maybe it was to keep my mind off of losing my father, my hero and best friend, or maybe it was because I promised him that I'd impact lives. One of my colleagues at the time told me that he'd do the morning meeting for about 145 sales representatives. I told him, "No, my dad would want me to do this." Personally I was hurting bad inside. I was destroyed at the loss of my hero, but I forced myself to do the meeting and made it about "time." How tomorrow isn't promised and how the loss of loved ones could happen in an instant. That creating the life for the people we love most shouldn't be pushed off. That we should move NOW, so we don't lose precious moments that can be taken from us before we believe something might happen. That meeting was about 20 minutes long. I broke down, cried, and could barely get through it. BUT, the impact was real, authentic, and personally driven by something bad that had just happened in my life and I used it as a positive to touch the hearts of those willing to listen.

I could've taken the easy road out and not showed up at all. I could've been negative, but my team would've seen me hurting and instead of inspiring them, I could've broken something that may have had the potential to be great. Well, guess what? GREAT isn't the word for production that day; it was EXTRAORDINARY! We had the best day in the history of the company.

Negativity can drive results down. So if you can't be inspirational and use it to empower, then keep it to yourself and always put a happy face on, as hard as that may be. Not just for your customers, but for your team as well. Why? you ask. Because you could easily bring another person's day down by spewing something that isn't positive.

A lot of people don't realize that when you say things like:

"I hope today doesn't suck like yesterday."

"The opportunities are horrible."

"These leads are so bad."

"Get ready for slow season. No one makes money this time of the year."

"This company only cares about itself. They could care less about our success."

"It never ends."

"When is the bad gonna stop?"

"I can't catch a break."

You get the drift, but things like this stated to another individual or team is a transfer of negative energy that will break someone or a team. These types of things make them resurface the hard that's in their lives and that's something that won't help anyone be more productive at work or at life.

Be a light, not a shadow. NO NEGATIVITY! This is a very serious problem in cultures in a lot of companies I've consulted. I've literally talked CEOs into getting rid of some top performers who are negative to others. What you don't realize is that the short decrease in sales when you lose them (and it's very short when managed) will net you massive results when the rest of your team starts getting empowered by top performers rather than not sharing their success tools or just constantly acting as if someone can never be like them.

It's a culture killer for sure. Be positive at all costs. The entire dynamic of your team and your culture will shift instantly.

3. TITLES DON'T MATTER

The only titles that should matter are our names. Now let's be honest, including me; we all love a great title and when it's earned it should be given. I see way too many bosses who have no business leading who use their title as a tool to direct people and talk down to them, rather than using it to elevate the lives of others.

If you're a chief in your organization and people are afraid to speak to you, what benefit does that give you? What if they had crucial information that can affect the outcome of your business? What if they wanted to suggest something, but don't feel as if you'd listen. I've worked in some pretty crazy atmospheres selling in the past, where a sales representative would go up to shake the CEO's or Chief or higher-level leader's hand and the leader doesn't even look them in the eyes, as if they're not worthy to speak to. It's disgusting.

Your title is your name. Your business title represents how the company believes you should be represented. It DOES NOT give you the right to talk down or feel as if you're above anyone.

You want a great culture? Be approachable. Let people get to know the real you. Serve them. Be there for them. Teach, guide, empower them without it feeling awkward.

Titles can destroy a culture if used improperly as well. You've earned it, now own up to what it stands for! Every leader should be leading with a SERVANT MINDSET! Your culture depends on you first!

4. CLEAR COMPANY VALUES AND VISION

Do you even have core values? Think real quick. Now recite them to yourself. Here's the thing, if you don't know what they are, you don't have them. Every company and every person should have 3 core values that they stand by. This drives culture to another level. When you and or your team understands the vision that your company has, the culture is organically better.

When they know this, they have a sense of purpose and you're giving them a direction that aligns with you and your company's growth. You should constantly reinforce this to your team. They don't only need to know who you are as a person, but they need to know who and what your company stands for as well.

Do this and you've already impacted your team's culture in a positive way.

5. HAVE FUN!

What are some things that set your work environment apart from the rest? Do you have fun midday activities? Do you offer fun incentives for training? Do you have interactive and intentional ways to make people laugh and enjoy their work environment?

When my partner Brandon Biskie and I were consulting for an insurance company, we started putting for $100 bills twice a week. The team looked forward to it. You won by whoever putted the ball closest the $100 bill. The entire team stood up and around the person putting and they'd be videoing the putting contest and posting it all over social media. Their friends and family would reach out and ask them where they worked and is that a normal thing? The truth? We did way more than that!

We'd make fun ways of incentivizing people in training. Contest one vs one to whoever handles the most common objections the best and more. Put together things that people would love to do, interactive things that they'd have so much fun on!

This is a HUGE DRIVING factor in building fun cultures that people want to be a part of. If you're not having fun, it's just work. When you're having fun, it becomes a passion-filled culture that people want to be a part of. When you do this, your retention will skyrocket and new talent will organically come to you!

6. THEY NEED TO KNOW THEY CAN TRUST YOU

Culture itself seems hard enough these days for some who don't put an emphasis on how important it is, but when you combine that with co-workers questioning whether they can trust you and whether you'll always be transparent with them through the good and bad times, it becomes a recipe for disaster for you and your company.

You've got to be able to trust the people you RUN WITH! You have to know that they're going to be honest and tell you when things are good and when it's time to have the hard talks so we can all elevate together.

This is absolutely essential for a healthy and productive sales environment. When there's trust, people will open up to you more about concerns they have, they will help you when they have ideas that can potentially impact your business in a positive way, they'll be more ALL-IN when it comes to taking more risks "together" to help guarantee the success of you and your business.

If your people trust you, retention goes up, success becomes intentionally driven, and your culture becomes a family. A family fights for each other through all the hard. Trust your people until that trust is broken. Give them a reason to trust you and be transparent at all times. This will also be an additive to culture that many think doesn't matter, but without trust, you're just another employee working for someone with unaligned visions and values.

7. LISTEN!!!!!!!!!!

I know we talk a lot about listening more than we speak in the sales process; well, it's the same thing when you're building an unmatched culture. Most bosses who hold a higher title than the sales representatives don't listen to them, and if they do, it's in a way that their opinions seem to hold no value. BIG MISTAKE!

Yes, as a leader, people are going to be drawn to you and want to speak to you more, share their ideas, talk to you about their concerns in business and personally. LISTEN TO THEM! You have no idea the power and positive fortune that adds to a culture.

Is it true that because someone doesn't have your experience, they might not have good ideas? Is it true that because you hold a title that's above theirs, they shouldn't have concerns that need answers? The answer to both is NO! People have value at any level, at any tenure, at any age. People need to know you hear them and will follow up on what they ask or say. Never tell them what they say has no value. Instead, have a good and transparent conversation about why their ideas may or may not make sense. But never make someone feel as if you don't want to hear what they have to say or that what they say doesn't matter.

If you did that in a sales presentation would you get more deals? We both know the answer to that, NO! So why not follow the same steps in listening to the people you have the luxury of working with? You should. If you want people to run with you, give them the same respect they give you, not because of your title, but because they matter just as much as you do.

8. SHARE YOUR KNOWLEDGE

This one is a hard one for me to not go off the deep end on, because I've consulted and been in some sales atmospheres where the top salespeople don't ever want to share how they're successful.

Why? you ask. OK, I'll tell ya:

o They're shady and lying to customers to get deals.

o They're afraid of competition.

o They don't like training other people.

o They're afraid if they share their trade "secrets," it'll become common and won't work anymore.

o And… They lie and deceive people to get deals….oh wait, I already said that… but it needs to be said again… JS.

I'm sure you know what I'm talking about and I'm sure there are more things you can add to this list above, but really… If you're having success, why not share how you're doing it?

It's crazy to me that people think serving other people doesn't add value to their lives. Most need to be compensated to serve, but I'll tell you this, when I started elevating my life, it came from serving people with no hidden agenda. I wasn't afraid of the competition. I was always top in sales, but there were times I was surpassed, and I couldn't have been more excited or proud.

Did that lead to money? It wasn't the intention, but yes it did. I made more money by serving people with money NOT on my mind. The truth is, when I did that, I made more money than I ever had before.

Create a workspace where teamwork is non-negotiable. If someone doesn't fit in culture-wise, don't hire them, and if they're not working with your team the way you'd like them to, help them first, but eliminate them if they won't change.

The moral of the story: create an environment, a CULTURE, where people want to serve their team and those around them. This type of culture is rare but needed now more than ever!

9. NO BAD EGO!

An egotistical scale is almost impossible with success-driven efficiencies that most try to reach. Ego-driven leaders, ego-driven salespeople, just DO NOT help culture at all. You can't have an environment where people believe they're better than others for any reason whatsoever. This kind of belief is simply offensive.

If you want to destroy success, promote bad egos. It's the dream killer of all companies and salespeople. Confidence is different from ego. Cocky is different from confidence. Arrogance is different from confidence. You get where I'm going here, right? You can't have people who make others feel less worthy of success. You can't have other people make someone feel as if they can't achieve at a high level.

You want to create a culture of high-level leaders who empower people to surpass their own success and applaud them when they do. I know, I know. Easier said than done. I promise you I get it, but this is a massive differentiator in how your culture grows. Remember, you are the sum of the people you surround yourselves with. You want good people? Be good people. You want empowering people? Be one. You want servant leaders? Be one.

At the end of the day, there's no room for ego maniacs in any sales environment, but there is tons of room for individuals who love to see other people win and who are happy when they do. Be this way. The culture you build will yield unparalleled results.

10. CONSISTENT LEARNING AND DEVELOPMENT

This section is crucial to your growth in culture and in sales and leadership development. You should have scheduled mandatory (although I hate that word) training and development for your team to give them the best chance at achieving their goals. Not just training from leaders, but get your team engaged. Get your salespeople to present something new and fresh weekly too.

Having everyone engaged in the training and development of your entire organization is key to your culture and success overall. Of course, if need be, present the training for approval with your leadership, but get them involved. It teaches you and your team how to speak and present, which allows them to be able to communicate better.

Overall a good culture needs good, consistent training and development.

11. AWARDS AND RECOGNITION ARE KEY

Do you like to get recognized? Do you need a pat on the back? You might've said no to both of those questions, but you do. You love it. Everyone loves to be recognized for their efforts, accomplishments, and their resilience.

When you celebrate individual or team success, it will automatically increase culture, happiness, and employee retention. It will prove that you as the leaders care about the people you run with.

When you do this, it not only helps the culture, but it will increase performance and morale and it motivates your team! Recognition is essential for an individual and a team structure. Keep recognizing everyone. Without it, you'll purposefully cause harm to you or your organization. You need this for a positive and influential sales culture.

12. LEADERSHIP IS KEY TO A THRIVING CULTURE.

According to a study by the *Harvard Business Review*, leaders are responsible for 70% of the variance in employee engagement levels. Employee engagement is closely tied to organizational culture, indicating that leadership significantly influences the overall cultural climate.

The percentage is insane, 70%! Think about that for a minute. Like, truly, sit back and take a look at how you lead yourself or if you lead others, you have to lead yourself first! When you master that, leading others will come easily.

There will be a bonus chapter on Leadership, but just know good leadership drives attitude and production and creates an environment where people don't just FEEL they're valued, THEY KNOW THEY ARE!

13. HOLD YOURSELF AND YOUR TEAM ACCOUNTABLE

In anything in life, accountability is key to your success. In a sales environment, it will make or break you. You have to learn to have a pattern, a sequence, a roadmap to success and that comes with you holding yourself accountable first, but also having someone keeping you on your "A" game as well! This could be anyone you surround yourself with who has a similar mindset.

Remember, who you surround yourself with matters very much. It's extremely important to track your success, measure your goals, get feedback from people you respect and who you know are accomplishing big things.

Having the right people in your life is huge for the culture you want to build your life around or your team. It will also force success on others and prove to them that with accountability at the forefront, you will win, earn an extraordinary living, and create an atmosphere that people want to be a part of.

14. PROMOTE A GREAT WORK–LIFE BALANCE

Simon Sinek, one of the world's greatest leadership experts who consults for the largest companies in the world, said this:

> "Everyone should have a duvet day. A duvet day is when someone wakes up in the morning and is perfectly healthy, everything is fine, but just decides they'd rather go to the beach. All they would do is call the office and say they were taking a duvet day and no one would bother them."

Now as crazy as this sounds, there were some parameters. They only had 10 duvet days throughout the year that was NOT their vacation or sick time. It was added days when they could dictate whether they wanted to come in to work or not and wouldn't get into any trouble if they didn't. The company agreed to this and the culture thrived and everyone wanted to work there.

He went on to say that when other people heard that this company was doing this, they were like "That's SO AMAZING that you guys do that!" But guess what? They were doing it anyway. LOL. They'd just lie and not come in. But what if they didn't have to lie? What if they had that leniency where they weren't looked down upon? What would it do for the culture?

Sometimes people need a break and it might not be something they can easily plan. I know this method isn't perfect, but building a culture where (and it doesn't have to be this model) people have flexibility, without taking advantage of it, gives them a feeling that the work environment that they're in, the leadership they work with, are the right ones and it drives production because they're allowed to have a balanced work-life balance.

Just do me a favor. You need to spend time with the people you love most, your friends, family and sometimes, just yourselves. Life's too short not to have the time to take a break. Don't work so hard that you forget to enjoy the fruits of your labor and if you're a company with sales representatives or anyone for that matter, LET THEM LIVE! When you do this, you can send me a message thanking me for how fast your efficiency has increased. You're welcome!

Once again, I don't have all the answers, but those 14 listed points above have helped me create some of the most amazing cultures in individuals and small to huge sales organizations. People have thoughts, suggestions, they have great ideas, they may want to speak to you but feel afraid to do so. You've got to make sure you're the person YOU want to be around and if you're leading anyone outside of yourself, you need to be the person other people want to be around.

Be humble enough to know other people matter just as much as you. Be grateful enough to know that running with anyone who is positive, has drive, and cares about others enough to create a great culture is a GIFT regardless of their title or tenure.

If you want to grow and crush goals, accomplishing things most never do, you have to be absolutely obsessed with building a culture that people want to be a part of.

How you treat others matters.

How you speak to others matters.

How you listen to others matters.

How you move with others matters.

Your body language matters.

Your facial expressions matter.

The time you give to others matters.

How you recognize others matters.

How you serve others matters.

How you lead others matters.

This list is ever growing and you can add to it. Just remember that people will work in a bad culture for a lot of money until what they once thought was "a lot" of money, isn't a lot anymore. You MUST HAVE BOTH! Opportunity combined with a great culture will change the game for you.

If you think culture doesn't matter and that you can build systems that drive success, you can to an extent, but you'll never reach the income level you could've or accomplish the things the elite do, without having a great culture as the foundation to your own and your people's success! Whether you're a new leader or an experienced one, master this chapter and the growth and development of your team will blow you away. I promise.

CHAPTER 37

DON'T GIVE UP EVER!

We all have a story, but it's not really the story that makes you great. It's how you use it! There are tons of books that push you, make you grind, and allow you to create a mindset to never, ever give up. There are tons of motivational videos online, on multiple different platforms, that you can watch and listen to that will help you stay on track. There are people you can surround yourselves with who will lift you up, encourage you, and make you think differently! But the hard truth is, YOU ARE THE ONLY ONE WHO CAN MAKE YOU MOVE!

You have to understand, whether it's in sales or anything you do in life, you have to make a decision. You either run hard or you don't, and not making a decision is a decision.

I was on stage keynoting at an event with over 4,000 of the best salespeople in the world and afterwards the conference had all the speakers on a panel for the attendees to ask questions. A young man in the crowd asked me a question.

He said: *"How do you keep going when you feel like you've done everything you can and you still seem to get nowhere?"*

Although there are different responses to this question depending on the person, I replied with a question.

I said: *"What's a goal you set that you weren't able to reach?"*

He replied: *"Well, I can't seem to get past 20 deals a month and I work 60 hours a week."*

I said: *"How would it change your life if you could?"*

He replied: *"For one, I'd make more money, which is the goal, right?"*

I said: *"Is it? Because what you're telling me is that the value behind you selling more is to make more money, but what if the loss was worth more?"*

He replied: *"What do you mean, the loss?"*

I said: *"Do you have someone in your life you love very much?"*

He replied: *"Yes sir, my wife and kids."*

I said: *"Let's say someone held one of the people you love hostage and the only way you'd ever see them again is if you sold 40 deals next month. Would you find a way to do it?"*

He replied: *"Well, obviously. Nothing would stop me."*

I said: *"So the loss of something or someone you love would force you to be successful?"*

After thinking, he replied: *"I guess so. Yes, sir."*

Too many times, we tie a goal or an achievement to a monetary outcome where the purpose doesn't mean enough or the effort you'd have to put in isn't worth the investment. But what if it was?

I said: *"So what you'd gain by selling more deals doesn't have enough value to put in the effort it'd take to close double the amount of deals you're selling per month now, is what you're telling me."*

He replied: *"I guess not."*

I said: *"So the money is irrelevant compared to spending time or seeing a loved one again, right?"*

He replied: *"Yes, sir, of course."*

See the mindset shift? The money doesn't matter enough. The reward isn't big enough to do what it takes to close more deals. That's just a byproduct of effort. But if the VALUE, the return on your effort, is big enough, there's nothing you wouldn't do to be successful.

He just told me to save a loved one, "NOTHING would stop me" from doubling the number of sales he's selling. You have to have a purpose, a goal, an outcome for the effort you put in. Most people don't think this way. Life can be going so great and then BOOM, one bad thing happens and the negativity takes you over. You start thinking about all the bad and seem to forget all the good you have in life.

What are you going to lose if you don't win at the level you know deep down inside you're capable of? Who suffers? Whose life is affected by your effort? What if that person is you? Do you love yourself enough? Do you really want more or are you complacent?

Complacency kills and will keep you down. If you're OK with your current income, the life you live, the car you drive, the house you have, the travel time you have, the time you get to spend with your family. If you're OK with all of that, then you'll never really push yourself to do more.

See, negative motivation isn't talked about enough. I didn't have the luxury of giving up. If I gave up, my family was in the streets, had no food on the table. I didn't have a fall back. I didn't have a choice to give up. GIVING UP IS A LUXURY too many people cash in on and the payoff is depression, anxiety, and an uncertainty I never want to feel again.

I had to hit rock bottom to win big. I've been held at gunpoint three times. I've been robbed. I've been in environments that I didn't want to be in and done things I've never wanted to do, because I didn't have a CHOICE but to earn. But the truth is, some of you have it too easy. You think you're suffering when you don't make more money or drive the nice car or have the materialistic things that others have. THAT'S NOT SUFFERING! That's why you give up.

Try talking to anyone who's been so depressed that they slept 12 hours a day and cried the other 12. Try speaking to someone who didn't have a home and would've been homeless if their friend didn't let them live in their basement until they got back on their feet. Try talking to someone who lived off of $1 boxes of mac and cheese with their family and questioned their existence as a parent or spouse. Talk to a parent who got divorced and couldn't afford gas money to see their kids who lived a few miles away, because they didn't have the confidence or the energy they needed to get back on their feet. Try being someone who has to tell their kids "no" they can't do something because they didn't have the funds to do so. Speak to a man who couldn't provide at the level he wanted to for his wife. Talk to someone who's had their cars repossessed, been evicted from their home, filed bankruptcy, and felt so down with life that they couldn't get out of bed. Speak with someone who drank their way into more excuses and lived life feeling sorry for themselves…

Would you like to speak to this person? It was me.

When I was on top, everyone loved me. When I lost everything, very few were there for me and the ones that were, couldn't get me out of my funk. They couldn't get me out of bed. They couldn't make me feel worthy. They couldn't prove to me that if I worked harder, my life would be better. You know the only person who could? Me.

Excuses will kill you mentally and eventually break you down physically. If you want to know ways not to give up, to push harder, to dig deep, to change your mindset.... You have to be BRUTALLY HONEST with yourself and find out what your purpose is. What is your why? Who and what are you fighting for? Why do you want a better life and what should you do to guarantee that the VALUE (return on your efforts) is worth so much that giving up isn't an option!

To me, at my worst, that was my daughters Averigh and Addyson. Then my amazing wife Michelle came along and my purpose got bigger. I wasn't going to let them down ever, NO CHANCE! Then my daughter Abriella came along. My purpose kept growing. The passion, the fight, the grit of being the man that creates wealth in LOVE, FINANCE, ABUNDANCE, FAITH and more, was something that I was going to live every second of my life working towards. Not just for me, but for them.

My mindset became different. My reasons for getting up every single day, creating a legacy and a life for them where they look at me proudly, became my purpose. My happiness, security in who I was as a man drove me to great accomplishments and soon gave me the courage to believe in myself. Fighting for them saved me, but it also created me!

My purpose doesn't have to be yours. You might have a family and you might not. You might have loved ones and you might not. In the end, you have to figure out what your purpose is where the outcome, the reward, the accomplishment will push you to never ever give up.

Don't be satisfied with mediocrity. The white picket fence, the 401k, the pension. That might be your dream, but it wasn't mine. I know I'm meant for more. I know I'm meant for greatness, but I didn't know that always. You have to convince yourself that you deserve it all, and you know what? You do.

You have a story, but your story, your past circumstances, does NOT mean you're meant to just be normal. You were put through the hard to build you. Don't use your story as an excuse, use it as fuel.

Why shouldn't you give up? I'm glad you asked. Let's dive in.

1. REGRET

Tim Grover said: *"If you think the cost of winning is high, wait til you get the bill for regret."*

The number one reason people die is regret. Don't believe me? Go ask anyone who works in hospice. People will literally lie on their death beds and say things like:

"I wish I would've done more."

"I wish I would've said sorry."

"I wish I went to …"

"I should've done more for you kids."

"I didn't live the life I wanted to and it went by so fast."

Ask any doctor. People choose to give up and the mental illness that regret creates when they're sick shortens the time they live. It's a fact. Live your life with no regrets. You want something, get it. You want to speak to someone, speak to them. Yep, we all make mistakes, but if you give up, you'll let regret shave years off your life that you can never get back. You can't give up! Not an option.

2. PEOPLE NEED YOU!

You may be reading this and living by yourself, but you have people in your life who love you, who want you to win, who can't wait for you to call them and tell them what you've accomplished. You owe them.

Your lack of commitment is an insult to the people who believe in you. Read that again!

Don't you dare think it's OK to be just OK. If you're mediocre, you're literally telling the world that knows you that it's OK to be mediocre. Is that what you want? Every day I live my life to prove to myself first, but to others who know me, read my posts, my books, watch my videos, that MORE IS REAL! I'll be damned if I'm going to set an example of average. No chance. I fight for more because I love others to see that more is out there.

3. QUITTING IS EASY.

People find every reason in the world why they should give up. It's crazy to me when I talk to someone and ask them why they didn't accomplish something and INSTANTLY they start listing all the reasons why it didn't work out.

If people took all the time and effort they spend on justifying why they didn't win and put it toward how they CAN WIN, they'd be winning! It's just easier to quit. They think the "hard" is too grueling when it's not.

Giving up is WAY HARDER. Try looking at your kids and imagine sitting down with them and telling them you're giving up. Who wants that? How would that make you feel? Try telling your spouse that you don't have what it takes to give them the life they deserve. Who wants that? Not you! Not me! That's way harder than failing. Still want to give up? Doubtful.

It's easier not to give up than it is to live a miserable life, wondering what would've happened if you didn't give up. That's a fact.

4. DON'T BE THE "WHAT IF" PERSON

I've said this for years after my depression when I started winning. I will never ever be the man lying on my death bed who says things like:

- What if I had done this?

- What if I had taken that chance?

- What if I had listened to the person who presented that opportunity?

- What if I had worked harder?

- What if I could've done more for my loved ones?

- What if I traveled more?

- What if I invested more?

You get where I'm going. I WILL NEVER BE THE "WHAT IF" GUY!

If you give up, if you stop trying, if you stay complacent… You'll be the what if person and I promise you, that's something you don't want to be. KEEP GOING! So you can at least die knowing you gave everything you had to live the best possible life.

5. IF YOU GIVE UP, YOU'RE CONVINCING YOURSELF YOU NEVER WILL SUCCEED

Giving up is a vicious cycle of mental destruction. You may not think you're strong enough to fight, but you are. I bet, right now, that if you start thinking of tough times you've had in your life that you've made it through, you can think of way more than one.

You're tough! You're just letting doubt terrorize your mind. Life is worth living. If your actions prove to your mind you're not capable, then you never will be.

MOVE DIFFERENTLY!

6. WAKING UP IS A GIFT.

Life is a gift. Tomorrow isn't promised, and if you take it for granted, life's going to go by so fast that one day you won't wake up. When you look down from the heavens above, seeing the people in your life who were affected by your lack of effort, you'll wish you had tried harder. Don't you dare take for granted what others have lost far too soon.

7. PEOPLE WANT YOU TO FAIL

I know, I know. Some of you are reading this and saying, "I don't care what other people think." I got news for ya, you do. You can tell yourself that all you want. You can give me fancy quotes like:

"When you realize how little people think about you, you'll stop caring about what they think."

"It doesn't matter what others think about me. What matters is how I think about me."

Oh, and one of my favorites.

"What you think about me is none of my business."

You care! You know you do. It doesn't have to change how you move, what you think about yourself, and it definitely shouldn't change your ability to win, but you care. I see so many videos online where people are preaching they don't care. What they should be saying is that they care, but it doesn't change their capacity to win.

I care and I use it as fuel. I have so many haters in my life and I use all the hate, all the doubt, all the trash-talk to KEEP DOING MORE! The people who doubt me, who want me to fail ARE THE REASON I WIN! To all of you who have doubted me, I thank you. You are the reason for all of my success. P.S. I'm smiling while I'm writing this.

Their opinions of you don't have to matter enough to stop you from winning, but let them matter enough to push you towards greatness. That reward is a phenomenal feeling. You'll want some of that, I promise.

If you lose, they win.

8. WHAT IF YOU KEPT GOING

Really, though, what if you did it?! What if you went after it all? What if you fought through all the hard, all the pain, all the sorrow? Who would you be? What would your life be?

You'll never know if you don't try! Why in the world would you ever give up!!!!!!!!!!!

I don't know about you, but I NEED to know what's on the other side of not giving up. My side has been pretty damn amazing. I know yours will be too.

9. YOU'RE CLOSER THAN YOU THINK!

There seems to be this common trend when I help people reach their goals. They were way closer than they thought. It's way easier, with guidance, than they thought and the reward you get from the fight is worth more than the pain you'll get from giving up.

All it takes is for you to keep going.

10. THE CHASE BECOMES FUN

The top, most elite, and successful people in the world have one thing in common: they all chase perfection. They never reach it, but they're constantly chasing it. This type of mindset always gives them something to run after. It gives them a daily challenge to keep going after the things others don't believe are possible to achieve. They never get complacent! Chase perfection. You'll never get there, but you'll get so much farther in life than those who are satisfied. Me, I'm never satisfied and never will be. Don't get me wrong, I'm proud of myself for all that I've accomplished, but I live every day knowing I can do more.

That's my top 10. Yours may not be the same and you know what? That's OK. Your reasons should be yours, but if you're in sales and you aren't hitting the goals you want or you're in a slump and not as consistent as you'd like to be, KEEP GOING! If not for my reasons, create your own top 10 and keep going for those.

Remember, some don't have the luxury of giving up. It's just not an option. Don't make it an option for you either.

I'll leave you with two questions:

Is there someone in your life right now whom you'd die for if it meant a lifetime of happiness and wealth for them?

That answer is usually always "yes."

So my last question would be: Then why are not you living for them to give them happiness and wealth?

That might be something you need to think about. They'd be much happier with you here. Don't take the easy way out; the hard is worth their happiness with you by their side. And you know what? You'll be happier too. It's time and you know it is. NEVER EVER THINK ABOUT GIVING UP AGAIN!

CHAPTER 38

GET RICH. STAY RICH.

This is the last chapter in this book, and it might be the most important one. I've probably said something like that numerous times throughout this book, BUT I really don't want you to make tons of money with the lessons and practices in this book and then just blow it all.

I'm speaking from personal experience here. The sales game is so lucrative and when you get really good at it, you spend your money like crazy, because you know you've got the talent to go out and earn more. It's very common that when a sales representative gets a fat commission check, they tend to fall off. You either don't see them until they run out of money, or they don't try as hard because they've got a nice cushion in the bank. Both of those things you should never do.

I had many years of my life where I'd get a huge check and go buy exotic vehicles, jewelry, clothes, pop bottles in VIP. I lived well beyond my means. Have you ever heard the phrase of someone being "rich poor"? That was me. I had money, but it was gone in an instant. Then there are people who didn't have money and could live off of 50k per year, because their bills allowed them to. There are also people who have money, who are just as broke, because when they started making it, they bought more stuff, the bills got bigger and their lifestyle and monthly nut need them to make more money. Is that why we work this hard? To stay struggling? Absolutely not.

You need to earn and invest. Cash in the bank is wasted money. Take your money, your fat commissions and bonuses and learn to live off of 30% of that income. Take the other 70% and invest it. Set your future up, so you can retire sooner and spend time with your family. Isn't that why we live? We should not live to work. We should work to set ourselves up with a life where we can make our own rules. If you keep spending the money that comes in on stuff that doesn't yield a return, then you're going to live life never getting ahead.

I added this chapter because I've been there. Pay your taxes. Invest your money. Get life insurance. Protect your money and your future! Learn to live beneath your means to live the life you deserve later.

I'm no financial advisor by any means, but I wanted to throw this chapter in because I've seen so many top-notch sales professionals live painful lives because they didn't know how to manage their money.

Listen, commission-based sales is as lucrative as it is scary. You have good weeks and bad weeks. You have great months and not so great months. You need to manage your money because it's going to fluctuate. I don't care what book you read where they're trying to convince you that you can be consistent in sales and not worry about variable earnings, but isn't it better to be prepared for a slow time than not? I think we both can agree that the answer is yes.

You need a minimum of 6 months' worth of money to cover your expenses when you're in sales. Budget properly and know your current expenses and upcoming ones. If you do this, you won't be so stressed out if you have a month or two where your performance didn't get you the income you're used to earning.

I'm not trying to sound like the boring dad. I'm so sick and tired of watching people I've trained earn millions of dollars and have nothing to show for it years later. It's sad and I promised myself that I'd say something about finance in this book to hopefully plant a seed for whoever reads this book to get a financial advisor or at least study enough to know how to manage your money. You don't work as hard as you do in business to be left with nothing. Please, if you take anything away from this book, don't put yourself in a financial burden that can be avoided. It's the worst feeling in the world. You and your family deserve better than that.

IN CLOSING

I want to thank you for taking the time to read this book. I promised my father that I would do everything in my power to leave a legacy to make him proud the day before he died. I will continue to fight to make the people in my world proud.

This book took over two and a half years to write. I wanted to put everything in it that could impact lives. Yes, it's a sales book, but I wanted to give you guys a book to use for a lifetime. Something where the practices could be retaught, learned over and over again, passed on for generations to come and I hope I've accomplished even a small portion of that.

I wrote this book from my knowledge, years of experience, through the mistakes I've made that I don't want others to make and most importantly from my heart. I didn't write this book for money or my brand. I wanted to write this book to teach people that sales is the best industry, the most lucrative career in the world, and when done with integrity and honesty, it's the most mentally and financially rewarding life move you will ever make.

MAKE SALES GREAT AGAIN is a way of life. If you read this book and you used to lie or stretch the truth to earn a living, I beg you to stop. You can earn just as much by serving people.

Reading a book this big is an accomplishment and I'm proud of you, but I'm equally grateful you chose my book. Please pass it on to others, wear it out, use it over and over again to help others get better and all that I ask in return is that you go after everything you want and never give up.

I'd like to thank everyone who stuck by me, who pushed me, who believed that I could write this book. Yes, I too, need good positive people in my life.

I'd like to thank my partner Brandon Biskie for your friendship, brotherhood, and your constant motivation. You're a genius, one of the best closers and trainers in the world, but you're an even better person. Thank you for being with me through this journey and you need the props for helping me create some of the best chapter titles I've seen yet. I'm truly grateful for you.

To my daughters, when I'm long gone, know that everything I do is for you. Thank you for making me the happiest man in the world, which drives me to accomplish things I didn't even think I could. A daughter's love can help you do some extraordinary things! Daddy loves you forever and always.

To my wife, Michelle, who gives me the ability to follow my passion, a thank you just doesn't seem like enough. You told me to never stop and that one day I'd look back at the lives this book would touch and smile knowing the work was worth the reward. I'm so beyond grateful for you. Through all the good and bad, we fought through it all side by side. You are my world, my wife, my life, and my love. Words just can't express what you mean to me. I know I wasn't always the easiest to be with, but I'll live a lifetime making sure whatever hard was worth the lifetime we have left together. You make me a better man.

Finally, to God. My faith over the years wasn't always the best, but it is now. I owe everything to you. Father God, I pray that anyone who reads this book will live a life of abundance and happiness, putting you first and being grateful for all that you allow us to have.

I pray that this book teaches people to serve others the right way, through integrity and honesty, to help bring back the good in what sales can be. Lord, please open the hearts and minds to those who aren't selling the right way. The ones who are being manipulative, saying whatever it takes to get a paycheck. I pray that you allow this book to change them, so they can finally see that serving people is the right thing to do.

Father God, please let this book reach anyone who needs to gain the knowledge and skills to create an extraordinary living in this amazing profession you've created for us all.

Thank you for giving me the time and the understanding to write this book. Lord, I pray it brings value to anyone who reads it.

In Jesus' mighty name. Amen.

FOR MORE INFORMATION

For more information about the book or consulting with Make Sales Great Again, please visit our website www.MakeSalesGreatAgain.com, email me at contact@msgaconsulting.com or find us at

IG @toddspeciale @msgaconsulting
LinkedIn: Todd Speciale
TikTok: @MakeSalesGreatAgain
FB Business Page: @makesalesgreatagain
YouTube: @MakeSalesGreatAgain
Websites: www.ToddSpeciale.com
www.MakeSalesGreatAgain.com

Printed in the USA
CPSIA information can be obtained
at www.ICGtesting.com
JSHW011910220324
59740JS00004B/4